HMH Georgia Science

This Interactive Student Edition belongs to

Teacher/Room

Houghton Mifflin Harcourt

Consulting Authors

Michael A. DiSpezio

Global Educator
North Falmouth, Massachusetts

Michael DiSpezio has authored many HMH instructional programs for science and mathematics. He has also authored numerous trade books and multimedia programs on various topics and hosted dozens of studio and location broadcasts for various organizations in the U.S. and worldwide. Most recently, he has been working with educators to provide strategies for implementing science and engineering practices, including engineering design challenges. To all his projects, he brings his extensive background in science, his expertise in classroom teaching at the elementary, middle, and high school levels, and his deep experience in producing interactive and engaging instructional materials.

Marjorie Frank

*Science Writer and
Content-Area Reading Specialist*
Brooklyn, New York

An educator and linguist by training, a writer and poet by nature, Marjorie Frank has authored and designed a generation of instructional materials in all subject areas, including past HMH Science programs. Her other credits include authoring science issues of an award-winning children's magazine, writing game-based digital assessments, developing blended learning materials for young children, and serving as instructional designer and co-author of pioneering school-to-work software. In addition, she has served on the adjunct faculty of Hunter, Manhattan, and Brooklyn Colleges, teaching courses in science methods, literacy, and writing.

All photos ©Houghton Mifflin Harcourt, Inc. unless otherwise noted.

Acknowledgments for Cover

Front cover: *DNA model* ©Carl Goodman/Science Source

ISBN 978-1-328-86820-6

7 8 9 10 0877 27 26 25 24 23 22 21

4500821056 B C D E F G

Michael R. Heithaus

Dean, College of Arts, Sciences & Education
Professor, Department of Biological Sciences
Florida International University
Miami, Florida

Mike Heithaus joined the FIU Biology Department in 2003, has served as Director of the Marine Sciences Program, and as Executive Director of the School of Environment, Arts, and Society, which brings together the natural and social sciences and humanities to develop solutions to today's environmental challenges. He now serves as Dean of the College of Arts, Sciences & Education. His research focuses on predator-prey interactions and the ecological importance of large marine species. He has helped to guide the development of Life Science content in this science program, with a focus on strategies for teaching challenging content as well as the science and engineering practices of analyzing data and using computational thinking.

Georgia Reviewers

C. Alex Alvarez, EdD
Director of STEM and Curriculum
Valdosta City Schools
Valdosta, Georgia

Suzanne Salter Brooks
Teacher
Lee Middle School
Sharpsburg, Georgia

Cindy Brown
Teacher
Coffee Middle School
Douglas, Georgia

Monica Dyess, EdD
Pine Grove Middle School
Valdosta, Georgia

Felecia Eckman
Teacher
Carl Scoggins Middle School
Dallas, Georgia

Theresa D. Flanagan
Physical Science Instructor
Arnall Middle School
Newnan, Georgia

Toppy R. Gurley, EdS
Science Dept. Chair
P.B. Ritch Middle School
Dallas, Georgia

Angel James
Middle Grades Educator
Midway Middle School
Midway, Georgia

Keith A. Peterman
Life Science Teacher
Lewis Frasier Middle School
Hinesville, Georgia

Monique Prince, EdD
East Paulding Middle School
Dallas, Georgia

Melanie Smith, MEd
Physical Science Instructor
Arnall Middle School
Newnan, Georgia

Cynthia L. Tupper
Science Teacher
Lewis Frasier Middle School
Hinesville, Georgia

Content Reviewers

Paul D. Asimow, PhD
*Professor of Geology
and Geochemistry*
Division of Geological and Planetary Sciences
California Institute of Technology
Pasadena, CA

Laura K. Baumgartner, PhD
Postdoctoral Researcher
Molecular, Cellular, and Developmental
Biology
University of Colorado
Boulder, CO

Eileen Cashman, PhD
Professor
Department of Environmental Resources
Engineering
Humboldt State University
Arcata, CA

Hilary Clement Olson, PhD
Research Scientist Associate V
Institute for Geophysics, Jackson School of
Geosciences
The University of Texas at Austin
Austin, TX

Joe W. Crim, PhD
Professor Emeritus
Department of Cellular Biology
The University of Georgia
Athens, GA

Elizabeth A. De Stasio, PhD
*Raymond H. Herzog Professor
of Science*
Professor of Biology
Department of Biology
Lawrence University
Appleton, WI

Dan Franck, PhD
Botany Education Consultant
Chatham, NY

Julia R. Greer, PhD
*Assistant Professor of Materials Science and
Mechanics*
Division of Engineering and Applied Science
California Institute of Technology
Pasadena, CA

John E. Hoover, PhD
Professor
Department of Biology
Millersville University
Millersville, PA

William H. Ingham, PhD
Professor (Emeritus)
Department of Physics and Astronomy
James Madison University
Harrisonburg, VA

Charles W. Johnson, PhD
*Chairman, Division of Natural Sciences,
Mathematics, and Physical Education*
Associate Professor of Physics
South Georgia College
Douglas, GA

Tatiana A. Krivosheev, PhD
Associate Professor of Physics
Department of Natural Sciences
Clayton State University
Morrow, GA

Joseph A. McClure, PhD
Associate Professor Emeritus
Department of Physics
Georgetown University
Washington, DC

Mark Moldwin, PhD
Professor of Space Sciences
Atmospheric, Oceanic, and Space Sciences
University of Michigan
Ann Arbor, MI

Russell Patrick, PhD
Professor of Physics
Department of Biology, Chemistry, and Physics
Southern Polytechnic State University
Marietta, GA

Patricia M. Pauley, PhD
Meteorologist, Data Assimilation Group
Naval Research Laboratory
Monterey, CA

Stephen F. Pavkovic, PhD
Professor Emeritus
Department of Chemistry
Loyola University of Chicago
Chicago, IL

L. Jeanne Perry, PhD
Director (Retired)
Protein Expression Technology Center
Institute for Genomics and Proteomics
University of California,
Los Angeles
Los Angeles, CA

Kenneth H. Rubin, PhD
Professor
Department of Geology and Geophysics
University of Hawaii
Honolulu, HI

Brandon E. Schwab, PhD
Associate Professor
Department of Geology
Humboldt State University
Arcata, CA

Marllin L. Simon, PhD
Associate Professor
Department of Physics
Auburn University
Auburn, AL

Larry Stookey, PE
Upper Iowa University
Wausau, WI

Kim Withers, PhD
Associate Research Scientist
Center for Coastal Studies
Texas A&M University-Corpus Christi
Corpus Christi, TX

Matthew A. Wood, PhD
Professor
Department of Physics & Space Sciences
Florida Institute of Technology
Melbourne, FL

Adam D. Woods, PhD
Associate Professor
Department of Geological Sciences
California State University, Fullerton
Fullerton, CA

Natalie Zayas, MS, EdD
Lecturer
Division of Science and Environmental Policy
California State University, Monterey Bay
Seaside, CA

© Houghton Mifflin Harcourt Publishing Company

Contents

Contents (continued)

© Houghton Mifflin Harcourt Publishing Company

Contents (continued)

Assignments:

_____

_____

_____

_____

_____

_____

_____

_____

_____

_____

_____

_____

_____

_____

_____

_____

_____

_____

_____

_____

_____

_____

Life over Time

Big Idea

The types and characteristics of organisms change over time.

S7L1., S7L1.a, S7L1.b, S7L5., S7L5.a, S7L5.b, S7L5.c

Fossils provide valuable information about life over time. Some species, such as the ginkgo tree, have lived on Earth for millions of years.

Modern ginkgo leaf

What do you think?

Over Earth's history, life forms change as the environment changes. What kinds of organisms lived in your area during prehistoric times? As you explore the unit, gather evidence to help you state and support claims to answer this question.

Unit 1
Life over Time

Prehistoric Life

Scientists have learned a lot about prehistoric times from fossils. We know that life on Earth was very different in the geologic past, and that it changes over time.
A changing environment causes changes in the types of organisms that are able to survive.

Jurassic Period
206 mya–140 mya

The central United States was covered by a huge ocean during the age of the dinosaurs! Many fossils from that time period are from aquatic organisms.

Mosasaurs found in the Midwest are fossils of extinct marine reptiles.

What clues does this fossil give you about the type of food the animal ate?

_____
_____
_____
_____
_____
_____
_____
_____
_____
_____
_____
_____
_____
_____

Wood fossilizes when minerals replace all the organic material.

Mammals such as this saber-toothed cat once roamed Indiana grasslands.

Great white egrets live in Indiana's wetlands.

Tertiary Period
65 mya–2 mya

Land began to emerge from the water. Early mammals and some plants left many kinds of fossils behind, telling us a lot about this period.

Early Holocene
12,000–10,000 years ago

As humans occupied the land, many large animals, including mammoths, mastodons, saber-toothed cats, and giant sloths, disappeared.

Present Day

Humans have a large impact on the organisms living in the Midwest. Some species, such as the piping plover, are threatened with extinction due to human activities. Protecting these species helps to ensure that Midwestern habitats will remain diverse.

Take It Home | Your Neighborhood over Time

Your neighborhood has also changed over time. Do some research to find out when your town was founded. Create a timeline similar to the one above that shows the details of what changes your neighborhood and town might have experienced in the time since it was founded. See **ScienceSaurus**® for more information about change and diversity of life.

Introduction to Living Things

ESSENTIAL QUESTION

What are living things?

By the end of this lesson, you should be able to describe the necessities of life and the characteristics that all living things share.

Living things need energy to survive. This bluebird gets energy by eating insects like this dragonfly.

Engage Your Brain

1 Compare Both of these pictures show living things. How are these living things different?

_____

_____

_____

_____

_____

2 List Many of the things that people need to stay alive are not found in space. List the things that the International Space Station must have to keep astronauts alive.

_____

_____

_____

_____

_____

_____

_____

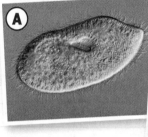

Active Reading

3 Synthesize Many English words have their roots in other languages. Use the Greek words below to make an educated guess about the meaning of the word *homeostasis*.

Greek word	Meaning
hómoios	similar
stásis	standing still

Example sentence
On a hot day, your body sweats to maintain homeostasis.

homeostasis:

_____

_____

Vocabulary Terms
- cell
- stimulus
- homeostasis
- DNA
- sexual reproduction
- asexual reproduction

4 Identify This list contains the vocabulary terms you'll learn in this lesson. As you read, underline the definition of each term.

Share and Share Alike

What characteristics do living things share?

An amazing variety of living things exists on Earth. These living things may seem very different, but they are all alike in several ways. What does a dog have in common with a bacterium? What does a fish have in common with a mushroom? There are five characteristics that all living things share.

Living Things Are Made of Cells

All living things are made of one or more cells. A **cell** is a membrane-covered structure that contains all of the materials necessary for life. Cells are the smallest unit of life, which means they are the smallest structures that can perform life functions. Most cells are so small they cannot be seen without a microscope. The membrane that surrounds a cell separates the cell's contents from its environment. Unicellular organisms are made up of only one cell. Multicellular organisms are made up of more than one cell. Some of these organisms have trillions of cells! Cells in a multicellular organism usually perform specialized functions.

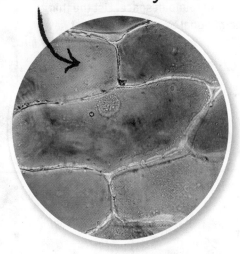

This is a microscopic view of cells in an onion root. An onion has many cells, so it is a multicellular organism.

Visualize It!

5 Categorize Identify each organism in the picture as unicellular or multicellular.

I'm an amoeba. I am:
☐ unicellular ☐ multicellular

I'm a cattail. I am:
☐ unicellular ☐ multicellular

I'm a turtle. I am:
☐ unicellular ☐ multicellular

Living Things Respond to Their Environment

All living things have the ability to sense change in their environment and to respond to that change. A change that affects the activity of an organism is called a **stimulus** (plural: stimuli). A stimulus can be gravity, light, sound, a chemical, hunger, or anything else that causes an organism to respond in some way. For example, when your pupils are exposed to light—a stimulus—they become smaller—a response.

Even though an organism's outside environment may change, conditions inside its body must stay relatively constant. Many chemical reactions keep an organism alive. These reactions can only happen when conditions are exactly right. An organism must maintain stable internal conditions to survive. The maintenance of a stable internal environment is called **homeostasis**. Your body maintains homeostasis by sweating when it gets hot and shivering when it gets cold. Each of these actions keeps the body at a stable internal temperature.

© Visualize It!

6 Claims • Evidence • Reasoning Why are these sunflowers all facing in the same direction? Explain your reasoning.

_____

_____

_____

_____

_____

Dogs respond to stimuli in their environment.

7 Infer Fill in the response that a dog might have to each stimulus listed in the table.

Stimulus	Response
Hunger	
Hot Day	
Owner with Leash	
Squirrel in Yard	
Friendly Dog	
Stranger	

Living Things Reproduce

Active Reading 8 **Identify** As you read, underline the ways in which organisms reproduce.

How does the world become filled with plants, animals, and other living things? Organisms make other organisms through the process of reproduction. When organisms reproduce, they pass copies of all or part of their DNA to their offspring. **DNA**, or deoxyribonucleic acid, is the genetic material that controls the structure and function of cells. DNA is found in the cells of all living things. Offspring share characteristics with their parents because they receive DNA from their parents.

Living things reproduce in one of two ways. Two parents produce offspring that share the characteristics of both parents through the process of **sexual reproduction**. Each offspring receives part of its DNA from each parent. Most animals and plants reproduce using sexual reproduction.

A single parent produces offspring that are identical to the parent through the process of **asexual reproduction**. Each offspring receives an exact copy of the parent's DNA. Most unicellular organisms and some plants and animals reproduce using asexual reproduction. Two methods of asexual reproduction are binary fission and budding. A unicellular organism splits into two parts during binary fission. During budding, a new organism grows on the parent organism until it is ready to separate.

A father pig is needed to produce piglets.

Visualize It!

9 **Identify** Use the check boxes to identify which offspring are identical to the parent or parents and which offspring are not identical.

A
Budding

B

A hydra produces offspring using asexual reproduction.

☐ identical ☐ not identical

A mother pig feeds her piglets. Pigs reproduce using sexual reproduction.

☐ identical ☐ not identical

Living Things Use Energy

Living things need energy to carry out the activities of life. Energy allows organisms to make or break down food, move materials into and out of cells, and build cells. Energy also allows organisms to move and interact with each other.

Where do living things get the energy they need for the activities of life? Plants convert energy from the sun into food. They store this food in their cells until they need to use it. Organisms that cannot make their own food must eat other organisms to gain energy. Some organisms eat plants. Others eat animals. Organisms such as fungi break down decaying material to gain energy.

10 Describe List three activities that you have done today that require energy.

_____

_____

_____

Living Things Grow and Mature

All living things grow during some period of their lives. When a unicellular organism grows, it gets larger and then divides, forming two cells. When a multicellular organism grows, the number of cells in its body increases, and the organism gets bigger.

Many living things don't just get larger as they grow. They also develop and change. Humans pass through different stages as they mature from childhood to adulthood. During these stages, the human body changes. Frogs and butterflies have body shapes that look completely different during different stages of development.

Visualize It!

11 Describe How does a frog grow and develop? Write a caption for each picture to describe each stage in a frog's life.

Younger Tadpoles (A)

_____

_____

Older Tadpole (B)

_____

_____

Adult Frog (C)

_____

_____

Stayin' Alive

Young eagles

What do living things need to survive?

Active Reading 12 **Identify** As you read, underline the four necessities of life.

Almost all organisms need water, air, food, and a place to live in order to survive. Water is essential for life. Cells are mostly made of water, and most chemical reactions in cells require water. Air contains gases that organisms need to survive. Cells use the oxygen in air to release energy from food. Organisms such as plants use the carbon dioxide in air to make food. Food provides organisms with the energy and nutrients that they need to survive. A place to live protects organisms from harm and contains the other necessities of life. Organisms often compete for food, water, and the best place to live.

Visualize It!

13 **Describe** How do the young eagles in the picture get each necessity of life?

Water: They get water from food that adult eagles bring to them.

Air: _____

_____

Food: _____

_____

Place to Live: _____

_____

_____

How do living things get food?

Food gives living things the energy and nutrients that they need to perform life processes. Nutrients include carbohydrates, lipids, and proteins. Fruits, vegetables, and grains provide carbohydrates. Nuts and fats provide lipids. Meats, nuts, and vegetables provide proteins.

Not all organisms get food in the same way. Producers make their own food. Consumers eat other organisms to get food. Decomposers break down dead organisms or wastes to get their food. Plants and algae are examples of producers. They use energy from the sun to make food. Animals such as deer are consumers that eat plants. Mice and squirrels are consumers that eat seeds from plants. Owls and eagles are consumers that eat other animals. Worms, bacteria, and fungi are examples of decomposers. They return nutrients to the soil, which other organisms can use.

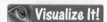 Visualize It!

14 Describe Look for these four organisms in the picture. How does each organism get its food?

Organism	Classification	Way of Getting Food
Barred Owl	Consumer	Eats mice and other small animals
Earthworm		
Red Squirrel		
Fern		

Visual Summary

To complete this summary, circle the correct word. Then use the key below to check your answers. You can use this page to review the main concepts of the lesson.

Introduction to Living Things

All living things are made of cells that contain DNA. Living things use energy, grow and develop, and reproduce. They also respond to changes in their environment.

15 Sunlight is an example of (a) homeostasis / stimulus.

16 Binary fission is an example of asexual / sexual reproduction.

Almost all living things need water, air, food, and a place to live.

17 Plants are producers / consumers.

18 Decomposers return organisms / nutrients to the environment.

Answers: 15 stimulus; 16 asexual; 17 producers; 18 nutrients

19 **Claims • Evidence • Reasoning** How do some producers and consumers each rely on light from the sun? State your claim. Summarize evidence to support your claim and explain your reasoning.

Lesson Review

Vocabulary

In your own words, define the following terms.

1 homeostasis

_____

_____

2 asexual reproduction

_____

_____

3 cell

_____

_____

Key Concepts

4 Explain What is the relationship between a stimulus and a response?

_____

_____

_____

_____

_____

5 Describe What happens to DNA during sexual reproduction?

_____

_____

_____

_____

6 Contrast What are the differences between producers, consumers, and decomposers?

_____

_____

_____

_____

_____

Critical Thinking

Use the pictures to answer the questions below.

7 Describe What is happening to the birds in the picture above?

_____

_____

_____

_____

8 Explain How do nutrients and energy allow the changes shown in the picture to happen?

_____

_____

_____

_____

_____

9 Compare How is a fish similar to an oak tree?

_____

_____

_____

10 Make Inferences Could life as we know it exist on Earth if air contained only oxygen? Explain your reasoning.

_____

_____

_____

_____

My Notes

Theory of Evolution by Natural Selection

ESSENTIAL QUESTION

What is the theory of evolution by natural selection?

By the end of this lesson, you should be able to describe the role of genetic variation and environmental factors in the theory of evolution by natural selection.

Because this grass snake's skin color looks like the plant stalk, it is able to hide from predators! This form of camouflage is the result of natural selection.

S7L5.a Natural selection and changes in traits

S7L5.b Genetic variation, environmental factors, and survival

Lesson Labs

Quick Labs
• Model Natural Selection
• Analyzing Survival Adaptations
• The Opposable Thumb

Exploration Lab
• Environmental Change and Evolution

Engage Your Brain

1 Predict Check T or F to show whether you think each statement is true or false.

T	F	
☐	☐	Fur color can help prevent an animal from being eaten.
☐	☐	The amount of available food can affect an organism's survival.
☐	☐	Your parents' characteristics are not passed on to you.
☐	☐	A species can go extinct if its habitat is destroyed.

2 Infer How do you think this bird and this flower are related? Explain your reasoning.

_____

_____

_____

_____

Active Reading

3 Synthesize You can often define an unknown word by clues provided in the sentence. Use the sentence below to make an educated guess about the meaning of the word *selective*.

Example sentence:
Many people are <u>selective</u> about the types of movies they like to watch.

selective:

_____

_____

_____

_____

Vocabulary Terms

• evolution
• selective breeding
• natural selection
• variation
• mutation
• adaptation
• extinction

4 Apply As you learn the definition of each vocabulary term in this lesson, create your own definition or sketch to help you remember the meaning of the term.

Darwin's Voyage

What did Darwin observe?

Charles Darwin was born in England in 1809. When he was 22 years old, Darwin graduated from college with a degree in theology. But he was also interested in plants and animals. Darwin became the naturalist—a scientist who studies nature—on the British ship HMS *Beagle*.

During his voyage, Darwin observed and collected many living and fossil specimens. He made some of his most important observations on the Galápagos Islands of South America. He kept a log that was later published as *The Voyage of the Beagle*. With the observations he made on this almost five-year journey, Darwin formed his idea about how biological evolution could happen.

In biology, **evolution** refers to the process by which populations change over time. A population is all of the individuals of a species that live in an area at the same time. A species is a group of closely related organisms that can mate to produce fertile offspring. Darwin developed a hypothesis, which eventually became a theory, of how evolution takes place.

Darwin left England on December 27, 1831. He returned 5 years later.

ENGLAND

EUROPE

NORTH AMERICA

The plants and animals on the Galápagos Islands differed from island to island. This is where Darwin studied birds called finches.

ATLANTIC OCEAN

AFRICA

Galápagos Islands

Equator

SOUTH AMERICA

Cape of Good Hope

Think Outside the Book [Inquiry]

5 Explore Trace Darwin's route on the map, and choose one of the following stops on his journey: Galápagos Islands, Andes Mountains, Australia. Do research to find out what plants and animals live there. Then write an entry in Darwin's log to describe what he might have seen.

Differences among Species

Darwin collected birds from the Galápagos Islands and nearby islands. He observed that these birds differed slightly from those on the nearby mainland of South America. And the birds on each island were different from the birds on the other islands. Careful analysis back in England revealed that they were all finches! Eventually, Darwin suggested that these birds may have evolved from one species of finch.

Darwin observed differences in beak size among finches from different islands. Many years later, scientists confirmed that these differences related to the birds' diets. Birds with shorter, heavier beaks could eat harder foods than those with thinner beaks.

This cactus finch has a narrow beak that it can use in many ways, including to pull grubs and insects from holes in the cactus.

This vegetarian finch has a curved beak, ideal for taking large berries from a branch.

Visualize It!

6 Infer How do you think the pointed beak of this woodpecker finch helps it to get food?

_____

_____

_____

Woodpecker finch

ASIA

INDIAN OCEAN

AUSTRALIA

Equator

Darwin saw many plants and animals that were found only on certain continents such as Australia.

NEW ZEALAND

km 0   1,000   2,000

mi 0   1,000   2,000

Darwin's Homework

What other ideas influenced Darwin?

The ideas of many scientists and observations of the natural world influenced Darwin's thinking. Darwin drew on ideas about Earth's history, the growth of populations, and observations of how traits are passed on in selective breeding. All of these pieces helped him develop his ideas about how populations could change over time.

Organisms Pass Traits Onto Offspring

Farmers and breeders have been producing many kinds of domestic animals and plants for thousands of years. These plants and animals have traits that the farmers and breeders desire. A *trait* is a form of an inherited characteristic. For example, the length of tail feathers is an inherited characteristic, and short or long tail feathers are the corresponding traits. The practice by which humans select plants or animals for breeding based on desired traits is **selective breeding**. Selective breeding, which is also called *artificial selection*, shows that traits can change. Traits can also spread through populations.

7 List Darwin studied selective breeding in the pigeons that he bred. List three other domestic animals that have many different breeds.

_____

_____

_____

_____

This chicken has been bred to have large tail feathers and a big red comb.

This chicken has been bred to have large head feathers.

This chicken has been bred to have feathers on its feet.

Organisms Acquire Traits

Scientist Jean-Baptiste Lamarck thought that organisms could acquire and pass on traits they needed to survive. For example, a man could develop stronger muscles over time. If the muscles were an advantage in his environment, Lamarck thought the man would pass on this trait to his offspring. Now we know that acquired traits are not passed onto offspring because these traits do not become part of an organism's DNA. But the fact that species change, and the idea that an organism's traits help it survive, shaped Darwin's ideas.

9 **Apply** Explain why the size of your muscles is partly an acquired trait and partly dependent on DNA.

_____

_____

_____

_____

These rock layers formed over millions of years.

Earth Changes over Time

The presence of different rock layers, such as those in the photo, show that Earth has changed over time. Geologist Charles Lyell hypothesized that small changes in Earth's surface have occurred over hundreds of millions of years. Darwin reasoned that if Earth were very old, then there would be enough time for very small changes in life forms to add up.

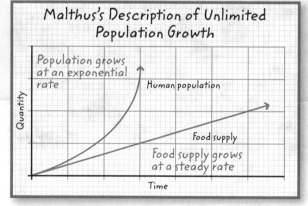

Malthus's Description of Unlimited Population Growth

Population grows at an exponential rate

Human population

Food supply

Food supply grows at a steady rate

Quantity

Time

A Struggle for Survival Exists

After his journey, Darwin read an essay about population growth by economist Thomas Malthus. The essay helped Darwin understand how the environment could influence which organisms survive and which organisms die. All populations are affected by factors that limit population growth, such as disease, predation, and competition for food. Darwin reasoned that the survivors probably have specific traits that help them survive and that some of these traits could be passed on from parent to offspring.

Visualize It!

10 **Summarize** What can you conclude from the two red growth lines on this graph?

_____

_____

_____

Natural Selection

What are the four parts of natural selection?

Darwin proposed that most evolution happens through the natural selection of advantageous traits. **Natural selection** is the process by which organisms that inherit advantageous traits tend to reproduce more successfully than other organisms do. There are four parts that contribute to the process of evolution by natural selection—overproduction, genetic variation, selection, and adaptation.

Overproduction

When a plant or animal reproduces, it usually makes more offspring than the environment can support. For example, a female jaguar may have up to four cubs at a time. Across the jaguar population, only some of them will survive to adulthood, and a smaller number of them will successfully reproduce.

11 Infer What might be a natural reason for low survival rates of jaguar cubs?

_____

_____

_____

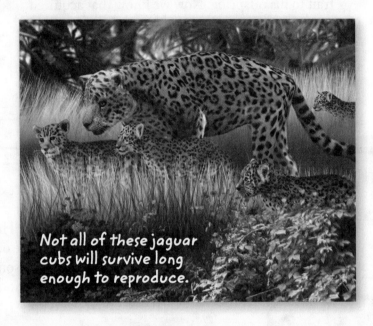

Not all of these jaguar cubs will survive long enough to reproduce.

Variation exists in the jaw sizes of these two jaguars. This variation will be passed onto the next generation.

Genetic Variation

Within a species there are naturally occurring differences, or **variations**, in traits. For example, in the two jaguar skulls to the left, one jaw is larger than the other. This difference results from a difference in the genetic material of the jaguars. Genetic variations can be passed on from parent to offspring. An important source of variation is a **mutation**, or change in genetic material.

With each new generation, genetic variation introduces changes to the traits of a population. Greater genetic variation in a population increases the chance that some individuals will have traits that can help them survive environmental changes or diseases. Traits that enhance an individual's ability to reproduce will also increase the probability of survival of a species.

Selection

Individuals try to get the resources they need to survive. These resources include food, water, space, and, in most cases, mates for reproduction. About 11,000 years ago, jaguars faced a shortage of food because the climate changed and many prey species died out. A genetic variation in jaw size then became important for survival. Jaguars with larger jaws could eat hard-shelled reptiles when other prey were hard to find.

Darwin reasoned that individuals with a particular trait, such as a large jaw, are more likely to survive long enough to reproduce. As a result, the trait is "selected" for, becoming more common in the next generation.

12 Summarize As you read, underline how large jaws become typical traits of jaguars.

A larger jaw makes it easier for this jaguar to eat hard-shelled turtles.

Adaptation

An inherited trait that helps an organism survive and reproduce in its environment is an **adaptation**. Adaptation is the selection of naturally occurring trait variations in populations. Jaguars with larger jaws survived and reproduced when food was hard to find. As natural selection continues, adaptations grow more common in populations over successive generations. Over time, the population becomes better adapted to the environment.

Large jaw size is one adaptation of jaguars.

Almost 150 years after Darwin was in the Galápagos Islands, Rosemary and Peter Grant studied the distribution of beak depths of medium ground finches on the island of Daphne Major. In 1977, a severe drought struck the island, significantly reducing the breeding population. A year later, the Grants measured the population again.

Medium Ground Finch Population—Daphne Major

Beak Depth (mm)	Number of Birds			
	1976		1978	
	Parents	Offspring	Parents	Offspring
7.3	1	2	0	2
7.8	12	8	1	2
8.3	30	15	3	6
8.8	47	27	3	21
9.3	46	16	7	34
9.8	40	10	8	37
10.3	26	2	9	18
10.8	3	2	1	15
11.3	0	1	0	3

Source: BioScience, 2003

Think Outside the Book Inquiry

13 Claims • Evidence • Reasoning Look at the data gathered by the Grants. Make a graph using the table. Then calculate the average beak depth in 1976 and 1978. Explain how genetic variation (beak depth) and environmental factors (drought) led to changes in the population of medium ground finches. How would these changes have affected the probability of survival of the finches? How did natural selection lead to a change in a trait that was passed over generations? Use your graph as evidence to support your claims and explain your reasoning.

Well-adapted

How do species change over time?

In order for a population to change, some individuals have to be genetically different from other members of the population. Mutations are one of the main sources of genetic variation. Offspring sometimes inherit a gene that has a slight mutation, or change, from the gene the parent has. Mutations can be harmful, helpful, or have no effect. Beneficial mutations help individuals survive and reproduce.

Over Generations, Adaptations Become More Common

Active Reading 14 **Identify** Underline examples of adaptations.

Adaptations are inherited traits that help organisms survive and reproduce. Some adaptations, such as a duck's webbed feet, are physical. Other adaptations are inherited behaviors that help an organism find food, protect itself, or reproduce. At first, an adaptation is rare in a population. Imagine a bird population in which some birds have short beaks. If more birds with shorter beaks survive and reproduce than birds with longer beaks, more birds in the next generation will probably have short beaks. The number of individuals with the adaptation would continue to increase.

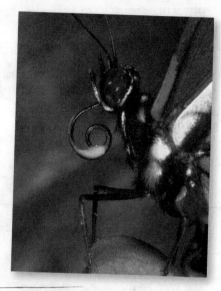

Visualize It!

15 Write a caption to describe how this butterfly's long mouth part helps it to survive.

_____

_____

_____

_____

Genetic Differences Add Up

Parents and offspring often have small differences in genetic material. Over many generations, the small differences can add up. These differences accumulate so that organisms alive now are often very different from their ancestors. As a result, there is great diversity among organisms. For example, the antibiotic penicillin was able to kill many types of bacteria in the 1950s. Today, some of those species of bacteria are now completely resistant to penicillin. The genetic makeup of these bacterial populations has changed. New fossil discoveries and new information about genes add to scientists' understanding of natural selection and evolution.

The male frigate bird uses his red throat pouch to attract a female, which could lead to reproduction.

What happens to species as the environment changes?

Certain environments favor certain traits. Consider a snake population with either brown- or green-colored snakes. In a forest that has many dead leaves on the ground, brown snakes will blend in better than green snakes will. But in an area with more grass, the green snakes may be better at hiding from predators. Changes in environmental conditions can affect the survival of organisms with a particular trait. Environmental changes can also lead to diversity of organisms by increasing the number of species.

Dinosaurs went extinct 65 million years ago.

Adaptations Can Allow a Species to Survive

All organisms have traits that allow them to survive in specific environments. For example, plants have xylem tissue that carries water up from the roots to the rest of the plant.

If the environment changes, a species is more likely to survive if it has genetic variation. For example, imagine a species of grass in which some plants need less water than others. If the environment became drier, many grass plants would die, but the plants that needed less water might survive. These plants might eventually become a new species if they cannot reproduce with the plants that needed more water.

Some Species May Become Extinct

If no individuals have traits that help them to survive and reproduce in the changed environment, a species will become extinct. **Extinction** occurs when all members of a species have died. Greater competition, new predators, and the loss of habitat are examples of environmental changes that can lead to extinction. Some extinctions are caused by natural disasters. Because a natural disaster can destroy resources quickly, organisms may die no matter what adaptations they have. The fossil record shows that many species have become extinct in the history of life on Earth.

Visualize It!

Environmental change has affected the environmental conditions near the North Pole.

16 Summarize How has ice cover near the North Pole changed in the last few decades?

_____

_____

17 Infer How do you think this environmental change will affect species that live in the area? Explain your reasoning.

_____

_____

_____

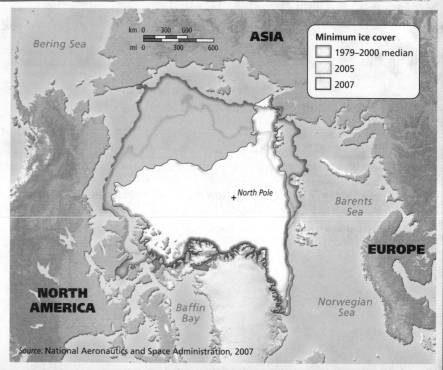

Minimum ice cover
- 1979–2000 median
- 2005
- 2007

Bering Sea
ASIA
North Pole
Barents Sea
EUROPE
NORTH AMERICA
Baffin Bay
Norwegian Sea

Source: National Aeronautics and Space Administration, 2007

Visual Summary

To complete this summary, circle the correct word. Then use the key below to check your answers. You can use this page to review the main concepts of the lesson.

Evolution is Change over Time

Darwin's theory of natural selection was influenced by his own observations and the work of other scientists.

18 Through natural selection / selective breeding, breeders choose the traits that are passed onto the next generation.

Many extinctions have occurred over the course of Earth's history.

20 Because of environmental change, dinosaurs eventually became mutated / extinct.

The theory of evolution by natural selection states that organisms with advantageous traits produce more offspring.

19 Natural selection can act only on acquired traits / inherited variation.

Answers: 18 selective breeding; 19 inherited variation; 20 extinct

21 **Claims • Evidence • Reasoning** How does the environment influence the likelihood of a species surviving and reproducing? State your claim. Summarize evidence to support your claim and explain your reasoning.

Lesson Review

Vocabulary

Use a term from the lesson to complete the sentences below.

1 The four parts of natural selection are overproduction, _____, selection, and adaptation.

2 _____ is the process by which populations change over time.

3 The hollow bones of birds, which keep birds lightweight for flying, is an example of a(n) _____

Key Concepts

4 Summarize Describe Darwin's observations on the Galápagos Islands during his voyage on the HMS *Beagle*.

_____

_____

_____

_____

5 Explain How does environmental change affect the survival of a species?

_____

_____

_____

_____

6 Compare Why are only inherited traits, not acquired ones, involved in the process of natural selection?

_____

_____

_____

7 Describe What is the relationship between mutation, natural selection, and adaptation?

_____

_____

_____

Critical Thinking

Use the diagram to answer the following question.

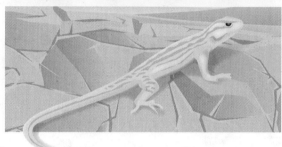

8 Apply How is each of these lizards adapted to its environment?

_____

_____

_____

_____

_____

_____

_____

_____

9 Infer What might happen to a population of rabbits in a forest if a new predator moved to the forest?

_____

_____

_____

_____

_____

My Notes

Scientific Debate

Not all scientific knowledge is gained through experimentation. It is also the result of a great deal of debate and confirmation.

Tutorial

As you prepare for a debate, look for information from the following sources.

Controlled Experiments Consider the following points when planning or examining the results of a controlled experiment.

- Only one factor should be tested at a time. A factor is anything in the experiment that can influence the outcome.

- Samples are divided into experimental group(s) and a control group. All of the factors of the experimental group(s) and the control group are the same except for one variable.

- A variable is a factor that can be changed. If there are multiple variables, only one variable should be changed at a time.

Independent Studies The results of a different group may provide stronger support for your argument than your own results. And using someone else's results helps to avoid the claim that your results are biased. Bias is the tendency to think about something from only one point of view. The claim of bias can be used to argue against your point.

Comparison with Similar Objects or Events If you cannot gather data from an experiment to help support your position, finding a similar object or event might help. The better your example is understood, the stronger your argument will be.

Read the passage below and answer the questions.

Many people want to protect endangered species but do not agree on the best methods to use. Incubating, or heating eggs to ensure hatching, is commonly used with bird eggs. It was logical to apply the same technique to turtle eggs. The Barbour's map turtle is found in Florida, Georgia, and Alabama. To help more turtles hatch, people would gather eggs and incubate them. However, debate really began when mostly female turtles hatched. Were efforts to help the turtles really harming them? Scientists learned that incubating eggs at 25°C (77°F) produces males and at 30°C (86°F) produces females. As a result, conservation programs have stopped artificially heating the eggs.

1 What is the variable described in the article about Barbour's map turtles?

_____

2 Write a list of factors that were likely kept the same between the sample groups described in the article.

_____

_____

_____

3 What argument could people have used who first suggested incubating the turtle eggs?

_____

_____

_____

© Houghton Mifflin Harcourt Publishing Company • Image Credits: (bl) ©Zigmund Leszczynski/age fotostock

You Try It!

Fossils from the Burgess Shale Formation in Canada include many strange creatures that lived over 500 million years ago. The fossils are special because the soft parts of the creatures were preserved. Examine the fossil of the creature *Marrella* and the reconstruction of what it might have looked like.

Fossil

Reconstruction

1 Recognizing Relationships Find four features on the reconstruction that you can also identify in the fossil. Write a brief description of each feature.

_____

_____

_____

_____

_____

_____

2 Applying Concepts *Marrella* is extinct. How do you think *Marrella* behaved when it was alive? What did it eat? How did it move? Summarize evidence to support your claims and explain your reasoning.

_____

_____

_____

_____

_____

_____

_____

_____

3 Communicating Ideas Share your description with a classmate. Discuss and debate your positions. Complete the table to show the points on which you agree and disagree.

Agree	Disagree

Take It Home

Research more about the creatures of the Burgess Shale Formation. Find at least one other fossil creature and its reconstruction. What do you think the creature was like?

Evidence of Evolution

ESSENTIAL QUESTION

What evidence supports the theory of evolution?

By the end of this lesson, you should be able to describe the evidence that supports the theory of evolution by natural selection.

S7L5.c Extinct and modern organisms

Fossils show us what a dinosaur looks like. This dinosaur lived millions of years ago!

© Houghton Mifflin Harcourt Publishing Company • Image Credits: ©Bill Varie/Corbis

🖐 Lesson Labs

Quick Labs
• Comparing Anatomy
• Genetic Evidence for Evolution

Field Lab
• Mystery Footprints

🧠 Engage Your Brain

1 Predict Check T or F to show whether you think each statement is true or false.

T	F	
☐	☐	Fossils provide evidence of organisms that lived in the past.
☐	☐	The wing of a bat has similar bones to those in a human arm.
☐	☐	DNA can tell us how closely related two organisms are.
☐	☐	Whales are descended from land-dwelling mammals.

2 Infer This is a Petoskey stone, which is made up of tiny coral fossils. What can you infer if you find a coral fossil on land? Explain your reasoning.

Petoskey stone

_____

_____

_____

_____

📖 Active Reading

3 Synthesize You can often define an unknown word if you understand the parts of the word. Use the words below to make an educated guess about the meaning of the word *fossil record*.

Word	Meaning
fossil	the remains or trace of once-living organisms
record	an account that preserves information about facts or events

Vocabulary Terms

• fossil
• fossil record

4 Apply As you learn the definition of each vocabulary term in this lesson, create your own definition or sketch to help you remember the meaning of the term.

fossil record:

_____

_____

_____

Fossil Hunt

How do fossils form?

Evidence that organisms have changed over time can be found in amber, ice, or sedimentary rock. Sedimentary rock is formed when particles of sand or soil are deposited in horizontal layers. Often this occurs as mud or silt hardens. After one rock layer forms, newer rock layers form on top of it. So, older layers are found below or underneath younger rock layers. The most basic principle of dating such rocks and the remains of organisms inside is "the deeper it is, the older it is."

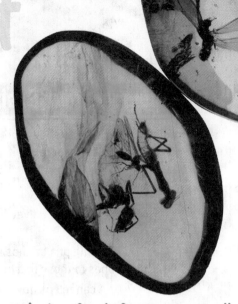

Amber fossils form when small creatures are trapped in tree sap and the sap hardens.

5 Examine What features of the organism are preserved in amber?

_____

_____

_____

This flying dinosaur is an example of a cast fossil.

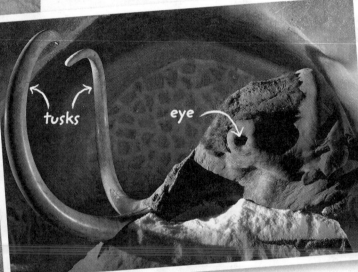

tusks

eye

Because this woolly mammoth was frozen in ice, its skin and hair were preserved.

Many Fossils Form in Sedimentary Rock

Rock layers preserve evidence of organisms that were once alive. The remains or imprints of once-living organisms are called **fossils**. Fossils commonly form when a dead organism is covered by a layer of sediment or mud. Over time, more sediment settles on top of the organism. Minerals in the sediment may seep into the organism and replace the body's material with minerals that harden over time. This process produces a cast fossil. Many familiar fossils are casts of hard parts, such as shells and bones. If the organism rots away completely after being covered, it may leave an imprint of itself in the rock. Despite all of the fossils that have been found, it is rare for an organism to become a fossil. Most often, the dead organism is recycled back into the biological world by scavengers, decomposers, or the process of weathering.

How do fossils show change over time?

All of the fossils that have been discovered make up the **fossil record**. The fossil record provides evidence about the existence of species, the order in which they have existed through time, and how they have changed over time. By examining the fossil record, scientists can learn about the history of life on Earth.

Despite all the fossils that have been found, there are gaps in the fossil record. These gaps represent chunks of geologic time for which a fossil has not been discovered. Also, the transition between two groups of organisms may not be well understood. Fossils that help fill in these gaps are *transitional fossils*.

Fossils found in newer layers of Earth's crust tend to have physical or molecular similarities to modern organisms. These similarities indicate that the fossilized organisms were close relatives of the modern organisms. Fossils from older layers are less similar to modern organisms than fossils from newer layers are. Most older fossils are of earlier life forms such as dinosaurs, which don't exist anymore because they are extinct.

Active Reading

6 Identify As you read, underline the steps that describe how a cast fossil forms.

Visualize It!

Ⓐ
Ⓑ
Ⓒ
Ⓓ

7 Claims • Evidence • Reasoning What do the patterns in this fossil record tell you about the existence and diversity of these extinct organisms? State your claim. Then, support your claim with evidence and explain your reasoning.

_____

_____

_____

_____

8 Synthesize How does the fossil record provide evidence of evolution? Summarize evidence to support your claim and explain your reasoning.

_____

_____

_____

_____

More clues . . .

What other evidence supports evolution?

Many fields of study provide evidence that modern species and extinct species share an ancestor. A *common ancestor* is the most recent species from which two different species have evolved. Structural data, DNA, developmental patterns, and fossils all support the theory that populations change over time. Sometimes these populations become new species. Biologists observe that all living organisms have some traits in common and inherit traits in similar ways. Evidence of when and where those ancestors lived and what they looked like is found in the fossil record.

Active Reading

9 List What is a common ancestor?

_____

_____

_____

Common Structures

Scientists have found that related organisms share structural traits. Structures reduced in size or function may have been complete and functional in the organism's ancestor. For example, snakes have traces of leglike structures that are not used for movement. These unused structures are evidence that snakes share a common ancestor with animals like lizards and dogs.

Scientists also consider similar structures with different functions. The arm of a human, the front leg of a cat, and the wing of a bat do not look alike and are not used in the same way. But as you can see, they are similar in structure. The bones of a human arm are similar in structure to the bones in the front limbs of a cat and a bat. These similarities suggest that cats, bats, and humans had a common ancestor. Over millions of years, changes occurred. Now, these bones perform different functions in each type of animal.

front limb of a bat

front limb of a cat

Visualize It!

10 Relate Do you see any similarities between the bones of the bat and cat limbs and the bones of the human arm? If so, use the colors of the bat and cat bones to color similar bones in the human arm. If you don't have colored pencils, label the bones with the correct color names.

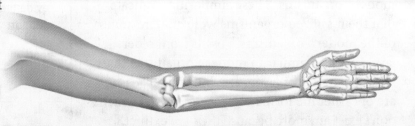

Similar DNA

The genetic information stored in an organism's DNA determines the organism's traits. Because an organism's DNA stays almost exactly the same throughout its entire lifetime, scientists can compare the DNA from many organisms. The greater the number of similarities between the molecules of any two species, the more recently the two species most likely shared a common ancestor.

Recall that DNA determines which amino acids make up a protein. Scientists have compared the amino acids that make up cytochrome c proteins in many species. Cytochrome c is involved in cellular respiration. Organisms that have fewer amino acid differences are more likely to be closely related.

Frogs also have cytochrome c proteins, but they're a little different from yours.

Cytochrome C Comparison	
Organism	Number of amino acid differences from human cytochrome c
Chimpanzee	0
Rhesus monkey	1
Whale	10
Turtle	15
Bullfrog	18
Lamprey	20

Source: M. Dayhoff, *Atlas of Protein Sequence and Structure*

Visualize It!

11 Infer The number of amino acids in human cytochrome c differs between humans and the species at left. Which two species do you infer are the least closely related to humans?

_____

_____

_____

_____

Developmental Similarities

The study of development is called *embryology*. Embryos undergo many physical and functional changes as they grow and develop. If organisms develop in similar ways, they also likely share a common ancestor.

Scientists have compared the development of different species to look for similar patterns and structures. Scientists think that such similarities come from an ancestor that the species have in common. For example, at some time during development, all animals with backbones have a tail. This observation suggests that they shared a common ancestor.

These embryos are at a similar stage of development.

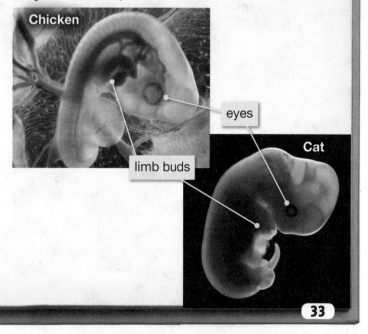

Chicken

Cat

eyes

limb buds

Visualize It!

How do we know organisms are related?

Scientists examine organisms carefully for clues about their ancestors. In a well-studied example, scientists looked at the characteristics of whales that made them different from other ocean animals. Unlike fish and sharks, whales breathe air, give birth to live young, and produce milk. Fossil and DNA evidence support the hypothesis that modern whales evolved from hoofed mammals that lived on land.

Fossil Evidence

Scientists have examined fossils of extinct species that have features in between whales and land mammals. These features are called *transitional characters*. None of these species are directly related to modern whales. But their skeletons suggest how a gradual transition from land mammal to aquatic whale could have happened.

A **Pakicetus** **52 million years ago**
- whale-shaped skull and teeth adapted for hunting fish
- ran on four legs
- ear bones in between those of land and aquatic mammals

B **Ambulocetus natans** **50 million years ago**
- name means "the walking whale that swims"
- hind limbs that were adapted for swimming
- a fish eater that lived on water and on land

C **Dorudon** **About 40 million years ago**
- lived in warm seas and propelled itself with a long tail
- tiny hind legs could not be used for swimming
- pelvis and hind limbs not connected to spine, could not support weight for walking

Unused Structures
Most modern whales have pelvic bones and some have leg bones. These bones do not help the animal move.

34

© Houghton Mifflin Harcourt Publishing Company

Molecular Evidence

The DNA of whales is very similar to the DNA of hoofed mammals. Below are some DNA fragments of a gene that makes a type of milk protein.

Hippopotamus   TCC TGGCA GTCCA GTGGT

Humpback whale   CCC TGGCA GTGCA GTGCT

12 Identify Circle the pairs of nitrogen bases (G, T, C, or A) that differ between the hippopotamus and humpback whale DNA.

13 Infer How do you think these bones are involved in a whale's movement?

_____

_____

_____

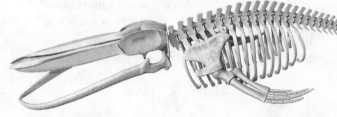

Modern Whale   *Present day*

- no hind limbs, front limbs are flippers
- some whales have tiny hip bones left over from their hoofed-mammal ancestors
- breathe air with lungs like other mammals do

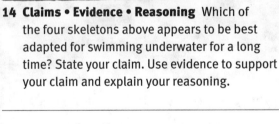

14 Claims • Evidence • Reasoning Which of the four skeletons above appears to be best adapted for swimming underwater for a long time? State your claim. Use evidence to support your claim and explain your reasoning.

_____

_____

_____

_____

_____

_____

_____

_____

Visual Summary

To complete this summary, circle the correct word. Then use the key below to check your answers. You can use this page to review the main concepts of the lesson.

Evidence of Evolution

Fossil evidence shows that life on Earth has changed over time.

15 The remains of once-living organisms are called fossils / ancestors.

Scientists use evidence from many fields of research to study the common ancestors of living organisms.

Evolutionary theory is also supported by structural, genetic, and developmental evidence.

16 Similarities / Differences in internal structures support evidence of common ancestry.

17 The tiny leg bones / large dorsal fins of modern whales are an example of unused structures.

Answers: 15 fossils; 16 similarities; 17 tiny leg bones

18 Summarize How does the fossil record provide evidence of the diversity of life?

Lesson Review

Vocabulary

1 Which word means "the remains or imprints of once-living organisms found in layers of rock?"

_____

2 Which word means "the history of life in the geologic past as indicated by the imprints or remains of living things?"

_____

Key Concepts

3 Identify What are two types of evidence that suggest that evolution has occurred?

_____

_____

_____

4 Explain How do fossils provide evidence that evolution has taken place?

_____

_____

_____

5 Apply What is the significance of the similar number and arrangement of bones in a human arm and a bat wing?

_____

_____

_____

Critical Thinking

6 Imagine If you were a scientist examining the DNA sequence of two unknown organisms that you hypothesize share a common ancestor, what evidence would you expect to find?

_____

_____

_____

Use this table to answer the following questions.

Cytochrome C Comparison	
Organism	Number of amino acid differences from human cytochrome c
Chimpanzee	0
Turtle	15
Tuna	21

Source: M. Dayhoff, *Atlas of Protein Sequence and Structure*

7 Identify What do the data suggest about how related turtles are to humans compared to tuna and chimpanzees?

_____

_____

_____

8 Infer If there are no differences between the amino acid sequences in the cytochrome c protein of humans and chimpanzees, why aren't we the same species? State your claim and provide evidence to support your reasoning.

_____

_____

_____

_____

_____

_____

9 Apply Explain why the pattern of differences that exists from earlier to later fossils in the fossil record supports the idea that evolution has taken place on Earth.

_____

_____

_____

_____

My Notes

Lesson **4**

The History of Life on Earth

ESSENTIAL QUESTION

How has life on Earth changed over time?

By the end of this lesson, you should be able to describe the evolution of life on Earth over time, using the geologic time scale.

Trilobites like this one lived on Earth about 400 million years ago. This fossil preserved great detail of the trilobite's body parts.

S7L5.c Extinct and modern organisms

🧠 Engage Your Brain

1 Predict Check T or F to show whether you think each statement is true or false.

T   F

☐ ☐ A mass extinction occurs when a large number of species go extinct during a relatively short amount of time.

☐ ☐ The largest division of the geologic time scale is the era.

☐ ☐ We currently live in the Cenozoic era.

☐ ☐ Fossils show that the first living things were very tiny.

2 Draw Imagine you find a fossil of a fish. Which parts of the fish could you see in the fossil? Draw what you think you would see below.

✏️ Active Reading

3 Apply Use context clues to write your own definition for the words *fossil record* and *extinction*.

Example sentence
Scientists develop hypotheses about Earth's history based on observable changes in the <u>fossil record</u>.

fossil record:

_____

_____

Example sentence
Endangered species are protected by law in an effort to preserve them from <u>extinction</u>.

extinction:

_____

_____

Vocabulary Terms
- fossil
- fossil record
- extinction
- geologic time scale

4 Identify As you read, place a question mark next to any words that you don't understand. When you finish reading the lesson, go back and review the text that you marked. If the information is still confusing, consult a classmate or a teacher.

Uncovering Clues

How do we learn about ancient life?

Paleontologists look for clues to understand what happened in the past. These scientists use fossils to reconstruct the history of life. A **fossil** is a trace or imprint of a living thing that is preserved by geological processes. Fossils of single-celled organisms date as far back as 3.8 billion years.

What can we learn from fossils?

All of the fossils that have been discovered worldwide make up the **fossil record**. By examining the fossil record, scientists can identify when different species lived and died. There are two ways to describe the ages of fossils. *Relative dating* determines whether a fossil formed before or after another fossil. When an organism is trapped in mud or sediment, the resulting fossil becomes part of that sedimentary layer of rock. In rock layers that are not disturbed, newer fossils are found in layers of rock that are above older fossils. *Absolute dating* estimates the age of a fossil in years. Estimations are based on information from radioactive elements in certain rocks near the fossil.

Visualize It!

The abbreviation Ma stands for mega annum. A mega annum is equal to 1 million years. Ma is often used to indicate "million years ago."

5 Infer What does absolute dating tell you about fossil A?

_____

_____

_____

_____

6 Claims • Evidence • Reasoning
Study the patterns in the layers. What conclusion might you draw if a layer contained a wider variety of fossilized organisms? State your claim. Support your claim with evidence and explain your reasoning.

_____

_____

_____

_____

_____

_____

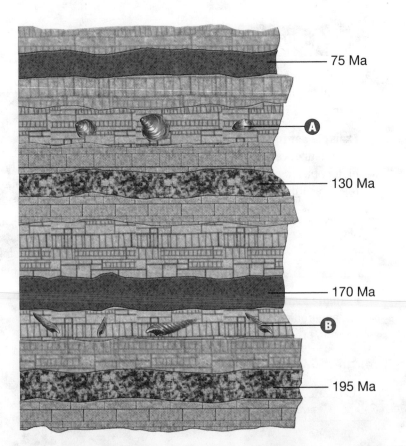

75 Ma

A

130 Ma

170 Ma

B

195 Ma

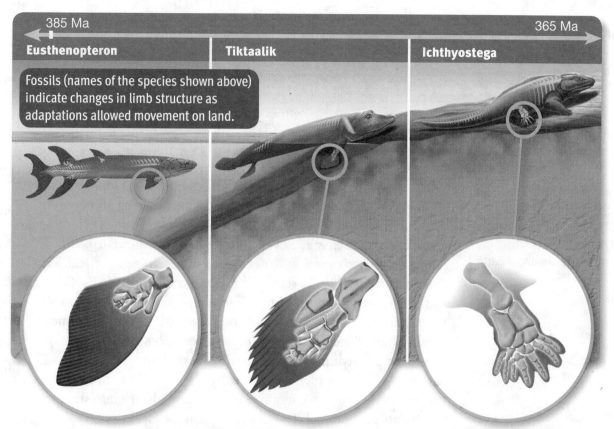

385 Ma

365 Ma

Eusthenopteron **Tiktaalik** **Ichthyostega**

Fossils (names of the species shown above) indicate changes in limb structure as adaptations allowed movement on land.

How Life Forms Have Changed over Time

The fossil record documents the existence of many different organisms that have lived during Earth's long history. Each fossil gives information about a single organism. But the overall fossil record helps us understand larger patterns of change.

Over many generations, populations change. These changes can be preserved in fossils. For example, fossils show the gradual change in limb structure, over many millions of years, of animals such as the ones shown in the drawing above.

Some species are present in the fossil record for a relatively short period of time. Other species have survived for long time spans without much change. The hard-plated horseshoe crab, for example, has changed little over the last 350 million years.

When Extinctions Occurred

An **extinction** happens when every individual of a species dies. A mass extinction occurs when a large number of species go extinct during a relatively short amount of time. Gradual environmental changes can cause mass extinctions. Catastrophic events, such as the impact of an asteroid, can also cause mass extinctions.

Extinctions and mass extinctions are documented in the fossil record. Fossils that were common in certain rock layers may decrease in frequency and eventually disappear altogether. Based on evidence in the fossil record, scientists form hypotheses about how and when species went extinct.

Visualize It!

7 Describe How does the pattern of change in the limb structure of the three animals above explain the relationship between modern reptiles and Eusthenopteron?

_____

_____

_____

_____

Active Reading

8 Describe How can the extinction of an organism be inferred from evidence in the fossil record? Use evidence to support your reasoning.

_____

_____

_____

_____

_____

_____

Way Back When

What is the geologic time scale?

After a fossil is dated, a paleontologist can place the fossil in chronological order with other fossils. This ordering allows scientists to hypothesize about relationships between species and how organisms changed over time. To keep track of Earth's long history, scientists have developed the geologic time scale. The **geologic time scale** is the standard method used to divide Earth's long 4.6-billion-year natural history into manageable parts.

Paleontologists adjust and add details to the geologic time scale when new evidence is found. The early history of Earth has been poorly understood, because fossils from this time span are rare. As new evidence about early life on Earth accumulates, scientists may need to organize Earth's early history into smaller segments of time.

![Active Reading]

9 Identify Underline one reason why it is hard for scientists to study the early history of Earth.

Visualize It!

10 Identify When did the Paleozoic era begin and end?

_____

_____

_____

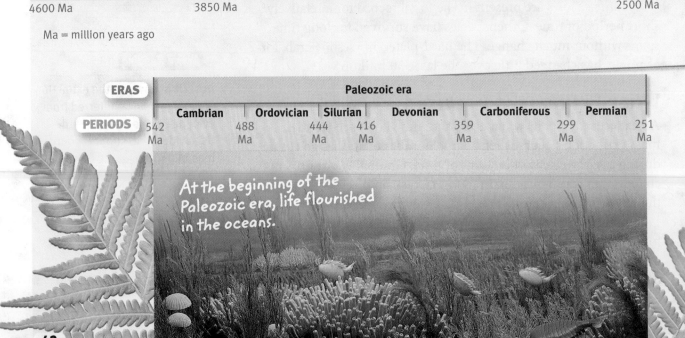

Precambrian time (4600 Ma to 542 Ma)

EONS	Hadean eon	Archean eon	
	4600 Ma	3850 Ma	2500 Ma

Ma = million years ago

ERAS	Paleozoic era					
PERIODS	Cambrian	Ordovician	Silurian	Devonian	Carboniferous	Permian
	542 Ma	488 Ma	444 Ma	416 Ma	359 Ma	299 Ma / 251 Ma

At the beginning of the Paleozoic era, life flourished in the oceans.

A Tool to Organize Earth's History

Boundaries between geologic time intervals correspond to significant changes in Earth's history. Some major boundaries are defined by mass extinctions or significant changes in the number of species. Other boundaries are defined by major changes in Earth's surface or climate.

The largest divisions of the geologic time scale are eons. Eons are divided into eras. Eras are characterized by the type of organism that dominated Earth at the time. Each era began with a change in the type of organism that was most dominant. Eras are further divided into periods, and periods are divided into epochs.

The four major divisions that make up the history of life on Earth are Precambrian time, the Paleozoic era, the Mesozoic era, and the Cenozoic era. Precambrian time is made up of the first three eons of Earth's history.

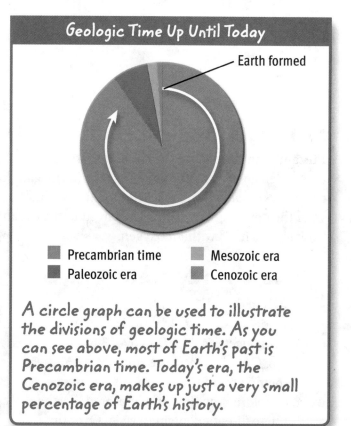

Geologic Time Up Until Today

Earth formed

- Precambrian time
- Paleozoic era
- Mesozoic era
- Cenozoic era

A circle graph can be used to illustrate the divisions of geologic time. As you can see above, most of Earth's past is Precambrian time. Today's era, the Cenozoic era, makes up just a very small percentage of Earth's history.

Visualize It!

11 List Which three periods make up the Mesozoic era?

_____

_____

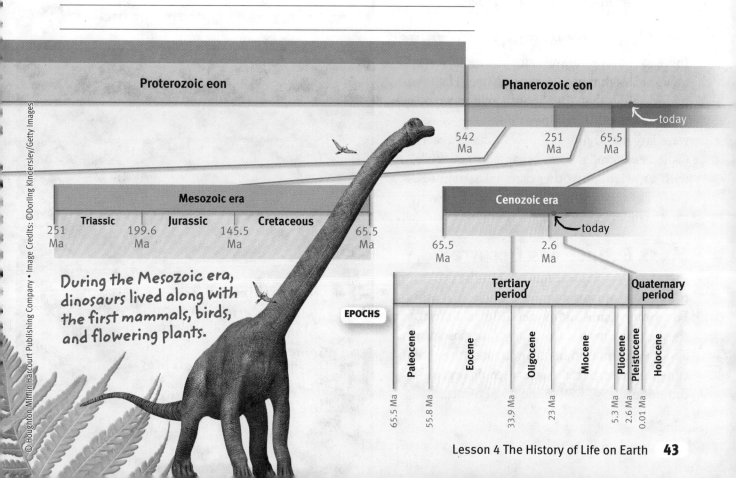

Proterozoic eon

Phanerozoic eon

today

542 Ma   251 Ma   65.5 Ma

Mesozoic era

| 251 Ma | Triassic | 199.6 Ma | Jurassic | 145.5 Ma | Cretaceous | 65.5 Ma |

Cenozoic era

65.5 Ma   today   2.6 Ma

During the Mesozoic era, dinosaurs lived along with the first mammals, birds, and flowering plants.

EPOCHS

Tertiary period

Quaternary period

| Paleocene | Eocene | Oligocene | Miocene | Pliocene | Pleistocene | Holocene |

65.5 Ma   55.8 Ma   33.9 Ma   23 Ma   5.3 Ma   2.6 Ma   0.01 Ma

Ancient Wisdom

What defined Precambrian time?

Precambrian time started 4.6 billion years ago, when Earth formed, and ended about 542 million years ago. Life began during this time. *Prokaryotes*—single-celled organisms without a nucleus—were the dominant life form. They lived in the ocean. The earliest prokaryotes lived without oxygen.

Life Began to Evolve and Oxygen Increased

Fossil evidence suggests that prokaryotes called *cyanobacteria* appeared over 3 billion years ago. Cyanobacteria use sunlight to make their own food. This process releases oxygen. Before cyanobacteria appeared, Earth's atmosphere did not contain oxygen. Over time, oxygen built up in the ocean and air. Eventually, the oxygen also formed *ozone,* a gas layer in the upper atmosphere. Ozone absorbs harmful radiation from the sun. Before ozone formed, life existed only in the oceans and underground.

Multicellular Organisms Evolved

Increased oxygen allowed for the evolution of new species that used oxygen to live. The fossil record shows that after about 1 billion years, new types of organisms evolved. These organisms were larger and more complex than prokaryotes. Called *eukaryotes,* these organisms have cells with a nucleus and other complex structures. Later, eukaryotic organisms evolved that were multicellular, or made up of more than one cell.

Mass Extinctions Occurred

Increased oxygen was followed by the evolution of some organisms, but the extinction of others. For some organisms, oxygen is toxic. Many of these organisms became extinct. Less is known about Precambrian life than life in more recent time intervals, because microscopic organisms did not preserve well in the fossil record.

12 Summarize How are cyanobacteria related to increases in oxygen in the atmosphere?

_____

_____

_____

Stromatolites are cyanobacteria that form colonies and build reefs. Some of the oldest known fossils are of stromatolites. The mounds in this photo are modern stromatolites.

What defined the Paleozoic era?

The word *Paleozoic* comes from Greek words that mean "ancient life." When scientists first named this era, they thought it was the time span in which life began.

The Paleozoic era began about 542 million years ago and ended about 251 million years ago. Rocks from this era are rich in fossils of animals such as sponges, corals, snails, and trilobites. Fish, the earliest animals with backbones, appeared during this era, as did sharks.

Think Outside the Book Inquiry

13 **Compose** Select one of the organisms that lived during the Paleozoic era and find out more about it. Make a poster with information about the organism.

Life Moved onto Land

Plants, fungi, and air-breathing animals colonized land during the Paleozoic era. Land dwellers had adaptations that allowed them to survive in a drier environment. All major plant groups except flowering plants appeared. Crawling insects were among the first animals to live on land, followed by large salamander-like animals. By the end of the era, forests of giant ferns covered much of Earth, and reptiles and winged insects appeared.

A Mass Extinction Occurred

The Permian mass extinction took place at the end of the Paleozoic era. It is the largest known mass extinction. By 251 million years ago, as many as 96% of marine species had become extinct. The mass extinction wiped out entire groups of marine organisms such as trilobites. Oceans were completely changed. Many other species of animals and plants also became extinct. However, this opened up new habitats to those organisms that survived.

Visualize It!

14 **Describe** Based on this drawing, describe the landscape that existed during the Carboniferous period of the Paleozoic era.

_____

_____

_____

_____

_____

_____

Giant winged insects such as this one were common during the Carboniferous period.

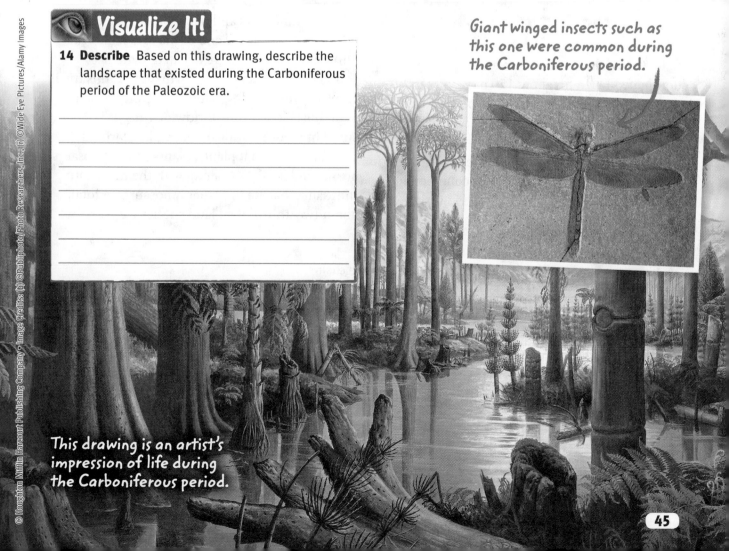

This drawing is an artist's impression of life during the Carboniferous period.

Time Marches On

What defined the Mesozoic era?

Active Reading

15 Identify As you read, underline the names of animals that lived in the Mesozoic era.

The Mesozoic era lasted about 185.5 million years. *Mesozoic* comes from Greek words that mean "middle life." Scientists think the reptiles that survived the Paleozoic era evolved into many different species during the Mesozoic era. Because of the abundance of reptiles, the Mesozoic era is commonly called the *Age of Reptiles*.

Dinosaurs and Other Reptiles Dominated Earth

Dinosaurs are the most well-known reptiles that evolved during the Mesozoic era. They dominated Earth for about 150 million years. A great variety of dinosaurs lived on Earth, and giant marine lizards swam in the ocean. The first birds and mammals also appeared. The most important plants during the early part of the Mesozoic era were conifers, or cone-bearing plants, which formed large forests. Flowering plants appeared later in the Mesozoic era.

A Mass Extinction Occurred

Why did dinosaurs and many other species become extinct at the end of the Mesozoic era? Different hypotheses are debated. Evidence shows that an asteroid hit Earth around this time. A main hypothesis is that this asteroid caused giant dust clouds and worldwide fires. With sunlight blocked by dust, many plants would have died. Without plants, plant-eating dinosaurs also would have died, along with the meat-eating dinosaurs that ate the other dinosaurs. In total, about two-thirds of all land species went extinct.

16 Summarize Make a cause-and-effect chart to explain the chain of events that, according to a main hypothesis, resulted in a mass extinction at the end of the Mesozoic era.

What defines the Cenozoic era?

The Cenozoic era began about 65 million years ago and continues today. *Cenozoic* comes from Greek words that mean "recent life." More is known about the Cenozoic era than about previous eras, because the fossils are closer to Earth's surface and easier to find.

Primates evolved during the Cenozoic era.

Birds, Mammals, and Flowering Plants Dominate Earth

We currently live in the Cenozoic era. Mammals have dominated the Cenozoic the way reptiles dominated the Mesozoic. Early Cenozoic mammals were small, but larger mammals appeared later. Humans appeared during this era. The climate has changed many times during the Cenozoic. During ice ages, many organisms migrated toward the equator. Other organisms adapted to the cold or became extinct.

Primates Evolved

Primates are a group of mammals that includes humans, apes, and monkeys. Primates' eyes are located at the front of the skull. Most primates have five flexible digits, one of which is an opposable thumb.

The ancestors of primates were probably nocturnal, mouse-like mammals that lived in trees. The first primates did not exist until after dinosaurs died out. Millions of years later, primates that had larger brains appeared.

---

17 Claims • Evidence • Reasoning How might the mass extinction that occurred at the end of the Mesozoic era relate to the dominance of mammals in the Cenozoic era? State your claim. Use evidence to support your claim and explain your reasoning.

The Cenozoic era has been dominated by mammals. Woolly mammoths were well-adapted to surviving in a cold climate.

Visual Summary

To complete this summary, circle the correct word. Then, use the key below to check your answers. You can use this page to review the main concepts of the lesson.

The fossil record provides evidence of ancient life.

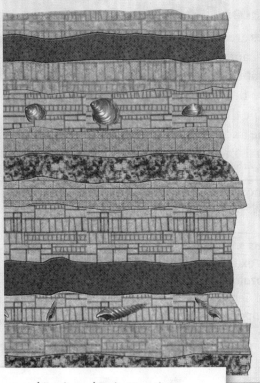

18 Absolute/Relative dating estimates the age of a fossil in years.

The geologic time scale divides Earth's history into eons, eras, periods, and epochs.

19 Epochs/Eras are characterized by the type of organism that dominated Earth at the time.

The History of Life on Earth

Four major divisions of Earth's past are Precambrian time, the Paleozoic era, the Mesozoic era, and the Cenozoic era.

20 Primates evolved during the Mesozoic era/Cenozoic era.

Answers: 18 Absolute; 19 Eras; 20 Cenozoic era

---

21 Synthesize Starting with Precambrian time, briefly describe how life on Earth has changed over Earth's long history.

© Houghton Mifflin Harcourt Publishing Company • Image Credits: ©Wide Eye Pictures/Alamy Images

Lesson Review

Vocabulary

Draw a line to connect the following terms to their definitions.

1 fossil

2 geologic time scale

3 fossil record

4 extinction

A all of the fossils that have been discovered worldwide

B death of every member of a species

C trace or remains of an organism that lived long ago

D division of Earth's history into manageable parts

Key Concepts

5 List What four major divisions make up the history of life on Earth in the geologic time scale?

_____

_____

_____

_____

6 Explain What is one distinguishing feature of each of the four major divisions listed in your previous answer?

_____

_____

_____

_____

_____

_____

_____

_____

_____

Critical Thinking

7 Contrast How do the atmospheric conditions near the beginning of Precambrian time contrast with the atmospheric conditions that are present now? Which organism is largely responsible for this change?

_____

_____

_____

_____

Use this drawing to answer the following question.

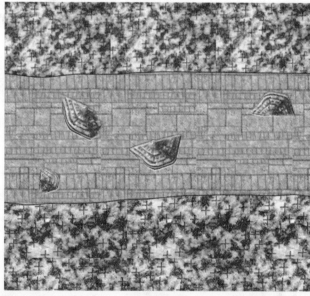

8 Explain The fossils shown are of a marine organism. In which of the three rock layers would you expect to find fossils of an organism that went extinct before the marine organism evolved? Explain your reasoning.

_____

_____

_____

_____

_____

_____

_____

My Notes

Dr. Erica Bree Rosenblum

EVOLUTIONARY BIOLOGIST

Think about watching a little frog hop around. Now, imagine a world of children who have neither seen nor heard of a frog, except in very old videos. It is true that the world's amphibian population is declining. But thanks to scientists such as Dr. Erica Bree Rosenblum, frogs will likely be part of the world for kids in future generations.

Dr. Rosenblum does research in the areas of biological diversity and adaptive evolution at the University of California, Berkeley. Her research includes studying both the emergence of new species and the extinction of existing species. In the case of frogs, her work will hopefully prevent their extinction.

A fungus known as Bd (*Batrachochytrium dendrobatidis*) is killing many amphibians, including frogs. Since the 1980s, amphibians have declined about 70%, and this fungus is partially responsible for the decline. Dr. Rosenblum and her colleagues are studying frogs' responses to the Bd fungus under certain conditions. With continued effort, these researchers may be able to help amphibians survive this widespread fungal infection.

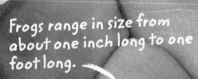

Frogs range in size from about one inch long to one foot long.

Social Studies Connection

Find ten different countries that report amphibian declines due to the Bd fungus. On a world map, shade in the countries you find. Which countries have experienced the largest amphibian declines? State your claim. Use evidence to support your claim and explain your reasoning.

JOB BOARD

Vet Technician

What You'll Do: Assist veterinarians in taking care of the health of animals.

Where You Might Work: In a veterinary clinic, animal humane society, pet hospital, or zoo.

Education: A veterinarian technician license is preferred.

Other Job Requirements: You should have compassion for animals and an ability to perform a variety of tasks, including surgical assistance, laundry and exam-room cleaning, animal feeding, and dog walking.

Student Research Assistant

What You'll Do: Assist in molecular/genome research under the supervision of university faculty by recording and inputting data into the computer.

Where You Might Work: In a lab within a university building on your college campus.

Education: You must be a student within a science-based degree program at the university.

Other Job Requirements: You should be willing to work odd hours with short notice, have attention to detail, excellent data-entry skills, and an ability to follow directions carefully.

Wildlife Photographer

What You'll Do: Take photos of wildlife in their natural habitat.

Where You Might Work: For a publishing company, advertising agency, magazine, or as a freelance photographer. If you work as a freelancer, you would have to secure contracts with companies in order to be paid for your work.

Education: No degree is required; however, having an associate's or bachelor's degree in photojournalism would make it easier to get a job as a wildlife photographer. With or without a degree, you will need a portfolio of your work to take to interviews.

Lesson 5

Classification of Living Things

ESSENTIAL QUESTION

How are organisms classified?

By the end of this lesson, you should be able to describe how people sort living things into groups based on common characteristics.

Scientists use physical and chemical characteristics to classify organisms. Is that a spider? Look again. It's an ant mimicking a jumping spider!

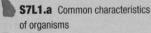 **S7L1.a** Common characteristics of organisms

S7L1.b Six-kingdom classification

Lesson Labs

Quick Labs
• Using a Dichotomous Key
• Investigate Classifying Leaves

Exploration Lab
• Developing Scientific Names

Engage Your Brain

1 Predict Check T or F to show whether you think each statement is true or false.

T   F

☐   ☐   The classification system used today has changed very little since it was introduced.

☐   ☐   To be classified as an animal, an organism must have a backbone.

☐   ☐   Organisms can be classified according to whether they have nuclei in their cells.

☐   ☐   Scientists can study genetic material to classify organisms.

☐   ☐   Organisms that have many physical similarities are always related.

2 Analyze The flowering plant shown above is called an Indian pipe. It could be mistaken for a fungus. Write down how the plant is similar to and different from other plants you know.

_____

_____

_____

_____

Active Reading

3 Word Parts Many English words have their roots in other languages. Use the Latin suffix below to make an educated guess about the meaning of the word *Plantae*.

Latin suffix	Meaning
-ae	a group of

Example sentence
Maples are part of the kingdom <u>Plantae</u>.

Plantae:

_____

_____

_____

Vocabulary Terms

• species   • Eukarya
• genus   • Protista
• domain   • Plantae
• Bacteria   • Fungi
• Archaea   • Animalia

4 Apply As you learn the definition of each vocabulary term in this lesson, write your own definition or make a sketch to help you remember the meaning of each term.

Sorting Things Out!

Why do we classify living things?

There are millions of living things on Earth. How do scientists keep all of these living things organized? Scientists *classify* organisms based on common characteristics that living things have. Classification helps scientists answer questions such as:

- How many kinds of organisms are there?
- What characteristics define each kind of organism?
- What are the relationships among organisms?

Sharks have fins and gills.

Dolphins also have fins, but not gills.

Visualize It!

5 Analyze The photos show two organisms. In the table, place a check mark in the box for each characteristic that the organisms have.

Yellow pansy butterfly

American goldfinch

	Wings	Antennae	Beak	Feathers
Yellow pansy butterfly				
American goldfinch				

6 Summarize What characteristics do yellow pansy butterflies have in common with American goldfinches? How do they differ?

_____

_____

_____

How do scientists know living things are related?

If two organisms look similar, are they related? To classify organisms, scientists compare physical characteristics. For example, they may look at size or bone structure. Scientists also compare the chemical characteristics of living things.

Physical Characteristics

How are chickens similar to dinosaurs? If you compare dinosaur fossils and chicken skeletons, you will see that chickens and dinosaurs share many physical characteristics. Scientists look at physical characteristics, such as skeletal structure. They also study how organisms develop from an egg to an adult. For example, animals with similar skeletons and development may be related.

Chemical Characteristics

Scientists can identify the relationships among organisms by studying genetic material such as DNA and RNA. They study mutations and genetic similarities to find relationships among organisms. Organisms that have very similar gene sequences or have the same mutations are likely related. Other chemicals, such as proteins and hormones, can also be studied to learn how organisms are related.

The two pandas below share habitats and diets. They look alike, but they have different DNA.

Red panda

The red panda is a closer relative to a raccoon than it is to a giant panda.

Raccoon

7 Claims • Evidence • Reasoning
How does DNA lead scientists to better classify organisms? Explain your reasoning.

_____

_____

_____

_____

_____

_____

_____

_____

Giant panda

The giant panda is a closer relative to a spectacled bear than it is to a red panda.

Spectacled bear

What's in a Name?

How are living things named?

Early scientists used names as long as 12 words to identify living things, and they also used common names. So, classification was confusing. In the 1700s, a scientist named Carolus Linnaeus (KAR•uh•luhs lih•NEE•uhs) simplified the naming of living things. He gave each kind of living thing a two-part *scientific name*.

Scientific Names

Each species has its own scientific name. A **species** (SPEE•sheez) is a group of organisms that are very closely related. They can mate and produce fertile offspring. Consider the scientific name for a mountain lion: *Puma concolor*. The first part, *Puma,* is the genus name. A **genus** (JEE•nuhs; plural, *genera*) includes similar species. The second part, *concolor,* is the specific, or species, name. No other species is named *Puma concolor.*

A scientific name always includes the genus name followed by the specific name. The first letter of the genus name is capitalized, and the first letter of the specific name is lowercase. The entire scientific name is written either in italics or underlined.

HELLO
my name is
Carolus Linnaeus

The A.K.A. Files

Some living things have many common names. Scientific names prevent confusion when people discuss organisms.

Scientific name:
Puma concolor

Common names:
Mountain lion
Puma
Cougar
Panther

Scientific name:
Acer rubrum

Common names:
Red maple
Swamp maple
Soft maple

8 Apply In the scientific names above, circle the genus name and underline the specific name.

What are the levels of classification?

Linnaeus's ideas became the basis for modern taxonomy (tak•SAHN•uh•mee). *Taxonomy* is the science of describing, classifying, and naming living things. At first, many scientists sorted organisms into two groups: plants and animals. But numerous organisms did not fit into either group.

Today, scientists use an eight-level system to classify living things. Each level gets more specific. Therefore, it contains fewer kinds of living things than the level above it. Living things in the lower levels are more closely related to each other than they are to organisms in the higher levels. From most general to more specific, the levels of classification are domain, kingdom, phylum (plural, *phyla*), class, order, family, genus, and species.

Classifying Organisms

Domain   **Domain Eukarya** includes all protists, fungi, plants, and animals.

Kingdom   **Kingdom Animalia** includes all animals.

Phylum   Animals in **Phylum Chordata** have a hollow nerve cord in their backs. Some have a backbone.

Class   Animals in **Class Mammalia**, or mammals, have a backbone and nurse their young.

Order   Animals in **Order Carnivora** are mammals that have special teeth for tearing meat.

Family   Animals in **Family Felidae** are cats. They are carnivores that have retractable claws.

Genus   Animals in **Genus *Felis*** are cats that cannot roar. They can only purr.

Species   The **species *Felis domesticus***, or the house cat, has unique traits that other members of genus *Felis* do not have.

From domain to species, each level of classification contains a smaller group of organisms.

Visualize It!

10 Apply What is true about the number of organisms as they are classified closer to the species level?

_____

_____

_____

_____

_____

Triple Play

What are the three domains?

Active Reading

11 Identify As you read, underline the first mention of the three domains of life.

Scientists use a six-kingdom system to classify organisms. Once, kingdoms were the highest level of classification. But scientists noticed that organisms in two of the kingdoms differed greatly from organisms in the other four kingdoms. So scientists added a new classification level: domains. A **domain** represents the largest differences among organisms. The three domains are Bacteria (bak•TIR•ee•uh), Archaea (ar•KEE•uh), and Eukarya (yoo•KAIR•ee•uh).

Bacteria

The only kingdom in the domain Bacteria is Eubacteria. Domain **Bacteria** is made up of prokaryotes that usually have a cell wall and reproduce by cell division. *Prokaryotes* are single-cell organisms that lack a nucleus in their cells. Bacteria live in almost any environment—soil, water, and even inside the human body!

Archaea

All organisms in the domain Archaea belong to the kingdom Archaebacteria. Domain **Archaea** is also made up of prokaryotes. They differ from bacteria in their genetics and in the makeup of their cell walls. Archaea live in harsh environments, such as hot springs and thermal vents, where other organisms could not survive. Some archaea are found in the open ocean and soil.

Bacteria from the genus Streptomyces are commonly found in soil.

Archaea from the genus Sulfolobus are found in hot springs.

Eukarya

What do algae, mushrooms, trees, and humans have in common? All of these organisms are *eukaryotes*. Eukaryotes are made up of cells that have a nucleus and membrane-bound organelles. The cells of eukaryotes are more complex than the cells of prokaryotes. For this reason, the cells of eukaryotes are usually larger than the cells of prokaryotes. Some eukaryotes, such as many protists and some fungi, are single-celled. Many eukaryotes are multicellular organisms. Some protists and many fungi, plants, and animals are multicellular eukaryotes. Domain **Eukarya** is made up of all eukaryotes.

It may look like a pinecone, but the pangolin is actually an animal from Africa. It is in Domain Eukarya.

Visualize It!

12 Identify Fill in the blanks with the missing labels.

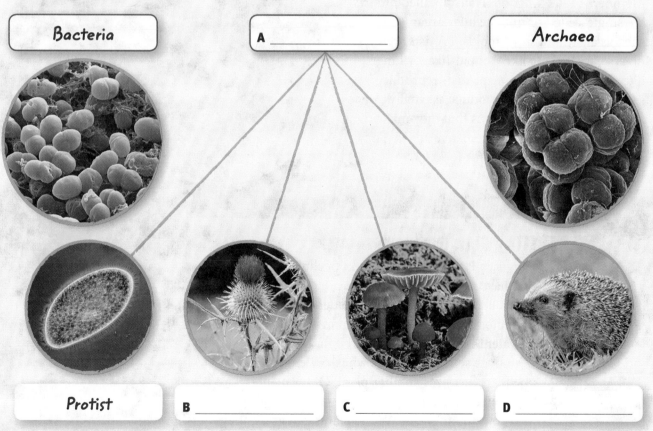

Bacteria

A _____

Archaea

Protist

B _____

C _____

D _____

13 Compare What are the differences between Bacteria and Eukarya?

_____

_____

_____

My Kingdom for a

What are the four kingdoms in Eukarya?

Scientists have classified four types of Eukarya. They ask questions to decide in which kingdom to classify an organism.

- Is the organism single-celled or multicellular?
- Does it make its food or get it from the environment?
- How does it reproduce?

Kingdom Protista

Members of the kingdom **Protista**, called *protists,* are single-celled or multicellular organisms such as algae and slime molds. Protists are very diverse, with plant-like, animal-like, or fungus-like characteristics. Some protists reproduce sexually, while others reproduce asexually. Algae are *autotrophs,* which means that they make their own food. Some protists are *heterotrophs.* They consume other organisms for food.

Kingdom Plantae

Kingdom **Plantae** consists of multicellular organisms that have cell walls, mostly made of cellulose. Most plants make their own food through the process of photosynthesis. Plants are found on land and in water that light can pass through. Some plants reproduce sexually, such as when pollen from one plant fertilizes another plant. Other plants reproduce asexually, such as when potato buds grow into new potato plants. While plants can grow, they cannot move by themselves.

14 Compare How are protists different from plants?

_____

_____

_____

Eukaryote!

Kingdom Fungi

The members of the kingdom **Fungi** get energy by absorbing materials. They have cells with cell walls but no chloroplasts. Fungi are single-celled or multicellular and include yeasts, molds, and mushrooms. Fungi use digestive juices to break down materials around them for food. Fungi reproduce sexually, asexually, or in both ways, depending on their type.

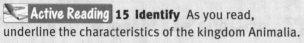

Active Reading **15 Identify** As you read, underline the characteristics of the kingdom Animalia.

Kingdom Animalia

Kingdom **Animalia** contains multicellular organisms that lack cell walls. They do not have chloroplasts like plants and algae, so they must get nutrients by consuming other organisms. Therefore, they are heterotrophic. Animals have specialized sense organs, and most animals are able to move around. Birds, fish, reptiles, amphibians, insects, and mammals are just a few examples of animals. Most animals reproduce sexually, but a few types of animals reproduce asexually, such as by budding.

16 Classify Place a check mark in the box for the characteristic that each kingdom in Eukarya displays.

Kingdom	Cells		Nutrients		Reproduction	
	Unicellular	Multicellular	Autotrophic	Heterotrophic	Sexual	Asexual
Protista						
Plantae						
Fungi						
Animalia						

It all began...

How did classification systems start?

Classification goes back to the beginning of time. Early humans classified animals into two groups: "Animals I can eat" and "Animals that can eat me." It didn't take long for them to learn which animals belonged in each group. There have been many classification systems since then. Most were created for a specific purpose, such as categorizing plants according to their uses.

Smilodon was a prehistoric mammal commonly known as saber-toothed tiger.

Death by Classification

One of the earliest written taxonomies is attributed to Shen Nung, who was emperor of China around 3000 BCE. Shen Nung is known as the father of Chinese medicine. He is said to have investigated and classified hundreds of herbs and plants so that he could educate his people in agriculture and medicine. Unfortunately, his work ultimately led to his death. He passed away while sampling a toxic plant as part of an investigation.

It's All Greek

Aristotle (384–322 BCE) was the first to attempt to classify all living things. He classified the organisms he could see into two major groups—plants and animals—that he called kingdoms. (Because there were no microscopes back then, he had no idea that unicellular organisms existed.)

Aristotle saw organisms as a hierarchy (HAHY•uh•rahr•kee). A *hierarchy* is a system that classifies by ranking. Aristotle called his hierarchy *Scala Naturae*, or the "Ladder of Nature." At the very bottom of this ladder were nonliving things, such as rocks. Human beings were at the top. Between rocks and people were plants and animals—although we now know that humans are also animals. Because animals can move to get what they need for survival while plants are completely dependent on what their environment delivers to them, Aristotle considered animals to be more complex and put them higher on the ladder.

Aristotle's Ladder of Nature

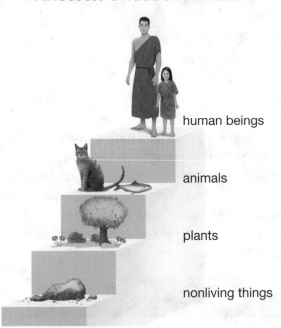

human beings

animals

plants

nonliving things

17 Synthesize Evaluate Aristotle's Ladder of Nature. How is it similar to and different from the six-kingdom classification system we use today? How did it lead to the current six-kingdom system?

_____

_____

_____

_____

The Birth of Modern Taxonomy

It took almost two thousand years for someone to outdo the work of Aristotle. In the 18th century, Carolus Linnaeus created a hierarchical classification system with six levels, or taxa. At the very top of his system were three kingdoms called *Minerae* (minerals), *Plantae* (plants), and *Animalia* (animals), although Linnaeus knew that minerals were not living organisms.

Although many of Linnaeus's classifications have changed as we have learned more about the world's life, his system's basic structure remains virtually the same.

New Organisms, New Classifications

With the invention of the microscope, a whole new world of previously unseen organisms was discovered. To accommodate many of those organisms, Kingdom Protista was created. In 1937, a French marine biologist named Edouard Chatton realized that all cells could be classified based on whether or not they had a nucleus. Thus, prokaryotes and eukaryotes were differentiated and Kingdom Prokaryotae was born. In 1969, R. H. Whittaker proposed Kingdom Fungi to accommodate "plants" like mushrooms that don't photosynthesize, reproduce through spores instead of seeds, and get their energy by absorbing it from other organisms.

In the mid-1990s, a whole new level was added to Linnaeus's system—domains. That happened because scientists discovered that what used to be Kingdom Prokaryotae actually contained two very different kinds of organisms. That development gave us the eight-level classification system we use today.

18 Claims • Evidence • Reasoning
How did the invention of the microscope change Linnaeus's classification system and lead to the six-kingdom system? Be sure to support your claim with evidence and explain your reasoning.

_____

_____

_____

_____

_____

Kingdom Fungi was created to accommodate those organisms that are similar to plants but don't photosynthesize.

Classification systems often reflect the needs of their creators. Zoos generally classify their animals based on natural habitats or eating habits. This makes it easier to determine which animals can be grouped together in an exhibit, which plants should accompany them, and what food the zoo will need to properly care for them.

Think Outside the Book Inquiry

19 Apply Work with a partner to list at least ten animals at your local zoo. Then, create a classification system based on their common characteristics. Finally, describe the method you used for categorizing organisms, justifying the decisions you made in creating the system.

How might classification systems continue to evolve?

Millions of organisms have been identified, but millions have yet to be named. Many new organisms fit into the existing system. However, scientists often find organisms that don't fit. Not only do scientists identify new species, but sometimes these species do not fit into existing genera or phyla. In fact, many scientists argue that protists are so different from one another that they should be classified into several kingdoms instead of one. Classification continues to change as scientists learn more about living things.

How do we show classification relationships?

One of the things historical classification systems of the past and current classification systems that we use today have in common is their attempt to understand the relationships among organisms. This has a lot to do with how information is organized.

How do you organize your closet? What about your books? People organize things in many different ways. Linnaeus' two-name system worked for scientists long ago, but the system does not represent what we know about living things today. Scientists use different tools to organize information about classification.

Scientists often use a type of branching diagram called a *cladogram* (KLAD•uh•gram). A cladogram shows relationships among species. Organisms are categorized according to common characteristics. Usually these characteristics are listed along a line. Branches of organisms extend from this line. Organisms on branches above each characteristic have the characteristic. Organisms on branches below lack the characteristic.

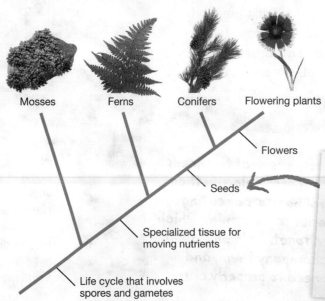

Mosses   Ferns   Conifers   Flowering plants

Flowers

Seeds

Specialized tissue for moving nutrients

Life cycle that involves spores and gametes

This branching diagram shows the relationships among the four main groups of plants.

Conifers and flowering plants are listed above this label, so they both produce seeds. Mosses and ferns, listed below the label, do not produce seeds.

Why It Matters

A Class by Themselves

As scientists find more living things to study, they find that they may not have made enough classifications, or that their classifications may not describe organisms well enough. Some living things have traits that fall under more than one classification. These organisms are very difficult to classify.

Sea spider

Sea Spider
The sea spider is a difficult-to-classify animal. It is an arthropod because it has body segments and an exoskeleton. The problem is in the sea spider's mouth. They eat by sticking a straw-like structure into sponges and sea slugs and sucking out the juice. No other arthropod eats like this. Scientists must decide if they need to make a new classification or change an existing one to account for this strange mouth.

Euglena

Euglena
An even stranger group of creatures is Euglena. Euglena make their own food as plants do. But, like animals, they have no cell walls. They have a flagellum, a tail-like structure that bacteria have. Despite having all of these characteristics, Euglena have been classified as protists.

Extend   Inquiry

22 Claims • Evidence • Reasoning In which domain would the sea spider be classified? Support your claim with evidence and explain your reasoning.

23 Research Investigate how scientists use DNA to help classify organisms such as the sea spider.

24 Debate Find more information on Euglena and sea spiders. Hold a class debate on how scientists should classify the organisms.

Keys to Success

How can organisms be identified?

Imagine walking through the woods. You see an animal sitting on a rock. It has fur, whiskers, and a large, flat tail. How can you find out what kind of animal it is? You can use a dichotomous key.

Dichotomous Keys

A *dichotomous key* (dy•KAHT•uh•muhs KEE) uses a series of paired statements to identify organisms. Each pair of statements is numbered. When identifying an organism, read each pair of statements. Then choose the statement that best describes the organism. Either the chosen statement identifies the organism, or you will be directed to another pair of statements. By working through the key, you can eventually identify the organism.

25 Apply Use the dichotomous key below to identify the animals shown in the photographs.

Dichotomous Key to Six Mammals in the Eastern United States

1	A	The mammal has no hair on its tail.	**Go to step 2**
	B	The mammal has hair on its tail.	**Go to step 3**
2	A	The mammal has a very short naked tail.	**Eastern mole**
	B	The mammal has a long naked tail.	**Go to step 4**
3	A	The mammal has a black mask.	**Raccoon**
	B	The mammal does not have a black mask.	**Go to step 5**
4	A	The mammal has a flat, paddle-shaped tail.	**Beaver**
	B	The mammal has a round, skinny tail.	**Possum**
5	A	The mammal has a long furry tail that is black on the tip.	**Long-tailed weasel**
	B	The mammal has a long tail that has little fur.	**White-footed mouse**

A _____

B _____

26 Apply Some dichotomous keys are set up as diagrams instead of tables. Work through the key below to identify the unknown plant.

Think Outside the Book Inquiry

27 Summarize With a partner, choose six plants or animals in a local ecosystem. Then design a dichotomous key that can be used to identify the organisms. When you have finished, trade keys with your classmates and work through their keys with your partner.

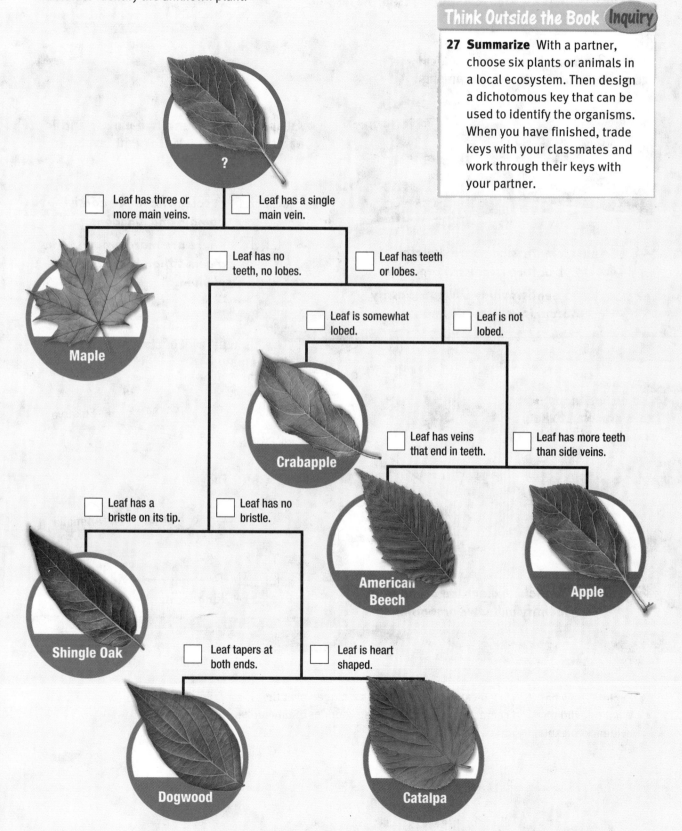

☐ Leaf has three or more main veins.

☐ Leaf has a single main vein.

☐ Leaf has no teeth, no lobes.

☐ Leaf has teeth or lobes.

☐ Leaf is somewhat lobed.

☐ Leaf is not lobed.

☐ Leaf has veins that end in teeth.

☐ Leaf has more teeth than side veins.

Maple

Crabapple

☐ Leaf has a bristle on its tip.

☐ Leaf has no bristle.

American Beech

Apple

Shingle Oak

☐ Leaf tapers at both ends.

☐ Leaf is heart shaped.

Dogwood

Catalpa

Visual Summary

To complete this summary, check the box that indicates true or false. Then, use the key below to check your answers. You can use this page to review the main concepts of the lesson.

Classification of Living Things

Scientists use physical and chemical characteristics to classify organisms.

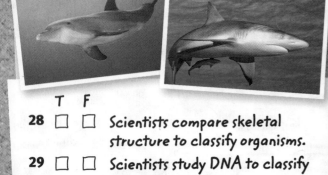

T F

28 ☐ ☐ Scientists compare skeletal structure to classify organisms.

29 ☐ ☐ Scientists study DNA to classify organisms.

All species are given a two-part scientific name and classified into eight levels.

T F

30 ☐ ☐ A scientific name consists of domain and kingdom.

31 ☐ ☐ There are more organisms in a genus than there are in a phylum.

Branching diagrams and dichotomous keys are used to help classify and identify organisms.

T F

32 ☐ ☐ Branching diagrams are used to identify unknown organisms.

The highest level of classification is the domain.

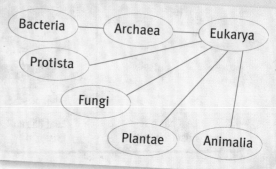

Bacteria — Archaea — Eukarya
Protista
Fungi
Plantae — Animalia

T F

33 ☐ ☐ Domains are divided into kingdoms.

Answers: 28 T; 29 T; 30 F; 31 F; 32 F; 33 T

34 **Explain** How has the classification of living things changed over time? What role did physical characteristics play in these changes? Summarize evidence to explain your reasoning.

Lesson Review

Vocabulary

Fill in the blanks with the term that best completes the following sentences.

1 A _____
contains paired statements that can be used to identify organisms.

2 The kingdoms of eukaryotes are
_____, Fungi, Plantae, and Animalia.

3 Domains _____ and
_____ are made up of prokaryotes.

Key Concepts

4 List Name the eight levels of classification from most general to most specific.

_____
_____
_____
_____

5 Explain Describe how scientists choose the kingdom in which a eukaryote belongs.

_____
_____
_____
_____

6 Identify What two types of evidence are used to classify organisms?

_____
_____

7 Compare Dichotomous keys and branching diagrams organize different types of information about classification. How are these tools used differently?

_____
_____
_____
_____

Critical Thinking

Use the figure to answer the following questions.

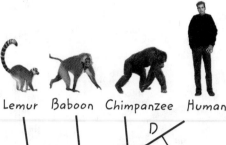
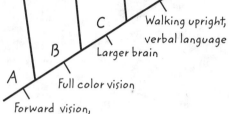

8 Identify Which traits do baboons have?

_____
_____

9 Analyze Which animal shares the most traits with humans?

_____

10 Synthesize Do both lemurs and humans have the trait listed at point D? Explain.

_____
_____
_____

11 Classify A scientist finds an organism that cannot move. It has many cells, produces spores, and gets food from its environment. In which kingdom does it belong? State your claim. Provide evidence to support your claim and explain your reasoning.

_____
_____
_____
_____

My Notes

Unit 1

Lesson 1

ESSENTIAL QUESTION
What are living things?

Describe the necessities of life and the characteristics that all living things share.

Lesson 2

ESSENTIAL QUESTION
What is the theory of evolution by natural selection?

Describe the role of genetic and environmental factors in the theory of evolution by natural selection.

Lesson 3

ESSENTIAL QUESTION
What evidence supports the theory of evolution?

Describe the evidence that supports the theory of evolution by natural selection.

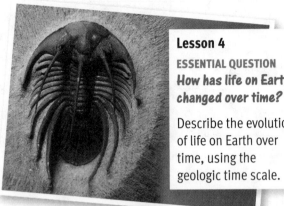

Lesson 4

ESSENTIAL QUESTION
How has life on Earth changed over time?

Describe the evolution of life on Earth over time, using the geologic time scale.

Lesson 5

ESSENTIAL QUESTION
How are organisms classified?

Describe how people sort living things into groups based on shared characteristics.

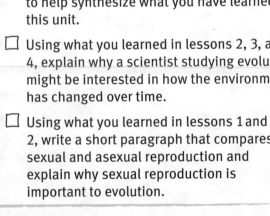

Connect ESSENTIAL QUESTIONS
Lessons 2 and 3

1 Identify Describe two types of evidence that support the theory of evolution.

_____

_____

_____

_____

Think Outside the Book

2 Synthesize Choose one of these activities to help synthesize what you have learned in this unit.

☐ Using what you learned in lessons 2, 3, and 4, explain why a scientist studying evolution might be interested in how the environment has changed over time.

☐ Using what you learned in lessons 1 and 2, write a short paragraph that compares sexual and asexual reproduction and explain why sexual reproduction is important to evolution.

Unit 1 Review

Name _____

Vocabulary

Fill in each blank with the term that best completes the following sentences.

1 A(n) _____ is a membrane-covered structure that contains all of the materials necessary for life.

2 In _____ reproduction, a single parent produces offspring that are genetically identical to the parent.

3 _____ is the difference in inherited traits an organism has from others of the same species.

4 The _____ is made up of fossils that have been discovered around the world.

5 In the most recent classification system, Bacteria, Archaea, and Eukarya are the three major _____ of life.

Key Concepts

Read each question below, and circle the best answer.

6 The teacher makes an argument to the class for why fire could be considered a living thing and then asks what is wrong with that argument. Tiana raises her hand and replies with one characteristic of life that fire does not have. Which of these could have been Tiana's response?

  A Fire does not grow and develop.

  B Fire cannot reproduce.

  C Fire does not have genetic material.

  D Fire does not use energy.

7 A mushroom grows on a dead, rotting oak tree lying in the forest. Which of the following best describes the tree and the mushroom?

  A The oak tree was a producer, and the mushroom is a producer.

  B The oak tree was a consumer, and the mushroom is a consumer.

  C The oak tree was a decomposer, and the mushroom is a producer.

  D The oak tree was a producer, and the mushroom is a decomposer.

8 Darwin's theory of natural selection consists of four important parts. Which of these correctly lists the four essential parts of natural selection?

A living space, adaptation, selection, and hunting

B overproduction, genetic variation, selection, and adaptation

C selection, extinction, underproduction, and competition

D asexual reproduction, genetic variation, selection, and adaptation

9 Charles Darwin studied the finches of the Galápagos Islands and found that their beaks vary in shape and size.

   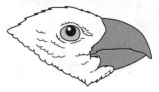

Darwin found that the finches that ate mostly insects had long, narrow beaks. Finches that ate mostly seeds had shorter, broad beaks to crush seeds. Which statement below best describes how natural selection resulted in the four types of finches shown above?

A The residents of the Galápagos Islands selectively bred together finches having the traits that they wanted them to have.

B The narrow-beaked finches came first and evolved into the broad-beaked finches through a series of natural mutations.

C The broad-beaked finches wore down their beaks digging for insects and passed these narrower beaks onto their offspring.

D Over time, the finches that were born with beaks better suited to the available food supply in their habitats survived and reproduced.

10 Which of these describes a likely reason why a species would become extinct after a major environmental change?

A There are not enough members of the species born with a trait necessary to survive in the new environment.

B The environmental changes mean fewer predators are around.

C The change in the environment opens new resources with less competition.

D There are more homes for the species in the changed environment.

11 Which of the following provides structural evidence for evolution?

A A fossil from the Mesozoic era shows an extinct animal similar to a modern animal.

B A comparison of similar bones in the legs of a human, a dog, and a bat.

C A genetic analysis of two animals shows similar sequences of DNA.

D The embryos of two animals look similar at similar stages.

12 How did the invention of the microscope change the way people classified organisms?

A People could classify nonliving things, such as rocks.

B People could finally classify plant as well as animal organisms.

C People could classify organisms they were never able to see.

D People could at last place humans and animals at the top of the classification ladder.

13 Which of the following happened in Precambrian time?

A Life began to evolve on Earth.

B The first mammals appeared.

C A mass extinction wiped out most dinosaurs.

D Life on Earth began to move from water to land.

Critical Thinking

Answer the following questions in the space provided.

14 The dichotomous key below helps identify the order of some sharks.

Orders of Sharks

Hexanchiformes

1 fin on back, 6–7 gill slits

Has third eyelid — Carcharhiniformes

Mouth behind eyes

Does not have spines in back fin

Does not have third eyelid — Lamniformes

Mouth in front of eyes — Orectolobiformes

2 fins on back, 5 gill slits

Has spines at front of back fin — Heterodontiformes

Use the diagram to determine the order to which this shark belongs. Then name its domain and kingdom.

Order: _____

Domain: _____ Kingdom: _____

15 Describe how the changes that happened during the first division of the geologic time scale affected the evolution of organisms on Earth. Provide evidence to support your reasoning.

_____

_____

_____

_____

Connect ESSENTIAL QUESTIONS
Lessons 2, 3, 4, and 5

Answer the following question in the space provided.

16 Explain why mass extinctions occur and why they often mark divisions of geologic time. Provide evidence and examples to support your reasoning.

_____

_____

_____

_____

Cells

© Houghton Mifflin Harcourt Publishing Company • Image Credits: (bkgd) ©Quest/Photo Researchers, Inc.; (br) ©Biophoto Associates / Photo Researchers, Inc.

Big Idea ◀

All organisms are made up of one or more cells.

▮ **S7L2., S7L2.a, S7L2.b**

Colorized picture of the organelles of a cell through a modern microscope

What do you think?

As microscopes have become more powerful, our understanding of cells and their functions has also increased. What kinds of questions can be answered by using a microscope? As you explore the unit, give examples that explain how a microscope might help to answer your questions.

Cells seen through an early microscope

Unit 2
Cells

Seeing through Microscopes

Microscopes have come a long way. Today, we can see the details of the surface of metals at the atomic level. Microscopes have allowed us to study our world at some of the smallest levels.

Circa 1000 CE
Although people may have used rock crystals to magnify things thousands of years ago, it wasn't until about 1000 CE that people were able to form and polish clear-glass partial spheres. Placing these reading stones on top of a page made it easier to read the words.

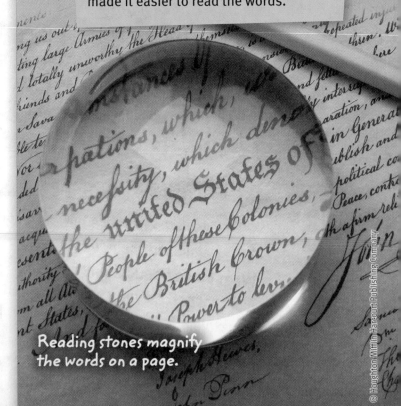

Reading stones magnify the words on a page.

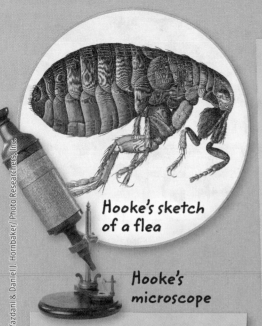

Hooke's sketch
of a flea

Hooke's
microscope

1931
Ernst Ruska developed the electron microscope, which shows much greater detail than do light microscopes. The electron microscope uses an electron beam instead of light to show things as small as the structure of viruses. Ruska received the Nobel Prize in Physics in 1986 for his breakthrough.

Ruska with
his electron
microscope

1665
Robert Hooke was interested in many areas of science. In 1665, Hooke invented a light microscope to look at small creatures such as fleas. Hooke's microscope was similar to a telescope, but it also had a way to shine light on the object.

Atoms at platinum's
surface

1981
The scanning tunneling microscope changed again the way scientists look at things. Using this microscope, we can look at images of surfaces at the atomic level. The microscope uses a beam of electrons to map a surface. This information is collected and processed so that it can be viewed on a computer screen.

What's in a Microscope?

1 Think About It

A What characteristics do different microscopes have?

_____

_____

_____

_____

B Why are microscopes used? Use examples to support your claim.

_____

_____

_____

_____

2 Conduct Research

Choose a specific kind of microscope and research how it is used, whether it is used to view live or dead samples, and its range of magnification.

_____

_____

_____

_____

_____

Take It Home

With an adult, prepare an oral presentation for your class on the microscope that you have researched. See *ScienceSaurus*® **for more information about microscopes.**

The Characteristics of Cells

ESSENTIAL QUESTION

What are living things made of?

By the end of this lesson, you should be able to explain the components of the scientific theory of cells.

People communicate to others through talking, signing, body language, and other methods. Inside your body, cells communicate too. Brain cells, like the ones shown here, control balance, posture, and muscle coordination.

© Houghton Mifflin Harcourt Publishing Company • Image Credits: ©J. Guerin, PhD, MRC Toxicology Unit/Photo Researchers, Inc.

Lesson Labs

Quick Labs
- How Do Tools that Magnify Help Us Study Cells?
- Investigating Cell Size

Exploration Lab
- Using a Microscope to Explore Cells

Engage Your Brain

1 Predict Check T or F to show whether you think each statement is true or false.

T	F	
☐	☐	All living things are made up of one or more cells.
☐	☐	Rocks are made up of cells.
☐	☐	All cells are the same size.
☐	☐	Cells perform life functions for living things.

2 Describe Sketch your idea of what a cell looks like. Label any parts you include in your sketch.

Active Reading

3 Synthesize Many English words have their roots in other languages. Use the Greek words below to make an educated guess about the meanings of the words *prokaryote* and *eukaryote*. Here *kernel* refers to the nucleus, where genetic material is contained in some cells.

Word part	Meaning
pro-	before
eu-	true
karyon	kernel

Vocabulary Terms

- cell
- organism
- cell membrane
- cytoplasm
- organelle
- nucleus
- prokaryote
- eukaryote

4 Apply As you learn the definition of each vocabulary term in this lesson, create your own sketches of a prokaryotic cell and a eukaryotic cell and label the parts in each cell.

prokaryote:

_____

_____

eukaryote:

_____

_____

Cell-ebrate!

What is a cell?

Like all living things, you are made up of cells. A **cell** is the smallest functional and structural unit of all living organisms. An **organism** is any living thing. All organisms are made up of cells. Some organisms are just one cell. Others, like humans, contain trillions of cells. An organism carries out all of its own life processes.

Robert Hooke was the first person to describe cells. In 1665, he built a microscope to look at tiny objects. One day, he looked at a thin slice of cork from the bark of a cork tree. The cork looked as if it was made of little boxes. Hooke named these boxes *cells*, which means "little rooms" in Latin.

Active Reading

5 **Identify** As you read, underline the reasons why cells are important.

Visualize It!

6 **Claims • Evidence • Reasoning** Look at the photos of the three different cells. Do the cells have any common features? Give examples to explain your reasoning.

_____

_____

_____

_____

_____

_____

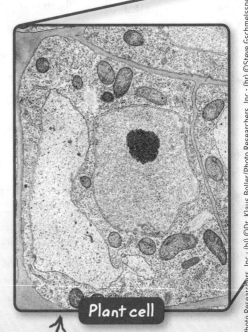

Plant cell

Bacterial cell

Plant cells range in size from 10 μm to 100 μm. They can be much larger than animal cells.

Human skin cell

The average size of a human cell is 10 μm. It would take about 50 average human cells to cover the dot on this letter i.

Bacterial cells are up to 1000 times smaller than human cells.

Microscope

Why are most cells small?

Most cells are too small to be seen without a microscope. Cells are small because their size is limited by their outer surface area. Cells take in food and get rid of wastes through their outer surface. As a cell grows, it needs more food and produces more waste. Therefore, more materials pass through its outer surface. However, as a cell grows, the cell's volume increases faster than the surface area. If a cell gets too large, the cell's surface area will not be large enough to take in enough nutrients or pump out enough wastes. The ratio of the cell's outer surface area to the cell's volume is called the *surface area-to-volume ratio*. Smaller cells have a greater surface area-to-volume ratio than larger cells.

![Do the Math]

Here's an example of how to calculate the surface area-to-volume ratio of the cube shown at the right.

Sample Problem

A Calculate the surface area.

surface area of cube =

number of faces × area of one face

surface area of cube = $6(2 \text{ cm} \times 2 \text{ cm})$

surface area of cube = 24 cm^2

B Calculate the volume.

volume of cube = side × side × side

volume of cube = $2 \text{ cm} \times 2 \text{ cm} \times 2 \text{ cm}$

volume of cube = 8 cm^3

C Calculate the surface area-to-volume ratio. A ratio is a comparison between numbers. It can be written by placing a colon between the numbers being compared.

surface area : volume = $24 \text{ cm}^2 : 8 \text{ cm}^3$

surface area : volume = $3 \text{ cm}^2 : 1 \text{ cm}^3$

You Try It

7 Calculate What is the surface area-to-volume ratio of a cube whose sides are 3 cm long?

A Calculate the surface area.

B Calculate the volume.

C Calculate the surface area-to-volume ratio.

Cell *Hall of Fame*

What is the cell theory?

Scientific knowledge often results from combining the work of several scientists. For example, the discoveries of Matthias Schleiden (muh•THY•uhs SHLY•duhn), Theodor Schwann (THEE•oh•dohr SHVAHN), and Rudolf Virchow (ROO•dawlf VIR•koh) led to one very important theory called the *cell theory*. The cell theory lists three basic characteristics of all cells and organisms:

- All organisms are made up of one or more cells.
- The cell is the basic unit of all organisms.
- All cells come from existing cells.

The cell theory is fundamental to the study of organisms, medicine, heredity, evolution, and all other aspects of life science.

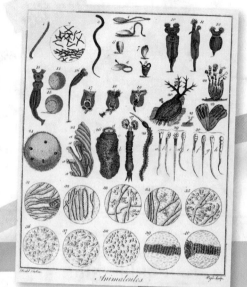

8 Provide As you read, fill in the missing events on the timeline.

Model of Hooke's microscope

1673
Anton van Leeuwenhoek made careful drawings of the organisms he observed.

1665
Robert Hooke sees tiny, box-like spaces when using a microscope like this to observe thin slices of cork. He calls these spaces cells.

1858
Rudolf Virchow _____
_____
_____
_____.

© Houghton Mifflin Harcourt Publishing Company • Image Credits: (b) ©Dave King/Getty Images; (tl) ©Dr. Jeremy Burgess/Photo Researchers, Inc.; (tr) ©The Print Collector/Alamy; (br) ©Time & Life Pictures/Getty Images

9 **Explain** How can microscopes help you see cells? First, think of a good place to collect a sample of cells. Then, in a paragraph, describe how to prepare a microscope slide to observe those cells.

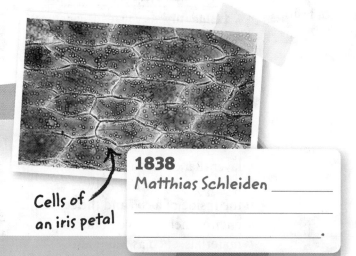

Cells of an iris petal

1838
Matthias Schleiden _____
_____
_____.

1839
Theodor Schwann _____
_____
_____
_____
_____
_____.

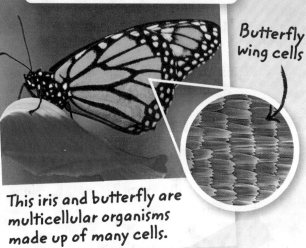

Butterfly wing cells

This iris and butterfly are multicellular organisms made up of many cells.

All Organisms Are Made Up of One or More Cells

Anton van Leeuwenhoek (AN•tahn VAN LAY•vuhn•huk) was the first person to describe actual living cells when he looked at a drop of pond water under a microscope. These studies made other scientists wonder if all living things were made up of cells. In 1838, Matthias Schleiden concluded that plants are made of cells. Then in 1839, Theodor Schwann determined that all animal tissues are made of cells. He concluded that all organisms are made up of one or more cells.

Organisms that are made up of just one cell are called *unicellular organisms*. The single cell of a unicellular organism must carry out all of the functions for life. Organisms that are made up of more than one cell are called *multicellular organisms*. The cells of multicellular organism often have specialized functions.

The Cell Is the Basic Unit of All Organisms

Based on his observations about the cellular make up of organisms, Schwann made another conclusion. He determined that the cell is the basic unit of all living things. Thus, Schwann wrote the first two parts of the cell theory.

All Cells Come from Existing Cells

In 1858, Rudolf Virchow, a doctor, proposed that cells could form only from the division of other cells. Virchow then added the third part of the cell theory that all cells come from existing cells.

Active Reading

10 **Summarize** What is the cell theory?

_____
_____
_____
_____
_____

On the Cellular

What parts do all cells have in common?

Different cells vary in size and shape. However, all cells have some parts in common, including cell membranes, cytoplasm, organelles, and DNA. These different parts help the cell to carry out all the tasks needed for life.

Cell Membrane

A **cell membrane** is a protective layer that covers a cell's surface and acts as a barrier between the inside of a cell and the cell's environment. It also controls materials, such as water and oxygen, that move into and out of a cell.

Cytoplasm

The region enclosed by the cell membrane that includes the fluid and all of the *organelles* of the cell is called the **cytoplasm** (SY•tuh•plaz•uhm).

Organelles

An **organelle** is a small body in a cell's cytoplasm that is specialized to perform a specific function. Cells can have one or more types of organelles. Most, but not all, organelles have a membrane.

DNA

Deoxyribonucleic acid, or DNA, is genetic material that provides instructions for all cell processes. Organisms inherit DNA from their parent or parents. In some cells, the DNA is contained in a membrane-bound organelle called the **nucleus**. In other types of cells, the DNA is not contained in a nucleus.

What are the two types of cells?

Although cells have some basic parts in common, there are some important differences. The way that cells store their DNA is the main difference between the two cell types.

Active Reading

12 Identify As you read, underline the differences between prokaryotes and eukaryotes.

Prokaryotic

A **prokaryote** (proh•KAIR•ee•oht) is a single-celled organism that does not have a nucleus or membrane-bound organelles. Its DNA is located in the cytoplasm. Prokaryotic cells contain organelles called *ribosomes* that do not have a membrane. Some prokaryotic cells have hairlike structures called *flagella* that help them move. Prokaryotes, which include all bacteria and archaea, are smaller than eukaryotes.

Eukaryotic

A **eukaryote** (yoo•KAIR•ee•oht) is an organism made up of cells that contain their DNA in a nucleus. Eukaryotic cells contain membrane-bound organelles, as well as ribosomes. Not all eukaryotic cells are the same. Animals, plants, protists, and fungi are eukaryotes. All multicellular organisms are eukaryotes. Most eukaryotes are multicellular. Some eukaryotes, such as amoebas and yeasts, are unicellular.

Visualize It!

13 Identify Use the list of terms below to fill in the blanks with the matching cell parts in each cell. Some terms are used twice.

DNA in cytoplasm
DNA in nucleus
Cytoplasm
Cell membrane
Organelles

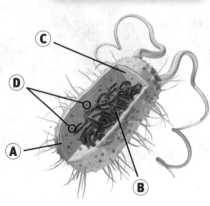

Prokaryotic

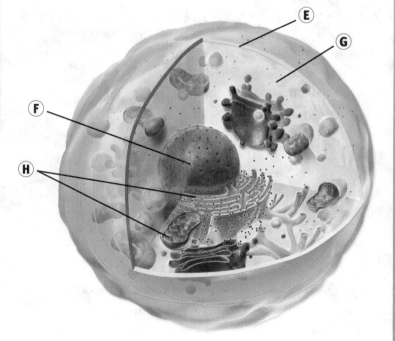

Eukaryotic

A _____
B _____
C _____
D _____

E _____
F DNA in nucleus
G _____
H _____

Visual Summary

To complete this summary, fill in the blanks with the correct word or phrase. Then use the key below to check your answers. You can use this page to review the main concepts of the lesson.

Cells and Cell Theory

A cell is the smallest unit that can perform all the processes necessary for life.

14 The cell of a(n) _____ organism must carry out all of its life functions; an organism made up of more than one cell is called a _____ organism.

The cell theory lists three basic principles of all cells and organisms.

15 All cells come from existing _____.

All cells have a cell membrane, cytoplasm, organelles, and DNA.

16 The organelle that contains DNA in eukaryotic cells is called a(n) _____.

Eukaryotic

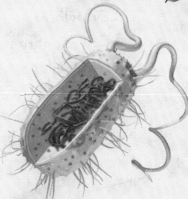

Prokaryotic

Answers: 14 unicellular, multicellular; 15 cells; 16 nucleus

17 Relate Choose an organism that you are familiar with. Do the three parts of the cell theory relate to that organism? Use evidence to support your claim.

Lesson Review

Vocabulary

Fill in the blank with the term that best completes the following sentences.

1 The _____ is the smallest functional and structural unit of all living things.

2 All cells are surrounded by a(n) _____.

3 A living thing is called a(n) _____.

Key Concepts

4 Describe Do all cells share any common features? Explain your reasoning and support your claim by giving two examples.

_____

_____

_____

_____

_____

_____

_____

5 List What are the main ideas of the cell theory?

_____

_____

_____

6 Compare How do prokaryotes differ from eukaryotes? How are they similar? Use evidence to support your claim.

_____

_____

_____

_____

_____

_____

_____

Critical Thinking

Use this figure to answer the following questions.

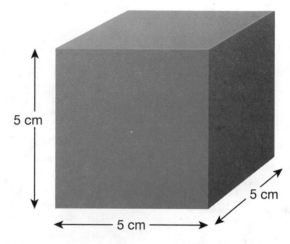

5 cm

5 cm

5 cm

7 Apply What is the surface area-to-volume ratio of this cube?

_____

_____

8 Apply Cells are not as large as this cube. Explain why in terms of a cell's surface area-to-volume ratio.

_____

_____

_____

_____

_____

9 Compare How is the structure of a unicellular organism different than the structure of a multicellular organism? How does this affect function?

_____

_____

_____

_____

_____

_____

My Notes

Chemistry of Life

ESSENTIAL QUESTION

What are the building blocks of organisms?

By the end of this lesson, you should be able to discuss the chemical makeup of living things.

These fungi are bioluminescent, which means they produce light from chemical reactions in their bodies. The light attracts insects that disperse the fungi's spores.

Engage Your Brain

1 Describe Fill in the blank with the word or phrase that you think correctly completes the following sentences.

The chemical formula for _____

is H_2O. The *H* stands for hydrogen and the

_____ stands for oxygen.

If you don't get enough water, you might

_____

_____ .

2 Relate What do you think you are made of?

_____

_____

_____

_____

_____

Active Reading

3 Synthesize You can often define an unknown word if you know the meaning of its word parts. Use the word parts and sentence below to make an educated guess about the meaning of the word *atom*.

Word part	Meaning
a–	not
tom	to cut

Example sentence
Air is mostly made up of oxygen and nitrogen <u>atoms</u>.

Vocabulary Terms
- atom
- molecule
- lipid
- protein
- carbohydrate
- nucleic acid
- phospholipid

4 Identify This list contains the key terms you'll learn in this lesson. As you read, circle the definition of each term.

atom: _____

_____

_____

It's Elementary

What are atoms and molecules?

Think about where you live. The streets are lined with many types of buildings. But these buildings are made from a lot of the same materials, such as bricks, glass, wood, and steel. Similarly, all cells are made from the same materials. The materials in cells are made up of atoms that can join together to form molecules.

Atoms Are the Building Blocks of Matter

The matter that you encounter every day, both living and nonliving, is made up of basic particles called **atoms.** Not all atoms are the same. There are nearly one hundred types of atoms that occur naturally on Earth. These different types of atoms are known as *elements.* Each element has unique properties. For example, oxygen is a colorless gas made up of oxygen atoms. The element gold is a shiny metal made up of gold atoms. Just six elements make up most of the human body. These and other elements are important for cell processes in all living things.

Active Reading

5 Relate How do atoms relate to cells?

_____

_____

_____

_____

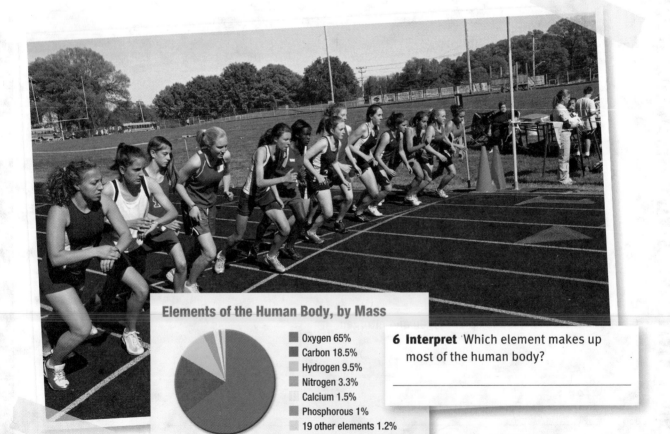

Elements of the Human Body, by Mass

- Oxygen 65%
- Carbon 18.5%
- Hydrogen 9.5%
- Nitrogen 3.3%
- Calcium 1.5%
- Phosphorous 1%
- 19 other elements 1.2%

6 Interpret Which element makes up most of the human body?

_____

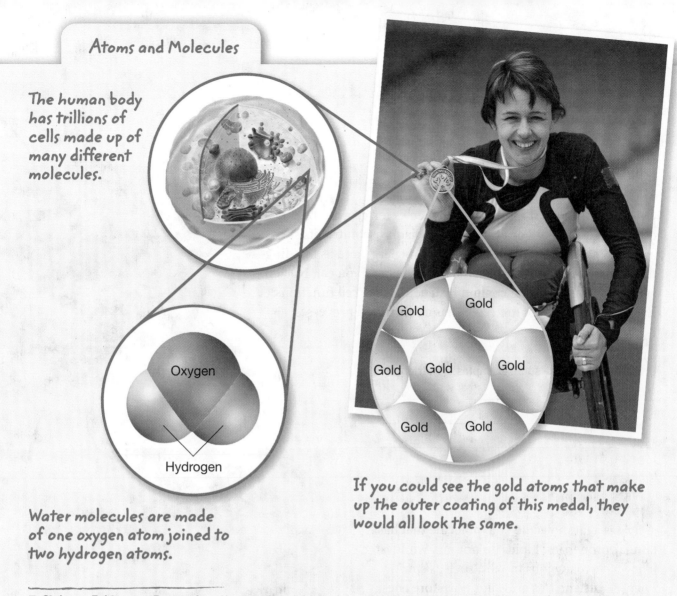

Atoms and Molecules

The human body has trillions of cells made up of many different molecules.

Oxygen

Hydrogen

Water molecules are made of one oxygen atom joined to two hydrogen atoms.

Gold Gold

Gold Gold Gold

Gold Gold

If you could see the gold atoms that make up the outer coating of this medal, they would all look the same.

7 Claims • Evidence • Reasoning How are the gold medal and the human cell similar? How do they differ? Summarize evidence to support your claim and explain your reasoning.

_____

_____

_____

Molecules Are Made of Two or More Atoms

A **molecule** is a group of atoms that are held together by chemical bonds. For example, the molecule of water shown above is made of one oxygen atom bonded to two hydrogen atoms. If you separated the oxygen and hydrogen atoms, then you would no longer have a water molecule.

Some molecules are made up of only one type of atom. For example, a molecule of oxygen gas is made of two oxygen atoms. Other molecules contain different types of atoms. A substance made up of atoms of two or more elements joined by chemical bonds is called a *compound.* Most of the molecules found in cells are also compounds.

Cell Fuel

What are some important types of molecules in cells?

Organisms need certain types of molecules for growth, repair, and other life processes. For example, organisms use nutrients such as lipids, proteins, and carbohydrates for energy and as building materials. You get these nutrients from the food you eat. Nucleic acids are molecules that contain instructions for cell functions. Each of these types of molecules has a role in cell processes.

 **Active Reading**

8 Identify What are some examples of nutrients?

_____

_____

_____

Lipids

A **lipid** is a fat molecule or a molecule that has similar properties. Lipids do not mix with water. They have many jobs in cells, such as storing energy. Fats and oils are lipids that store energy that organisms can use when they need it. Your cells get lipids from foods such as olive oil and fish. Waxes and steroids are other types of lipids.

Proteins

A **protein** is a molecule made up of smaller molecules called *amino acids*. When you eat foods high in proteins, such as peanut butter and meat, the proteins are broken down into amino acids. Amino acids are used to make new proteins. Proteins are used to build and repair body structures and to regulate body processes. Proteins called *enzymes* (EHN•zymz) help chemical processes happen in cells.

9 Describe What are the building blocks of proteins?

_____

© Houghton Mifflin Harcourt Publishing Company • Image Credits: (c) ©Purestock/Alamy; (b) © MBI/Alamy

Carbohydrates

Molecules that include sugars, starches, and fiber are called **carbohydrates**. Cells use carbohydrates as a source of energy and for energy storage. Cells break down carbohydrates to release the energy stored in them. Carbohydrates contain carbon, hydrogen, and oxygen atoms. Simple carbohydrates, such as table sugar, are made up of one sugar molecule or a few sugar molecules linked together. Complex carbohydrates, such as starch, are made of many sugar molecules linked together. Pasta, made from grains, is a good source of complex carbohydrates.

Nucleic Acids

A **nucleic acid** is a molecule that carries information in cells. Nucleic acids are made up of smaller molecules called *nucleotides* (NOO•klee•oh•TYDZ). Deoxyribonucleic acid, or DNA, is one type of nucleic acid that is found in all cells. DNA contains the information that cells need to make molecules, such as proteins. The order of nucleotides in DNA reads like a recipe. Each nucleotide tells the cell the order of amino acids needed to build a certain protein.

DNA

10 Summarize Fill in the table with a function of each nutrient in the cell.

Nutrient	Function in the cell
Lipids	
Proteins	
Carbohydrates	
Nucleic acids	

Waterworks

What are phospholipids?

All cells are surrounded by a cell membrane. The cell membrane helps protect the cell and keep the internal conditions of the cell stable. A lipid that contains phosphorus is called a **phospholipid** (FOSS•foh•LIH•pyd). Phospholipids form much of the cell membrane. The head of a phospholipid molecule is attracted to water. The tail repels water, or pushes it away. Because there is water inside and outside the cell, the phospholipids form a double layer. One layer lines up so that the heads face the outside of the cell. A second layer of phospholipids line up so the heads face the inside of the cell. The tails from both layers face each other, forming the middle of the cell membrane. Molecules, such as water, are regulated into and out of a cell through the cell membrane.

Active Reading **11 Explain** Describe how phospholipids form a barrier between water inside the cell and water outside the cell.

_____

_____

_____

_____

12 Identify Write *attracts* next to the end of the phospholipid that attracts water. Write *repels* next to the end that repels water.

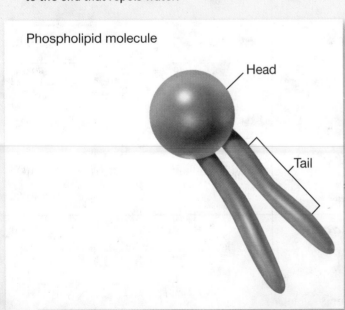

Phospholipid molecule

Head

Tail

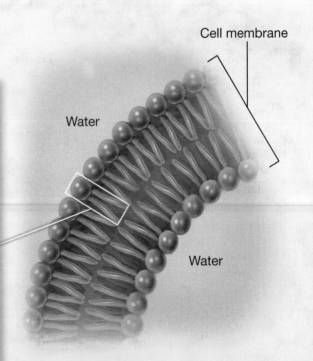

Cell membrane

Water

Water

Why is water important?

Many cell processes require water, which makes up nearly two-thirds of the mass of the cell. Thus, water is an important nutrient for life. Water moves through the cell membrane by a process called *osmosis*. Osmosis depends on the concentration of the water inside and outside of the cell. Pure water has the highest concentration of water molecules. If the water concentration inside the cell is lower than the water concentration outside the cell, then water will move into the cell. If the environment outside a cell has a low concentration of water, such as in a salty solution, water will move out of the cell.

14 Associate Think of an object that could be an analogy to the cell membrane. Draw a picture of the object and explain how it is similar to and different from a cell membrane.

Losing too much water can cause a cell to shrivel and die.

The right balance of water allows a cell to function normally.

If too much water enters a cell, it may swell up and burst.

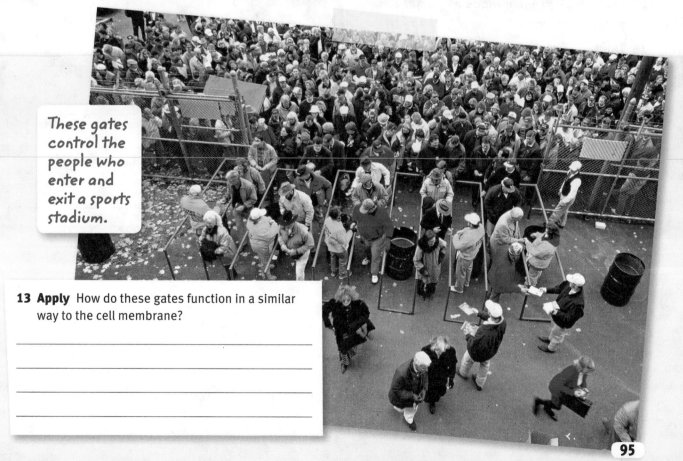

These gates control the people who enter and exit a sports stadium.

13 Apply How do these gates function in a similar way to the cell membrane?

_____

_____

_____

_____

Visual Summary

To complete this summary, circle the correct word and fill in the blanks with the correct word or phrase. Then, use the key below to check your answers. You can use this page to review the main concepts of the lesson.

Cell Chemistry

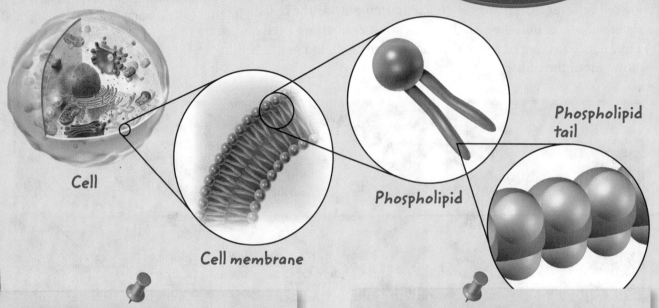

Cell

Cell membrane

Phospholipid

Phospholipid tail

Cells are made up of atoms and molecules.

15 A cell membrane is made of phospholipid atoms / molecules.

16 The tail of the phospholipid is made up of carbon and hydrogen atoms / molecules.

Cells use different molecules for life processes.

17 List four types of molecules important for cell processes.

_____

_____

_____

_____

18 Water moves into and out of a cell through the

_____ .

Answers: 15 molecules; 16 atoms; 17 lipids, carbohydrates, proteins, nucleic acids; 18 cell membrane

19 Relate Explain how atoms and molecules are important to cell processes. Summarize evidence to support your claim and explain your reasoning.

Lesson Review

Vocabulary

Fill in the blank with the term that best completes the following sentences.

1 The smallest unit of an element is a(n)

_____.

2 A(n) _____ is a group of atoms joined by chemical bonds.

Key Concepts

3 Contrast What is the difference between atoms and molecules?

_____

_____

_____

_____

4 Identify What are the functions of proteins in organisms?

_____

_____

_____

_____

5 List Name four important types of molecules found in cells.

_____

_____

_____

6 Describe How does the structure of the cell membrane help the cell regulate water?

_____

_____

_____

_____

_____

_____

Critical Thinking

Use this diagram to answer the following questions.

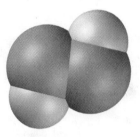

7 Identify Is this an atom or a molecule? Explain.

_____

_____

_____

_____

8 Recognize The red spheres represent oxygen atoms, and the blue spheres represent hydrogen atoms. Is this substance a compound? Explain.

_____

_____

_____

_____

_____

_____

9 Summarize Why is water important in cells? Clearly state your claim, support it with evidence, and explain your reasoning.

_____

_____

_____

_____

_____

_____

_____

My Notes

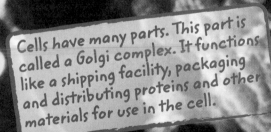

Cell Structure and Function

ESSENTIAL QUESTION

What are the different parts that make up a cell?

By the end of this lesson, you should be able to compare the structure and function of cell parts in plant and animal cells.

Cells have many parts. This part is called a Golgi complex. It functions like a shipping facility, packaging and distributing proteins and other materials for use in the cell.

S7L2.a Cell structures and functions

Lesson Labs

Quick Labs
- Comparing Cells
- Making a 3-D Cell Model
- Cell Walls and Wilting

Engage Your Brain

1 Predict Check T or F to show whether you think each statement is true or false.

T   F

☐   ☐   All cells have the same structure and function.

☐   ☐   Prokaryotes do not have a nucleus.

☐   ☐   Plant cells are the same as animal cells.

☐   ☐   All organisms are multicellular.

2 Relate How does the structure of this umbrella relate to its function?

_____

_____

_____

_____

_____

Active Reading

3 Synthesis You can often define an unknown word if you know the meaning of its word parts. Use the word parts and sentence below to make an educated guess about the meaning of the word *chloroplast*.

Word part	Meaning
chloro-	green
plast	structure

Example sentence
Plant cells have <u>chloroplasts</u>, which contain a green pigment used for making their own food.

Vocabulary Terms

- cytoskeleton
- mitochondrion
- ribosome
- endoplasmic reticulum
- Golgi complex
- cell wall
- vacuole
- chloroplast
- lysosome

4 Apply As you learn the definition of each vocabulary term in this lesson, create your own definition or sketch to help you remember the meaning of the term.

chloroplast:

_____

_____

Being Eu-nique

What are the characteristics of eukaryotic cells?

Active Reading

5 Identify As you read, underline the characteristics of eukaryotic cells.

All organisms are made up of one or more cells, but what kinds of cells? There are two types of organisms: prokaryotes and eukaryotes. Prokaryotes are made up of a single prokaryotic cell. Eukaryotes are made up of one or more eukaryotic cells. Prokaryotic cells do not have a nucleus or membrane-bound organelles. Eukaryotic cells have membrane-bound organelles, including a nucleus.

Eukaryotic cells can differ from each other depending on their *structure* and *function*. A cell's structure is the arrangement of its parts. A cell's function is the activity the parts carry out. For example, plant cells and animal cells have different parts that have different functions for the organism. This is what makes plants and animals so different from each other. Even cells within the same organism can differ from each other depending on their function. Most of the cells in multicellular organisms are specialized to perform a specific function. However, all eukaryotic cells share some characteristics. They all have a nucleus, membrane-bound organelles, and parts that protect and support the cell.

Visualize It!

6 Apply A euglena is a unicellular organism. Why is it a eukaryote like the plant and animal cells shown here?

_____

_____

_____

_____

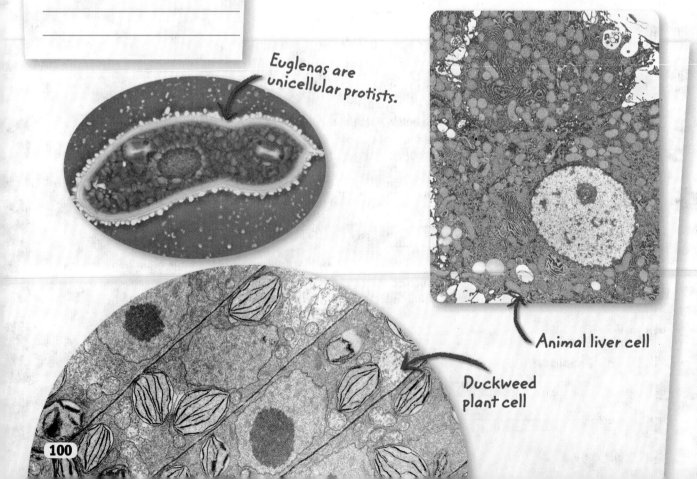

Euglenas are unicellular protists.

Animal liver cell

Duckweed plant cell

Parts that Protect and Support the Cell

Every cell is surrounded by a cell membrane. The cell membrane acts as a barrier between the inside of a cell and the cell's environment. This membrane protects the cell and regulates what enters and leaves the cell.

The cytoplasm is the region between the cell membrane and the nucleus that includes fluid and all of the organelles. Throughout the cytoplasm of eukaryotic cells is a **cytoskeleton**. The cytoskeleton is a network of protein filaments that gives shape and support to cells. The cytoskeleton is also involved in cell division and in movement. It may help parts within the cell to move. Or it may form structures that help the whole organism to move.

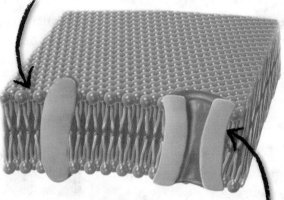

The cell membrane is a double layer of phospholipids. Water molecules and some gas molecules can pass through the cell membrane.

Other larger materials must pass through protein channels in the membrane.

Genetic Material in the Nucleus

In eukaryotic cells, the nucleus is the organelle that contains the cell's genetic material. Deoxyribonucleic acid, or DNA, is stored in the nucleus. DNA is genetic material that contains information needed for cell processes, such as making proteins. Proteins perform most actions of a cell. Although DNA is found in the nucleus, proteins are not made there. Instead, instructions for how to make proteins are stored in DNA. These instructions are sent out of the nucleus through pores in the nuclear membrane. The nuclear membrane is a double layer. Each layer is similar in structure to the cell membrane.

7 Describe What are two functions of the cell membrane?

_____

_____

_____

_____

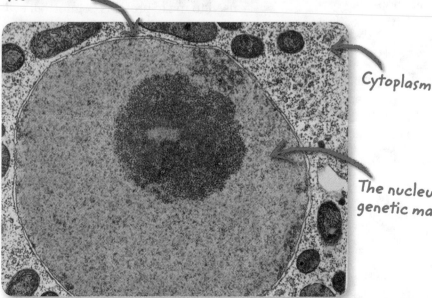

Nuclear membrane

Cytoplasm

The nucleus contains genetic material.

Part-iculars

What organelles are found in plant and animal cells?

Even though plant and animal cells are microscopic, they are very complex. They have many parts that function to keep the cell alive. Many of these parts are membrane-bound organelles that perform a specific function.

Mitochondria

Organisms need energy for life processes. Cells carry out such processes for growth and repair, movement of materials into and out of the cell, and chemical processes. Cells get energy by breaking down food using a process called *cellular respiration*. Cellular respiration occurs in an organelle called the **mitochondrion** (my•TOH•kahn•dree•ahn). In cellular respiration, cells use oxygen to release energy stored in food. For example, cells break down the sugar glucose to release the energy stored in the sugar. The mitochondria then transfer the energy released from the sugar to a molecule called *adenosine triphosphate*, or ATP. Cells use ATP to carry out cell processes.

Mitochondria have their own DNA, and they have two membranes. The outer membrane is smooth. The inner membrane has many folds. Folds increase the surface area inside the mitochondria where cellular respiration occurs.

---

8 Claims • Evidence • Reasoning Would "powerhouse of cells" be a good name for mitochondria? Why or why not? Provide evidence or examples to support your reasoning.

_____

_____

_____

_____

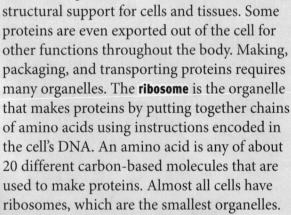

Ribosomes

Ribosomes

Proteins control most chemical reactions of cells and provide structural support for cells and tissues. Some proteins are even exported out of the cell for other functions throughout the body. Making, packaging, and transporting proteins requires many organelles. The **ribosome** is the organelle that makes proteins by putting together chains of amino acids using instructions encoded in the cell's DNA. An amino acid is any of about 20 different carbon-based molecules that are used to make proteins. Almost all cells have ribosomes, which are the smallest organelles.

Ribosomes are not enclosed in a membrane. In prokaryotes, the ribosomes are suspended freely in the cytoplasm. In eukaryotes, some ribosomes are free, and others are attached to another organelle called the *endoplasmic reticulum*.

9 Describe How do ribosomes make proteins?

_____

_____

_____

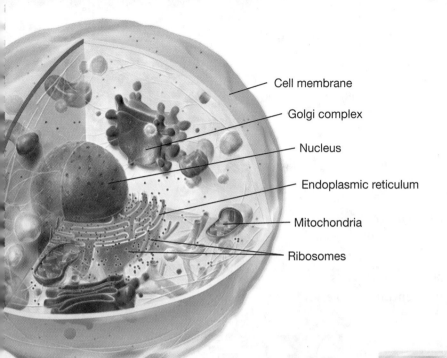

Cell membrane

Golgi complex

Nucleus

Endoplasmic reticulum

Mitochondria

Ribosomes

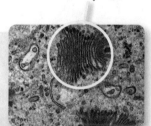

Golgi complex

Endoplasmic Reticulum

In the cytoplasm is a system of membranes near the nucleus called the **endoplasmic reticulum** (ehn•doh•PLAHZ•mick rhett•ICK•yoo•luhm), or ER. The ER assists in the production, processing, and transport of proteins and in the production of lipids. The ER is either smooth or rough. Rough ER has ribosomes attached to its membrane, while smooth ER does not. Ribosomes on the rough ER make many of the cell's proteins. Some of these proteins move through the ER to different places in the cell. The smooth ER makes lipids and breaks down toxic materials that could damage the cell.

10 Claims • Evidence • Reasoning Do rough ER and smooth ER differ? Summarize evidence to support your claim and explain your reasoning.

_____

_____

_____

_____

Golgi Complex

The membrane-bound organelle that packages and distributes materials, such as proteins, is called the **Golgi complex** (GOHL•ghee COHM•plehkz). It is named after Camillo Golgi, the Italian scientist who first identified the organelle.

The Golgi complex is a system of flattened membrane sacs. Lipids and proteins from the ER are delivered to the Golgi complex where they may be modified to do different jobs. The final products are enclosed in a piece of the Golgi complex's membrane. This membrane pinches off to form a small bubble, or vesicle. The vesicle transports its contents to other parts of the cell or out of the cell.

11 Describe What is the function of the Golgi complex?

_____

_____

_____

Now Showing: The Plant Cell

What additional parts are found in plant cells?

Think about some ways that plants are different from animals. Plants don't move around, and some have flowers. Plant cells do have a cell membrane, cytoskeleton, nucleus, mitochondria, ribosomes, ER, and a Golgi complex, just like animal cells do. In addition, plant cells have a cell wall, a large central vacuole, and chloroplasts.

Active Reading

12 Identify As you read, underline the functions of the cell wall, large central vacuole, and the chloroplasts.

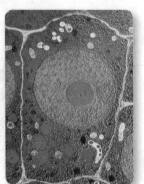

Cell Wall

In addition to the cell membrane, plant cells have a **cell wall**. The cell wall is a rigid structure that surrounds the cell membrane, identified by the yellow line around the plant cell in this photo. Cell walls provide support and protection to the cell. Plants don't have a skeleton like many animals do, so they get their shape from the cell wall. The cells of fungi, archaea, bacteria, and some protists also have cell walls.

Large Central Vacuole

A **vacuole** (VAK•yoo•ohl) is a fluid-filled vesicle found in the cells of most animals, plants, and fungi. A vacuole may contain enzymes, nutrients, water, or wastes. Plant cells also have a large central vacuole that stores water. A central vacuole full of water helps support the cell. Plants may wilt when the central vacuole loses water.

13 Compare How do large central vacuoles differ from vacuoles?

_____

_____

_____

Visualize It!

14 Identify Label these cell parts on the plant cell shown here:
- Mitochondrion
- Golgi complex
- Nucleus
- Endoplasmic reticulum
- Ribosomes
- Cell wall
- Cell membrane
- Cytoskeleton

F _____

G _____

A _____

B _____

C _____

D _____

E _____

H _____

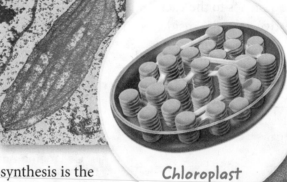

Chloroplast

Chloroplasts

Animals must eat food to provide their cells with energy. However, plants and some protists can make their own food using photosynthesis. These organisms have **chloroplasts** (KLOHR•oh•plahstz), organelles where photosynthesis occurs. Photosynthesis is the process by which cells use sunlight, carbon dioxide, and water to make sugar and oxygen. Chloroplasts are green because they contain a green pigment called *chlorophyll* (KLOHR•oh•fill). Chlorophyll absorbs the energy in sunlight. This energy is used to make sugar, which is then used by mitochondria to make ATP. Chloroplasts have two outer membranes.

15 Describe What is the role of chlorophyll inside chloroplasts?

_____

_____

_____

Think Outside the Book Inquiry

16 Describe Cyanobacteria and green algae are similar to plants. Choose one of these organisms. Why is it similar to plants, but is not classified as a plant? Summarize the evidence to support your claim and explain your reasoning.

© Houghton Mifflin Harcourt Publishing Company • Image Credits: (bkgd) ©Peter Finger/Corbis; (b) ©Dr Jeremy Burgess/SPL/Photo Researchers, Inc.

Introducing:
The Animal Cell

What additional part is found in animal cells?

Animal cells are eukaryotic cells that contain a nucleus and are surrounded by a cell membrane. They contain many of the same organelles as most plant cells, including mitochondria, ribosomes, ER, and a Golgi complex. Most animal cells also contain a membrane-bound organelle called a *lysosome*.

Active Reading 17 **Recognize** As you read, underline the function of lysosomes.

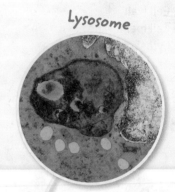

Lysosome

Lysosomes

Organelles called **lysosomes** (LY•soh•zohmz) contain digestive enzymes, which break down worn-out or damaged organelles, waste materials, and foreign invaders in the cell. Some of these materials are collected in vacuoles. A lysosome attaches to the vacuole and releases the digestive enzymes inside. Some of these materials are recycled and reused in the cell. For example, a human liver cell recycles half of its materials each week.

18 Compare How are lysosomes similar to vacuoles?

_____

_____

_____

_____

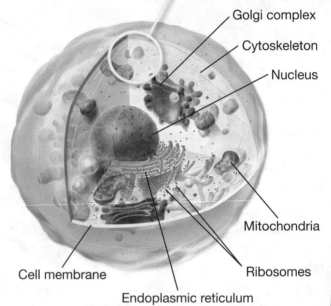

Golgi complex

Cytoskeleton

Nucleus

Mitochondria

Ribosomes

Cell membrane

Endoplasmic reticulum

19 Compare Draw a model of a plant cell and an animal cell. Label the models with the appropriate structures identified in the *Structure* column. Then, read the *Function* column and complete the missing information. Finally, refer to your model to explain how the nucleus, cytoplasm, cell membrane, cell wall, chloroplasts, lysosome, and mitochondria interact and work together to allow the cell to grow, reproduce, make needed materials, and process waste.

Structure	Function
Nucleus	
Endoplasmic reticulum	Processes and transports proteins and makes lipids
Golgi complex	Packages and distributes materials within or out of the cell
Ribosome	Makes proteins
Chloroplast	
Mitochondrion	
Lysosome	
Large central vacuole	Stores water and helps give shape to the cell
Cytoplasm	
Cell membrane	
Cell wall	

Visual Summary

To complete this summary, fill in the blanks to identify the organelles in each cell. Then, use the key below to check your answers. You can use this page to review the main concepts of the lesson.

Compare
Plant Cells and Animal Cells

Structures in plant cells

20 _____

21 _____

Structures in animal cells

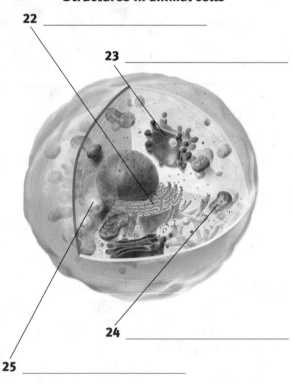

22 _____

23 _____

24 _____

25 _____

Plants and animals are eukaryotes. The structures inside a eukaryotic cell work together to keep the cell and the entire organism alive.

Answers: 20 large central vacuole; 21 cell wall; 22 endoplasmic reticulum; 23 Golgi complex; 24 mitochondrion; 25 lysosome

---

26 Summarize How do eukaryotic cells differ from each other?

Lesson Review

Vocabulary

Circle the term that best completes the following sentences.

1 A *Golgi complex / ribosome* makes proteins that are transported through the endoplasmic reticulum.

2 The *nucleus / large central vacuole* contains the genetic material of a eukaryotic cell.

3 The *cell membrane / cytoplasm* acts as a barrier between the inside of a cell and the cell's environment.

4 The organelle in which photosynthesis takes place is the *cell wall / chloroplast*.

Key Concepts

5 Recognize What do all eukaryotic cells have in common?

_____

_____

_____

6 Compare Are the functions of the cytoskeleton and the cell wall similar? Provide evidence to support your claim and explain your reasoning.

_____

_____

_____

_____

_____

_____

7 Contrast What structures are found in plant cells that are not found in animal cells?

_____

_____

_____

Critical Thinking

Use this diagram to answer the following questions.

8 Identify What is this organelle?

_____

9 Explain How does its structure affect its function?

_____

_____

_____

_____

_____

_____

10 Compare Which cells contain this organelle: plant cells, animal cells, or both?

_____

11 Apply Explain the function of ribosomes and why cells need them.

_____

_____

_____

_____

_____

_____

_____

My Notes

Making Predictions

Scientists try to answer questions about the world by developing hypotheses, making predictions, and conducting experiments to test those predictions. To make a prediction, a scientist will analyze a general idea and then predict specific results. Predictions often take the form of "if–then" statements. For example, "If living organisms are made of small units called cells, then we predict that we will see cells if we look at organisms up close under a microscope."

A dividing frog cell showing microtubules (green) and DNA (blue)

Tutorial

For an organism to grow and reproduce, chromosomes must replicate and cells must divide. The following steps will teach you how to make predictions from hypotheses about the role of protein fibers, called microtubules, in cell division.

Question: How do chromosomes move and separate during cell division?

Hypothesis: Microtubules play an important role in the movement of the chromosomes during cell division.

Prediction: If microtubules were inhibited during cell division, then chromosomes would not be able to move and separate from each other during cell division.

Observations: When microtubules are exposed to a drug that blocks microtubule formation, movement of chromosomes is inhibited and cell division stops.

What is the hypothesis? A hypothesis is a plausible answer to a scientific question. Form a hypothesis based on prior experience, background knowledge, or your own observations.

What would we expect or predict to see if the hypothesis were true? When scientists summarize their data, they look for observations and measurements that will support their hypothesis.

Does the prediction match the observations? If the data match the predictions generated by the hypothesis, then the hypothesis is supported. Sometimes, errors occur during the scientific investigation, which can lead to incorrect results. There is also the possibility that correct data will not match the hypothesis. When this happens, generate a new hypothesis.

You Try It!

Scientists often propose hypotheses about the causes of events they observe. Read the following scenario, and answer the questions that follow.

Scenario: A cell biologist has three cell cultures of human skin cells. The cells in each culture are taken from the same cell line. Each cell culture is placed in a solution for observation. The cells in culture A are growing faster than the cells in cultures B and C.

Question: Why are the cells in culture A growing at a faster rate than the cells in cultures B and C?

Hypothesis 1: The waste level is higher in cultures B and C than in culture A.

Hypothesis 2: The nutrient levels are higher in culture A than in cultures B and C.

1 Making Predictions Read each of the hypotheses above, and then make a prediction for each about what might be observed.

Hypothesis 1:

_____

_____

_____

Hypothesis 2:

_____

_____

_____

2 Testing a Hypothesis Identify a possible experiment for each hypothesis that you can perform or observations that you can make to find out whether the hypothesis is supported.

Hypothesis 1:

_____

_____

_____

Hypothesis 2:

_____

_____

_____

3 Predicting Outcomes Fill in the two tables below with plausible data that support each hypothesis.

Culture	Waste level	Rate of growth (cells/hour)
A		
B		
C		

Culture	Nutrient level	Rate of growth (cells/hour)
A		
B		
C		

Take It Home

Find a recent newspaper or magazine article that makes a conclusion based on a scientific study. Carefully evaluate the study, and identify the predictions that were tested in the study. Bring the article to class, and be prepared to discuss your analysis of the article.

Levels of Cellular Organization

ESSENTIAL QUESTION

How are living things organized?

By the end of this lesson, you should be able to describe the different levels of organization in living things.

S7L2.b Organization of tissues, organs, systems, and organisms

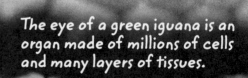

The eye of a green iguana is an organ made of millions of cells and many layers of tissues.

Lesson Labs

Quick Labs
• Evaluating Specialization
• Observing Plant Organs

Exploration Lab
• The Organization of Organisms

 Engage Your Brain

1 Describe Fill in the blank with the word or phrase you think correctly completes the following sentences.

Your body has many organs, such as a

heart and a(n) _____.

Plant organs include stems and

_____.

Animal and plant organs are organized into

organ systems, thus resembling the way you

organize your homework in _____

_____.

2 Explain How is the structure of a hammer related to its function?

_____

_____

_____

_____

_____

Active Reading

3 Relate Many scientific words, such as *organ* and *tissue,* also have everyday meanings. Use context clues to write your own definition for each underlined word.

It is helpful to use a <u>tissue</u> when sneezing to prevent the spread of droplets carrying bacteria.

tissue:

_____

_____

_____

An <u>organ</u> can be very difficult to play.

organ:

_____

_____

_____

Vocabulary Terms

• organism   • organ system
• tissue   • structure
• organ   • function

4 Apply As you learn the definition of each vocabulary term in this lesson, create your own definition or sketch to help you remember the meaning of the term.

Body Building

How are living things organized?

An **organism** is a living thing that can carry out life processes by itself. *Unicellular organisms* are made up of just one cell that performs all of the functions necessary for life. Unicellular organisms do not have levels of organization. Having only one cell has advantages and disadvantages. For example, unicellular organisms need fewer resources, and some can live in harsh conditions, such as hot springs and very salty water. However, a disadvantage of being unicellular is that the entire organism dies if the single cell dies.

Active Reading

5 Identify As you read, underline the characteristics of unicellular and multicellular organisms.

Into Cells

Multicellular organisms are made up of more than one cell. These cells are grouped into different levels of organization, including tissues, organs, and organ systems. The cells that make up a multicellular organism, such as humans and plants, are specialized to perform specific functions. Many multicellular organisms reproduce through sexual reproduction, during which a male sex cell fertilizes a female sex cell. The single cell that results from fertilization divides repeatedly. This cell division forms the basic tissues of an embryo, which further develop into all of the specialized tissues and organs within a multicellular organism. Other characteristics of multicellular organisms include a larger size and a longer lifespan than unicellular organisms.

There are some disadvantages to being multicellular. Multicellular organisms need more resources than do unicellular organisms. Also, the cells of multicellular organisms are specialized for certain jobs, which means that cells must depend on each other to perform all of the functions that an organism needs to live.

Diatoms are microscopic unicellular organisms that live in water.

Humpback whales are multicellular organisms.

Into Tissues

A **tissue** is a group of similar cells that perform a common function. Humans and many other animals are made up of four basic types of tissue: nervous, epithelial, connective, and muscle. Nervous tissue functions as a messaging system within the body. Epithelial tissue is protective and forms boundaries, such as skin. Connective tissue, including bones and blood, holds parts of the body together and provides support and nourishment to organs. Muscle tissue helps produce movement.

Plants have three types of tissue: transport, protective, and ground. Transport tissue moves water and nutrients through the plant. Protective tissue protects the outside of the plant. Ground tissue provides internal support and storage and absorbs light energy to make food in photosynthesis (foh•toh•SIN•thuh•sis).

Plant leaf tissue

Animal skin tissue

6 Compare Fill in the Venn diagram to compare the functions of animal tissues and plant tissues. What functions do they share?

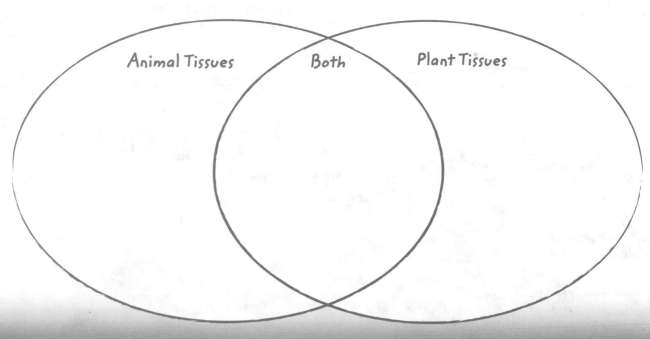

Animal Tissues   Both   Plant Tissues

Visualize It!

7 Apply Does either one of the organisms shown on the opposite page contain cells that are organized into tissues? Use evidence to support your answer.

_____

_____

_____

_____

_____

_____

Into Organs

A structure made up of a collection of tissues that carries out a specialized function is called an **organ**. The stomach is an organ that breaks down food for digestion. Different types of tissues work together to accomplish this function. For example, nervous tissue sends messages to the stomach's muscle tissue to tell the muscle tissue to contract. When the muscle tissue contracts, food and stomach acids are mixed, and the food breaks down.

Plants also have organs that are made up of different tissues working together. For example, a leaf is an organ that contains protective tissue to reduce water loss, ground tissue for photosynthesis, and transport tissue to move nutrients from leaves to stems. Stems and roots are organs that function to transport and store water and nutrients in the plant. The trunk of most trees is a stem. Roots are usually below the ground.

Active Reading

8 Apply How do organs relate to cells and tissues?

_____

_____

_____

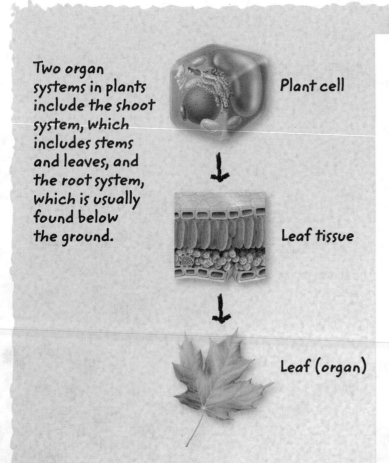

Two organ systems in plants include the shoot system, which includes stems and leaves, and the root system, which is usually found below the ground.

Plant cell

Leaf tissue

Leaf (organ)

Visualize It!

9 Identify Label the organ system shown in the tree below. Then draw and label the tree's root system.

The digestive system is an organ system found in most animals, including humans.

Stomach
muscle cell

Stomach
muscle tissue

Stomach (organ)

Human digestive system

10 Claims • Evidence • Reasoning Voluntary muscles can be controlled, while involuntary muscles cannot. Do you think stomach muscle is voluntary or involuntary? Provide evidence to support your reasoning.

_____

_____

_____

_____

_____

Into Organ Systems

An **organ system** is a group of organs that work together to perform body functions. Each organ system has a specific job to do for the organism. For example, the stomach works with other organs of the digestive system to digest and absorb nutrients from food. Other organs included in the digestive system are the esophagus and the small and large intestines.

Humans are made up of many organ systems. All of the systems have specific functions to keep the body alive.

Think Outside the Book Inquiry

11 Illustrate Research an organ system of the human body other than the digestive system. Draw a conceptual model of how the cells, tissues, organs, and systems are organized hierarchically. Then, use the model to conclude how the organization of the human body supports specific functions. (You can refer to resources in your library or to Unit 4.)

What's Your Function?

What is the connection between structure and function?

Cells, tissues, organs, and organ systems make up the structure of a multicellular organism. **Structure** is the arrangement of parts in an organism or an object. The structure of a cell, tissue, or organ determines its **function**, or the activity of each part in an organism. In fact, the structure of any object determines its function.

**Active Reading**

12 Recognize As you read, underline examples of multicellular structures.

Structure Determines Function

Cells, tissues, and organs vary in structure. For example, bone cells look different from plant leaf cells. A lung differs from a stomach because the two organs have different functions. Cells, tissues, and organs are specialized to perform specific functions. For example, a lung is an organ made up of cells and tissues that work together to help you breathe. The lungs are made up of millions of tiny air sacs called *alveoli* (singular, *alveolus*). The large number of alveoli increases the surface area of the lungs to let enough oxygen and carbon dioxide move between the lungs and the blood.

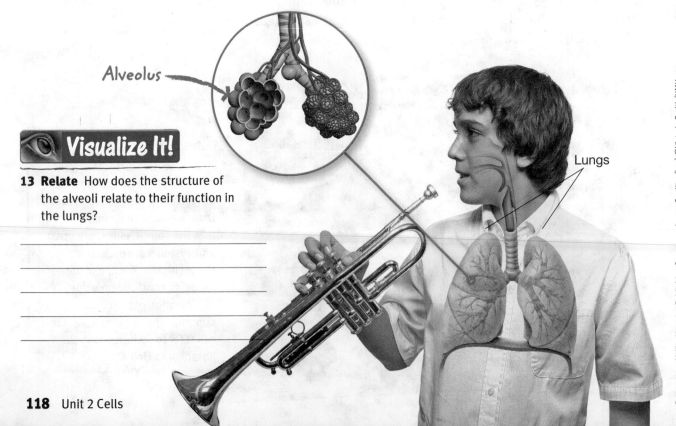

Alveolus

Visualize It!

13 Relate How does the structure of the alveoli relate to their function in the lungs?

_____

_____

_____

_____

Lungs

© Houghton Mifflin Harcourt Publishing Company • Image Credits: (boy) ©Victoria Smith/HMH

WEIRD SCIENCE

Odd Bodies

With millions of different organisms that exist on Earth, it's no wonder there are so many different body structures. Some organisms have special structures that can help them eat—or not be eaten!

Night Vision

The tarsier's huge eyes provide excellent vision for hunting insects at night. Its eyes average 16 mm in diameter, but the tarsier's overall body size ranges from 85 mm to 165 mm. In comparison, your eyes would be the size of apples! When the tarsier spots its prey, it leaps through the air to pounce on it. The tarsier's long fingers help it grasp branches when it's on the move.

Can't Touch This!

Named for its prickly body, the spiny katydid doesn't make much of a meal for its predator. Male katydids sing loudly at night to attract female katydids. The singing can also attract predators, such as bats, who hunt for food at night. Its spines provide the katydid with some protection from being eaten.

Blow on Your Food

The longhorn cowfish is a marine organism that lives on the sandy ocean bottom at depths up to 50 m. Its permanently puckered mouth helps the cowfish find food. The cowfish blows jets of water into the sand to find and feed on tiny organisms.

Extend

Inquiry

14 Relate How does the body structure of each of these organisms contribute to a particular function?

15 Contrast How do structures in living organisms compare with structures of nonliving things such as construction cranes, buildings, ships, airplanes, or bridges?

16 Claims • Evidence • Reasoning Describe an organism that might live in an extreme environment such as inside a volcano, deep in the ocean, or in an icy cave. What type of organism is it? What special structures would it have in order to survive in that environment? Summarize evidence to support your claim and explain your reasoning.

Systems at Work

What tasks do systems perform to meet the needs of cells?

Complex organisms are made up of many systems. These systems work together to perform actions needed by cells to function properly. Whether it is a bone cell or a skin cell, each cell in the organism needs to receive nutrients, exchange carbon dioxide and oxygen, and have waste products taken away.

A unicellular organism must perform all functions necessary for life, such as getting nutrients, exchanging gases, and removing wastes. The functions must be performed by a single cell, because there is no opportunity for cell specialization.

Multicellular organisms face different challenges. Multicellular organisms have different cell types that can work together in groups to perform specific functions. Groups of cells that work together form tissues. Groups of tissues that work together form organs, and groups of organs that work together form systems. Systems work with other systems. In most animals, the digestive, respiratory, and excretory systems interact with the circulatory system to maintain healthy cells. A circulatory system delivers nutrients to body cells and carries away wastes. It carries oxygen to cells and removes carbon dioxide.

Some plants have a vascular system that transports water and nutrients to and from cells throughout the plant. Xylem and phloem are tissues that make up the vascular system. Xylem transports water from roots to cells. Phloem transports nutrients made in leaf cells to all parts of the plant.

17 Compare How do unicellular organisms and multicellular organisms compare in meeting their needs to stay alive?

_____

_____

_____

_____

_____

Visualize It!

18 Analyze This diagram shows the xylem and phloem that make up the plant's vascular system. How does a vascular system serve the needs of plant cells?

_____

_____

_____

Leaf

Water   Food

Stem

Xylem   Phloem

Roots

Delivering Nutrients

The digestive system in most animals breaks down food mechanically and chemically. In most animals, the digestive system works with a circulatory system. In the small intestine, nutrients are absorbed through thousands of finger-like projections in the wall of the small intestine, called villi, and then into the blood vessels of the circulatory system. Once in the blood, the nutrients are delivered to cells throughout the body.

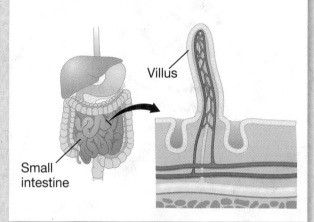

Villus

Small intestine

Delivering Oxygen

In animals, taking in oxygen is a function of the respiratory system. Depending on the animal, oxygen enters a body through skin, gills, spiracles, or lungs. There, it comes in contact with the circulatory system. Oxygen enters the bloodstream and is carried to the cells of the body. Once in the cells, oxygen is used to release energy from nutrients from digestion.

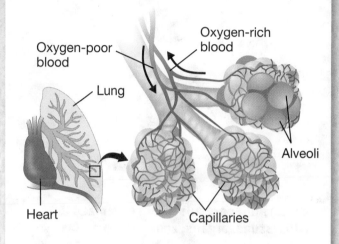

Oxygen-poor blood

Oxygen-rich blood

Lung

Alveoli

Heart

Capillaries

Removing Wastes

Skin, lungs, the digestive system, and the kidneys all have processes for removing waste products from the body. Sweat evaporates from the skin. Solid wastes and some water move out as part of the digestive system. Carbon dioxide and some water are breathed out through the respiratory system. In humans, the largest amount of excess water and waste products from cells is carried by the blood to the kidneys. There, wastes are filtered out of the blood through a complex series of tubules in the kidneys and leave the body as urine.

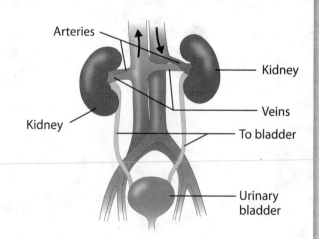

Arteries

Kidney

Veins

Kidney

To bladder

Urinary bladder

Visualize It!

19 **Synthesize** Notice that oxygen-poor blood (blue) and oxygen-rich blood (red) are shown in all three diagrams. Describe the role of blood in the transportation of materials throughout the body.

_____

_____

_____

_____

_____

_____

_____

Visual Summary

To complete this summary, fill in the blanks with the correct word. Then, use the key below to check your answers. You can use this page to review the main concepts of the lesson.

Cellular Organization

All organisms are made up of one or more cells.

T F
20 ☐ ☐ A plant is a unicellular organism.

The structures of cells, tissues, and organs determine their functions.

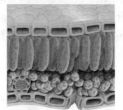

T F
21 ☐ ☐ The protective tissue on a leaf has a structure that keeps the leaf from drying out.

Multicellular organisms are organized into tissues, organs, and organ systems.

T F
22 ☐ ☐ This leaf is an example of a plant organ.

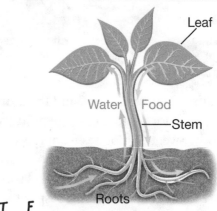

Leaf

Water Food
Stem

Roots

T F
23 ☐ ☐ A plant obtains water from its environment through the root system.

Answers: 20 False; 21 True; 22 True; 23 True

---

24 Synthesize How do cells, tissues, organs, and organ systems work together in a multicellular organism?

Lesson Review

Vocabulary

Fill in the blank with the term that best completes the following sentences.

1 Animals have four basic types of

_____: nervous, epithelial, muscle, and connective.

2 Together, the esophagus, stomach, and

intestines are part of a(n) _____.

Key Concepts

3 Describe What are the levels of organization in multicellular organisms?

_____

_____

_____

_____

4 Analyze Multicellular organisms have specialized cells. Would such organisms be better served by cells that are all the same instead? Use evidence to support your claim and explain your reasoning.

_____

_____

_____

_____

_____

_____

_____

5 Relate How do the structures in an organism relate to their functions?

_____

_____

_____

Critical Thinking

Use the figure to answer the next two questions.

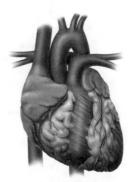

Human heart

6 Apply What level of organization is shown here?

_____

7 Relate How does this level of organization relate to cells? To organ systems?

_____

_____

_____

_____

_____

_____

8 Analyze Explain why a circulatory system is important in meeting the needs of all cells throughout an animal's body.

_____

_____

_____

_____

_____

_____

_____

_____

My Notes

Homeostasis and Cell Processes

ESSENTIAL QUESTION

How do organisms maintain homeostasis?

By the end of this lesson, you should be able to explain the important processes that organisms undergo to maintain stable internal conditions.

These American alligators are warming themselves in the sun. Temperature is one factor that an organism can control to maintain stable internal conditions.

Lesson Labs

Quick Labs
• Investigate Microorganisms
• Homeostasis and Adaptations

Exploration Lab
• Diffusion

Engage Your Brain

1 Explain How is this person able to stay on the skateboard?

_____
_____

2 Describe Fill in the blanks with the word or phrase that you think correctly completes the following sentences.

Eating _____ provides your body with nutrients it needs for energy.

Cells can _____ to make more cells.

Trucks, airplanes, and trains are used to _____ people and supplies from one place to another.

Active Reading

3 Synthesis You can often define an unknown word if you know the meaning of its word parts. Use the word parts and sentence below to make an educated guess about the meaning of the word *photosynthesis*.

Word part	Meaning
photo-	light
synthesis	to make

Example sentence
Plants use a process called <u>photosynthesis</u> to make their own food.

photosynthesis:

_____
_____

Vocabulary Terms

- **homeostasis**
- **photosynthesis**
- **cellular respiration**
- **mitosis**
- **passive transport**
- **diffusion**
- **osmosis**
- **active transport**
- **endocytosis**
- **exocytosis**

4 Identify As you read, place a question mark next to any words that you don't understand. When you finish reading the lesson, go back and review the text that you marked. If the information is still confusing, consult a classmate or a teacher.

Stayin' Alive

What is homeostasis?

We all feel more comfortable when our surroundings are ideal—not too hot, not too cold, not too wet, and not too dry. Cells are the same way. However, a cell's environment is constantly changing. **Homeostasis** (hoh•mee•oh•STAY•sis) is the maintenance of a constant internal state in a changing environment. In order to survive, your cells need to be able to obtain and use energy, make new cells, exchange materials, and eliminate wastes. Homeostasis ensures that cells can carry out these tasks in a changing environment.

Active Reading **6 Summarize** What are four things that cells can do to maintain homeostasis?

_____

_____

_____

Visualize It!

7 Apply Think about how this girl is feeling after she exercises. What things can you see that are helping to keep her body temperature stable?

_____

_____

_____

Balance in Organisms

All cells need energy and materials in order to carry out life processes. A unicellular organism exchanges materials directly with its environment. The cell membrane and other parts of the cell regulate what materials get into and out of the cell. This is one way that unicellular organisms maintain homeostasis.

Cells in multicellular organisms must work together to maintain homeostasis for the entire organism. For example, multicellular organisms have systems that transport materials to cells from other places in the organism. The main transport system in your body is your cardiovascular system. The cardiovascular system includes the heart, blood vessels, and blood. The heart pumps blood through branched blood vessels that come close to every cell in the body. Blood carries materials to the cells and carries wastes away from the cells. Other multicellular organisms have transport systems, too. For example, many plants have two types of vascular tissues that work together as a transport system. *Xylem* is the tissue that transports water and minerals from the roots to the rest of the plant. Another tissue called *phloem* transports food made within plant cells.

© Houghton Mifflin Harcourt Publishing Company • Image Credits: (t) ©Biophoto Associates/Photo Researchers, Inc.; (b) ©Steve Gschmeissner/Photo Researchers, Inc.

Active Reading

8 Compare As you read, underline how unicellular organisms and multicellular organisms exchange materials.

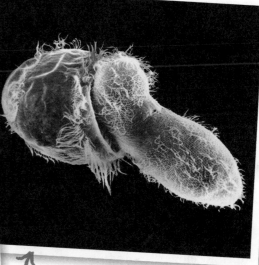

A unicellular organism, **Didinium**, is eating another unicellular organism, called a **Paramecium**.

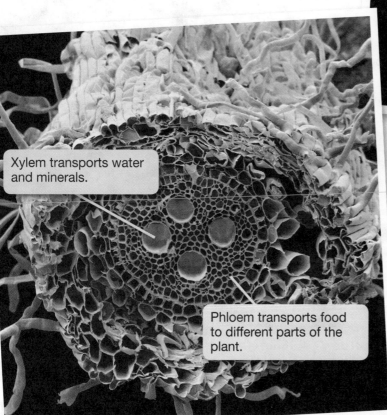

Xylem transports water and minerals.

Phloem transports food to different parts of the plant.

Plants have two types of vascular tissue that they use to transport materials.

Get Growing!

How do cells get energy?

Cells need energy to perform cell functions. Cells get energy by breaking down materials, such as food, in which energy is stored. Breaking down food also provides raw materials the cell needs to make other materials for cell processes.

Photosynthesis

The sun provides the energy for plants to grow and make food. Plants use sunlight to change carbon dioxide and water into sugar and oxygen. This process by which plants, algae, and some bacteria make their own food is called **photosynthesis**. Inside plant and algal cells are special organelles, called chloroplasts, where photosynthesis takes place.

Cellular Respiration

All living things need food to produce energy for cell processes. The process by which cells use oxygen to produce energy from food is called **cellular respiration**. Plants, animals, and most other organisms use cellular respiration to get energy from food.

Nearly all the oxygen around us is made by photosynthesis. Animals and plants use oxygen during cellular respiration to break down food. Cellular respiration also produces carbon dioxide. Plants need carbon dioxide to make sugars. So, photosynthesis and respiration are linked, each one depending on the products of the other.

Plants provide the food for nearly all living things on land. Some organisms eat plants for food. Other organisms eat animals that eat plants.

9 Synthesize Fill in the blanks with the materials that are involved in photosynthesis and cellular respiration.

Photosynthesis	_____ + carbon dioxide —sunlight→ _____ + oxygen
Cellular respiration	sugar + _____ ———→ water + _____ + energy

How do cells divide?

Cells grow, divide, and die. Some cells divide more often than others. For example, cells in the skin are constantly dividing to replace those that have died or are damaged. Some cells, such as nerve cells, cannot divide to produce new cells once they are fully formed. Multicellular organisms grow by adding more cells. These new cells are made when existing cells divide.

The Cell Cycle

Cell division in eukaryotes is a complex process. Before a cell can divide, its DNA is copied. Then, the DNA copies are sorted into what will become two new cells. In order to divide up the DNA evenly between the new cells, the DNA needs to be packaged. The packages are called *chromosomes* (croh•moh•SOHMS). Equal numbers of chromosomes are separated, and the nucleus splits to form two identical nuclei. This process is called **mitosis**. Then, the rest of the cell divides, resulting in two identical cells. Because the two new cells have DNA identical to that found in the original cell, all the cells in an organism have the same genetic material.

Active Reading

10 Explain Why is it important for DNA to be copied before cell division?

_____

_____

_____

_____

Visualize It!

11 Compare How do new cells form in plants and animal?

_____

_____

_____

_____

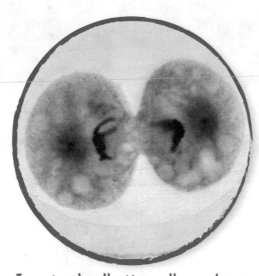

In animal cells, the cell membrane pinches inward through the cell to form two new cells.

When a plant cell divides, a cell plate forms and the cell splits into two cells.

Move It!

How do cells exchange materials?

What would happen to a factory if its supply of raw materials never arrived or it couldn't get rid of its garbage? Like a factory, an organism must be able to obtain materials for energy, make new materials, and get rid of wastes. The exchange of materials between a cell and its environment takes place at the cell's membrane. Cell membranes are *semi-permeable* because they allow only certain particles to cross into or out of the cell.

Passive Transport

The movement of particles across a cell membrane without the use of energy by the cell is called **passive transport**. For example, when a tea bag is added to a cup of water, the molecules in the tea will eventually spread throughout the water. **Diffusion** is the movement of molecules from high concentrations to low concentrations. Some nutrients move into a cell by diffusion. Some waste products move out of the cell by diffusion. **Osmosis** is the diffusion of water through a semi-permeable membrane. Many molecules are too large to diffuse through the cell membrane. Some of these molecules enter and exit cells through protein channels embedded in the cell membrane. When molecules move through these protein channels from areas of higher concentration to areas of lower concentration, the process usually requires no energy.

The tea has a higher concentration of molecules in the tea bag than in the rest of the mug.

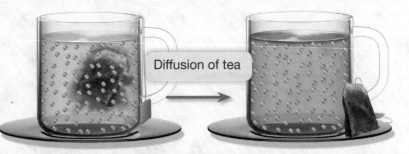

Diffusion of tea

Tea moves into areas of lower concentration, spreading out evenly in the mug.

13 Apply How is diffusion related to smelling the odor of a skunk that is far away? Support your claim with evidence.

_____

_____

_____

_____

_____

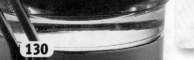

Active Transport

Cells often need to move materials across the cell membrane from areas of low concentration into areas of higher concentration. This is the opposite direction of passive transport. **Active transport** is the movement of particles against a concentration gradient and requires the cell to use energy. Some large particles that do not fit through the protein channels may require active transport across the cell membrane by processes called *endocytosis* and *exocytosis*.

Visualize It!

14 Identify Place a check mark next to the box that describes diffusion. Explain your answer.

_____

_____

_____

_____

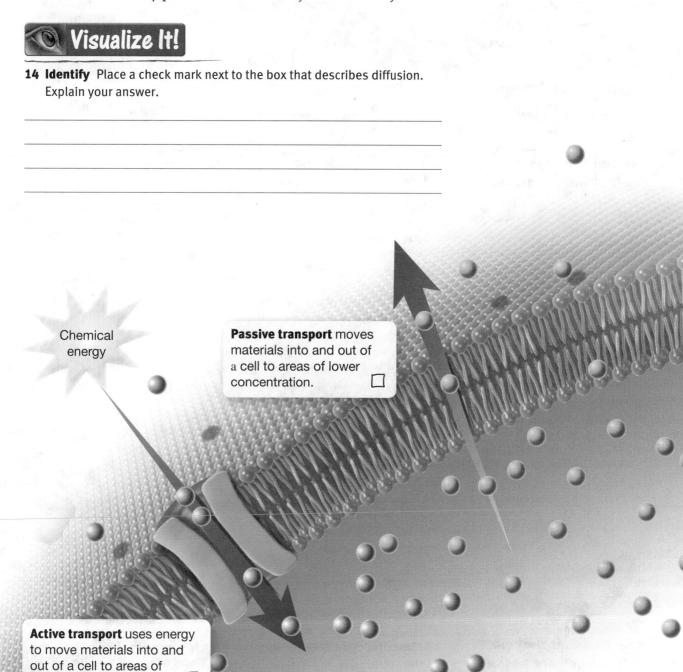

Chemical energy

Passive transport moves materials into and out of a cell to areas of lower concentration. ☐

Active transport uses energy to move materials into and out of a cell to areas of higher concentration. ☐

Endocytosis

The process by which a cell uses energy to surround a particle and enclose the particle in a vesicle to bring the particle into the cell is called **endocytosis** (en•doh•sye•TOH•sis). Vesicles are sacs formed from pieces of the cell membrane. Unicellular organisms, such as amoebas, use endocytosis to capture smaller organisms for food.

The cell comes into contact with a particle.

The cell membrane begins to wrap around the particle.

15 Describe What is happening in this step?

_____

_____

_____

_____

Exocytosis

When particles are enclosed in a vesicle and released from a cell, the process is called **exocytosis** (ek•soh•sye•TOH•sis). Exocytosis is the reverse process of endocytosis. Exocytosis begins when a vesicle forms around particles within the cell. The vesicle fuses to the cell membrane and the particles are released outside of the cell. Exocytosis is an important process in multicellular organisms.

Large particles that must leave the cell are packaged in vesicles.

16 Describe What is happening in this step?

_____

_____

_____

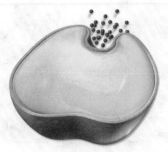

The cell releases the particles to the outside of the cell.

How do organisms maintain homeostasis?

As you have read, cells can obtain energy, divide, and transport materials to maintain stable internal conditions. In multicellular organisms, the cells must work together to maintain homeostasis for the entire organism. For example, when some organisms become cold, the cells respond in order to maintain a normal internal temperature. Muscle cells will contract to generate heat, a process known as shivering.

Some animals adapt their behavior to control body temperature. For example, many reptiles bask in the sun or seek shade to regulate their internal temperatures. When temperatures become extremely cold, some animals hibernate. Animals such as ground squirrels are able to conserve their energy during the winter when food is scarce.

Some trees lose all their leaves around the same time each year. This is a seasonal response. Having bare branches during the winter reduces the amount of water loss. Leaves may also change color before they fall. As autumn approaches, chlorophyll, the green pigment used for photosynthesis, breaks down. As chlorophyll is lost, other yellow and orange pigments can be seen.

The leaves of some trees change colors when the season changes.

17 Identify As you read, underline the different ways that organisms can respond to changes in the environment.

Visualize It!

18 Describe How is this boy's body responding to the cold weather?

_____

_____

_____

Visual Summary

To complete this summary, fill in the blanks with the correct word or phrase. Then use the key below to check your answers. You can use this page to review the main concepts of the lesson.

Cells need energy to perform cell functions.

19 Food is made during _____.
   Energy is produced from food during

   _____.

Cell division allows organisms to grow and repair damaged parts.

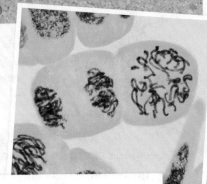

20 _____ occurs when cells divide to form two new nuclei that are identical to each other.

Maintaining Homeostasis: Balance In Organisms

Materials move into and out of cells through the cell membrane.

21 _____ uses energy to release particles from a cell.

Organisms respond to changes in the environment.

22 The change in leaf color on these trees is one way the trees maintain _____.

Answers: 19 photosynthesis; cellular respiration; 20 Mitosis; 21 Active transport; 22 homeostasis

23 **Summarize** Explain why organisms need to maintain homeostasis. Provide evidence to support your claim and explain your reasoning.

Lesson Review

Vocabulary

In your own words, define the following terms.

1 homeostasis

_____

_____

2 endocytosis

_____

_____

Key Concepts

3 Compare What is the difference between passive and active transport?

_____

_____

_____

_____

4 List List four things that cells do to maintain homeostasis.

_____

_____

_____

_____

5 Describe What happens during mitosis?

_____

_____

_____

_____

6 Apply How do the cells in your body get energy?

_____

_____

_____

_____

_____

_____

Critical Thinking

Use the graphs to answer the next two questions.

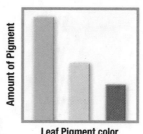

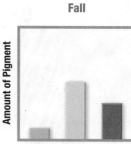

7 Compare How do the amounts of green pigment, chlorophyll, differ from summer to fall?

_____

_____

8 Infer How do you think the change in chlorophyll levels is a response to changes in the length of day from summer to fall?

_____

_____

_____

_____

_____

_____

9 Claims • Evidence • Reasoning Why is homeostasis important for cells as well as for an entire organism? Summarize the evidence to support your claim and explain your reasoning.

_____

_____

_____

_____

_____

_____

_____

My Notes

S.T.E.M. Engineering & Technology

Analyzing Technology

Skills
✓ Identify risks
✓ Identify benefits
Evaluate cost of technology
Evaluate environmental impact
Propose improvements
Propose risk reduction
Plan for technology failures
✓ Compare technology
✓ Communicate results

Objectives
• Identify different resources for nutritional values.
• Compare the nutritional value of common foods.

Analyzing Nutrients

Technology includes products, processes and systems developed to meet people's needs. Therefore, food is a kind of technology. Food supplies materials, called *nutrients*, that the body needs to perform its life functions. Your body gets nutrients from the food that you eat and the beverages that you drink. Each nutrient plays a role in keeping your body healthy. To make good decisions about what to eat, use nutrition guidelines such as the ChooseMyPlate.gov recommendations and the Nutrition Facts panels and ingredient labels on food packages.

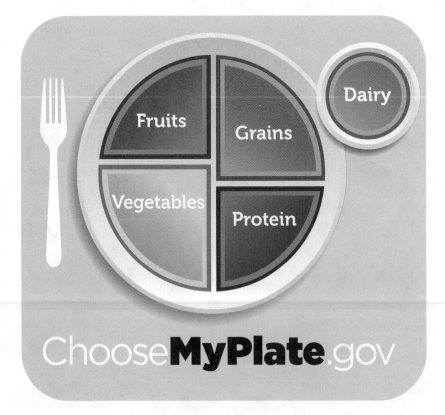

The MyPlate image was designed to help people make healthy food choices. As shown on the MyPlate icon, a healthy meal should be made up primarily of fruits and vegetables. The rest should be made up of lean protein, whole grains, and low-fat dairy products.

1 Infer According to the MyPlate icon, what kinds of food should you eat to maintain a healthy body?

_____

_____

_____

What's in Your Food?

Nutrients are listed on food labels by amounts and as percentages of Daily Values. The Daily Value (DV) of a nutrient is the recommended amount that a person should consume in a day. The percentage of the DV of a nutrient tells you what percentage of the recommended amount is provided by one serving of the food if your diet contains 2,000 Calories. A Calorie is a measurement of the amount of energy your body gets from a food. Your body gets energy from carbohydrates, proteins, and fats. So when is the amount of a nutrient in a food item low, and when is it high? If a food item has less than 5% of the DV of a nutrient, the Food and Drug Administration (FDA) says it's low in that nutrient. If the item has more than 20% of the DV of a nutrient, the FDA says it's high in that nutrient.

2 Calculate If a person consumes an entire can of this product, what percentage of his or her Daily Value of saturated fat would he or she consume?

_____

_____

_____

_____

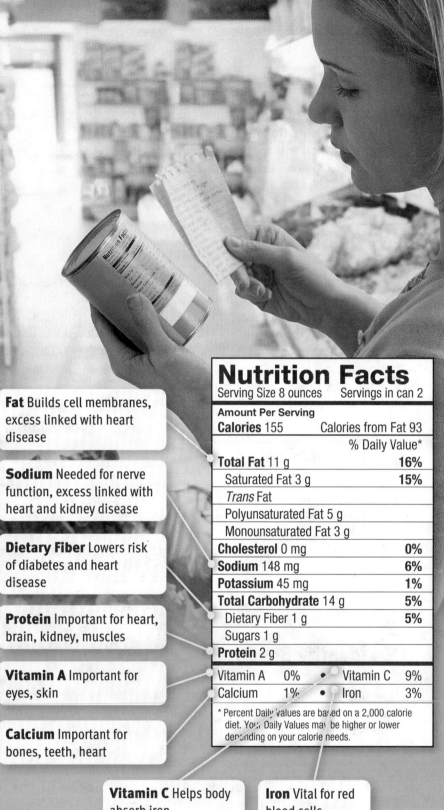

Fat Builds cell membranes, excess linked with heart disease

Sodium Needed for nerve function, excess linked with heart and kidney disease

Dietary Fiber Lowers risk of diabetes and heart disease

Protein Important for heart, brain, kidney, muscles

Vitamin A Important for eyes, skin

Calcium Important for bones, teeth, heart

Vitamin C Helps body absorb iron

Iron Vital for red blood cells

Nutrition Facts

Serving Size 8 ounces   Servings in can 2

Amount Per Serving	
Calories 155	Calories from Fat 93

	% Daily Value*
Total Fat 11 g	**16%**
Saturated Fat 3 g	**15%**
Trans Fat	
Polyunsaturated Fat 5 g	
Monounsaturated Fat 3 g	
Cholesterol 0 mg	**0%**
Sodium 148 mg	**6%**
Potassium 45 mg	**1%**
Total Carbohydrate 14 g	**5%**
Dietary Fiber 1 g	**5%**
Sugars 1 g	
Protein 2 g	

Vitamin A	0%	•	Vitamin C	9%
Calcium	1%	•	Iron	3%

* Percent Daily Values are based on a 2,000 calorie diet. Your Daily Values may be higher or lower depending on your calorie needs.

 **You Try It!** ———→

Now it's your turn to compare the nutritional value of some food items.

 **You Try It!**

Now it's your turn to use a Pugh chart and to compare the nutritional value of some common food items. You will analyze which foods are most likely to provide better nutrition, which allows you to make objective comparisons.

You Will Need

✔ Make a list of 5 common foods that you like to eat, including some that you think are healthy and some that you think are not very healthy.

_____

_____

_____

_____

_____

① Identify Risks

Using Nutrition Facts labels from Internet or supermarket resources, find out what nutrients are in each food on your list. Which foods are high in nutrients that are associated with health risks, such as saturated fat and cholesterol? Are there other health risks in these foods—for example, few healthy nutrients, or too many calories based on your recommended daily allowance? Use the information you find to fill in the table.

Food item	Unhealthy nutrients	Other health risks
1		
2		
3		
4		
5		

② Identify Benefits

Now use the same resources to identify which foods from your list are high in nutrients associated with health benefits. Are there other benefits you should consider for your foods? Use your information to fill in the table.

Food item	Healthy nutrients	Other health benefits
1		
2		
3		
4		
5		

③ Compare Technologies

Now make a Pugh chart to compare nutritional values numerically. Write the names of the five foods you chose in the top row of the chart below. Fill in the boxes under each food item, ranking the food on a scale of 1–5, based on how it compares to the other foods for each nutrient.

Key for Ranking:
Each food is assigned 1 if it has the least of the listed nutrient and a 5 if it has the most.

1= lowest

5= highest

Fiber				
Protein				
Vitamin A				
Calcium				
Vitamin C				
Iron				
Total				

④ Communicate Results

Summarize your comparison of your food items, and interpret the information. Which of your foods has the highest total? Which has the lowest? What do your results tell you about the nutritional value of these foods?

_____

_____

_____

_____

_____

Lesson 6

Photosynthesis and Cellular Respiration

ESSENTIAL QUESTION

How do cells get and use energy?

By the end of this lesson, you should be able to explain how cells capture and release energy.

Sunflowers capture light energy and change it to chemical energy, but people need to eat to get energy.

Lesson Labs

Quick Labs
• Plant Cell Structures
• Investigate Carbon Dioxide

S.T.E.M. Lab
• Investigate Rate of Photosynthesis

Engage Your Brain

1 Predict Check T or F to show whether you think each of the following statements is true or false.

T F

☐ ☐ All living things must eat other living things for food.

☐ ☐ Plants can make their own food.

☐ ☐ Plants don't need oxygen, only carbon dioxide.

☐ ☐ Animals eat plants or other animals that eat plants.

☐ ☐ Many living things need oxygen to release energy from food.

2 Infer Look at the photo. Describe the differences between the plants. What do you think caused these differences? Explain your reasoning.

_____

_____

_____

_____

_____

_____

_____

_____

Active Reading

3 Synthesize You can often define an unknown word if you know the meaning of its word parts. Use the word parts and sentence below to make an educated guess about the meaning of the term *chlorophyll*.

Word part	Meaning
chloro-	green
-phyll	leaf

Example sentence
Chlorophyll is a pigment that captures light energy.

chlorophyll:

_____

_____

Vocabulary Terms

• photosynthesis   • cellular respiration
• chlorophyll

4 Apply As you learn the definition of each vocabulary term in this lesson, write your own definition or make a sketch to help you remember the meaning of the term.

Energize!

How do the cells in an organism function?

![Active Reading] **5 Identify** As you read, underline sources of energy for living things.

How do you get the energy to run around and play soccer or basketball? How does a tree get the energy to grow? All living things, from the tiniest single-celled bacterium to the largest tree, need energy. Cells must capture and use energy or they will die. Cells get energy from food. Some living things can make their own food. Many living things get their food by eating other living things.

Your cells use energy all the time, whether you are active or not.

Cells Need Energy

Growing, moving, and other cell functions use energy. Without energy, a living thing cannot replace cells, build body parts, or reproduce. Even when a living thing is not very active, it needs energy. Cells constantly use energy to move materials into and out of the cell. They need energy to make different chemicals. And they need energy to get rid of wastes. A cell could not survive for long if it did not have the energy for all of these functions.

![Active Reading] **6 Relate** Why do living things need energy at all times?

_____

_____

_____

Cells Get Energy from Food

The cells of all living things need chemical energy. Food contains chemical energy. Food gives living things the energy and raw materials needed to carry out life processes. When cells break down food, the energy of the chemical bonds in food is released. This energy can be used or stored by the cell. The atoms and molecules in food can be used as building blocks for the cell.

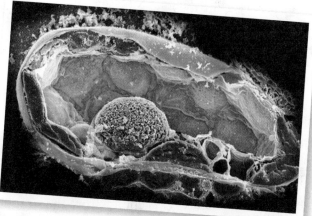

Plant cells make their own food using energy from the sun.

Living things get food in different ways. In fact, they can be grouped based on how they get food. Some living things, such as plants and many single-celled organisms, are called *producers* (proh•DOO•suhrz). Producers can make their own food. Most producers use energy from the sun. They capture and store light energy from the sun as chemical energy in food. A small number of producers, such as those that live in the deepest parts of the ocean, use chemicals to make their own food. Producers use most of the food they produce for energy. The unused food is stored in their bodies.

Many living things, such as people and other animals, are *consumers* (kun•SOO•muhrz). Consumers must eat, or consume, other living things to get food. Consumers may eat producers or other consumers. The cells of consumers break down food to release the energy it contains. A special group of consumers is made up of *decomposers* (dee•cum•POH•zhurhz). Decomposers break down dead organisms or the wastes of other organisms. Fungi and many bacteria are decomposers.

7 Compare Use the Venn diagram below to describe how producers and consumers get energy.

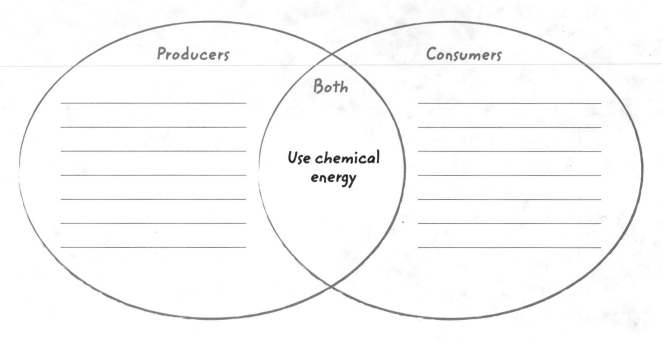

Producers

Consumers

Both

Use chemical energy

Cooking with Chloroplasts

How do plant cells make food?

Nearly all life on Earth gets energy from the sun. Plants make food with the energy from the sun. So, plants use energy from the sun directly. Animals use energy from the sun indirectly when they eat a plant or another animal.

In a process called **photosynthesis** (foh•toh•SYN•thuh•sys), plants use energy from sunlight, carbon dioxide, and water to make sugars. Plants capture light energy from the sun and change it to chemical energy in sugars. These sugars are made from water and carbon dioxide. In addition to sugars, photosynthesis also produces oxygen gas. The oxygen gas is given off into the air.

 **Active Reading**

8 Identify What is the source of energy for nearly all life on Earth?

 **Visualize It!**

Photosynthesis In many plants, photosynthesis takes place in the leaf. Chlorophyll, which is located in chloroplasts, captures light energy from the sun. This light energy is converted to chemical energy in sugars.

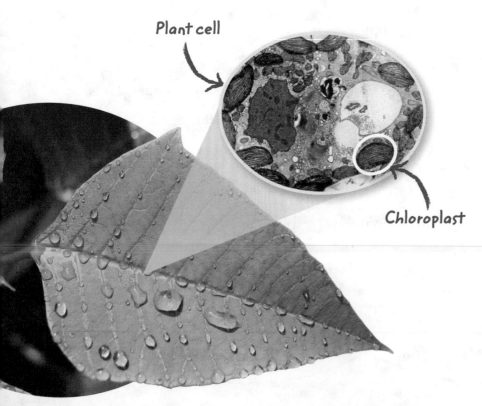

Plant cell

Chloroplast

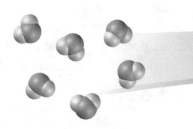

Water

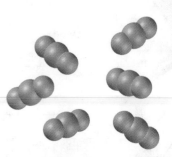

Carbon dioxide

Capturing Light Energy

Energy from sunlight powers the process of photosynthesis. The light energy is converted to chemical energy, which is stored in the bonds of the sugar molecules made during photosynthesis.

Photosynthesis takes place in organelles called *chloroplasts* (KLOHR•oh•plahstz). These organelles are found only in the cells of plants and other organisms that undergo photosynthesis. They are not found in animal or fungal cells. Chloroplasts contain a green pigment called **chlorophyll** (KLOHR•oh•fill). Chlorophyll captures energy from sunlight. This energy is used to combine carbon dioxide (CO_2) and water (H_2O), forming the sugar glucose ($C_6H_{12}O_6$) and oxygen gas (O_2). Photosynthesis is a series of reactions summarized by the following chemical equation:

$$6CO_2 + 6H_2O + light\ energy \rightarrow C_6H_{12}O_6 + 6O_2$$

Chloroplast   Light energy

Oxygen

Sugar

9 Claims • Evidence • Reasoning How do you think water and carbon dioxide used for photosynthesis get into the plant's leaf? Clearly state your claim. Then, use evidence to support your claim and explain your reasoning.

_____

_____

_____

_____

_____

_____

Storing Chemical Energy

Glucose (GLOO•kohs) is a sugar that stores chemical energy. It is the food that plants make. Plant cells break down glucose for energy. Excess sugars are stored in the body of the plant. They are often stored as starch in the roots and stem of the plant. When another organism eats the plant, the organism can use these stored sugars for energy.

Mighty Mitochondria

How do cells get energy from food?

When sugar is broken down, energy is released. It is stored in a molecule called *adenosine triphosphate* (ATP). ATP powers many of the chemical reactions that enable cells to survive. The process of breaking down food to produce ATP is called **cellular respiration** (SELL•yoo•lahr ress•puh•RAY•shuhn).

Active Reading

10 Identify As you read, underline the starting materials and products of cellular respiration.

Mitochondria are found in both plant cells and animal cells.

Mitochondrion

Visualize It!

Cellular Respiration During cellular respiration, cells use oxygen gas to break down sugars and release energy.

Oxygen

Using Oxygen

Cellular respiration takes place in the cytoplasm and cell membranes of prokaryotic cells. In eukaryotic cells, cellular respiration takes place in organelles called *mitochondria* (singular, *mitochondrion*). Mitochondria are found in both plant and animal cells. The starting materials of cellular respiration are glucose and oxygen.

In eukaryotes, the first stage of cellular respiration takes place in the cytoplasm. Glucose is broken down into two 3-carbon molecules. This releases a small amount of energy. The next stage takes place in the mitochondria. This stage requires oxygen. Oxygen enters the cell and travels into the mitochondria. As the 3-carbon molecules are broken down, energy is captured and stored in ATP.

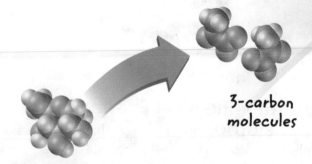

Sugar from photosynthesis

3-carbon molecules

Releasing Energy

The products of cellular respiration are chemical energy (ATP), carbon dioxide, and water. The carbon dioxide formed during cellular respiration is released by the cell. In many animals, the carbon dioxide is carried to the lungs and exhaled during breathing.

Some of the energy produced during cellular respiration is released as heat. However, much of the energy produced during cellular respiration is transferred to ATP. ATP can be carried throughout the body. When ATP is broken down, the energy released is used for cellular activities. The steps of cellular respiration can be summarized by the following equation:

$$C_6H_{12}O_6 + 6O_2 \rightarrow 6CO_2 + 6H_2O + \text{chemical energy (ATP)}$$

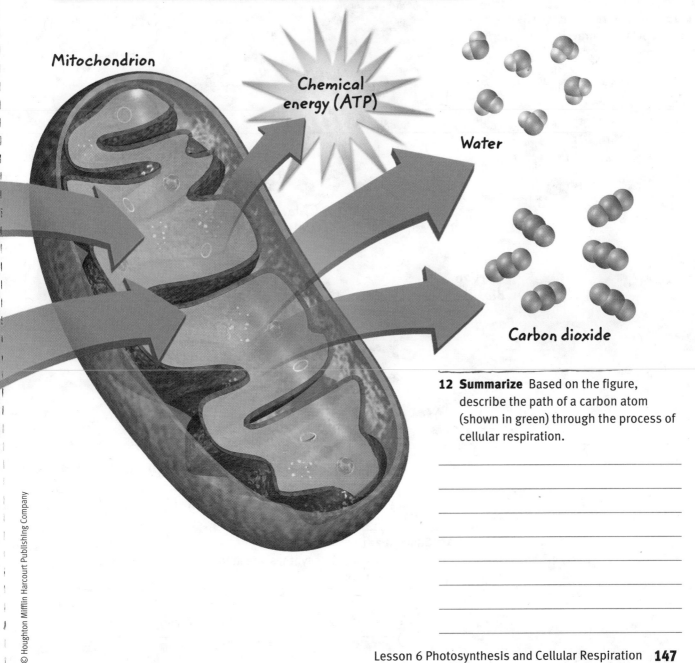

Mitochondrion

Chemical energy (ATP)

Water

Carbon dioxide

Think Outside the Book Inquiry

11 Identify With a partner, write a creative story or play that describes the process of cellular respiration.

12 Summarize Based on the figure, describe the path of a carbon atom (shown in green) through the process of cellular respiration.

_____

_____

_____

_____

_____

_____

_____

_____

Merry-Go-Round!

How are photosynthesis and cellular respiration connected?

Most of the oxygen in the atmosphere was made during photosynthesis. Nearly all organisms use this oxygen during cellular respiration. They produce carbon dioxide and release it into the environment. In turn, plants use the carbon dioxide to make sugars. So, photosynthesis and respiration are linked, each depending on the products of the other.

Ⓐ _____
energy

👁 Visualize It!

13 Synthesize Fill in the missing labels, and draw in the missing molecules.

Ⓓ _____

Used in

Produces

Chloroplast
(in plant cells)

Oxygen

Carbon
dioxide

Ⓑ _____

Used in

Produces

Mitochondrion
(in plant and
animal cells)

Ⓒ _____
energy

14 Summarize How are the starting materials and products of cellular respiration and photosynthesis related?

_____

_____

_____

© Houghton Mifflin Harcourt Publishing Company

Why It Matters

Out of Air

When there isn't enough oxygen, living things can get energy by anaerobic respiration (AN•uh•roh•bick ress•puh•RAY•shuhn). *Anaerobic* means "without oxygen." Like cellular respiration, anaerobic respiration produces ATP. However, it does not produce as much ATP as cellular respiration.

Rising to the Top

Fermentation is a type of anaerobic respiration. Many yeasts rely on fermentation for energy. Carbon dioxide is a product of fermentation. Carbon dioxide causes bread to rise, and gives it air pockets.

Feel the Burn!

The body uses anaerobic respiration during hard exercise, such as sprinting. This produces lactic acid, which can cause muscles to ache after exercise.

Extend

Inquiry

15 Compare What products do both cellular and anaerobic respiration have in common?

16 Research Blood delivers oxygen to the body. If this is the case, why does the body rely on anaerobic respiration during hard exercise? Research the reasons why the body switches between cellular and anaerobic respiration. Provide evidence to support your reasoning.

17 Compare Research and compare cellular respiration and fermentation. How are they similar? How do they differ? Summarize your results by doing one of the following:
- make a poster
- write a brochure
- draw a comic strip
- make a table

Visual Summary

To complete this summary, check the box that indicates true or false. Then, use the key below to check your answers. You can use this page to review the main concepts of the lesson.

Cells get and use energy

Living things need energy to survive.

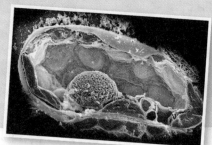

	T	F	
18	☐	☐	Organisms get energy from food.
19	☐	☐	A producer eats other organisms.

Plants make their own food.

	T	F	
20	☐	☐	Photosynthesis is the process by which plants make their own food.
21	☐	☐	Chlorophyll captures light energy during photosynthesis.

Cells release energy from food during cellular respiration.

	T	F	
22	☐	☐	Carbon dioxide is required for cellular respiration.
23	☐	☐	Cellular respiration takes place in chloroplasts.

Photosynthesis and cellular respiration are interrelated.

	T	F	
24	☐	☐	The products of photosynthesis are the starting materials of cellular respiration.

Answers: 18 T; 19 F; 20 T; 21 T; 22 F; 23 F; 24 T

25 Identify Describe how the cells in your body get energy and then use that energy.

© Houghton Mifflin Harcourt Publishing Company • Image Credits: (t) © Dr David Furness, Keele University/SPL/Photo Researchers, Inc.

Lesson Review

Vocabulary

Fill in the blank with the term that best completes the following sentences.

1 _____ takes place in organelles called *chloroplasts*.

2 Light energy is captured by the green pigment _____.

3 Cells use oxygen to release energy during _____.

Key Concepts

Use the figure to answer the following questions.

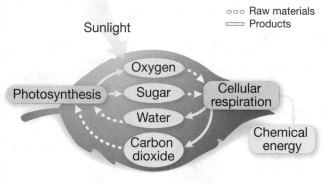

4 Identify What are the starting materials and products of photosynthesis and cellular respiration?

_____

_____

_____

_____

5 Relate What does the diagram above reveal about the connections between photosynthesis and cellular respiration?

_____

_____

_____

_____

6 Contrast How do plants and animals get their energy in different ways?

_____

_____

_____

_____

Critical Thinking

7 Infer Does your body get all its energy from the sun? Explain.

_____

_____

_____

_____

_____

8 Synthesize Could cellular respiration happen without photosynthesis? Summarize evidence to support your claim and explain your reasoning.

_____

_____

_____

_____

_____

_____

_____

9 Apply Plants don't move around, so why do they need energy?

_____

_____

_____

_____

My Notes

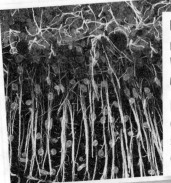

Lesson 1
ESSENTIAL QUESTION
What are living things made of?

Explain the components of the scientific theory of cells.

Lesson 4
ESSENTIAL QUESTION
How are living things organized?

Describe the different levels of organization in living things.

Lesson 2
ESSENTIAL QUESTION
What are the building blocks of organisms?

Discuss the chemical makeup of living things.

Lesson 5
ESSENTIAL QUESTION
How do organisms maintain homeostasis?

Explain the important processes that organisms undergo to maintain stable internal conditions.

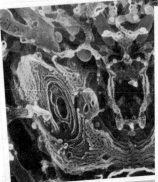

Lesson 3
ESSENTIAL QUESTION
What are the different parts that make up a cell?

Compare the structure and function of cell parts in plant and animal cells.

Lesson 6
ESSENTIAL QUESTION
How do cells get and use energy?

Explain how cells capture and release energy.

Connect ESSENTIAL QUESTIONS
Lessons 3 and 5

1 Synthesize Explain the role of a cell membrane and how it aids in maintaining homeostasis.

_____

_____

_____

_____

Think Outside the Book

2 Synthesize Choose one of the activities to help synthesize what you learned in this unit.

☐ Using what you learned in lessons 2 and 3, choose a plant or an animal and create a poster that shows its levels of organization from a single cell to the whole organism. Include a diagram of a cell and one example of the organism's tissues, organs, and organ systems.

☐ Using what you learned in lessons 3 and 6, draw a diagram of cellular respiration and photosynthesis. Identify what organelles are involved in each process.

© Houghton Mifflin Harcourt Publishing Company • Image Credits: (tl) ©C.J. Guerin, PhD, MRC Toxicology Unit/Photo Researchers, Inc.; (cl) ©Ben Nottidge/Alamy; (bl) ©Professors Pietro M. Motta & Tomonori Naguro/Photo Researchers, Inc; (tr) ©David Maitland/Workbook Stock/Getty Images; (cr) ©Arco Images GmbH/Alamy; (br) ©Getty Images

Name _____

Vocabulary

Check the box to show whether each statement is true or false.

T	F	
☐	☐	**1** <u>Photosynthesis</u> is the process in which cells use oxygen to break down food and release stored energy.
☐	☐	**2** A <u>molecule</u> is made up of atoms that are joined together.
☐	☐	**3** A <u>eukaryote</u> has cells that do not contain a nucleus, whereas a <u>prokaryote</u> has cells that have a nucleus.
☐	☐	**4** A cell organelle that is found in animal cells but usually not in plant cells is a <u>lysosome</u>.
☐	☐	**5** A <u>tissue</u> is a group of similar cells that perform a common function.

Key Concepts

Read each question below, and circle the best answer.

6 Prem finds an unusual object on the forest floor. After he examines it under a microscope and performs several lab tests, he concludes that the object is a living thing. Which of the following observations most likely led to Prem's conclusion?

A The object contained carbon.

B Prem saw cells in the object.

C The object had a green color.

D Prem saw minerals inside the object.

7 Which of the following substances must animal cells take in from the environment to maintain homeostasis?

A DNA

B oxygen

C chlorophyll

D carbon dioxide

8 Juana made the following table.

Organelle	Function
Mitochondrion	Cellular respiration
Ribosome	DNA synthesis
Chloroplast	Photosynthesis
Endoplasmic reticulum	Makes proteins and lipids
Golgi complex	Packages proteins

Juana's table lists several cell organelles and their functions, but she made an error. Which of the organelles shown in the table is listed with the wrong function?

A mitochondrion

C cell membrane

B ribosome

D Golgi complex

9 Which molecule is a source of energy, a store of energy in the body, and can mix with water?

A lipid

C nucleic acid

B chlorophyll

D carbohydrate

10 Which method of material exchange uses up energy?

A osmosis

C active transport

B diffusion

D passive transport

11 The following diagram shows a common cell organelle.

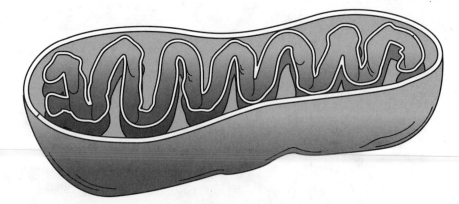

What process takes place in the organelle shown?

A photosynthesis

C cellular respiration

B protein synthesis

D packaging of proteins

12 Plants contain xylem and phloem tissue. What organ system in animals performs a similar function as the xylem and phloem of plants?

A digestive system

B excretory system

C respiratory system

D circulatory system

13 Which statement correctly tells why the cells of unicellular and multicellular organisms divide?

A The cells of unicellular organisms divide to reproduce; those of multicellular organisms divide to replace cells and to grow.

B The cells of unicellular organisms divide to replace cells and to grow; those of multicellular organisms divide to reproduce.

C The cells of both kinds of organisms divide to reproduce.

D The cells of both kinds of organisms divide to replace cells and to grow.

14 The following picture shows *Escherichia coli* cells, a species of bacterium.

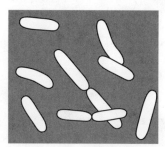

Which of the following statements correctly compares the cells shown in the picture with a human cell?

A Both types of cells divide by mitosis.

B Human cells contain proteins, but *E. coli* cells do not.

C Both cells contain ribosomes and a cell membrane.

D Human cells contain DNA, but *E. coli* cells do not.

15 A plant leaf is an organ that traps light energy to make food. In what way is an animal stomach similar to a plant leaf?

A Both organs make food.

B Both organs are made up of only one kind of cell.

C Both organs are made up of several kinds of tissues.

D Both organs take in oxygen and release carbon dioxide.

16 The following table shows the surface area-to-volume ratio of four cube-shaped cell models.

Cell Model	Surface Area	Volume	Surface Area-to-Volume Ratio
A	6 cm^2	1 cm^3	$6 : 1 \ = 6$
B	24 cm^2	8 cm^3	$24 : 8 \ = 3$
C	54 cm^2	27 cm^3	$54 : 27 \ = 2$
D	96 cm^2	64 cm^3	$96 : 64 \ = 1.5$

Cells are small, and their surface area is large in relation to their volume. This is an important feature for the proper transport of nutrients and water into and out of the cell. Which of the four model cells do you think will be best able to supply nutrients and water to its cell parts?

A cell model A

B cell model B

C cell model C

D cell model D

17 Cells of a multicellular organism are specialized. What does this statement mean?

A Cells of a multicellular organism are adapted to perform specific functions.

B Cells of a multicellular organism perform all life functions but not at the same time.

C Cells of a multicellular organism are specialized because they have a complex structure.

D Cells of a multicellular organism can perform all the life functions the organism needs to survive.

Critical Thinking

Answer the following questions in the space provided.

18 Can unicellular organisms combine to create tissues, organs, and organ systems? Explain your answer and support it with evidence.

_____

_____

_____

_____

_____

_____

19 The following diagram shows a cell that Dimitri saw on his microscope slide.

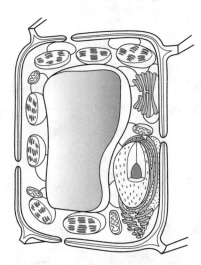

Dimitri's teacher gave him an unlabeled slide of some cells and asked him to identify whether the cells were plant cells or animal cells. Dimitri examined the slide under a microscope and concluded that the cells were plant cells.

How did Dimitri reach his conclusion? Is his conclusion correct? What life process can these cells carry out that a cell from another kind of multicellular organism cannot?

_____

_____

_____

_____

_____

_____

20 One of the characteristics of living things is that they respond to external changes in their environment so that their internal environment stays as stable as possible. Why must an organism do this? Name an environmental change that an animal must respond to in order to keep a stable internal environment. What might happen to an organism if it could not adapt to an external change?

_____

_____

_____

_____

Connect **ESSENTIAL QUESTIONS**
Lessons 2, 3, 4, 5, and 6

Answer the following question in the space provided.

21 The following picture shows the process of photosynthesis.

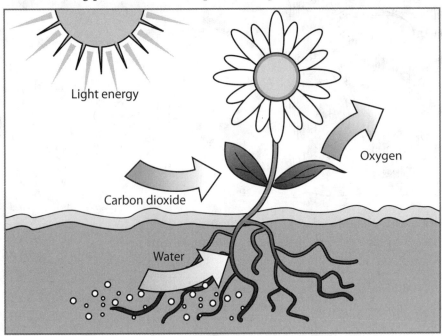

In which plant organ and organelle does photosynthesis take place? One of the products of photosynthesis is missing from the diagram. What is this missing product? Describe the role of this substance in cells. How do animals get this substance?

_____

_____

_____

_____

Reproduction and Heredity

Big Idea
Characteristics from parents are passed to offspring in predictable ways.

S7L3., S7L3.a, S7L3.b, S7L3.c

What do you think?

Every organism—including orange trees and dogs—shares traits with its offspring. How are qualities passed on from generation to generation? As you explore the unit, gather evidence to help you support claims to answer this question.

Unit 3
Reproduction and Heredity

Pass It On

Heredity was a mystery that scientists worked to crack over hundreds of years. The modern field of genetics is vital to the understanding of hereditary diseases. The study of genetics can also predict which traits will be passed from parent to offspring.

1856–1863
Many people consider Gregor Mendel to be the father of modern genetics. His famous pea plant experiments, conducted from 1856–1863, helped to illustrate and establish the laws of inheritance.

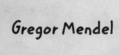

Gregor Mendel

Can you predict the traits Mendel might have examined in pea plants? What traits might a fruit or vegetable plant inherit from a parent plant?

_____

_____

_____

_____

_____

Fruit fly

Pairs of chromosomes viewed under a microscope

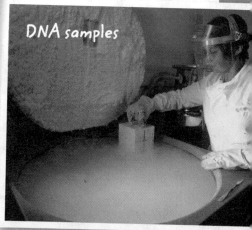

DNA samples

1882
Walther Flemming discovered chromosomes while observing the process of cell division. He didn't know it, but chromosomes pass characteristics from parents to offspring.

1908
Thomas Hunt Morgan was the first to actually realize that chromosomes carry traits. Morgan's fruit fly studies established that genes are located on chromosomes. Scientists still use fruit flies in research today.

2003
Our DNA carries information about all of our traits. In fact, the human genome is made up of 20,000–25,000 genes! In 2003, the Human Genome Project successfully mapped the first human genome.

Take It Home · Making Trait Predictions

See *ScienceSaurus*® for more information about genes and heredity.

① Think About It

Different factors influence appearance. Family members may look similar in some ways but different in others. What factors influence a person's appearance?

_____

_____

_____

② Ask Some Questions

Can you spot any physical traits, such as bent pinky fingers, that people in your family share?

_____

_____

_____

③ Make a Plan

A Consider the traits that are most distinctive in your family. How can you trace the way specific traits have been passed through the family? Design an investigation and construct an explanation about hereditary characteristics in your family.

_____

_____

_____

_____

B Describe how these characteristics might be the same or different as they are transferred to offspring. What factors might influence this? Make notes here, and illustrate your descriptions on a separate sheet of paper.

_____

_____

_____

Mitosis

ESSENTIAL QUESTION

How do cells divide?

By the end of this lesson, you should be able to relate the process of mitosis to its functions in single-celled and multicellular organisms.

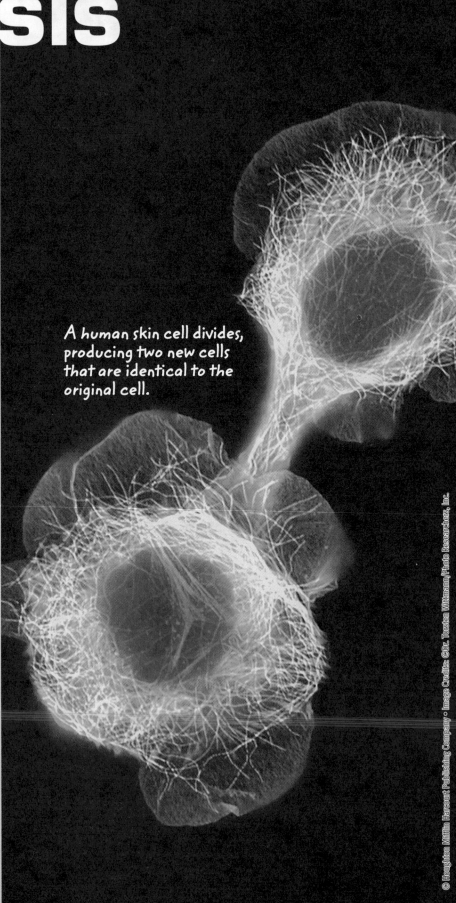

A human skin cell divides, producing two new cells that are identical to the original cell.

Lesson Labs

Quick Labs
• Modeling Mitosis
• Mitosis Flipbooks
• DNA, Chromosomes, and Cell Division

Exploration Lab
• Stages of the Cell Cycle

Engage Your Brain

1 Predict Check T or F to show whether you think each statement is true or false.

T	F	
☐	☐	Single-celled organisms can reproduce by cell division.
☐	☐	The only function of cell division is reproduction.
☐	☐	In multicellular organisms, cell division can help repair injured areas.
☐	☐	Cell division produces two cells that are different from each other.

2 Infer An old sequoia tree weighs many tons and has billions of cells. These trees start out as tiny seeds. Predict how these trees get so large. Use evidence or examples to support your reasoning.

_____
_____
_____
_____
_____

Active Reading

3 Synthesize You can often define an unknown word if you know the meaning of its word parts. Use the word parts and sentence below to make an educated guess about the meaning of the word *cytokinesis*.

Word part	Meaning
cyto-	hollow vessel
-kinesis	division

Example sentence
When a dividing cell undergoes <u>cytokinesis</u>, two cells are produced.

cytokinesis:
_____
_____
_____

Vocabulary Terms

• DNA	• interphase
• chromosomes	• mitosis
• cell cycle	• cytokinesis

4 Apply As you learn the definition of each vocabulary term in this lesson, write your own definition or make a sketch to help you remember the meaning of the term.

Splitsville!

Why do cells divide?

Cell division happens in all organisms. Cell division takes place for different reasons. For example, single-celled organisms reproduce through cell division. In multicellular organisms, cell division is involved in growth, development, and repair, as well as reproduction.

Reproduction

Cell division is important for asexual reproduction, which involves only one parent organism. In single-celled organisms, the parent divides in two, producing two identical offspring. In single-celled and some multicellular organisms, offspring result when a parent organism buds, producing offspring. In multicellular organisms, reproduction by cell division can include plant structures such as runners and plantlets.

Growth and Repair

One characteristic of all living things is that they grow. You are probably bigger this year than you were last year. Your body is made up of cells. Although cells themselves grow, most growth in multicellular organisms happens because cell division produces new cells.

Cell division also produces cells for repair. If you cut your hand or break a bone, the damaged cells are replaced by new cells that form during cell division.

 **Visualize It!**

5 Apply Take a look at the photos below. Underneath each photo, describe the role of cell division in what is taking place.

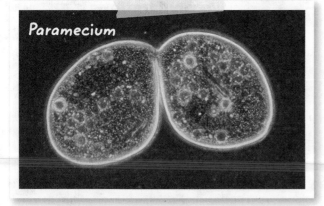

Paramecium

Starfish

Role of cell division:

_____

_____

_____

Role of cell division:

_____

_____

_____

What happens to genetic material during cell division?

The genetic material in cells is called DNA (deoxyribonucleic acid). A **DNA** molecule contains the information that determines the traits that a living thing inherits and needs to live. It contains instructions for an organism's growth, development, and activities. In eukaryotes, DNA is found in the nucleus.

During most of a cell's life cycle, DNA, along with proteins, exists in a complex material called *chromatin* (KROH•muh•tin). Before cell division, DNA is duplicated, or copied. Then, in an early stage of cell division, the chromatin is compacted into visible structures called **chromosomes** (KROH•muh•sohmz). A duplicated chromosome consists of two identical structures called *chromatids* (KROH•muh•tidz). The chromatids are held together by a *centromere* (SEN•truh•mir).

6 Describe What happens to DNA before cell division?

_____

_____

_____

_____

Chromosome
A duplicated chromosome has two chromatids, which are held together by a centromere.

Centromere

Chromatid

A chromosome is made of compacted chromatin.

Chromatin
Chromatin is made up of DNA and proteins.

Protein

DNA

DNA
DNA is found in the nucleus of a eukaryotic cell.

Visualize It!

7 Analyze What happens to chromatin in the early stages of cell division?

_____

_____

_____

Around and Around

What are the stages of the cell cycle?

The life cycle of an organism includes birth, growth, reproduction, and death. The life cycle of a eukaryotic cell, called the **cell cycle**, can be divided into three stages: interphase, mitosis, and cytokinesis. During the cell cycle, a parent cell divides into two new cells. The new cells are identical to the parent.

Active Reading

8 Identify As you read, underline the main characteristics of each stage of the cell cycle.

Interphase

The part of the cell cycle during which the cell is not dividing is called **interphase** (IN•ter•fayz). A lot of activity takes place in this stage of the cell's life. The cell grows to about twice the size it was when it was first produced. It also produces various organelles. The cell engages in normal life activities, such as transporting materials into the cell and getting rid of wastes.

Changes that occur during interphase prepare a cell for division. Before a cell can divide, DNA must be duplicated. This ensures that, after cell division, each new cell gets an exact copy of the genetic material in the original cell.

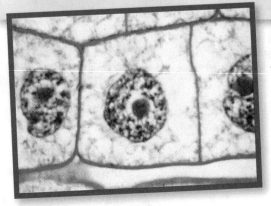

During interphase, the cell carries out normal life activities.

INTERPHASE

Active Reading

9 Describe What happens during interphase?

_____

_____

_____

_____

_____

Mitosis

In eukaryotic cells, **mitosis** (my•TOH•sis) is the part of the cell cycle during which the nucleus divides. Prokaryotes do not undergo mitosis because they do not have a nucleus. Mitosis results in two nuclei that are identical to the original nucleus. So, the two new cells formed after cell division have the same genetic material. During mitosis, chromosomes condense from chromatin. When viewed with a microscope, chromosomes are visible inside the nucleus. At the end of mitosis, the cell has two identical sets of chromosomes in two separate nuclei.

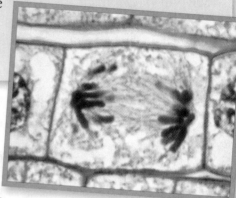

During mitosis, the cell's nucleus divides into two identical nuclei.

MITOSIS

Prophase
Metaphase
Anaphase
Telophase

CYTOKINESIS

Cytokinesis

Cytokinesis (sy•toh•kuh•NEE•sis) is the division of the parent cell's cytoplasm. Cytokinesis begins during the last step of mitosis. During cytokinesis, the cell membrane pinches inward between the new nuclei. Eventually, it pinches all the way, forming two complete cells.

In a cell that has a cell wall, such as a plant cell, a cell plate forms. The cell plate becomes cell membranes that separate the new cells. New cell walls form where the plate was.

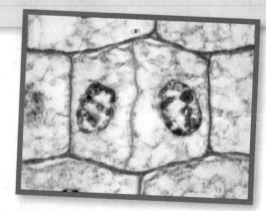

During cytokinesis, the cytoplasm divides and two new cells are produced.

Visualize It!

10 Interpret Based on this diagram, in what stage does a cell spend most of its time? What evidence is there to support your claim?

_____
_____
_____
_____
_____

Phasing Out

What are the phases of mitosis?

Mitosis has four phases: prophase (PROH•fayz), metaphase (MET•uh•fayz), anaphase (AN•uh•fayz), and telophase (TEE•luh•fayz). By the end of these phases, the cell will have two identical nuclei and cytokinesis will begin.

📖 Active Reading

11 Identify As you read, underline the major events that take place in each phase of mitosis.

During interphase, DNA is duplicated.

Prophase

During prophase, the chromatin in the nucleus of a cell condenses and becomes visible under a microscope. Each chromosome consists of two chromatids held together by a centromere. The membrane around the nucleus breaks down.

Prophase

Metaphase

During metaphase, chromosomes line up in the middle of the cell. Centromeres of the chromosomes are the same distance from each side of the cell.

Metaphase

Anaphase

Anaphase

During anaphase, the chromatids separate. They are pulled to opposite sides of the cell. Each side of the cell ends up with a complete set of chromosomes.

Think Outside the Book (Inquiry)

12 Model With a small group, write a play that acts out the steps of mitosis. Trade your play with another group, and perform the play for your classmates.

13 Apply Use the table below to draw a picture for each step of the cell cycle.

Step	Drawing
Interphase	
Mitosis: Prophase	
Mitosis: Metaphase	
Mitosis: Anaphase	
Mitosis: Telophase	
Cytokinesis	

Both new cells start the cycle again.

After mitosis, cytokinesis results in two new cells.

Telophase

Telophase

The last phase of mitosis is telophase. A new nuclear membrane forms around each group of chromosomes. So, the cell now has two identical nuclei. The chromosomes become less condensed. Cytokinesis begins during this phase.

Visual Summary

To complete this summary, fill in the blanks with the correct word or phrase. Then, use the key below to check your answers. You can use this page to review the main concepts of the lesson.

During the cell cycle, cells divide to produce two identical cells.

14 Three reasons that cells divide are

_____

_____

_____.

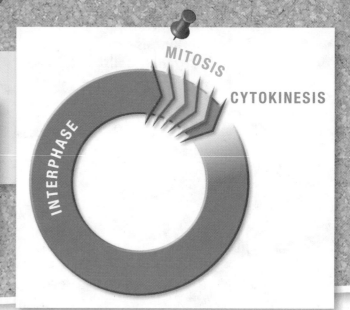

DNA is duplicated before cell division.

15 Loose chromatin is compacted into

_____,

each of which has two

_____ that are

held together by a centromere.

Mitosis

The cell cycle is the life cycle of a cell.

16 They lack nuclei, so prokaryotes do not undergo _____.

17 The cell produces organelles during _____.

18 _____ results in the formation of two new cells.

INTERPHASE

MITOSIS

CYTOKINESIS

19 Summarize Briefly describe the four phases of mitosis.

Lesson Review

Vocabulary

Fill in the blanks with the term that best completes the following sentences.

1 _____ provides the information for cell growth and function.

2 The cell spends most of its time in the _____ stage of the cell cycle.

3 After _____ , the nucleus of the parent cell has divided into two new nuclei.

4 A _____ is the condensed, visible form of chromatin.

Key Concepts

5 Relate What happens in a cell during interphase?

_____

_____

_____

_____

6 Compare Describe the functions of cell division in single-celled and multicellular organisms.

_____

_____

_____

7 Explain Why is it important for DNA to be duplicated before mitosis? Explain your reasoning.

_____

_____

_____

_____

_____

_____

Critical Thinking

Use the figures below to answer the questions that follow.

8 Sequence Starting with prophase, what is the correct order of the four diagrams above?

_____

9 Identify What phase is shown in each of the diagrams above?

_____

_____

_____

_____

10 Describe What is happening to the cell in diagram B?

_____

_____

_____

_____

11 Claims • Evidence • Reasoning What would happen if the cell went through mitosis but not cytokinesis? Explain your reasoning.

_____

_____

_____

_____

_____

_____

My Notes

Meiosis

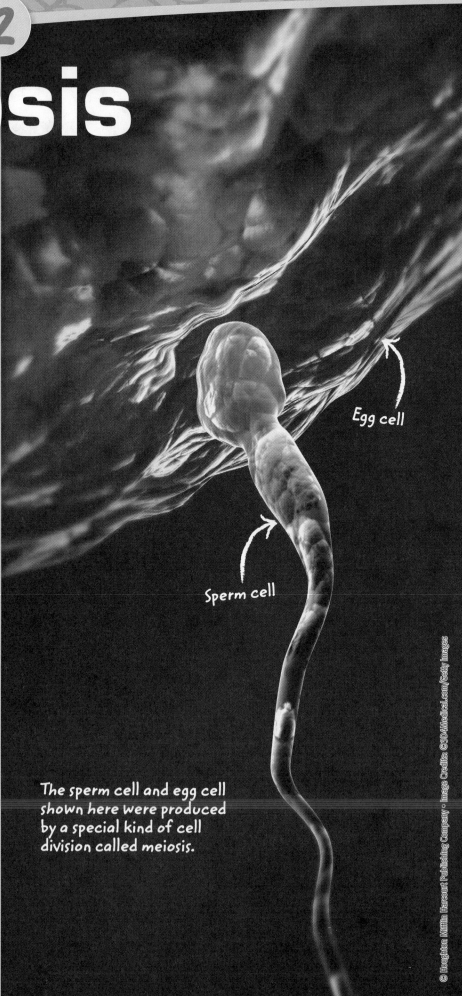

ESSENTIAL QUESTION

How do cells divide for sexual reproduction?

By the end of this lesson, you should be able to describe the process of meiosis and its role in sexual reproduction.

Egg cell

Sperm cell

The sperm cell and egg cell shown here were produced by a special kind of cell division called meiosis.

Engage Your Brain

1 Predict Check T or F to show whether you think each statement is true or false.

T	F	
☐	☐	The offspring of sexual reproduction have fewer chromosomes than their parents have.
☐	☐	During sexual reproduction, two cells combine to form a new organism.
☐	☐	Sex cells are produced by cell division.
☐	☐	Sex cells have half the normal number of chromosomes.

2 Calculate Organisms have a set number of chromosomes. For example, humans have 46 chromosomes in body cells and half that number (23) in sex cells. In the table below, fill in the number of chromosomes for different organisms.

Organism	Full set of chromosomes	Half set of chromosomes
Human	46	23
Fruit fly		4
Chicken		39
Salamander	24	
Potato	48	

 Active Reading

3 Synthesize You can often define an unknown word if you know the meaning of its word parts. Use the word parts and the sentence below to make an educated guess about the meaning of the term *homologous*.

Word part	Meaning
homo-	same
-logos	word, structure

Example sentence
Homologous chromosomes are a pair of chromosomes that look similar and have the same genes.

homologous:

_____

_____

_____

Vocabulary Terms

- **homologous chromosomes**
- **meiosis**

4 Apply As you learn the definition of each vocabulary term in this lesson, write your own definition or make a sketch to help you remember the meaning of the term.

Number Off!

How do sex cells differ from body cells?

Before sexual reproduction can take place, each parent produces sex cells. *Sex cells* have half of the genetic information that body cells have. Thus, when the genetic information from two parents combines, the offspring have a full set of genetic information. The offspring will have the same total number of chromosomes as each of its parents.

 **Active Reading** **5 Relate** Describe sex cells.

_____

_____

Chromosome Number

In body cells, most chromosomes are found in pairs that have the same structure and size. These **homologous chromosomes** (huh•MAHL•uh•guhs KROH•muh•sohmz) carry the same genes. A homologous chromosome pair may have different versions of the genes they carry. One chromosome pair is made up of *sex chromosomes*. Sex chromosomes control the development of sexual characteristics. In humans, these chromosomes are called X and Y chromosomes. Cells with a pair of every chromosome are called *diploid* (DIP•loyd). Many organisms, including humans, have diploid body cells.

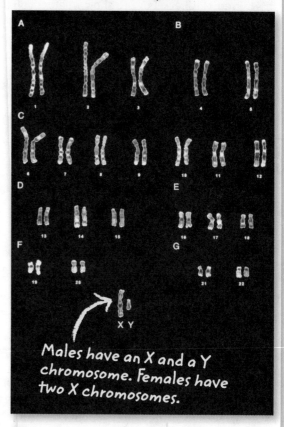

This photo shows the 23 chromosome pairs in a human male. Body cells contain all of these chromosomes. Sex cells contain one chromosome from each pair.

Males have an X and a Y chromosome. Females have two X chromosomes.

Visualize It! **Inquiry**

6 Predict The cell shown is a body cell that has two pairs of homologous chromosomes. Use the space to the right to draw a sex cell for the same organism.

Body cell

Sex cell

Why do organisms need sex cells?

Most human body cells contain 46 chromosomes. Think about what would happen if two body cells were to combine. The resulting cell would have twice the normal number of chromosomes. A sex cell is needed to keep this from happening.

Sex cells are also known as *gametes* (GAM•eetz). Gametes contain half the usual number of chromosomes—one chromosome from each homologous pair and one sex chromosome. Cells that contain half the usual number of chromosomes are known as *haploid* (HAP•loyd).

Gametes are found in the reproductive organs of plants and animals. An egg is a gamete that forms in female reproductive organs. The gamete that forms in male reproductive organs is called a sperm cell.

How are sex cells made?

You know that body cells divide by the process of mitosis. Mitosis produces two new cells, each containing exact copies of the chromosomes in the parent cell. Each new cell has a full set of chromosomes. But to produce sex cells, a different kind of cell division is needed.

Meiosis

A human egg and a human sperm cell each have 23 chromosomes. When an egg is joined with, or *fertilized* by, a sperm cell, a new diploid cell is formed. This new cell has 46 chromosomes, or 23 pairs of chromosomes. One set is from the mother, and the other set is from the father. The newly formed diploid cell may develop into an offspring. **Meiosis** (my•OH•sis) is the type of cell division that produces haploid sex cells such as eggs and sperm cells.

Visualize It!

For the example of fertilization shown, the egg and sperm cells each have one chromosome.

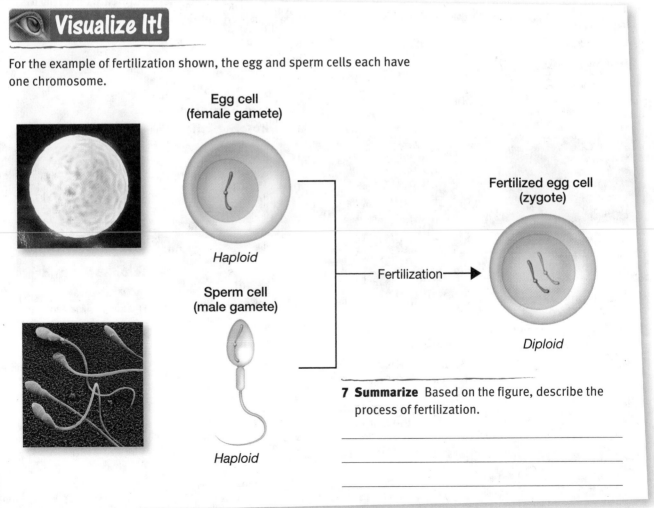

Egg cell
(female gamete)

Haploid

Sperm cell
(male gamete)

Haploid

Fertilization

Fertilized egg cell
(zygote)

Diploid

7 Summarize Based on the figure, describe the process of fertilization.

_____

_____

_____

What are the stages of meiosis?

Meiosis results in the formation of four haploid cells. Each haploid cell has half the number of chromosomes found in the original cell. Meiosis has two parts: meiosis I and meiosis II.

Meiosis I

Remember that homologous chromosomes have the same genes, but they are not exact copies of each other. Before meiosis I begins, each chromosome is duplicated, or copied. Each half of a duplicated chromosome is called a *chromatid* (KROH•muh•tid). Chromatids are connected to each other by *centromeres* (SEN•truh•mirz). Duplicated chromosomes are drawn in an **X** shape. Each side of the **X** represents a chromatid, and the point where they touch is the centromere.

During meiosis I, pairs of homologous chromosomes and sex chromosomes split apart into two new cells. These cells each have one-half of the chromosome pairs and their duplicate chromatids. The steps of meiosis I are shown below.

Active Reading

8 **Sequence** As you read, underline what happens to chromosomes during meiosis.

Duplicated homologous chromosomes

Half of a homologous chromosome pair

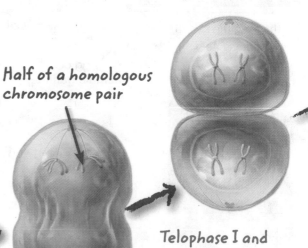

Prophase I
The chromosomes are copied before meiosis begins. The duplicated chromosomes, each made up of two chromatids, pair up.

Metaphase I
After the nuclear membrane breaks down, the chromosome pairs line up in the middle of the cell.

Anaphase I
The chromosomes separate from their partners, and then move to opposite ends of the cell.

Telophase I and cytokinesis
The nuclear membranes re-form, and the cell divides into two cells. The chromatids are still joined.

9 Contrast How does meiosis II differ from meiosis I? Gather evidence to help you state and support your claim.

_____

_____

_____

_____

_____

Telophase II and cytokinesis
The nuclear membranes re-form and the cells divide. Four new haploid cells are formed. Each has half the usual number of chromosomes.

Anaphase II
The chromatids are pulled apart and move to opposite sides of the cell.

Centromere

Chromatid

Metaphase II
The chromosomes line up in the middle of each cell.

Prophase II
The chromosomes are not copied again before meiosis II. The nuclear membrane breaks down.

Think Outside the Book

10 Summarize Work with a partner to make a poster that describes all the steps of meiosis.

Meiosis II

Meiosis II involves both of the new cells formed during meiosis I. The chromosomes of these cells are not copied before meiosis II begins. Both of the cells divide during meiosis II. The steps of meiosis II are shown above.

Meiosis II results in four haploid sex cells. In male organisms, these cells develop into sperm cells. In female organisms, these cells become eggs. In females of some species, three of the cells are broken down and only one haploid cell becomes an egg.

11 Identify At the end of meiosis II, how many cells have formed?

_____

How does meiosis compare to mitosis?

The processes of meiosis and mitosis are similar in many ways. However, they also have several very important differences.

- Only cells that will become sex cells go through meiosis. All other cells divide by mitosis.
- During meiosis, chromosomes are copied once, and then the nucleus divides twice. During mitosis, the chromosomes are copied once, and then the nucleus divides once.
- The cells produced by meiosis contain only half of the genetic material of the parent cell—one chromosome from each homologous pair and one sex chromosome. The cells produced by mitosis contain exactly the same genetic material as the parent—a full set of homologous chromosomes and a pair of sex chromosomes.

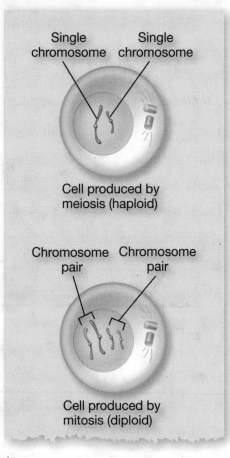

Single chromosome   Single chromosome

Cell produced by meiosis (haploid)

Chromosome pair   Chromosome pair

Cell produced by mitosis (diploid)

12 Summarize Using the table below, compare meiosis and mitosis.

Characteristic	Meiosis	Mitosis
Number of nuclear divisions		
Number of cells produced		
Number of chromosomes in new cells (diploid or haploid)		
Type of cell produced (body cell or sex cell)		
Steps of the process		

Down Syndrome

Down syndrome is a genetic disease. It is usually caused by an error during meiosis. During meiosis, the chromatids of chromosome 21 do not separate. So, a sex cell gets two copies of chromosome 21 instead of one copy. When this sex cell joins with a normal egg or sperm, the fertilized egg has three copies of chromosome 21 instead of two copies.

Beating the Odds

Down syndrome causes a number of health problems and learning difficulties, but many people with Down syndrome have fulfilling lives.

One Too Many

Someone who has Down syndrome has three copies of chromosome 21 instead of two copies.

Extend

Inquiry

13 Identify What type of error in meiosis causes Down syndrome?

14 Investigate Research the characteristics of Down syndrome. How can some of the difficulties caused by the disorder be overcome?

15 Recommend Research the Special Olympics. Then make an informative brochure, poster, or oral presentation that describes how the Special Olympics gives people with Down syndrome and other disabilities the chance to compete in sports.

Visual Summary

To complete this summary, fill in the blanks with the correct word or phrase. Then use the key below to check your answers. You can use this page to review the main concepts of the lesson.

Meiosis

Meiosis produces haploid cells that can become sex cells.

16 List the steps of meiosis I.

_____

_____

_____

_____

17 List the steps of meiosis II.

_____

_____

_____

_____

Sex cells have half as many chromosomes as body cells.

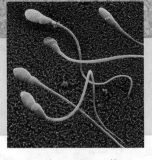

18 Sex cells produced by males are called _____, and sex cells produced by females are called _____.

Mitosis and meiosis have similarities and differences.

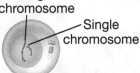

Single chromosome

Single chromosome

Cell produced by meiosis (haploid)

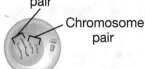

Chromosome pair

Chromosome pair

Cell produced by mitosis (diploid)

19 During _____, chromosomes are copied once and the nucleus divides twice.

20 During _____, chromosomes are copied once and the nucleus divides once.

Answers: 16 prophase I, metaphase I, anaphase I, telophase I and cytokinesis; 17 prophase II, metaphase II, anaphase II, telophase II and cytokinesis; 18 sperm cells, eggs; 19 meiosis; 20 mitosis

21 Summarize Briefly describe what happens during meiosis I and meiosis II.

Lesson Review

Vocabulary

Fill in the blanks with the term that best completes the following sentences.

1 _____ chromosomes are found in body cells but not sex cells.

2 The process of _____ produces haploid cells.

Key Concepts

3 Compare How does the number of chromosomes in sex cells compare with the number of chromosomes in body cells?

_____

_____

_____

4 Identify What is the function of meiosis?

_____

_____

_____

5 List Identify the steps of meiosis.

_____

_____

_____

_____

_____

_____

6 Compare How are mitosis and meiosis alike and different?

_____

_____

_____

_____

_____

_____

_____

Critical Thinking

Use the figure to answer the following questions.

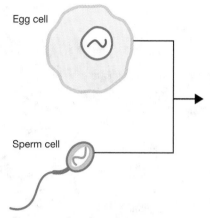

Egg cell

Sperm cell

7 Identify By what process did these cells form?

_____

_____

8 Identify How many chromosomes does a body cell for the organism shown have?

_____

_____

9 Predict Draw a picture of the cell that would form if the sperm cell fused with the egg cell. What is this cell called?

10 Claims • Evidence • Reasoning What would happen if meiosis did not occur? State your claim and explain your reasoning.

_____

_____

_____

_____

_____

_____

_____

My Notes

People in Science

Michael Coble

GENETICIST

Michael Coble's interest in genetics began when, as young child, he learned about Gregor Mendel's discoveries. While Coble was in college, his interest increased due to a science project in which he had to find dominant and recessive genes in fruit flies. Little did Coble know at the time that his work in genetics would lead him to solve one of history's greatest mysteries: What happened to Russia's royal family, the Romanovs, during the Russian revolution?

The whole family had supposedly been executed in 1918. However, many people believed there was a chance that at least one of the children had escaped.

Coble says that "since 1918, over 200 individuals have claimed to be one of the five 'surviving' Romanov children." Fueling the mystery was the fact that there were no remains in the Romanov's grave for two of the children.

However, in 2007, a grave with the remains of two people was found. Coble and his team used the DNA evidence to identify the remains as the missing Romanov children.

Coble continues his work in genetics today. He says, "It is very rewarding to know that something you were involved with will be used for finding criminals, exonerating the innocent, or helping to identify missing persons."

If the bands of DNA on the film line up correctly, you have a match.

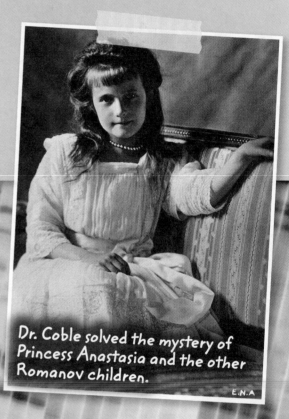

Dr. Coble solved the mystery of Princess Anastasia and the other Romanov children.

Social Studies Connection

Research Find out more about what happened to the Romanovs, including the mystery around Princess Anastasia. Put together a slideshow or a video to report your findings.

JOB BOARD

Genetic Counselor

What You'll Do: Analyze a family's risk factors for inherited conditions and disorders

Where You Might Work: At a doctor's office, a health clinic, or a hospital

Education: A graduate degree in genetic counseling

Other Job Requirements: Certification from the American Board of Genetic Counseling

Plant Nursery Manager

What You'll Do: Grow plants from seeds, cuttings, or by other methods. Manage a plant-related business or organization.

Where You Might Work: At a botanical garden, a garden center, or a plant nursery

Education: A degree in plant science and/or business management

Other Job Requirements: A green thumb!

PEOPLE IN SCIENCE NEWS

MULTIPLE Births

Not so rare anymore

Dr. Brian Kirshon and his medical team made history in December 1998. They delivered the world's first known set of surviving octuplets. Octuplets are a very rare type of multiple birth in which the mother carries eight fetuses in her uterus at once. There have been only 19 recorded instances of octuplets. Only two of those sets survived past birth—the first in 1998, and another in 2009. Considering how rare octuplets are, how is it possible that two pairs were born so recently?

The birth rate for twins increased by 70% from 1980 to 2004. In 2006, the birth rate for twins was up to 32 for every 1,000 births. The birth rate in 2006 for having triplets or a larger birth was 153 for every 100,000 births.

What's going on? Doctors point to modern fertility drugs and treatments. In addition, many women are now waiting until later in life to have children. This increases the chance of having a multiple birth.

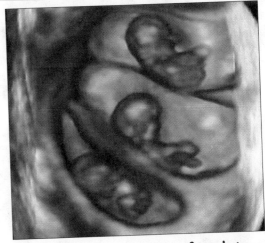

3D ultrasound image of triplets

Sexual and Asexual Reproduction

ESSENTIAL QUESTION

How do organisms reproduce?

By the end of this lesson, you should be able to describe asexual and sexual reproduction and list the advantages and disadvantages of each.

Female wolf spiders carry their young on their backs for a short period of time after the young hatch.

S7L3.b Reproduction and genetic variation

 **Lesson Labs**

Quick Labs
• Reproduction and Diversity
• Egg vs. Sperm
• Create a Classification System

Field Lab
• Investigate Asexual Reproduction

Engage Your Brain

1 Predict Check T or F to show whether you think each statement is true or false.

T F

☐ ☐ Reproduction requires two parents.

☐ ☐ Some organisms reproduce by cell division.

☐ ☐ New plants can grow from parts of a parent plant, such as roots and stems.

☐ ☐ Offspring of two parents always look like one of their parents.

2 Describe How is the young wolf in the photo below similar to its mother?

_____

_____

_____

_____

Active Reading

3 Synthesize You can often define an unknown word if you know the meaning of its word parts. Use the word parts and sentence below to make an educated guess about the meaning of the word *reproduction*.

Word part	Meaning
re-	again
produce	to make
-ion	act or process

Example sentence
Flowers are plant organs that are used for reproduction.

reproduction:

_____

_____

Vocabulary Terms

• asexual reproduction
• sexual reproduction
• fertilization

4 Apply As you learn the definition of each vocabulary term in this lesson, write your own definition or make a sketch to help you remember the meaning of the term.

One Becomes Two

What is asexual reproduction?

An individual organism does not live forever. The survival of any species depends on the ability to reproduce. Reproduction lets genetic information be transferred to new organisms. Reproduction involves various kinds of cell division.

Most single-celled organisms and some multicellular organisms reproduce asexually. In **asexual reproduction** (ay•SEHK•shoo•uhl ree•pruh•DUHK•shuhn), one organism produces one or more new organisms that are identical to itself. These organisms live independently of the original organism. The organism that produces the new organism or organisms is called a *parent*. Each new organism is called an *offspring*. The parent transfers all of its genetic information to the offspring. So, the offspring produced by asexual reproduction are genetically identical to their parents. They may differ only if a genetic mutation happens.

Active Reading

5 Relate Describe the genetic makeup of the offspring of asexual reproduction.

_____

_____

_____

Dandelions usually reproduce asexually. The dandelions in this field may all be genetically identical!

Think Outside the Book (Inquiry)

6 Summarize Research five organisms that reproduce asexually. Create flashcards that describe how asexual reproduction in each organism results in offspring that have identical genetic information. When you have finished, trade flashcards with a classmate to learn about five more organisms.

© Houghton Mifflin Harcourt Publishing Company • Image Credits: (bkgd) ©Peter Cade/Iconica/Getty Images

How do organisms reproduce asexually?

Organisms reproduce asexually in many ways. In prokaryotes, which include bacteria and archaea, asexual reproduction happens by cell division. In eukaryotes, which include single-celled and multicellular organisms, asexual reproduction is a more involved process. It often involves a type of cell division called *mitosis* (my•TOH•sis). Mitosis produces genetically identical cells.

Binary Fission

Binary fission (BY•nuh•ree FISH•uhn) is the form of asexual reproduction in prokaryotes. It is a type of cell division. During binary fission, the parent organism splits in two, producing two new cells. Genetically, the new cells are exactly like the parent cell.

Budding

During *budding*, an organism develops tiny buds on its body. A bud grows until it forms a new full-sized organism that is genetically identical to the parent. Budding is the result of mitosis. Eukaryotes such as single-celled yeasts and multicellular hydras reproduce by budding.

Spores

A *spore* is a specialized cell that can survive harsh conditions. Both prokaryotes and eukaryotes can form spores. Spores are produced asexually by one parent. Spores are light and can be carried by the wind. In the right conditions, a spore develops into an organism, such as a fungus.

Vegetative Reproduction

Some plants are able to reproduce asexually by *vegetative reproduction*. Mitosis makes vegetative reproduction possible. New plants may grow from stems, roots, or leaves. Runners are aboveground stems from which a new plant can grow. Tubers are underground stems from which new plants can grow. Plantlets are tiny plants that grow along the edges of a plant's leaves. They drop off the plant and grow on their own.

Visualize It!

7 Infer Pick one of the pictures below. How does the specific type of asexual reproduction help the organism reproduce quickly? Explain your reasoning.

_____

_____

_____

Bacteria reproduce by binary fission.

Hydras reproduce by budding.

Spores can survive long periods of time in harsh conditions.

New potato plants can grow from tubers.

Two Make One

What is sexual reproduction?

Most multicellular organisms can reproduce sexually. In **sexual reproduction** (SEHK•shoo•uhl ree•pruh•DUHK•shuhn), two parents each contribute a sex cell to the new organism. Half the genes in the offspring come from each parent. So, the offspring are not identical to either parent. Instead, they have a combination of traits from each parent.

Active Reading

8 Identify As you read, underline the male and female sex cells.

Fertilization

Usually, one parent is male and the other is female. Males produce sex cells called *sperm cells.* Females produce sex cells called *eggs.* Sex cells are produced by a type of cell division called *meiosis* (my•OH•sis). Sex cells have only half of the full set of genetic material found in body cells.

A sperm cell and an egg join together in a process called **fertilization** (fer•tl•i•ZAY•shuhn). When an egg is fertilized by a sperm cell, a new cell is formed. This cell is called a *zygote* (ZY•goht). It has a full set of genetic material. The zygote develops into a new organism. The zygote divides by mitosis, which increases the number of cells. This increase in cells produces growth. You are the size that you are today because of mitosis.

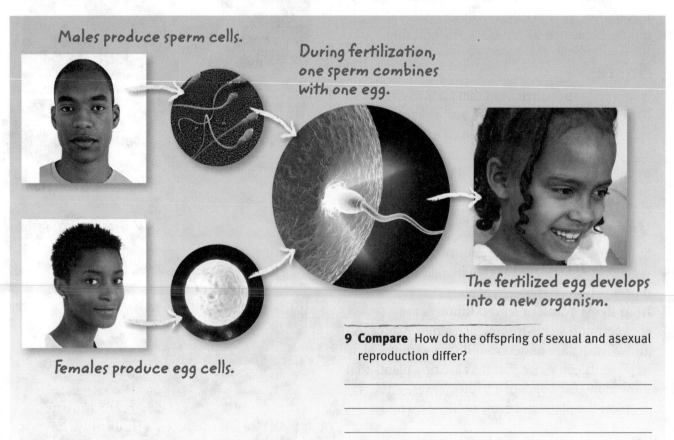

Males produce sperm cells.

During fertilization, one sperm combines with one egg.

The fertilized egg develops into a new organism.

Females produce egg cells.

9 Compare How do the offspring of sexual and asexual reproduction differ?

_____

_____

_____

Odd Reproduction

It may seem like only single-celled organisms undergo asexual reproduction. However, many multicellular organisms reproduce asexually.

Original arm

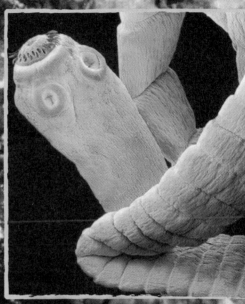

Appearing Act
Some organisms, such as aphids, reproduce asexually by *parthenogenesis*. A female produces young without fertilization.

Newly grown body and arms

Falling to Pieces
Tapeworms can reproduce asexually by *fragmentation*. Each segment of the worm can become a new organism if it breaks off of the worm.

Seeing Stars
Organisms such as starfish reproduce asexually by *regeneration*. Even a small part of the starfish can grow into a new organism.

Extend

Inquiry

10 Identify Which types of asexual reproduction involve part of an organism breaking off?

11 Claims • Evidence • Reasoning Research the advantages and disadvantages of a type of reproduction shown on this page. Gather evidence to support your claims and explain your reasoning.

12 Hypothesize A female shark was left alone in an aquarium tank. She was not pregnant when placed in the tank. But scientists were surprised one morning to find a baby shark in the tank. Form a hypothesis about what type of reproduction took place in this scenario.

Added Advantage

What are the advantages of each type of reproduction?

Organisms reproduce asexually, sexually, or both. Each type of reproduction has advantages. For example, sexual reproduction involves complex structures, such as flowers and other organs. These are not needed for asexual reproduction. But the offspring of sexual reproduction may be more likely to survive in certain situations. Read on to find out more about the advantages of each.

13 Compare Complete the Venn diagram below to compare asexual and sexual reproduction.

Asexual Reproduction
_____
_____
_____
_____

Both
_____
_____
_____

Sexual Reproduction
_____
_____
_____
_____

Advantages of Asexual Reproduction

Asexual reproduction has many advantages. First, an organism can reproduce very quickly. Offspring are identical to the parent. So, it also ensures that any favorable traits the parent has are passed on to offspring. Also, a parent organism does not need to find a partner to reproduce. Finally, all offspring—not just females—are able to produce more offspring.

14 List Identify four advantages of asexual reproduction.

_____
_____
_____
_____

Cholla cactuses reproduce asexually by vegetative reproduction. They drop off small pieces that grow into new plants.

Cats reproduce sexually. Offspring are similar to, but not exactly like, their parents.

Advantages of Sexual Reproduction

Sexual reproduction is not as quick as asexual reproduction. Nor does it produce as many offspring. However, it has advantages. First, it increases genetic variation. Offspring have different traits that improve the chance that at least some offspring will survive. This is especially true if the environment changes. Offspring are not genetically identical to the parents. So, they may have a trait that the parents do not have, making them more likely to survive.

15 Explain How can increased genetic variation help some offspring survive? State your claim. Summarize evidence to support your claim and explain your reasoning.

_____

_____

_____

_____

_____

_____

Advantages of Using Both Types of Reproduction

Some organisms can use both types of reproduction. For example, when conditions are favorable, many plants and fungi will reproduce asexually. Doing so lets them spread quickly and take over an area. When the environment changes, these organisms will switch to sexual reproduction. This strategy increases the chance that the species will survive. Because of genetic variation, at least some of the offspring may have traits that help them make it through the environmental change.

16 Compare In the table below, place a check mark in the cells that describe a characteristic of asexual or sexual reproduction.

	Quick	Increases chance of survival in changing environments	Produces genetic variation	Doesn't need a partner	Requires complex structures
Asexual reproduction					
Sexual reproduction					

© Houghton Mifflin Harcourt Publishing Company • Image Credits: ©Petra Wegner/Alamy

Visual Summary

To complete this summary, circle the correct word that completes each statement. Then use the key below to check your answers. You can use this page to review the main concepts of the lesson.

Asexual reproduction involves one parent.

Reproduction

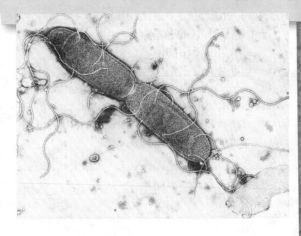

17 The offspring of asexual reproduction are genetically identical / similar to the parent organisms.

18 Prokaryotes reproduce by budding / binary fission.

19 Specialized reproductive structures called runners / spores can survive harsh conditions.

20 A benefit of asexual reproduction is that it is fast / slow.

Sexual reproduction involves two parents.

21 Male organisms produce sex cells called eggs / sperm cells.

22 Male and female sex cells join during fertilization / meiosis.

23 Sexual reproduction increases genetic variation / similarity.

Answers: 17 identical; 18 binary fission; 19 spores; 20 fast; 21 sperm cells; 22 fertilization; 23 variation

---

24 Explain How can both asexual reproduction and sexual reproduction allow for the survival of a species? Summarize evidence to support your claim and explain your reasoning.

Lesson Review

Vocabulary

Fill in the blanks with the term that best completes the following sentences.

1 After _____ , the zygote develops into a larger organism.

2 An advantage of _____ reproduction is the ability to reproduce quickly.

3 The offspring of _____ reproduction are more likely to survive changes in the environment.

Key Concepts

4 **Identify** What are some advantages of asexual and sexual reproduction?

_____

_____

_____

_____

_____

5 **Compare** In sexual reproduction, how do the offspring compare to the parents?

_____

_____

_____

6 **Identify** List four types of asexual reproduction.

_____

7 **Claims • Evidence • Reasoning** Why do some organisms use both types of reproduction? State your claim. Summarize evidence to support your claim and explain your reasoning.

_____

_____

_____

_____

_____

_____

Critical Thinking

Use the graph to answer the following questions.

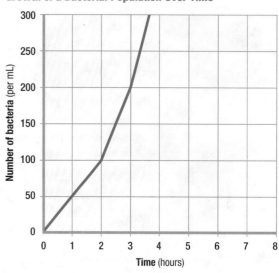

Growth of a Bacterial Population Over Time

8 **Infer** What type of reproduction is most likely taking place?

_____

_____

9 **Analyze** Which advantage of reproduction does the graph show? Explain.

_____

_____

_____

_____

10 **Predict** How might the graph change if the environmental conditions of the bacteria suddenly change? Explain.

_____

_____

_____

_____

_____

_____

My Notes

Heredity

ESSENTIAL QUESTION

How are traits inherited?

By the end of this lesson, you should be able to analyze the inheritance of traits in individuals.

Members of the same family share certain traits. Can you think of some traits that family members share?

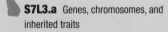
S7L3.a Genes, chromosomes, and inherited traits

S7L3.b Reproduction and genetic variation

© Houghton Mifflin Harcourt Publishing Company • Image Credits: © Steve Bloom Images/Alamy

Lesson Labs

Quick Labs
- Dominant Alleles
- What's the Difference Between a Dominant Trait and a Recessive Trait?

Engage Your Brain

1 Predict Check T or F to show whether you think each statement is true or false.

T	F	
☐	☐	Siblings look similar because they each have some traits of their parents.
☐	☐	Siblings always have the same hair color.
☐	☐	Siblings have identical DNA.

2 Describe Do you know any identical twins? How are they similar? How are they different?

_____

_____

_____

_____

_____

Active Reading

3 Infer Use context clues to write your own definition for the words *exhibit* and *investigate*.

Example sentence
A person with brown hair may also <u>exhibit</u> the trait of brown eye color.

exhibit:

_____

_____

Example sentence
Gregor Mendel began to <u>investigate</u> the characteristics of pea plants.

investigate:

_____

_____

Vocabulary Terms

- heredity
- gene
- allele
- genotype
- phenotype

- dominant
- recessive
- incomplete dominance
- codominance

4 Identify This list contains the key terms you'll learn in this lesson. As you read, circle the definition of each term.

Give Peas a Chance

What is heredity?

Imagine a puppy. The puppy has long floppy ears like his mother has, and the puppy has dark brown fur like his father has. How did the puppy get these traits? The traits are a result of information stored in the puppy's genetic material. The passing of genetic material from parents to offspring is called **heredity**.

What did Gregor Mendel discover about heredity?

The first major experiments investigating heredity were performed by a monk named Gregor Mendel. Mendel lived in Austria in the 1800s. Before Mendel became a monk, he attended a university and studied science and mathematics. This training served him well when he began to study the inheritance of traits among the pea plants in the monastery's garden. Mendel studied seven different characteristics of pea plants: plant height, flower and pod position, seed shape, seed color, pod shape, pod color, and flower color. A *characteristic* is a feature that has different forms in a population. Mendel studied each pea plant characteristic separately, always starting with plants that were true-breeding for that characteristic. A true-breeding plant is one that will always produce offspring with a certain trait when allowed to self-pollinate. Each of the characteristics that Mendel studied had two different forms. For example, the color of a pea could be green or yellow. These different forms are called *traits*.

Characteristics of Pea Plants

Characteristic	Traits	
Seed color		
Seed shape		
Pod color		
Flower position		

5 Apply Is flower color a characteristic or a trait?

_____

Traits Depend on Inherited Factors

In his experiments with seed pod color, Mendel took two sets of plants, one true-breeding for plants that produce yellow seed pods and the other true-breeding for plants that produce green seed pods. Instead of letting the plants self-pollinate as they do naturally, he paired one plant from each set. He did this by fertilizing one plant with the pollen of another plant. Mendel called the plants that resulted from this cross the first generation. All of the plants from this first generation produced green seed pods. Mendel called this trait the *dominant* trait. Because the yellow trait seemed to recede, or fade away, he called it the *recessive* trait.

Then Mendel let the first-generation plants self-pollinate. He called the offspring that resulted from this self-pollination the second generation. About three-fourths of the second-generation plants had green seed pods, but about one-fourth had yellow pods. So the trait that seemed to disappear in the first generation reappeared in the second generation. Mendel hypothesized that each plant must have two heritable "factors" for each trait, one from each parent. Some traits, such as yellow seed pod color, could only be observed if a plant received two factors—one from each parent—for yellow pod color. A plant with one yellow factor and one green factor would produce green pods because producing green pods is a dominant trait. However, this plant could still pass on the yellow factor to the next generation of plants.

Active Reading

6 Identify As you read, underline Mendel's hypothesis about how traits are passed from parents to offspring.

Visualize It!

7 Apply Which pod color is recessive? Explain your reasoning.

_____

_____

_____

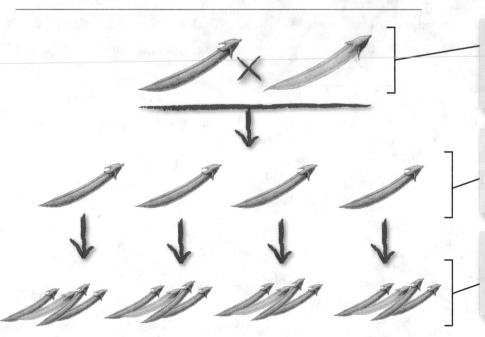

Parent plants Mendel crossed true-breeding green-pod plants with true-breeding yellow-pod plants.

First generation All of the first generation plants had green pods. Mendel let these plants self-pollinate.

Second generation About three-fourths of the second generation had green pods, and one-fourth had yellow pods.

© Houghton Mifflin Harcourt Publishing Company

It's in your genes!

Genes are made up of DNA.

How are traits inherited?

Mendel's experiments and conclusions have been the basis for much of the scientific thought about heredity. His ideas can be further explained by our modern understanding of the genetic material DNA. What Mendel called "factors" are actually segments of DNA known as genes!

Genes Are Passed from Parents to Offspring

Genes are segments of DNA found in chromosomes that give instructions for producing a certain characteristic. Humans, like many other organisms, inherit their genes from their parents. Each parent gives one set of genes to the offspring. The offspring then has two versions, or forms, of the same gene for every characteristic—one version from each parent. The different versions of a gene are known as **alleles** (uh•LEELZ). Genes are often represented by letter symbols. Dominant alleles are shown with a capital letter, and recessive alleles are shown with a lowercase version of the same letter. An organism with two dominant or two recessive alleles is said to be *homozygous* for that gene. An organism that has one dominant and one recessive allele is *heterozygous*.

Humans have 23 pairs of chromosomes.

In humans, cells contain pairs of chromosomes. One chromosome of each pair comes from each of two parents. Each chromosome contains sites where specific genes are located.

A gene occupies a specific location on both chromosomes in a pair.

 Visualize It!

8 Apply Circle a gene pair for which this person is heterozygous.

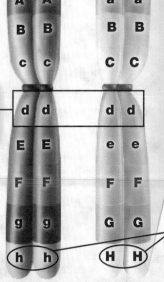

Alleles are alternate forms of the same gene.

© Houghton Mifflin Harcourt Publishing Company • Image Credits: (cr) ©L. Willatt/Photo Researchers, Inc.

This girl has dimples.

This girl does not have dimples.

9 Apply The girls in this photograph have different types of hair. Is hair type a genotype or a phenotype?

Genes Influence Traits

The alternate forms of genes, called alleles, determine the traits of all living organisms. The combination of alleles that you inherited from your parents is your **genotype** (JEEN•uh•typ). Your observable traits make up your **phenotype** (FEEN•uh•typ). The phenotypes of some traits follow patterns similar to the ones that Mendel discovered in pea plants. That is, some traits are dominant over others. This is the case both for sexual and asexual reproduction. For example, consider the gene responsible for producing dimples, or creases in the cheeks. This gene comes in two alleles: one for dimples and one for no dimples. If you have even one copy of the allele for dimples, you will have dimples. This happens because the allele for producing dimples is dominant. The **dominant** allele contributes to the phenotype if one or two copies are present in the genotype. The no-dimples allele is recessive. The **recessive** allele contributes to the phenotype only when two copies of it are present. If one chromosome in the pair contains a dominant allele and the other contains a recessive allele, the phenotype will be determined by the dominant allele. If you do not have dimples, it is because you inherited two no-dimples alleles—one from each parent. This characteristic shows *complete dominance*, because one trait is completely dominant over another. However, not all characteristics follow this pattern.

Active Reading

11 Identify What is the phenotype of an individual with one allele for dimples and one allele for no dimples?

_____

_____

Visualize It!

10 Identify There is a dominant allele for cats having curled ears *(C)*, and a recessive allele for cats having straight ears *(c)*. Complete the following chart by classifying combinations of alleles according to whether they are homozygous or heterozygous. Then assign the correct symbols to them. Finally, refer to your chart to describe why an organism that reproduces asexually would have the same alleles as the parent.

_____

_____

_____

_____

_____

_____

Description	Genotype	Symbols
Two of the same allele	Homozygous	CC or cc
One dominant allele, one recessive allele		
Two dominant alleles		
Two recessive alleles		

Many Genes Can Influence a Single Trait

Some characteristics, such as the color of your skin, hair, and eyes, are the result of several genes acting together. Different combinations of alleles can result in different shades of eye color. Because there is not always a one-to-one relationship between a trait and a gene, many traits do not have simple patterns of inheritance.

A Single Gene Can Influence Many Traits

Sometimes, one gene influences more than one trait. For example, a single gene causes the tiger shown below to have white fur. If you look closely, you will see that the tiger also has blue eyes. The gene that affects fur color also influences eye color.

Many genetic disorders in humans are linked to a single gene but affect many traits. For example, the genetic disorder sickle cell anemia occurs in individuals who have two recessive alleles for a certain gene. This gene carries instructions for producing a protein in red blood cells. When a person has sickle cell anemia alleles, the body makes a different protein. This protein causes red blood cells to be sickle or crescent shaped when oxygen levels are low. Sickle-shaped blood cells can stick in blood vessels, sometimes blocking the flow of blood. These blood cells are also more likely to damage the spleen. With fewer healthy red blood cells, the body may not be able to deliver oxygen to the body's organs. All of the traits associated with sickle cell anemia are due to a single gene.

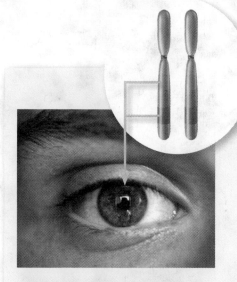

12 Identify How many genes are responsible for eye color in this example?

_____

_____

This single gene affects the tiger's fur color and eye color.

The Environment Can Influence Traits

Sometimes, the environment influences an organism's phenotype. For example, the arctic fox has a gene that is responsible for coat color. This gene is affected by light. In the winter, there are fewer hours of daylight, and the hairs that make up the arctic fox's coat grow in white. In the summer, when there are more daylight hours, the hairs in the coat grow in brown. In this case, both genes and the environment contribute to the organism's phenotype. The environment can influence human characteristics as well. For example, your genes may make it possible for you to grow to be tall, but you need a healthy diet to reach your full height potential.

Traits that are learned in one's environment are not inherited. For example, your ability to read and write is an acquired trait—a skill you learned. You were not born knowing how to ride a bike, and if you have children, they will not be born knowing how to do it either. They will have to learn the skill just as you did.

 **Active Reading**

13 Identify Give an example of an acquired trait.

_____

_____

In the summer, the arctic fox has a brown coat.

In the winter, the arctic fox has a white coat.

14 Predict What advantage does white fur give the arctic fox in winter?

_____

_____

_____

Bending the Rules

What are the exceptions to complete dominance?

The characteristics that Mendel chose to study demonstrated complete dominance, meaning that heterozygous individuals show the dominant trait. Some human traits, such as freckles and dimples, follow the pattern of complete dominance, too. However, other traits do not. For traits that show incomplete dominance or codominance, one trait is not completely dominant over another.

Incomplete Dominance

In **incomplete dominance**, each allele in a heterozygous individual influences the phenotype. The result is a phenotype that is a blend of the phenotypes of the parents. One example of incomplete dominance is found in the snapdragon flower, shown below. When a true-breeding red snapdragon is crossed with a true-breeding white snapdragon, all the offspring are pink snapdragons. Both alleles of the gene have some influence. Hair texture is an example of incomplete dominance in humans. A person with one straight-hair allele and one curly-hair allele will have wavy hair.

Active Reading

15 Identify As you read, underline examples of incomplete dominance and codominance.

Visualize It!

16 Analyze Construct an explanation of why these snapdragons do not follow the pattern of complete dominance.

_____

_____

_____

_____

Pink snapdragons are produced by a cross between a red snapdragon and a white snapdragon.

Codominance

For a trait that shows **codominance**, both of the alleles in a heterozygous individual contribute to the phenotype. Instead of having a blend of the two phenotypes, heterozygous individuals have both of the traits associated with their two alleles. An example of codominance is shown in the genes that determine human blood types. There are three alleles that play a role in determining a person's blood type: *A, B,* and *O.* The alleles are responsible for producing small particles on the surface of red blood cells called antigens. The *A* allele produces red blood cells coated with A antigens. The *B* allele produces red blood cells coated with B antigens. The *O* allele does not produce antigens. The *A* and *B* alleles are codominant. So, someone with one *A* allele and one *B* allele will have blood cells that are coated with A antigens and B antigens. This person would have type AB blood.

Active Reading **18 Identify** What antigens coat the red blood cells of a person with type AB blood?

_____

Think Outside the Book *Inquiry*

17 Research Blood type is an important factor when people give or receive blood. Research the meanings of the phrases "universal donor" and "universal recipient." What are the genotypes of each blood type?

Visualize It!

19 Predict The color of these imaginary fish is controlled by a single gene. Sketch or describe their offspring if the phenotypes follow the pattern of complete dominance, incomplete dominance, or codominance.

 X

Complete dominance (Blue is dominant to yellow.)	Incomplete dominance	Codominance

Visual Summary

To complete this summary, circle the correct word or phrase. Then use the key below to check your answers. You can use this page to review the main concepts of the lesson.

Heredity

Gregor Mendel studied patterns of heredity in pea plants.

20 Traits that seemed to disappear in Mendel's first-generation crosses were dominant / recessive traits.

Inherited genes influence the traits of an individual.

21 An individual with the genotype BB is heterozygous / homozygous.

Phenotypes can follow complete dominance, incomplete dominance, or codominance.

22 When these imaginary fish cross, their offspring are all green. This is an example of codominance / incomplete dominance.

Answers: 20 recessive; 21 homozygous; 22 incomplete dominance

23 Claims • Evidence • Reasoning If a child has blonde hair and both of her parents have brown hair, what does that tell you about the allele for blonde hair? Summarize the evidence to support your claim and explain your reasoning.

Lesson Review

Vocabulary

Draw a line to connect the following terms to their definitions.

1 heredity   **A** an organism's appearance or other detectable characteristic

2 gene   **B** a section of DNA that contains instructions for a particular characteristic

3 phenotype

   C the passing of genetic material from parent to offspring

Key Concepts

4 Describe What did Mendel discover about genetic factors in pea plants? Use evidence to support your claim.

_____

_____

_____

_____

_____

_____

5 Describe Construct an explanation of the role of DNA in determining an organism's traits. Support your explanation with scientific evidence.

_____

_____

_____

6 Apply Imagine that a brown horse and a white horse cross to produce an offspring whose coat is made up of some brown hairs and some white hairs. Which pattern of dominance is this an example of?

_____

7 Identify Give an example of a trait that is controlled by more than one gene.

_____

Use this diagram to answer the following questions.

8 Identify What is the genotype at the Q gene?

_____

9 Apply For which genes is this individual heterozygous?

_____

Critical Thinking

10 Describe Marfan syndrome is a genetic disorder caused by a dominant allele. Provide evidence to explain how Marfan syndrome is inherited.

_____

_____

_____

11 Describe Jenny, Jenny's mom, and Jenny's grandfather are all good basketball players. Give an example of an inherited trait and an acquired trait that could contribute to their skill at basketball.

_____

_____

_____

My Notes

Interpreting Tables

Visual displays, such as diagrams, tables, or graphs, are useful ways to show data collected in an experiment. A table is the most direct way to communicate this information. Tables are also used to summarize important trends in scientific data. Making a table may seem easy. However, if tables are not clearly organized, people will have trouble reading them. Below are a few strategies to help you improve your skills in interpreting scientific tables.

Tutorial

Use the following instructions to study the parts of a table about heredity in Brittanies and to analyze the data shown in the table.

Offspring from Cross of Black Solid and Liver Tricolor Brittanies		
Color	**Pattern**	**Number of Offspring**
orange and white	solid	1
black and white	solid	1
	tricolor	3
liver and white	solid	1
	tricolor	3

Reading the Title
Every table should have an informative title. By reading the title of the table to the left, we know that the table contains data about the offspring of a cross between a black solid Brittany and a liver tricolor Brittany.

Summarizing the Title
Sometimes it is helpful to write a sentence to summarize a table's title. For example, you could write, "This table shows how puppies that are the offspring of a black solid Brittany and a liver tricolor Brittany might look."

Analyzing the Headings
Row and column headings describe the data in the cells. Headings often appear different from the data in the cells, such as being larger, bold, or being shaded. The row headings in the table to the left organize three kinds of data: the coat color of the puppies, the coat pattern of the puppies, and the number of puppies that have each combination of coat color and pattern.

Describing the Data
In complete sentences, record the information that you read in the table. For example, you could write, "There are five different kinds of offspring. Tricolor puppies are most common, and puppies with a solid coat pattern are least common. There are twice as many tricolor puppies as solid puppies."

Analyzing the Data
Now that you have seen how the table is organized, you can begin to look for trends in the data. Which combinations are most common? Which combinations are least common?

You Try It!

The table below shows the characteristics of Guinea pig offspring. Look at the table, and answer the questions that follow.

Characteristics of Guinea Pig Offspring from Controlled Breeding			
Hair Color	Coat Texture	Hair Length	Number of Guinea Pigs
black	rough	short	27
		long	9
	smooth	short	9
		long	3
white	rough	short	9
		long	3
	smooth	short	3
		long	1

1 Summarizing the Title Circle the title of the table. Write a one-sentence description of the information shown in the table.

_____

_____

_____

2 Analyzing the Headings Shade the column headings in the table. What information do they show? How many combinations of hair color, coat texture, and hair length are shown?

_____

_____

_____

3 Analyzing the Data Circle the most common type of Guinea pig. Box the least common type of Guinea pig. Write sentences to describe the characteristics of each.

_____

_____

_____

_____

_____

4 Applying Mathematics Calculate the total number of Guinea pig offspring. Write this total at the bottom of the table. What percentage of the total number of Guinea pigs has short hair? What percentage of the total number of Guinea pigs has long hair?

_____

_____

_____

5 Observing Trends Based on your data from Step 4, which characteristic is dominant in Guinea pigs: long hair or short hair?

_____

_____

6 Applying Concepts What is one advantage of displaying data in tables? What is one advantage of describing data in writing?

_____

_____

_____

Take It Home

With an adult, practice making tables. You can categorize anything that interests you. Make sure your table has a title and clearly and accurately organizes your data using headings. If possible, share your table with your class.

Punnett Squares and Pedigrees

ESSENTIAL QUESTION

How are patterns of inheritance studied?

By the end of this lesson, you should be able to explain how patterns of heredity can be predicted by Punnett squares and pedigrees.

S7L3.b Reproduction and genetic variation

These cattle are bred for their long, curly hair, which keeps them warm in cold climates. This trait is maintained by careful breeding of these animals.

 **Lesson Labs**

Quick Labs
- Gender Determination
- Interpreting Pedigree Charts
- Completing a Punnett Square

S.T.E.M. Lab
- Matching Punnett Square Predictions

Engage Your Brain

1 Infer Why do you think that children look like their parents?

_____

_____

_____

_____

_____

_____

_____

_____

2 Apply Color or label each circle with the color that results when the two paints mix. As you read the lesson, think about how this grid is similar to and different from a Punnett square.

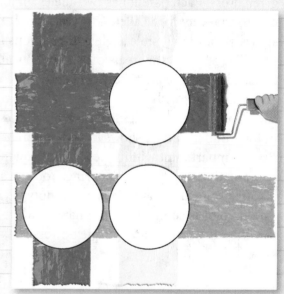

Active Reading

3 Apply Use context clues to write your own definition for the words *occur* and *outcome*.

Example sentence
Tools can be used to predict the likelihood that a particular genetic combination will <u>occur</u>.

occur:

_____

_____

Example sentence
A Punnett square can be used to predict the <u>outcome</u> of a genetic cross.

outcome:

_____

_____

Vocabulary Terms

- **Punnett square**
- **probability**
- **ratio**
- **pedigree**

4 Apply As you learn the definition of each vocabulary term in this lesson, create your own definition or sketch to help you remember the meaning of the term.

Squared Away

How are Punnett squares used to predict patterns of heredity?

When Gregor Mendel studied pea plants, he noticed that traits are inherited in patterns. One tool for understanding the patterns of heredity is a diagram called a *Punnett square*. A **Punnett square** is a graphic used to predict the possible genotypes of offspring in a given cross. Each parent has two alleles for a particular gene. An offspring receives one allele from each parent. A Punnett square shows all of the possible allele combinations in the offspring.

The Punnett square below shows how alleles are expected to be distributed in a cross between a pea plant with purple flowers and a pea plant with white flowers. The top of the Punnett square shows one parent's alleles for this trait (*F* and *F*). The left side of the Punnett square shows the other parent's alleles (*f* and *f*). Each compartment within the Punnett square shows an allele combination in potential offspring. You can see that in this cross, all offspring would have the same genotype (*Ff*). Because purple flower color is completely dominant to white flower color, all of the offspring would have purple flowers.

Active Reading

5 Identify In a Punnett square, where are the parents' alleles written?

_____

_____

_____

_____

_____

This Punnett square shows the possible offspring combinations in pea plants with different flower colors.

Key:

F Purple flower allele

f White flower allele

Genotype: FF
Phenotype: purple flower

Genotype: ff
Phenotype: white flower

One parent's alleles

The other parent's alleles

	F	F
f	Ff	Ff
f	Ff	Ff

6 Apply Fill in the genotypes and phenotypes of the parents and offspring in this Punnett square. Sketch the resulting offspring possibilities in the white boxes below. (Hint: Assume complete dominance.)

Genotype: _____

Phenotype: _____

Key:

R Round pea allele

r Wrinkled pea allele

Genotype: _____

Phenotype: _____

	R	r
R	Genotype: _____ Phenotype: _____	Genotype: _____ Phenotype: _____
r	Genotype: _____ Phenotype: _____	Genotype: _____ Phenotype: _____

7 Analyze What does each compartment of the Punnett square represent? Support your claim with evidence.

_____

_____

_____

_____

_____

_____

How can a Punnett square be used to make predictions about offspring?

A Punnett square does not tell you what the exact results of a certain cross will be. A Punnett square only helps you find the probability that a certain genotype will occur. **Probability** is the mathematical chance of a specific outcome in relation to the total number of possible outcomes.

Probability can be expressed in the form of a **ratio** (RAY•shee•oh), an expression that compares two quantities. A ratio written as 1:4 is read as "one to four." The ratios obtained from a Punnett square tell you the probability that any one offspring will get certain alleles. Another way of expressing probability is as a *percentage*. A percentage is like a ratio that compares a number to 100. A percentage states the number of times a certain outcome might happen out of a hundred chances.

1:4 is the ratio of red squares to total squares.

![Do the Math] **Sample Problem**

In guinea pigs, the dominant *B* allele is responsible for black fur, while the recessive *b* allele is responsible for brown fur. Use the Punnett square to find the probability of this cross resulting in offspring with brown fur.

	B	b
b	Bb	bb
b	Bb	bb

Identify

A. What do you know?

Parent genotypes are Bb and bb. Possible offspring genotypes are Bb and bb.

B. What do you want to find out?

Probability of the cross resulting in offspring with brown fur

---

Plan

C. Count the total number of offspring allele combinations: 4

D. Count the number of allele combinations that will result in offspring with brown fur: 2

Solve

E. Write the probability of offspring with brown fur as a ratio: 2:4

F. Rewrite the ratio to express the probability out of 100 offspring by multiplying each side of the ratio by the same number (such as 25): 50:100

G. Convert the ratio to a percentage: 50%

Answer: 50% chance of offspring with brown fur

![Do the Math] **You Try It**

8 Calculate This Punnett square shows a cross between two *Bb* guinea pigs. What is the probability of the cross resulting in offspring with black fur?

	B	b
B	BB	Bb
b	Bb	bb

Identify

A. What do you know?

B. What do you want to find out?

Plan

C. Count the total number of offspring allele combinations:

D. Count the number of allele combinations that will result in offspring with black fur:

Solve

E. Write the probability of offspring with black fur as a ratio:

F. Rewrite the ratio to express the probability out of 100 offspring by multiplying each side of the ratio by the same number:

G. Convert the ratio to a percentage:

Answer:

9 Graph In the cross above, what is the ratio of each of the possible genotypes? Show your results by filling in the pie chart at the right. Fill in the key with color or shading to show which pieces of the chart represent the different genotypes.

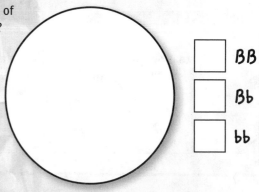

☐ BB

☐ Bb

☐ bb

How can a pedigree trace a trait through generations?

A pedigree is another tool used to study patterns of inheritance. A **pedigree** traces the occurrence of a trait through generations of a family. Pedigrees can be created to trace any inherited trait—even hair color!

Pedigrees can be useful in tracing a special class of inherited disorders known as *sex-linked disorders*. Sex-linked disorders are associated with an allele on a sex chromosome. Many sex-linked disorders, such as hemophilia and colorblindness, are caused by an allele on the X chromosome. Women have two X chromosomes, so a woman can have one allele for colorblindness without being colorblind. A woman who is heterozygous for this trait is called a *carrier*, because she can carry or pass on the trait to her offspring. Men have just one X chromosome. In men, this single chromosome determines if the trait is present.

The pedigree below traces a disease called *cystic fibrosis*. Cystic fibrosis causes serious lung problems. Carriers of the disease have one recessive allele. They do not have cystic fibrosis, but they are able to pass the recessive allele on to their children. If a child receives a recessive allele from each parent, then the child will have cystic fibrosis. Other genetic conditions follow a similar pattern.

Think Outside the Book Inquiry

10 Model Work in pairs to collect information about your partner's family. Identify a particular trait, such as dimples or freckles, that occurs in that family. Develop and use a model in the form of a pedigree chart to trace this trait identifying genetic variation in offspring through generations. Describe how this genetic variation is linked to sexual reproduction.

Visualize It!

Pedigree for Cystic Fibrosis

	Males ○ Females
	Vertical lines connect children to their parents.
or ●	A solid square or circle indicates that the person has a certain trait.
or ◨	A half-filled square or circle indicates that the person is a carrier of the trait.

11 Analyze Does anyone in the third generation have cystic fibrosis? Explain.

_____

_____

12 Calculate What is the probability that the child of two carriers will have cystic fibrosis?

_____

_____

Why It Matters

Saving the European Mouflon

The European mouflon is an endangered species of sheep. Scientists at the University of Teramo in Italy used genetic tools and techniques to show how the population of mouflon could be preserved.

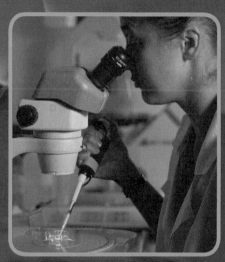

Maintaining Genetic Diversity

When a very small population of animals interbreeds, there is a greater risk that harmful genetic conditions can appear in the animals. This is one issue that scientists face when trying to preserve endangered species. One way to lower this risk is to be sure that genetically-similar animals do not breed.

Genetics to the Rescue!

Researchers combined the sperm and egg of genetically-dissimilar European mouflons in a laboratory. The resulting embryo was implanted into a mother sheep. By controlling the combination of genetic material, scientists hope to lower the risk of inherited disorders.

Extend

Inquiry

13 Claims • Evidence • Support Why are small populations difficult to preserve? State your claim and explain your reasoning.

14 Research Research another population of animals that has been part of a captive breeding program.

15 Describe Describe these animals and the results of the breeding program by doing one of the following:
- make a poster
- write a song
- write a short story
- draw a graphic novel

Visual Summary

To complete this summary, fill in the blanks with the correct word or phrase. Then use the key below to check your answers. You can use this page to review the main concepts of the lesson.

Punnett squares can be used to make predictions about possible offspring.

	F	F
f	Ff	Ff
f	Ff	Ff

16 A Punnett square shows combinations of different _____ received from each parent.

Pedigrees trace a trait through generations.

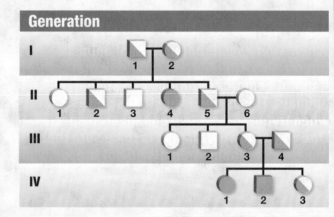

Generation

I   1 2

II   1 2 3 4 5 6

III 1 2 3 4

IV   1 2 3

17 An allele responsible for a _____ is found on a sex chromosome.

18 Compare How is a heterozygous individual represented in the Punnett square and pedigree shown above?

Lesson Review

Vocabulary

Circle the term that best completes the following sentences.

1 A *Punnett square / ratio* is a tool that can be used to predict the genotypes of potential offspring in a given cross.

2 The results from a Punnett square can be used to find the *pedigree / probability* that a certain allele combination will occur in offspring.

3 A mathematical expression that compares one number to another is called a *pedigree / ratio*.

Key Concepts

Use this diagram to answer the following questions.

	G	G
g	Gg	Gg
g	Gg	Gg

4 Analyze What is gene G responsible for in these fruit flies?

_____

_____

5 Analyze What is the ratio of heterozygous offspring to total offspring in the Punnett square?

_____

6 Define What is a sex-linked disorder?

_____

_____

_____

_____

Critical Thinking

7 Infer Imagine a pedigree that traces an inherited disorder found in individuals with two recessive alleles for gene D. The pedigree shows three siblings with the genotypes *DD*, *Dd*, and *dd*. Did the parents of these three children have the disorder? Explain your reasoning.

_____

_____

_____

_____

_____

8 Explain A *Bb* guinea pig crosses with a *Bb* guinea pig, and four offspring are produced. All of the offspring are black. Explain how this could happen.

_____

_____

_____

9 Synthesize You have developed a pedigree to trace dimples or freckles, a recessive trait, in a friend's family. You have found out which of her family members have dimples or freckles and which do not. After completing this model, what information have you obtained about members of your friend's family that you could not tell just by looking at them?

_____

_____

_____

My Notes

DNA Structure and Function

ESSENTIAL QUESTION

What is DNA?

By the end of this lesson, you should be able to describe the structure and main functions of DNA.

This bacterium was treated with a special chemical, causing a twisted maze of DNA to burst from the cell.

S7L3.a Genes, chromosomes, and inherited traits

🖐 Lesson Labs

Quick Labs
• Modeling DNA
• Building a DNA Sequence
• Mutations Cause Diversity

Exploration Lab
• Extracting DNA

🧠 Engage Your Brain

1 Predict Check T or F to show whether you think each statement is true or false.

T	F	
☐	☐	DNA is found in the cells of all living things.
☐	☐	All DNA mutations are harmful.
☐	☐	The cell can make copies of its DNA.

2 Describe DNA is sometimes called the *blueprint of life*. Why do you think that is?

_____

_____

_____

_____

_____

_____

✏️ Active Reading

3 Synthesize Many English words have their roots in other languages. Use the Latin words below to make an educated guess about the meanings of the words *replication* and *mutation*.

Latin word	Meaning
mutare	to change
replicare	to repeat

Example sentence
DNA can undergo <u>mutation</u>.

mutation:

_____

_____

Example sentence
Before cell division, DNA <u>replication</u> occurs.

replication:

_____

_____

Vocabulary Terms

• DNA
• nucleotide
• replication
• mutation
• RNA
• ribosome

4 Identify This list contains the key terms you'll learn in this lesson. As you read, circle the definition of each term.

Cracking the CODE

ATTAGCGATCACTAAATTAGC

Active Reading

5 Identify As you read, underline the meaning of the word *code*.

What is DNA?

The genetic material of a cell is carried by chromosomes in the form of genes. Genes contain information needed for the cell's growth and other activities. Genetic material also determines the inherited characteristics of an organism. The genetic material in cells is contained in a molecule called deoxyribonucleic (dee•OK•see•ry•boh•noo•KLAY•ik) acid, or **DNA** for short. DNA is found within each chromosome. You could compare the information in DNA to the books in your local library. You might find a book describing how to bake a cake or complete your favorite video game. The books, however, don't actually do any of those things—you do. Similarly, the "books" that make up the DNA "library" carry the information that a cell needs to function, grow, and divide. However, DNA doesn't do any of those things. Proteins do most of the work of a cell and also make up much of the structure of a cell.

Scientists describe DNA as containing a code. A *code* is a set of rules and symbols used to carry information. For example, your computer uses a code of ones and zeroes that is translated into numbers, letters, and graphics on a computer screen. To understand how DNA functions as a code, you first need to learn about the structure of the DNA molecule.

DNA Timeline

Review this timeline to learn about some of the important scientific contributions to our understanding of DNA.

1875   **1900**   **1925**

1869 Friedrich Miescher identifies a substance that will later be known as DNA.

1919 Phoebus Levene publishes a paper on nucleic acids. His research helps scientists determine that DNA is made up of sugars, phosphate groups, and four nitrogen-containing bases: adenine, thymine, guanine, and cytosine. Bases are often referred to by their first letter: A, T, C, or G. Each base has a different shape.

6 Analyze In this model, what do *P*, *S*, and *A bases* represent?

_____

_____

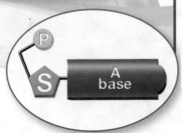

How was DNA discovered?

The discovery of the structure and function of DNA did not happen overnight. Many scientists from all over the world contributed to our current understanding of this important molecule. Some scientists discovered the chemicals that make up DNA. Others learned how these chemicals fit together. Still others determined the three-dimensional structure of the DNA molecule. The timeline below shows some of the key steps in this process of discovery.

Think Outside the Book (Inquiry)

7 Research Use the Internet or library resources to research a scientist who contributed to the discovery of DNA. Then, create a poster about the scientist. Share your findings with your class.

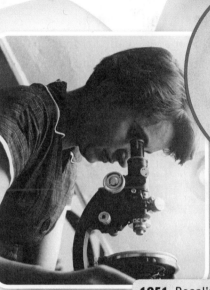

An image of DNA produced by using x-rays.

1951 Rosalind Franklin and Maurice Wilkins make images of DNA using x-rays. When an x-ray passes through the molecule, the ray bends and creates a pattern that is captured on film.

1953 James Watson and Francis Crick use Chargaff's rules and the x-ray images of DNA to conclude that DNA looks like a long, twisted ladder. They build a large-scale model of DNA using simple materials from their laboratory.

1950

1975

1950 Erwin Chargaff observes that the amount of guanine always equals the amount of cytosine, and the amount of adenine equals the amount of thymine. His findings are now known as *Chargaff's rules*.

1952 Alfred Hershey and Martha Chase perform experiments with viruses to confirm that DNA, not proteins, carries genetic information.

Unraveling DNA

What does DNA look like?

The chemical components that make up DNA are too small to be observed directly. But experiments and imaging techniques have helped scientists to infer the shape of DNA and the arrangement of its parts.

The Shape of DNA Is a Double Helix

The structure of DNA is a twisted ladder shape called a *double helix*. The two sides of the ladder, often referred to as the DNA backbone, are made of alternating sugars and phosphate groups. The rungs of the ladder are made of a pair of bases, each attached to one of the sugars in the backbone.

Active Reading **8 Describe** Where are phosphate groups found in a DNA molecule?

_____

_____

DNA is found in the nucleus of eukaryotic cells.

The DNA molecule has a double-helix shape.

Visualize It!

9 Compare How is the double-helix structure of DNA like a spiral staircase? Explain your reasoning.

_____

_____

_____

_____

_____

© Houghton Mifflin Harcourt Publishing Company • Image Credits: (bl) ©mediacolor's/Alamy

DNA Is Made Up of Nucleotides

A base, a sugar, and a phosphate group make a building block of DNA known as a **nucleotide**. These repeating chemical units join together to form the DNA molecule. There are four different nucleotides in DNA, identified by their bases: adenine (A), thymine (T), cytosine (C), and guanine (G). Because of differences in size and shape, adenine always pairs with thymine (A-T) and cytosine always pairs with guanine (C-G). These paired, or *complementary,* bases fit together like two pieces of a puzzle.

The order of the nucleotides in DNA is a code that carries information. The DNA code is read like a book. *Genes* are segments of DNA that are organized and carried on the chromosomes. The thousands of genes arranged in each chromosome are the same in each cell, and relate to particular traits, such as eye color, blood type, and handedness. Each gene has a starting point and an ending point, with the DNA code being read in one direction. The bases A, T, C, and G form the alphabet of the code. The code stores information about which proteins the cells should build. The types of proteins your body makes help to determine your traits.

10 Apply Place boxes around the bases that pair with each other.

Adenine (A) — P S A base

Thymine (T) — P S T base

Cytosine (C) — P S C base

Guanine (G) — P S G base

11 Devise The bases are often referred to simply by their initials—A, T, C, and G. The phrase "all tigers can growl" may help you remember them. Think of another phrase that uses words starting with A, T, C, and G that could help you remember the bases. Write your phrase below.

_____

_____

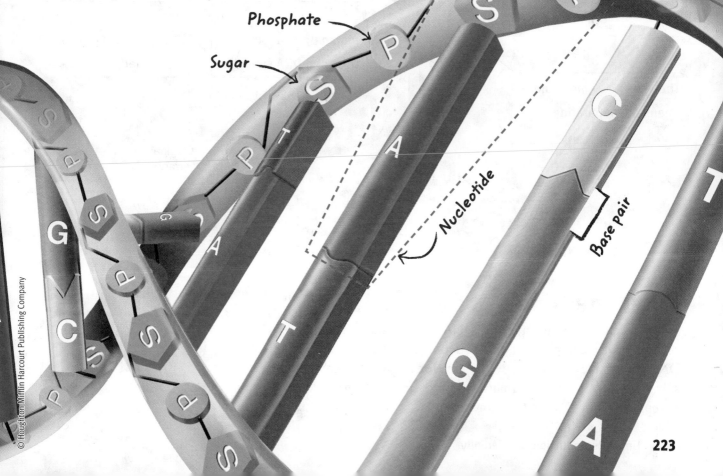

Phosphate

Sugar

Nucleotide

Base pair

How are copies of DNA made?

The cell is able to make copies of DNA molecules through a process known as **replication**. During replication, the two strands of DNA separate, almost like two threads in a string being unwound. The bases on each side of the molecule are used as a pattern for a new strand. As the bases on the original molecule are exposed, complementary nucleotides are added. For example, an exposed base containing adenine attaches to a nucleotide containing thymine. When replication is complete, there are two identical DNA molecules. Each new DNA molecule is made of one strand of old DNA and one strand of new DNA.

Visualize It!

12 Apply Fill in the blanks to complete the labels on this model of replicating DNA.

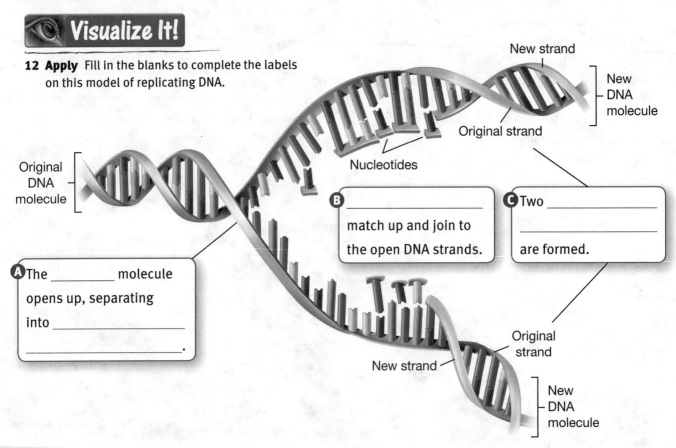

New strand

New DNA molecule

Original strand

Nucleotides

Original DNA molecule

B _____ match up and join to the open DNA strands.

C Two _____ _____ are formed.

A The _____ molecule opens up, separating into _____ _____.

New strand

Original strand

New DNA molecule

When are copies of DNA made?

Before a cell divides, it copies the DNA so that each new daughter cell will have a complete set of instructions. Our cells can replicate DNA in just a few hours. How? Replication begins in many places along the DNA strand. So, many groups of proteins are working to replicate your DNA at the same time.

Mutation

What are mutations?

Changes in the number, type, or order of bases on a piece of DNA are known as **mutations**. Sometimes, a base is left out. This kind of change is known as a *deletion*. Or, an extra base might be added. This kind of change is an *insertion*. The most common mutation happens when one base replaces another. This kind of change is known as a *substitution*.

How do mutations happen? Given the large number of bases in an organism's DNA, it is not surprising that random errors can occur during replication. However, DNA can also be damaged by physical or chemical agents called *mutagens*. Ultraviolet light and the chemicals in cigarette smoke are examples of mutagens.

Cells make proteins that can fix errors in DNA. But sometimes a mistake isn't corrected, and it becomes part of the genetic code. Mutations to DNA may be beneficial, neutral, or harmful. A *genetic disorder* results from mutations that harm the normal function of a cell. Some of these disorders, such as Tay-Sachs disease and sickle-cell anemia, are *inherited*, or passed on from parent to offspring. Other genetic disorders result from mutations that occur during a person's lifetime. Most cancers fall into this category.

Visualize It!

13 Apply Place a check mark in the box to indicate which type of mutation is being shown.

Original sequence

Ⓐ

☐ deletion   ☐ insertion   ☐ substitution

Ⓑ

☐ deletion   ☐ insertion   ☐ substitution

Ⓒ

☐ deletion   ☐ insertion   ☐ substitution

This snake has albinism, a condition in which the body cannot make the pigments that give color to the skin and eyes.

14 Explain Albinism is an inherited genetic disorder. Explain what is meant by "inherited genetic disorder."

_____

_____

_____

_____

ProteinFactory

What is the role of DNA and RNA in building proteins?

Imagine that you are baking cookies. You have a big cookbook that contains the recipe. If you take the book with you into the kitchen, you risk damaging the book and losing important instructions. You only need one page from the book, so you copy the recipe on a piece of paper and leave the cookbook on the shelf. This process is similar to the way that the cell uses DNA to build proteins. First, some of the information in the DNA is copied to a separate molecule called ribonucleic acid, or **RNA**. Then, the copy is used to build proteins. Not all the instructions are needed all the time. In eukaryotes, the DNA is protected inside the cell's nucleus.

Like DNA, RNA has a sugar-phosphate backbone and the bases adenine (A), guanine (G), and cytosine (C). But instead of thymine (T), RNA contains the base uracil (U). Also, the sugar found in RNA is different from the one in DNA. There are three types of RNA: messenger RNA, ribosomal RNA, and transfer RNA. Each type of RNA has a special role in making proteins.

Active Reading **15 Identify** As you read, number the sentences that describe the steps of transcription.

Transcription: The Information in DNA Is Copied to Messenger RNA

When a cell needs a set of instructions for making a protein, it first makes an RNA copy of the necessary section of DNA. This process is called *transcription*. Transcription involves DNA and messenger RNA (mRNA). Only individual genes are transcribed, not the whole DNA molecule. During transcription, DNA is used as a template to make a complementary strand of mRNA. The DNA opens up where the gene is located. Then RNA bases match up to complementary bases on the DNA template. When transcription is complete, the mRNA is released and the DNA molecule closes.

RNA uses the genetic information stored in DNA to build proteins.

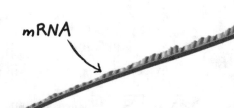

Cell nucleus

mRNA

A During transcription, DNA is used as a template to make a complementary strand of mRNA. In eukaryotes, the mRNA then exits the nucleus.

Translation: The Information in Messenger RNA Is Used to Build Proteins

Once the mRNA has been made, it is fed through a protein assembly line within a ribosome. A **ribosome** is a cell organelle made of ribosomal RNA (rRNA) and protein. As mRNA passes through the ribosome, transfer RNA (tRNA) molecules deliver amino acids to the ribosome. Each group of three bases on the mRNA strand codes for one amino acid. So the genetic code determines the order in which amino acids are brought to the ribosome. The amino acids join together to form a protein. The process of making proteins from RNA is called *translation*.

B A ribosome attaches to an mRNA strand at the beginning of a gene.

tRNA

Amino acid

Ribosome

C A tRNA molecule enters the ribosome. Three bases on the tRNA match up to 3 complementary bases on the mRNA strand. The bases on the mRNA strand determine which tRNA and amino acid move into the ribosome.

Chain of amino acids

Chain of amino acids released

D The tRNA transfers its amino acid to a growing chain. Then, the tRNA is released. The ribosome moves down the mRNA and the process repeats.

E Once the ribosome reaches the end of the gene, the chain of amino acids is released.

16 Apply Fill in the table below by placing check marks in the appropriate boxes and writing the product of transcription and translation.

Process	What molecules are involved?				What is the product?
Transcription	☐ DNA	☐ mRNA	☐ tRNA	☐ ribosome	
Translation	☐ DNA	☐ mRNA	☐ tRNA	☐ ribosome	

Visual Summary

To complete this summary, fill in the blanks with the correct word or phrase. Then use the key below to check your answers. You can use this page to review the main concepts of the lesson.

DNA Structure and Function

DNA has a double-helix shape and is made up of nucleotides.

17 The four bases in DNA nucleotides are

_____

_____

_____ .

The cell can make copies of DNA.

18 DNA replication happens before cells _____ .

DNA can mutate.

19 Three types of DNA mutations are _____

_____

_____ .

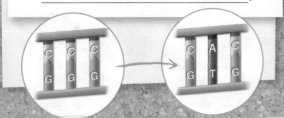

DNA and RNA are involved in making proteins.

20 The two processes involved in making proteins from the DNA code are:

21 Explain How could a mutation in the DNA affect what proteins are made by the cell? Summarize the evidence to support your claim.

Lesson Review

Vocabulary

Fill in the blanks with the term that best completes the following sentences.

1 A(n) _____ of DNA consists of a sugar, a phosphate, and a nitrogen-containing base.

2 A(n) _____ is a change in the base sequence of a DNA molecule.

Key Concepts

Draw a line to connect the following scientists to their contributions to our understanding of DNA.

3 Erwin Chargaff

4 Rosalind Franklin and Maurice Wilkins

5 James Watson and Francis Crick

A took x-ray images of DNA molecule

B proposed a double-helix model of DNA

C found that the amount of adenine equals the amount of thymine and that the amount of guanine equals the amount of cytosine

6 Identify How does the structure of RNA differ from the structure of DNA?

_____

_____

7 Identify When does DNA replication occur?

_____

_____

8 Describe Name the three types of RNA and list their roles in making proteins.

_____

_____

9 Identify What can cause DNA mutations?

_____

_____

Critical Thinking

Use this diagram to answer the following questions.

a A C T C C T G A A
b

10 Describe What is the sequence of bases on DNA strand *b*, from left to right?

_____

11 Apply This segment of DNA is transcribed to form a complementary strand of mRNA. The mRNA then undergoes translation. How many amino acids would the RNA code for?

_____

12 Claims • Evidence • Reasoning After many cell divisions, a segment of DNA has more base pairs than it originally did. Why do you think this happens? Provide evidence for your claim and explain your reasoning.

_____

_____

_____

13 Explain Why must DNA replicate?

_____

14 Explain Considering that chromosomes are structures that carry genetic material, what role do chromosomes and genes play in inheritance and the determination of traits? Construct an explanation with evidence to support your answer.

_____

_____

_____

My Notes

Identifying Variables

When you are analyzing or designing a scientific experiment, it is important to identify the variables in the experiment. Usually, an experiment is designed to discover how changing one variable affects another variable. In a scientific investigation, the independent variable is the factor that is purposely changed. The dependent variable is the factor that changes in response to the independent variable.

Tutorial

Use the following strategies to help you identify the variables in an experiment.

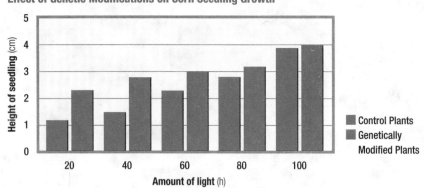

Summary: We genetically modified corn plants to increase growth in low-light conditions.

Effect of Genetic Modifications on Corn Seedling Growth

Control Plants
Genetically Modified Plants

Reading a Summary
The published results of an experiment usually include a brief summary. You should be able to identify the variables from it. In the summary to the left, the independent variable is the DNA of the corn plants, and the dependent variable is the height of the plants.

Analyzing a Graph Making a graph can be a very effective way to show the relationship between variables. For a line graph, the independent variable is usually shown on the *x*-axis, or the horizontal axis. The dependent variable is usually shown on the *y*-axis, or the vertical axis.

Describing the Data When you read a graph, describing the information in complete sentences can help you to identify the variables. For example, you could write, "In the first 80 hours, the genetically modified corn plants grew much more quickly than the control plants grew. But by 100 hours, both kinds of plants were about the same height. This shows that the effect of the independent variable was greatest during the first 80 hours of plant growth."

Identifying the Effects of Variables Look closely at the graph. Notice that the genetically modified seedlings grew more quickly than the control seedlings, but the effects were greatest in the early part of the experiment. A variable's effect is not always constant throughout an experiment.

You Try It!

The passage below describes the process of gel electrophoresis.
Use the description to answer the question that follows.

During gel electrophoresis, DNA is broken into separate fragments.
These fragments are added to a gel. When an electric current is
applied to the gel, the fragments travel different distances through
the gel. The size of the DNA fragments determines how far they
travel. Smaller fragments travel farther than larger fragments do.
Scientists can use these data to identify unknown samples of DNA.

1 Reading a Summary Identify the variables described in
the passage.

_____

_____

**The graph below shows the results of DNA
analysis using gel electrophoresis. Look at the
graph, and answer the questions that follow.**

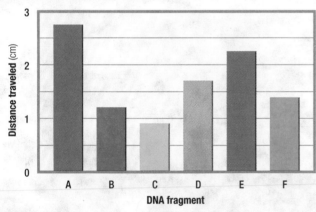

Distance Traveled by DNA Fragments

2 Analyzing a Graph Which variables are shown
in the graph? Circle the axis that shows the
dependent variable.

_____

_____

3 Analyzing the Data What is the relationship
between the size of the DNA fragments and the
distance they traveled? Circle the DNA fragment
that is the smallest.

_____

_____

_____

4 Applying Mathematics Calculate the average
distance that the DNA fragments traveled. How
much farther than the average distance did the
smallest DNA fragment travel?

5 Applying Concepts Why is it important to limit
the number of variables in an experiment?

_____

_____

_____

_____

Take It Home

**With an adult, plan and conduct a simple
experiment that includes an independent
variable and a dependent variable. Record
your results and graph your data if possible.
Then share your results with the class.**

Biotechnology

S7L3.c Selective breeding and inherited traits

ESSENTIAL QUESTION

How does biotechnology impact our world?

By the end of this lesson, you should be able to explain how biotechnology impacts human life and the world around us.

These glowing bands contain fragments of DNA that have been treated with a special chemical. This chemical glows under ultraviolet light, allowing scientists to see the DNA.

🧠 Engage Your Brain

1 Predict Fill in the blanks with the word or phrase you think correctly completes the following sentences.

A medical researcher might study DNA in order to learn _____

_____

_____.

A crime scene investigator might study DNA in order to learn _____

_____

_____.

2 Apply *GMO* stands for "genetically modified organism." Write a caption to accompany the following photo.

_____

_____

_____

📖 Active Reading

3 Apply Use context clues to write your own definition for the words *inserted* and *technique*.

Example sentence
Using special technologies, a gene from one organism can be <u>inserted</u> into the DNA of another.

inserted:

_____

_____

Example sentence
Cloning is a <u>technique</u> in which the genetic information of an organism is copied.

technique:

_____

_____

Vocabulary Terms

- **biotechnology**
- **selective breeding**
- **genetic engineering**
- **clone**

4 Apply As you learn the definition of each vocabulary term in this lesson, create your own definition or sketch to help you remember the meaning of the term.

BioTECHNOLOGY

Protective clothing keeps this geneticist safe as he works with infectious particles.

This scientist works inside of a greenhouse. He breeds potato plants.

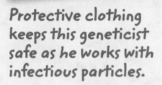

Think Outside the Book

5 Research Research careers in biotechnology. Choose a career that you might like to have and share it with your class. You may choose to present your findings in one of the following ways:
- a poster
- a computer presentation
- a play
- a short essay

What is biotechnology?

A forensic scientist makes copies of DNA from a crime scene. A botanist breeds flowers for their bright red blooms. A geneticist works to place a human gene into the DNA of bacteria. What do these processes have in common? They are all examples of biotechnology. **Biotechnology** is the use and application of living things and biological processes. In the past 40 years, new technologies have allowed scientists to directly change DNA. But biotechnology is not a new scientific field. For thousands of years, humans have been breeding plants and animals and using bacteria and yeast to ferment foods. These, too, are examples of biotechnology.

Active Reading **6 Identify** Name three examples of biotechnology.

_____

_____

_____

7 Infer If you wanted to produce a dog that nobody (or at least very few people) would be allergic to, how would you go about doing this? Create a poster or slide show in which you describe the way humans control the inheritance of certain traits in organisms by means of selective breeding and outline the steps required to breed a hypoallergenic dog.

Different dog breeds are produced by selective breeding.

What are some applications of biotechnology?

Biotechnology processes fall into some broad categories. Selective breeding, genetic engineering, and cloning are some of the most common techniques.

Selective Breeding

For thousands of years, humans have been carefully selecting and breeding certain plants and animals that have desirable traits. Over many generations, horses have gotten faster, pigs have gotten leaner, and corn has become sweeter. **Selective breeding** is the process of selecting and breeding organisms that have certain desired traits. Unlike *natural selection*, which takes place naturally, selective breeding occurs through human intervention. Selective breeding is also known as *artificial selection*.

Selective breeding can be successful as long as the desirable traits are controlled by genes. Animal and plant breeders select for alleles, which are different versions of a gene. The alleles being selected must already be present in the population. People do not change DNA during selective breeding. Instead, they cause certain alleles to become more common in a population. The different dog breeds are a good example of selective breeding. All dogs share a common ancestor, the wolf. However, thousands of years of selection by humans have produced dogs with a variety of characteristics.

Visualize It!

These vegetables have been developed through selective breeding. Their common ancestor is the mustard plant.

kale

broccoli

cabbage

cauliflower

Brussels sprouts

8 Infer Why might farmers use selective breeding to develop different types of vegetables? State your claim and explain your reasoning.

_____

_____

_____

_____

_____

_____

_____

Genetic Engineering

Within the past 40 years, it has become possible to directly change the DNA of an organism. **Genetic engineering** is the process in which a piece of DNA is modified for use in research, medicine, agriculture, or industry. The DNA that is engineered often codes for a certain trait of interest. Scientists can isolate a segment of DNA, change it in some way, and return it to the organism. Or, scientists can take a segment of DNA from one species and transfer it to the DNA of an organism from another species.

Active Reading 9 **Describe** For what purposes can genetic engineering be used?

_____

_____

_____

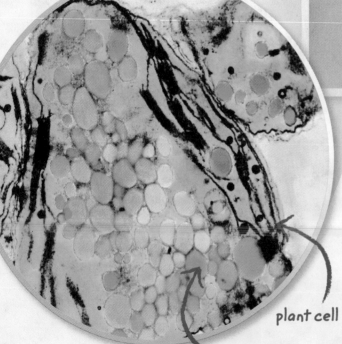

Scientists have disabled a gene in the mouse on the right. As a result, this mouse cannot control how much food it eats.

These genetically modified plant cells produce tiny, biodegradable plastic pellets. The pellets are then collected to make plastic products.

plant cell

plastic pellets

10 Infer Traditional plastics are made from petroleum, a nonrenewable resource. What benefit could plastic made by plants have over traditional plastic? Explain your reasoning.

_____

_____

_____

_____

_____

_____

_____

Cloning

A **clone** is an organism, cell, or piece of genetic material that is genetically identical to the one from which it was derived. Cloning has been used to make copies of small traces of DNA found at crime scenes or on ancient artifacts. Also, cloning can be used to copy segments of DNA for genetic engineering.

In 1996, scientists cloned the DNA from one sheep's body cell to produce another sheep named Dolly. The ability to clone a sheep, which is a mammal, raised many concerns about the future uses of cloning, because humans are also mammals. It is important that people understand the science of genetics. Only then can we make informed decisions about how and when the technology should be used.

Dolly was cloned from a body cell of an adult sheep.

11 Apply Review each of the examples of biotechnology below. Then classify each as selective breeding, genetic engineering, or cloning.

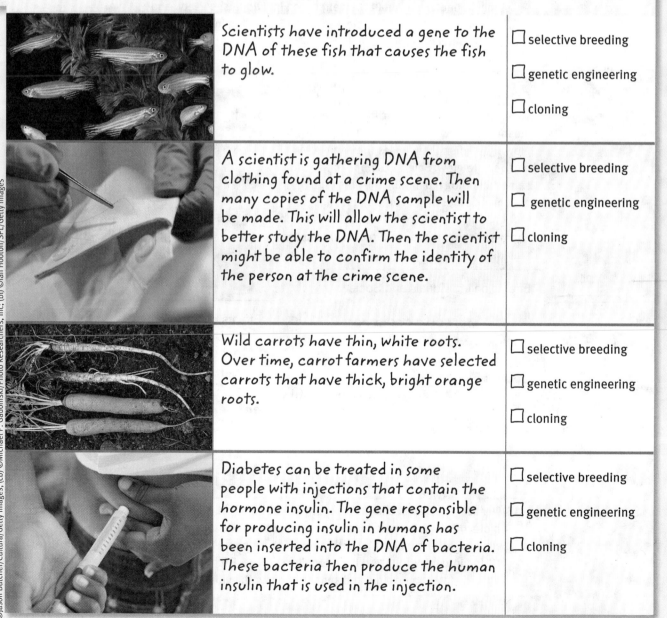

Scientists have introduced a gene to the DNA of these fish that causes the fish to glow.

☐ selective breeding

☐ genetic engineering

☐ cloning

A scientist is gathering DNA from clothing found at a crime scene. Then many copies of the DNA sample will be made. This will allow the scientist to better study the DNA. Then the scientist might be able to confirm the identity of the person at the crime scene.

☐ selective breeding

☐ genetic engineering

☐ cloning

Wild carrots have thin, white roots. Over time, carrot farmers have selected carrots that have thick, bright orange roots.

☐ selective breeding

☐ genetic engineering

☐ cloning

Diabetes can be treated in some people with injections that contain the hormone insulin. The gene responsible for producing insulin in humans has been inserted into the DNA of bacteria. These bacteria then produce the human insulin that is used in the injection.

☐ selective breeding

☐ genetic engineering

☐ cloning

Feel the IMPACT!

How does biotechnology impact our world?

Scientists are aware that there are many ethical, legal, and social issues that arise from the ability to use and change living things. Biotechnology can impact both our society and our environment. We must decide how and when it is acceptable to use biotechnology. The examples that follow show some concerns that might be raised during a classroom debate about biotechnology.

12 Evaluate Read the first two examples of biotechnology and what students had to say about their effects on individuals, society, and the environment. Then complete Example 3 by filling in questions or possible effects of the technology.

Example 1

A Glowing Mosquito?

This is the larva of a genetically engineered mosquito. Its DNA includes a gene from a glowing jellyfish that causes the engineered mosquito to glow. Scientists hope to use this same technology to modify the mosquito's genome in other ways. For example, it is thought that the DNA of the mosquito could be changed so that the mosquito could not spread malaria.

Effects on Individuals and Society

"If the mosquito could be engineered so that it does not spread malaria, many lives could be saved."

Effects on Environment

"Mosquitoes are a food source for birds and fish. Are there health risks to animals that eat genetically modified mosquitoes?"

Think Outside the Book (Inquiry)

13 Debate As a class, choose a current event that involves biotechnology. Prepare for a debate about the benefits and risks of this technology by gathering evidence about it. Divide into two groups taking opposing stances. Each group should state their claims and support them with evidence.

© Houghton Mifflin Harcourt Publishing Company • Image Credits: ©Sinclair Stammers/Photo Researchers, Inc.

Example 2

Cloning the Gaur

The gaur is an endangered species. In 2001, a gaur was successfully cloned. The clone, named Noah, died of a bacterial infection 2 days after birth.

Effects on Individuals and Society

"How will we decide when it is appropriate to clone other types of organisms?"

Effects on Environment

"Cloning could help increase small populations of endangered species like the gaur and save them from extinction."

Example 3

Tough Plants!

Much of the corn and soybeans grown in the United States is genetically engineered. The plants have bacterial genes that make them more resistant to plant-eating insects.

Effects on Individuals and Society

Effects on Environment

Visual Summary

To complete this summary, circle the correct word or phrase. Then use the key below to check your answers. You can use this page to review the main concepts of the lesson.

Biotechnology

Biotechnology is the use of living things and biological processes.

14 Modern biotechnology techniques can change an organism's DNA / environment.

Selective breeding, genetic engineering, and cloning are three types of biotechnology.

15 The DNA of the mouse on the right has been modified through a technique called cloning / genetic engineering.

Biotechnology impacts individuals, society, and the environment.

16 Creating a clone / gene of an endangered species could impact the environment.

Answers: 14 DNA; 15 genetic engineering; 16 clone

17 Compare Both selective breeding and genetic engineering produce organisms that have traits that are different from the original organism. Explain how these two techniques differ. How are they different from natural selection?

Lesson Review

Vocabulary

In your own words, define the following terms.

1 biotechnology

_____

_____

_____

2 selective breeding

_____

_____

_____

3 clone

_____

_____

_____

Key Concepts

4 Identify Wheat has been bred by farmers for thousands of years to improve its ability to be ground into flour. This is an example of what kind of biotechnology?

A selective breeding

B genetic engineering

C cloning

D PCR

5 Identify Which of the following statements correctly describes why society must carefully consider the use of biotechnology?

A Biotechnology is a relatively new scientific field.

B Biotechnology can impact individuals and the environment.

C The methods of genetic engineering are not well understood.

D Selective breeding is an example of biotechnology.

Critical Thinking

Use this graph to answer the following questions.

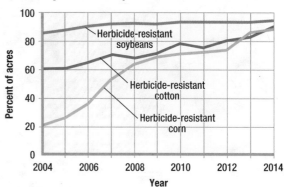

Genetically Modified Crops Grown in the United States

Source: USDA, 2009

6 Analyze In 2004, what percentage of soybean crops in the United States were genetically engineered to be herbicide resistant?

_____

7 Analyze From 2004 to 2014, which genetically engineered crop had the greatest increase in acreage? Explain your reasoning.

_____

_____

_____

_____

_____

8 Claims • Evidence • Reasoning Some salmon have been genetically engineered to grow more quickly. The salmon are raised in pens set in rivers or in the sea. What impacts do you think these salmon might have on society and the environment? Summarize the evidence to support your claim and explain your reasoning.

_____

_____

_____

_____

_____

_____

My Notes

Unit 3 Big Idea > Characteristics from parents are passed to offspring in predictable ways.

Lesson 1
ESSENTIAL QUESTION
How do cells divide?

Relate the process of mitosis to its function in single-celled and multicellular organisms.

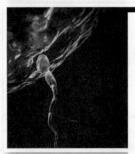

Lesson 2
ESSENTIAL QUESTION
How do cells divide for sexual reproduction?

Describe the process of meiosis and its role in sexual reproduction.

Lesson 3
ESSENTIAL QUESTION
How do organisms reproduce?

Describe sexual and asexual reproduction, and list the advantages and disadvantages of each.

Lesson 4
ESSENTIAL QUESTION
How are traits inherited?

Analyze the inheritance of traits in individuals.

Lesson 5
ESSENTIAL QUESTION
How are patterns of inheritance studied?

Explain how patterns of heredity can be predicted by Punnett squares and pedigrees.

Lesson 6
ESSENTIAL QUESTION
What is DNA?

Describe the structure and main functions of DNA.

Lesson 7
ESSENTIAL QUESTION
How does biotechnology impact our world?

Explain how biotechnology impacts human life and the world around us.

Think Outside the Book

2 Synthesize Choose one of these activities to help synthesize what you have learned in this unit.

☐ Using what you learned in lessons 2, 3, 4, and 6, develop a computer slideshow presentation to explain how genes are passed down from parents to offspring.

☐ Using what you learned in lessons 1–7, develop a poster showing the different processes in which DNA is duplicated.

Connect ESSENTIAL QUESTIONS
Lessons 1 and 2

1 Synthesize How are meiosis and mitosis similar? How are they different?

_____

_____

_____

Unit 3 Review

Name _____

Vocabulary

Fill in each blank with the term that best completes the following sentences.

1 The genetic material of all cells is _____.

2 A(n) _____ compares or shows the relationship between two quantities.

3 A(n) _____ is an organism, cell, or piece of genetic material that is genetically identical to the one from which it was derived.

4 _____ is the process of cell division that results in the formation of cells with half the usual number of chromosomes.

5 The type of reproduction that results in offspring that are genetically identical to the single parent is known as _____ reproduction.

Key Concepts

Read each question below, and circle the best answer.

6 A mouse breeder crosses a black-furred mouse with a white-furred mouse. All of the offspring have gray fur. What kind of inheritance pattern explains how fur color is inherited in mice?

A sex-linked

B codominance

C complete dominance

D incomplete dominance

7 What process does a multicellular organism use to replace its damaged body cells?

A mitosis

B meiosis

C replication

D transcription

8 The following diagram shows one way a mutation can form during DNA replication.

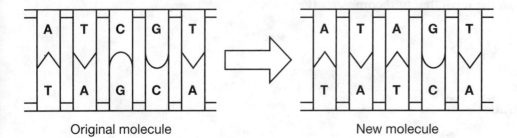

Original molecule   New molecule

What kind of mutation has occurred during the DNA replication shown in the diagram?

A deletion

B insertion

C substitution

D transcription

9 How does a sex cell differ from a body cell?

A A sex cell does not contain chromosomes.

B A sex cell contains homologous chromosomes.

C A sex cell has the same number of chromosomes as a body cell.

D A sex cell has half the amount of genetic material as a body cell.

10 How do the chromosomes at the end of meiosis I compare with the chromosomes at the end of meiosis II?

A Chromosomes have one chromatid at the end of both meiosis I and meiosis II.

B Chromosomes have two chromatids at the end of both meiosis I and meiosis II.

C Chromosomes have one chromatid at the end of meiosis I and two chromatids at the end of meiosis II.

D Chromosomes have two chromatids at the end of meiosis I and one chromatid at the end of meiosis II.

Name _____

11 The following table shows the percentage of each base in a sample of DNA.

Base	Percentage of total bases
A	12%
C	38%
T	12%
G	38%

Which of the following statements explains the data in the table?

A A pairs only with C, and T pairs only with G.

B A pairs only with T, and C pairs only with G.

C DNA is made up of nucleotides that consist of a sugar, a phosphate, and a base.

D The bases in DNA are arranged in the interior of a double helix, like rungs of a ladder.

12 Which of the following is an advantage of asexual reproduction?

A It is a slow process. **C** The organism can increase in number quickly.

B Two parents are needed. **D** It introduces genetic diversity in the offspring.

13 The diagram below shows a cross that is similar to one of Mendel's pea plant crosses.

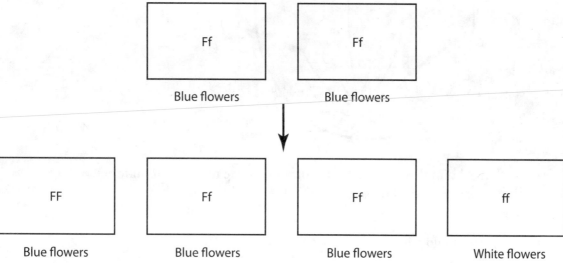

How is blue flower color inherited in the cross shown?

A as a codominant trait **C** as a dominant trait

B as a recessive trait **D** as an incompletely dominant trait

14 Which of the following statements correctly describes the function of cell division in unicellular organisms?

A Cell division allows the organism to grow.

B Cell division allows the organism to reproduce.

C Cell division allows the organism to produce sex cells.

D Cell division allows the organism to repair damage to the cell.

15 Which statement about zygotes, which form by fertilization, is correct?

A Zygotes have a full set of chromosomes, receiving half from each parent.

B Zygotes have half the set of chromosomes from one parent only.

C Zygotes have two full sets of chromosomes, one set from each parent.

D Zygotes have half the set of chromosomes, one-fourth from each parent.

16 The diagram shows a cell during the anaphase stage of mitosis.

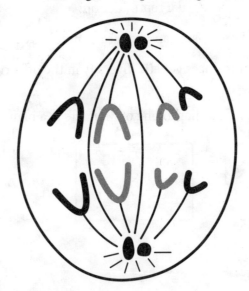

Justin's teacher showed him this slide of a stage of mitosis. He noticed the slide contains two homologous pairs of chromosomes. How would this diagram be different if it showed anaphase I of meiosis instead of anaphase of mitosis?

A Each chromosome would still have two chromatids.

B The chromosomes would look the same as in mitosis.

C You would be able to see DNA in the chromosomes during meiosis.

D Homologous chromosomes would be moving to the same end of the cell.

17 If the sequence of bases in one strand of DNA is ATTCGAC, what will be the base sequence on the strand that is formed during replication?

A ATTCGAC   **C** UAAGCUG

B TAAGCTG   **D** AUUCGAC

Critical Thinking

Answer the following questions in the space provided.

18 Describe the major steps of gene transcription and translation. What molecules and organelles are involved in the processes?

_____

_____

_____

_____

_____

19 Jake made a pedigree to trace the traits of straight and curly hair in his family.

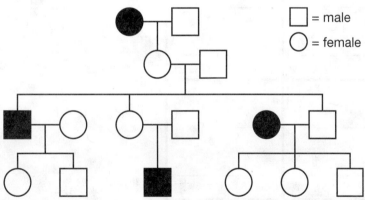

☐ = male

○ = female

A shaded circle or square in Jake's pedigree represents a person with straight hair. Is straight hair controlled by a dominant allele or a recessive allele? What led to your conclusion? How do you know that straight hair is not sex-linked?

_____

_____

_____

_____

_____

_____

20 Rachel's class is debating the impact of biotechnology on people, society, and the environment. Give one example of how biotechnology can have a positive impact. Give one example of how biotechnology can have a negative impact.

_____

_____

_____

_____

Connect ESSENTIAL QUESTIONS
Lessons 4 and 5

Answer the following question in the space provided.

21 The following diagram shows a Punnett square made to predict the earlobe shape of the offspring of two parents.

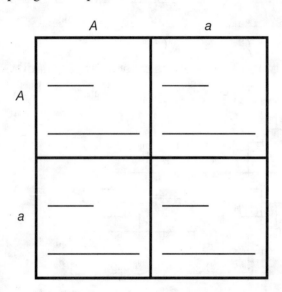

A stands for the trait of free-hanging earlobes and *a* stands for the trait of attached earlobes. Write the genotype of each offspring on the first line in each box of the Punnett square. What will be the phenotype of each offspring? Write either *attached* or *free-hanging* on the second line in each box. Describe how the trait of free-hanging earlobes is inherited. What is the expected ratio of free-hanging earlobes to attached earlobes in the offspring?

_____

_____

_____

_____

_____

_____

Human Body Systems

Big Idea

The human body is made up of systems that have different functions, and these systems interact to carry out life processes.

S7L2., S7L2.c

A brain scan can show whether the brain is functioning normally.

What do you think?

Technology like the MRI scanner allows us to study the living body. How does the living body work? As you explore the unit, gather evidence to help you state and support claims to answer this question.

A patient must stay still to get an accurate MRI scan.

CITIZEN SCIENCE

Muscles at Work

Design a test for muscle endurance or strength.

① Define The Problem

Unlike many things that wear out with use, our muscles actually get stronger the more often they are used. Doing different kinds of exercises helps different groups of muscles. But how can you tell if you are improving? How can you tell how strong a group of muscles are?

Muscles become larger as they become stronger.

Strength moves like this hold take practice and training.

© Houghton Mifflin Harcourt Publishing Company • Image Credits: (bkgd) ©Floresco Productions/Corbis; (tr) ©Ron Chapple Stock/Alamy

② Think About It

Design a test for a group of muscles.

Choose a group of muscles that you would like to work with. Then, come up with one or two simple exercises that can be done to show either how strong the muscles are or how well they are able to work continuously. Place a time limit on your tests so that the tests don't take too long.

Check off the points below as you use them to design your test.

☐ The kind of action the muscles can do.

☐ To do the test safely, remember to isolate the group of muscles. (Research how to do an exercise safely.)

☐ The equipment you will need for the test.

③ Plan and Test Your Design

A Write out how you will conduct your test in the space below. Check your plan with your teacher before proceeding.

_____
_____
_____
_____
_____

B Conduct the test on yourself. Have a classmate time you, help you count, or make any other measurements that you might need help with. Briefly state your findings.

_____
_____
_____
_____
_____

Take It Home

Do the same exercises at home for two weeks. Do strength training exercises every second day to avoid injury. Do continuous movement exercises, such as running, every day. Then, conduct your test again. See if there is any improvement. Report your findings to the class. See *ScienceSaurus*® for more information about muscular systems.

Introduction to Body Systems

ESSENTIAL QUESTION

How do the body systems interact to maintain homeostasis?

By the end of this lesson, you should be able to describe the functions of the human body systems, including how they interact to maintain homeostasis.

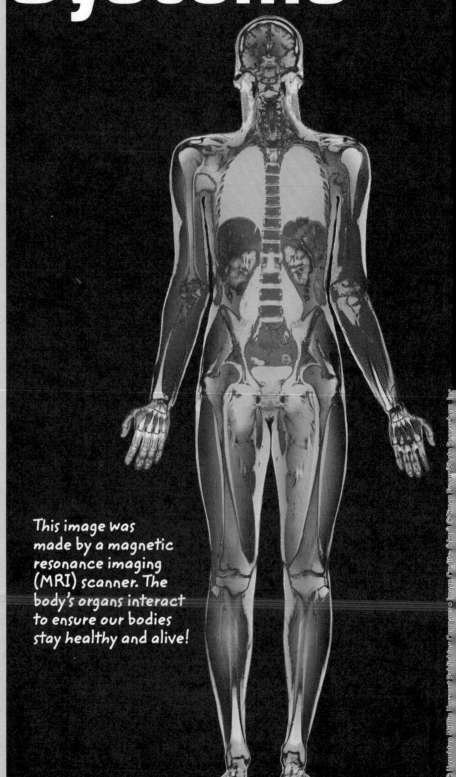

This image was made by a magnetic resonance imaging (MRI) scanner. The body's organs interact to ensure our bodies stay healthy and alive!

S7L2.c Body systems interactions

Lesson Labs

Quick Labs
- Balancing Act
- Body Systems: Their Structures and Functions

Engage Your Brain

1 Predict Check T or F to show whether you think each statement is true or false.

T   F

☐ ☐ Your muscles provide a framework that supports and protects your body.

☐ ☐ When you breathe in and out, you're using your lungs.

☐ ☐ Your nervous system gets rid of wastes from your body.

☐ ☐ When you eat food, it enters your digestive system.

2 Identify Draw a diagram of your body showing at least four organs. As you read the lesson, write down the organ system that each organ is a part of.

Active Reading

3 Synthesize You can often define an unknown word if you know the meaning of its word parts. Use the word parts and sentence below to make an educated guess about the meaning of the word *homeostasis*.

Greek word	Meaning
homoios	same
stasis	standing

Example sentence

In order to maintain <u>homeostasis</u>, the cardiovascular system and the respiratory system interact to move oxygen-carrying blood around the body.

homeostasis:

_____

_____

_____

_____

Vocabulary Term

- **homeostasis**

4 Apply As you learn the definition of the vocabulary term in this lesson, make a sketch that shows the meaning of the term or an example of that term. Next to your drawing, write your own definition of the term.

What do the body systems do?

Humans and other organisms need to get energy. They need to use energy to run their bodies and move. They need to reproduce. They need to get rid of waste and protect their bodies. Body systems, also called *organ systems*, help organisms do all of these things. They interact to carry out life processes, and they also coordinate all the functions of a body.

Groups of organs that interact form body systems. Nerves detect a stimulus in the environment and send a signal through the spinal cord to the brain. The brain sends a signal to respond. Without all the parts, the system would not work. Some organs work in more than one organ system.

Active Reading 5 **Identify** As you read about body systems on these pages, underline the main function of each body system.

Inside Out

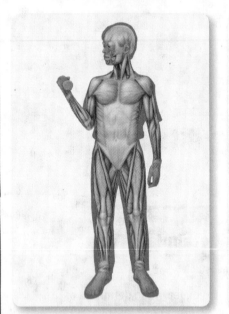

The muscular system allows movement of body parts. It interacts with the skeletal system to help you move.

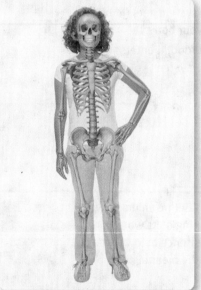

The skeletal system is made up of bones, ligaments, and cartilage. It supports the body and protects important organs. It also makes blood cells.

The respiratory system gathers oxygen from the environment and gets rid of carbon dioxide from the body. The exchange occurs in the lungs.

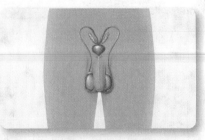

The male reproductive system produces sperm and delivers it to the female reproductive system.

The female reproductive system produces eggs and nourishes a developing fetus.

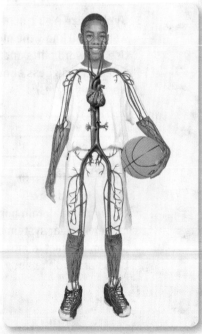

The cardiovascular system moves blood through the body. The heart is the pump for this system. Blood flows through blood vessels.

6 Analyze Look closely at the body systems shown on these pages. Then circle the two parts that make up the immune system and explain how this system of the body interacts with other systems.

_____

_____

The lymphatic system returns leaked fluid back to the blood. As a major part of the immune system, it has cells that help get rid of invading bacteria and viruses.

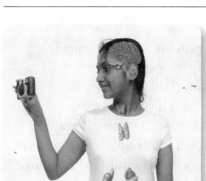

The endocrine system makes chemical messages. These messages help to regulate conditions inside the body. They also influence growth and development.

The integumentary system is the protective covering of the body. It includes the skin, hair, and nails. As part of the immune system, the skin acts as a barrier that protects the body from infection.

The excretory system gets rid of the body's wastes. The urinary system, shown here, removes wastes from blood. The skin, lungs, and digestive system also remove wastes from the body.

The digestive system breaks down food into nutrients that can be used by the body. The stomach breaks down food into tiny pieces. Nutrients are absorbed in the small intestine.

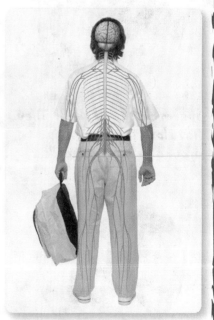

The nervous system collects information and responds to it by sending electrical messages. This information may come from outside or inside the body. The brain is the center of the nervous system.

A Closer Look

How are structure and function linked?

Even though animals may look very different on the outside, on the inside, their cells, tissues, and organs look very similar. This is because these structures do the same basic job. For example, a frog's heart, a bird's heart, and a human's heart all have the same function, to pump blood around the body. They are all made of the same type of muscle tissue, which is made up of the same type of muscle cells. The structure of the hearts is similar, too. Though their shape may be a little different from each other, they are all muscular pumps that push blood around the body.

The shapes and sizes of cells are related to their function. For example, sperm cells have long tails that are used to move. Nerve cells are long and thin to send messages long distances. Surface skin cells are broad and flat. The diagram below shows how skin cells form the skin, which covers and protects the body.

Skin is made up of different cells in many layers. The epidermis is the outer layer of skin. The dermis is the second layer of skin and contains glands, hair follicles, and blood vessels.

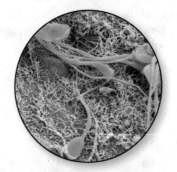

Sperm cells can "swim." They have long tails that whip around to move the cells.

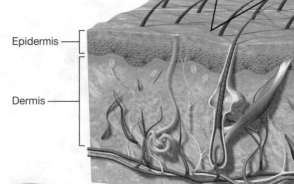

Epidermis

Dermis

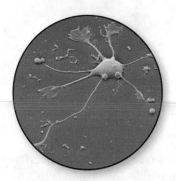

Nerve cells have long, thin branches to send electrical messages between the brain and far-away body parts.

Inquiry

7 Infer Muscle cells can get longer and shorter. How does this ability fit in with their job in the body? State your claim. Give examples to support your reasoning.

_____

_____

_____

_____

Watching the pitcher

- The endocrine system releases hormones to prepare the body for action.
- The eyes, part of the nervous system, see the ball coming. They send electrical messages to the brain.

Swinging the bat

- The brain sends electrical messages to the muscles.
- The bones and muscles grip the bat tightly.
- The eyes stay focused on the pitcher.
- The muscles contract to swing the arms.

Running the bases

- The muscles and bones help the legs move quickly.
- The heart of the cardiovascular system pumps quickly to move blood from the lungs to the body.
- The muscles use oxygen from the blood to keep moving.

© Houghton Mifflin Harcourt Publishing Company

How do body systems interact?

Our body systems can do a lot, but they can't work alone! Almost everything we need for our bodies to work properly requires many body systems to interact. For example, the nervous system may sense danger. The endocrine system releases hormones that cause the heart to beat faster to deliver more oxygen through the circulatory system to muscles. The muscular system and skeletal system interact to run away from danger.

Active Reading **8 Identify** As you read the captions on the left, underline examples of body systems interacting.

Body Systems Share Organs

Many organs are part of several body systems. Reproductive organs are part of the reproductive system and part of the endocrine system. The liver works in the digestive system, but it is also part of the excretory system. The heart is part of the muscular system and the cardiovascular system. Blood vessels, too, are shared. For example, blood vessels transport chemical messages from the endocrine system and cells from the lymphatic and cardiovascular systems.

Body Systems Communicate

There are two basic ways cells communicate: by electrical messages and by chemical messages. Nerve cells transfer information between the body and the spinal cord and brain. Nerves pass electrical messages from one cell to the next along the line. The endocrine system sends chemical messages through the bloodstream to certain cells.

9 Apply When you are finished running the bases, you are sweating and you feel thirsty. What body systems are interacting in this case?

_____

_____

_____

_____

Keeping the Balance

What is homeostasis?

Cells need certain conditions to work properly. They need food and oxygen and to have their wastes taken away. If body conditions were to change too much, cells would not be able to do their jobs. **Homeostasis** (hoh•mee•oh•STAY•sis) is the maintenance of a constant internal environment when outside conditions change. Responding to change allows all systems to work properly.

Responding to Change

If the external environment changes, body systems interact to keep conditions stable within the body. For example, if body cells were to get too cold, they would not work properly and they could die. So, if the brain senses the body temperature is getting too low, it tells the muscles to shiver. Shivering muscles release energy as heat, which warms the body. Your brain will also tell you to put on a sweater!

Maintaining a Balance

To maintain homeostasis, the body has to recognize that conditions are changing and then respond in the right way. In order to work, organ systems need to communicate properly. The electrical messages of the nervous system and chemical signals of the endocrine system tell the body what changes to make. If the body cannot respond properly to the internal messages or to an external change, a disease may develop.

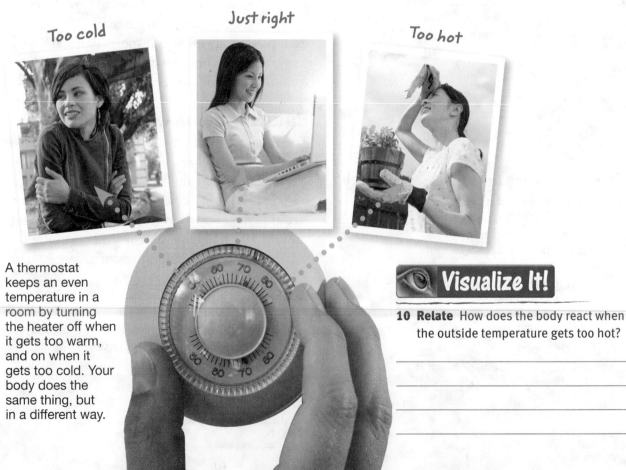

Too cold   Just right   Too hot

A thermostat keeps an even temperature in a room by turning the heater off when it gets too warm, and on when it gets too cold. Your body does the same thing, but in a different way.

Visualize It!

10 Relate How does the body react when the outside temperature gets too hot?

_____

_____

_____

What can go wrong with homeostasis?

If one body system does not work properly, other systems of the body can be affected. For example, body cells that do not get enough energy or nutrients cannot work properly. A lack of food harms many systems and may cause disease or even death. The presence of toxins or pathogens also can disrupt homeostasis. Toxins can prevent cells from carrying out life processes and pathogens can break down cells. Problems also occur if the body's messages do not work, or they are not sent when or where they are needed. Many diseases which affect homeostasis are hereditary.

Active Reading

11 Identify As you read this page, underline what can happen if homeostasis is disrupted.

Structure or Function Diseases

Problems with the structure or function of cells, tissues, or organs can affect the body. For example, diabetes is a disease that affects cell function. Certain changes in body cells stop them from taking glucose in from the blood as they normally do. If cells cannot get energy in the form of glucose, they cannot work properly.

Pathogens and Disease

When the body cannot maintain homeostasis, it is easier for pathogens to invade the body. Pathogens can also cause a disruption in homeostasis. For example, tuberculosis is a lung disease caused by bacteria. It weakens the lungs and body. Weakened lungs cannot take in oxygen well. Low oxygen levels affect the whole body.

12 Apply Alcoholism is a disease that disrupts homeostasis. Below are three body systems that are affected by alcohol. The effects on the nervous system are filled in. In the space provided, predict what might happen when the function of the two remaining systems is affected.

Body systems affected	What are the effects?
Nervous system	Disrupts proper functioning of the brain. The brain cannot respond properly to internal or external messages.
Digestive system	
Reproductive system	

Alcoholism can damage the structure and function of the liver and reduce its ability to remove toxins from the blood.

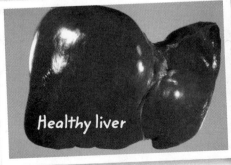
Healthy liver

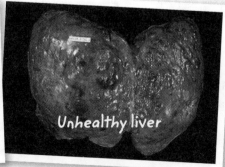
Unhealthy liver

Visual Summary

To complete this summary, fill in the blanks with the correct word or phrase. Then use the key below to check your answers. You can use this page to review the main concepts of the lesson.

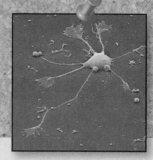

Body systems each have specific jobs.

13 The _____ system brings oxygen into the blood and releases carbon dioxide from the body.

The structure of cells, tissues, and organs are linked to their functions.

14 The long, thin cells of the _____ system help transmit electrical messages around the body.

The muscular heart pushes _____ around the body.

Body Systems and Homeostasis

Body systems interact, which allows the body to work properly.

15 The _____ and _____ systems interact to allow the player to swing the bat.

The body maintains homeostasis by adjusting to change.

16 If body temperature goes up, the _____ senses the change and will work to reduce the body temperature to normal.

Answers: 13 respiratory; 14 nervous, blood; 15 nervous, muscular (either order); 16 brain

17 **Claims • Evidence • Reasoning** How might disruption of the respiratory system affect homeostasis of the body? State your claim. Summarize evidence to support your claim and explain your reasoning.

Lesson Review

Vocabulary

Use a term from the lesson to complete each sentence below.

1 _____ is maintaining stable conditions inside the body.

2 A group of organs that interact is called a(n) _____ .

Key Concepts

3 Compare How are the functions of the skeletal and muscular systems related?

_____

_____

_____

_____

4 Identify What body system receives information from inside and outside the body and responds to that information?

_____

_____

5 Explain How is skin part of the integumentary system and the excretory system?

_____

_____

_____

_____

6 Describe What are the basic needs of all cells in the body?

_____

_____

_____

7 Relate Give an example of how a cell's structure relates to its function in the body.

_____

_____

_____

_____

Critical Thinking

Use the graph to answer the following questions.

Body Temperature over Time

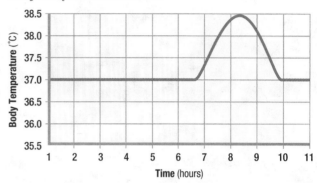

8 Analyze Is the body in homeostasis during the entire time shown in the graph? Explain.

_____

_____

_____

9 Predict What would happen to the body if the body temperature continued to decrease during the tenth hour instead of leveling off?

_____

_____

_____

10 Apply Make a claim about how drinking large volumes of plain water after exercising may affect the salt balance in the body. Summarize evidence and explain your reasoning.

_____

_____

_____

11 Infer Reflect on how the failure of a specific body system to function properly would affect other body systems. Build an argument for why all body systems must interact to carry out life processes based on your example. Provide evidence and give details.

_____

_____

_____

_____

My Notes

The Skeletal and Muscular Systems

The Skeletal and Muscular Systems

ESSENTIAL QUESTION

How do your skeletal and muscular systems work?

By the end of this lesson, you should be able to explain how the skeletal and muscular systems interact to allow movement of the body.

By interacting, your muscular and skeletal systems allow you to do many things such as stand up, sit down, type a note, or run a race.

Lesson Labs

Quick Labs
- Power in Pairs
- Speed of a Reflex

Exploration Lab
- A Closer Look at Muscles

Engage Your Brain

1 Identify Circle the terms that best complete the following sentences.

The *skeletal / muscular* system is responsible for supporting the body.

Bones are part of your *skeletal / muscular* system.

Your heart is made up of *bone / muscle* tissue.

You can increase your flexibility by stretching your *bones / muscles*.

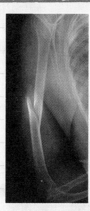

2 Infer This x-ray shows a broken arm. How might this injury affect your ability to move?

_____

_____

_____

_____

Active Reading

3 Synthesize You can often identify functions of a body part if you know what its name means. Use the Latin words below and context clues to make an educated guess about a function of *ligaments* and *tendons*.

Latin word	Meaning
ligare	to tie
tendere	to stretch

Example sentence
Ligaments are found at the ends of bones.

ligament:

_____

Example Sentence
Tendons connect muscles to bones.

tendon:

_____

Vocabulary Terms

- skeletal system
- ligament
- joint
- muscular system
- tendon

4 Apply As you learn the definition of each vocabulary term in this lesson, create your own definition or sketch it to help you remember the meaning of the term.

What's Inside?

What are the main functions of the skeletal system?

When you hear the word *skeleton*, you might think of the dry, white bones that you see in the models in your science class. You might think your bones are lifeless, but they are very much alive. The **skeletal system** is the organ system that supports and protects the body and allows it to move. Its other jobs include storing minerals and producing red blood cells. A human's skeleton is inside the body, so it is called an *endoskeleton*.

5 Identify As you read, underline the main functions of the skeletal system.

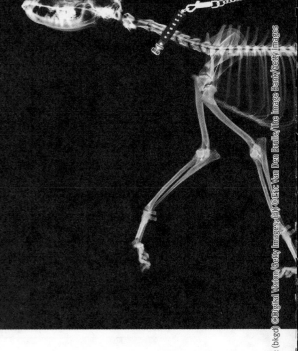

Visualize It!

6 Relate How might a suit of armor be a good analogy for a function of the skeletal system? State your claim. Summarize evidence to support your claim.

_____

_____

_____

_____

Protection

Bones provide protection to organs. For example, your ribs protect your heart and lungs, your vertebrae protect your spinal cord, and your skull protects your brain.

Storage

The hard outer layer of bone, called *compact bone*, stores important minerals such as calcium. These minerals are necessary for nerves and muscles to work properly.

Support

Bones provide support for your body and make it possible for you to sit or stand upright. If you did not have bones, you would be a mass of soft tissue, like a slug. However, unlike a slug, you would not be able to move around without your bones.

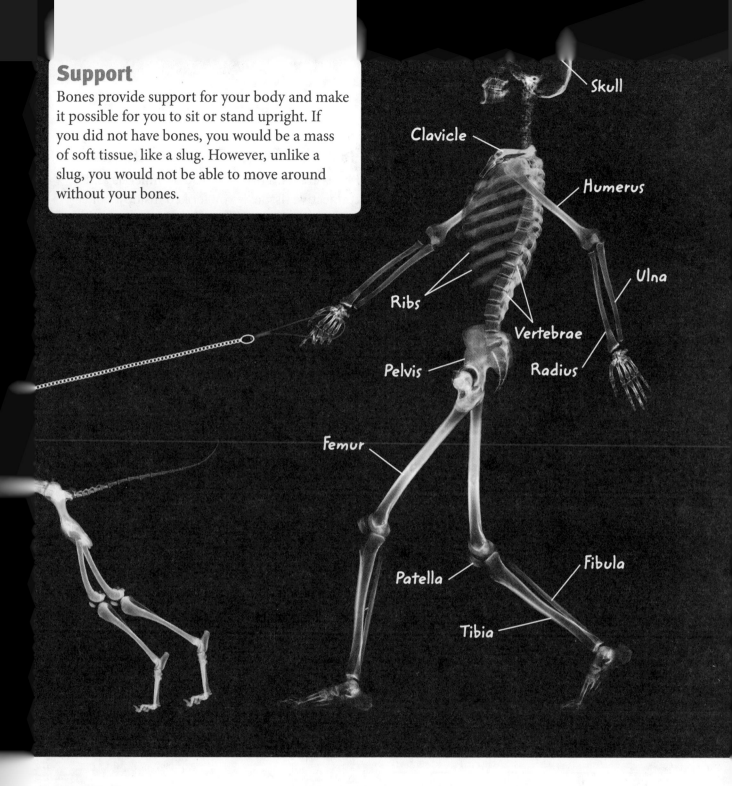

Skull

Clavicle

Humerus

Ulna

Ribs

Vertebrae

Radius

Pelvis

Femur

Fibula

Patella

Tibia

Blood Cell Production

At the center of bones, such as the long bones in the man's and dog's legs, is soft tissue called *marrow*. Red marrow, a type of marrow that makes blood cells, is found mostly in flat bones, such as the ribs, pelvis, and skull. The red and white blood cells shown here are made in the red bone marrow.

Movement

Bones play an important role in movement by providing a place for muscles to attach. Muscles pull on bones to move the body. Without bones, muscles could not do their job of moving the body.

No Bones About It!

What are the parts of the skeletal system?

Bones, ligaments, and cartilage make up your skeletal system. The skeletal system is divided into two parts. The skull, vertebrae, and ribs make up the *axial skeleton*, which supports the body's weight and protects internal organs. The arms, legs, shoulders, and pelvis make up the *appendicular skeleton*, which allows for most of the body's movement.

Bones

Bones are alive! They have blood vessels, which supply nutrients, and nerves, which signal pain. The body of a newborn baby has about 300 bones, but the average adult has only 206 bones. As a child grows, some bones fuse together.

Ligaments

The tough, flexible strand of connective tissue that holds bones together is a **ligament**. Ligaments allow movement, and are found at the end of bones. Some ligaments, such as the ones on your vertebrae, prevent too much movement of bones.

7 Compare How does the axial skeleton differ from the appendicular skeleton?

_____

_____

_____

_____

Cartilage

Cartilage is a strong, flexible, and smooth connective tissue found at the end of bones. It allows bones to move smoothly across each other. The tip of your nose and your ears are soft and bendy because they contain only cartilage. Cartilage does not contain blood vessels.

What are bones made of?

Bones are hard organs made of minerals and connective tissue. If you looked inside a bone, you would notice two kinds of bone tissue. One kind, called *compact bone*, is dense and does not have any visible open spaces. Compact bone makes bones rigid and hard. Tiny canals within compact bone contain blood capillaries. The other kind of bone tissue, called *spongy bone*, has many open spaces. Spongy bone provides most of the strength and support for a bone. In long bones, such as those of the arm or the leg, an outer layer of compact bone surrounds spongy bone and another soft tissue called *marrow*.

Active Reading **8 Identify** As you read, underline the name of a protein found in bone.

Minerals

Calcium is the most plentiful mineral in bones. The minerals in bones are deposited by bone cells called *osteoblasts*. Minerals, such as calcium, make the bones strong and hard.

Connective Tissue

The connective tissue in bone is made mostly of a protein called *collagen*. Minerals make the bones strong and hard, but the collagen in bones allows them to be flexible enough to withstand knocks and bumps. Otherwise, each time you bumped a bone, it would crack like a china cup.

Marrow

Bones also contain a soft tissue called *marrow*. There are two types of marrow. Red marrow is the site of platelet and red and white blood cell production. Red marrow is in the center of flat bones such as the ribs. Yellow marrow, which is found in the center of long bones such as the femur, stores fat.

Bones, such as the femur shown here, are made mostly of connective tissue. They also contain minerals such as calcium.

Ligament

Spongy bone

Compact bone

Marrow

Blood vessels

Cartilage

9 Summarize In the chart below, fill in the main functions of each part of the skeletal system.

Structure	Function
Spongy bone	
Compact bone	
Cartilage	
Ligaments	

How do bones grow?

The skeleton of a fetus growing inside its mother's body does not contain hard bones. Instead, most bones start out as flexible cartilage. When a baby is born, it still has a lot of cartilage. As the baby grows, most of the cartilage is replaced by bone.

The bones of a child continue to grow. The long bones lengthen at their ends, in areas called *growth plates*. Growth plates are areas of cartilage that continue to make new cells. Bone cells called *osteocytes* move into the cartilage, hardening it and changing it into bone. Growth continues into adolescence and sometimes even into early adulthood. Most bones harden completely after they stop growing. Even after bones have stopped growing, they can still repair themselves if they break.

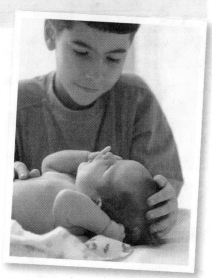

This baby's skeleton has more cartilage than his older brother's skeleton has.

Bone Connections

How are bones connected?

The place where two or more bones connect is called a **joint**. Some joints allow movement of body parts, others stop or limit movement. Just imagine how difficult it would be to do everyday things such as tying your shoelaces if you could not bend the joints in your arms, legs, neck, or fingers!

Joints

Bones are connected to each other at joints by strong, flexible ligaments. The ends of the bone are covered with cartilage. Cartilage is a smooth, flexible connective tissue that helps cushion the area in a joint where bones meet. Some joints allow little or no movement. These *fixed joints* can be found in the skull. Other joints, called *movable joints*, allow movement of the bones.

Your joints allow you to do everyday tasks easily.

Some Examples of Movable Joints

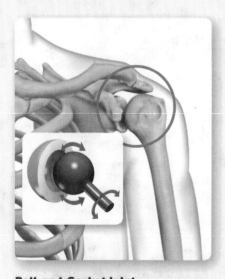

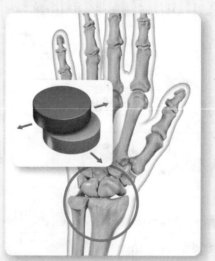

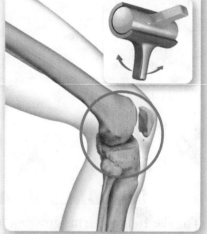

Ball-and-Socket joint
Shoulders and hips are ball-and-socket joints. Ball-and-socket joints allow one of the bones of the joint to rotate in a large circle.

Gliding joint
Wrists and ankles are gliding joints. Gliding joints allow a great deal of flexibility in many directions.

Hinge joint
Knees and elbows are hinge joints. Hinge joints work like door hinges, allowing bones to move back and forth.

10 **Apply** Some joints, such as the ones in your skull, do not move at all. Why do you think it is important that skull joints cannot move?

_____

_____

_____

_____

© Houghton Mifflin Harcourt Publishing Company • Image Credits: (t) ©Chris Clinton/Taxi/Getty Images

What are some injuries and disorders of the skeletal system?

Sometimes the skeletal system can become injured or diseased. Injuries and diseases of the skeletal system affect the body's support system and ability to move. Hereditary factors may play a role in the incidence of diseases such as osteoporosis and arthritis.

 **Active Reading**

11 Identify As you read, underline the characteristics of each injury and disease.

Fractures

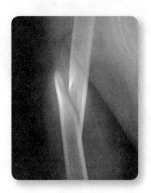

Bones may be fractured, or broken. Bones can be broken by a high-force impact such as a fall from a bike. A broken bone usually repairs itself in six to eight weeks.

Sprains

A sprain is an injury to a ligament that is caused by stretching a joint too far. The tissues in the sprained ligament can tear and the joint becomes swollen and painful to move. Sprains are common sports injuries.

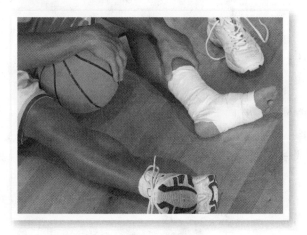

12 Apply How could someone sprain a ligament?

_____

_____

_____

_____

_____

Osteoporosis

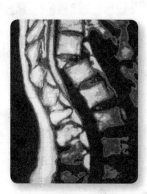

Osteoporosis is a disease that causes bone tissue to become thin. The bones become weak and break more easily. It is most common among adults who do not get enough calcium in their diet. What you eat now can affect your risk of developing osteoporosis later in life.

13 Claims • Evidence • Reasoning Is it important to get enough calcium in your diet? State your claim. Summarize evidence to support your claim and explain your reasoning.

_____

_____

_____

_____

_____

_____

Arthritis

Arthritis is a disease that causes joints to swell, stiffen, and become painful. It may also cause the joint to become misshapen, as shown in the photo. A person with arthritis finds it difficult to move the affected joint. Arthritis can be treated with drugs that reduce swelling.

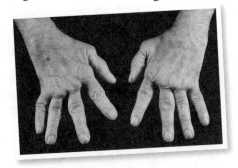

Keep Moving!

What are the main functions of the muscular system?

Muscles pump blood through your body, enable you to breathe, hold you upright, and allow you to move. All animals, except the simplest invertebrates, have muscles for movement. The **muscular system** is mostly made of the muscles that allow your body to move and be flexible. Other muscles move materials inside your body. *Muscle* is the tissue that contracts and relaxes, making movement possible. Muscle tissue is made up of muscle cells. Muscle cells contain special proteins that allow them to shorten and lengthen.

Active Reading 14 **Identify** How do muscles make movement possible?

_____

_____

_____

What are the three types of muscles?

Your body has three kinds of muscle tissue: *skeletal muscle, smooth muscle*, and *cardiac muscle*. Each muscle type has a specific function in your body.

You are able to control the movement of skeletal muscle, so it is called *voluntary muscle*. You are not able to control the movement of smooth muscle and cardiac muscles. Muscle action that is not under your control is *involuntary*. Smooth muscle and cardiac muscle are called *involuntary muscles*.

Smooth Muscle

Smooth muscle is found in internal organs and blood vessels. It helps move materials through the body. Arteries and veins contain a layer of smooth muscle that can contract and relax. This action controls blood flow through the blood vessel. Smooth muscle movement in your digestive system helps move food through your intestines. Smooth muscle is involuntary muscle.

Smooth muscle cells are spindle-shaped. They are fat in the middle with thin ends.

Cardiac muscle cells are long, thin, and branched.

Cardiac Muscle

Cardiac muscle is the tissue that makes up the heart. Your heart never gets tired like your skeletal muscle can. This is because cardiac muscle cells are able to contract and relax without ever getting tired. In order to supply lots of energy to the cells, cardiac muscle cells contain many mitochondria. Your cardiac muscles do not stop moving your entire lifetime!

The contractions of cardiac muscle push blood out of the heart and pump it around the body. Cardiac muscle is involuntary; you cannot consciously stop your heart from pumping.

Skeletal muscle cells are long and thin with stripes, or striations.

Skeletal Muscle

Skeletal muscle is attached to your bones and allows you to move. You have control over your skeletal muscle. For example, you can bring your arm up to your mouth to take a bite from an apple. The tough strand of tissue that connects a muscle to a bone is called a **tendon**. When a muscle contracts, or shortens, the attached bones are pulled closer to each other. For example, when the bicep muscle shortens, the arm bends at the elbow.

Most skeletal muscles work in pairs around a joint, as shown below. One muscle in the pair, called a *flexor*, bends a joint. The other muscle, the *extensor*, straightens the joint. When one muscle of a pair contracts, the other muscle relaxes to allow movement of the body part. Muscle pairs are found all around the body.

 **Visualize It!**

15 Apply What would happen to the arm if the flexor was not able to contract?

_____

_____

_____

_____

_____

_____

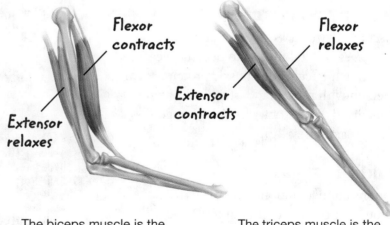

Flexor contracts

Extensor relaxes

Flexor relaxes

Extensor contracts

The biceps muscle is the flexor that contracts to bend the arm.

The triceps muscle is the extensor that contracts to straighten the arm.

 **Visualize It!**

16 Compare How do the three muscle tissue types look similar and different?

_____

_____

_____

_____

_____

_____

Move It or Lose It!

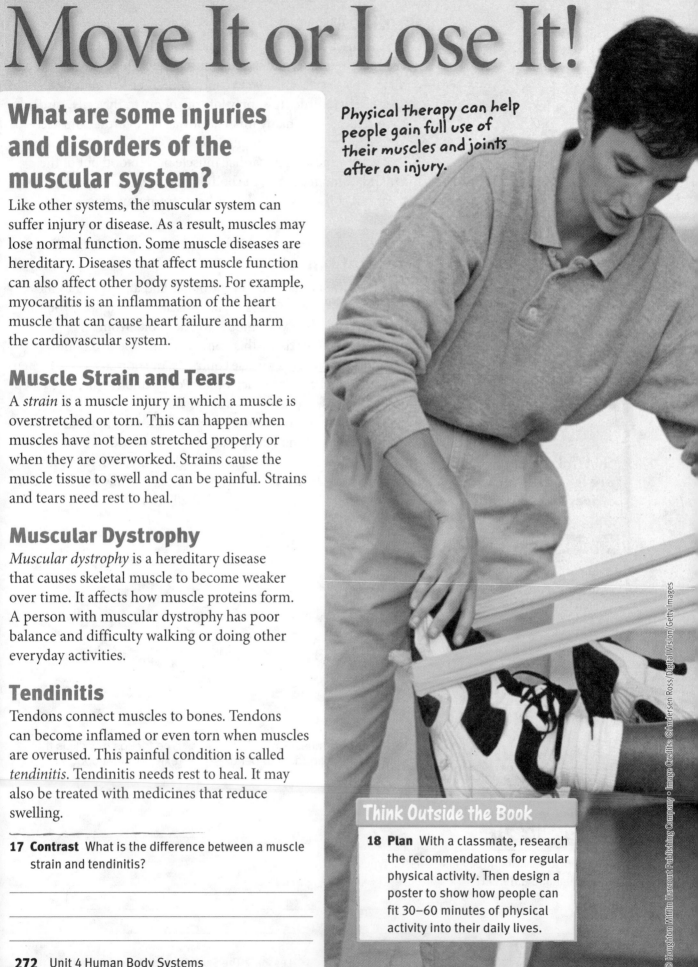

Physical therapy can help people gain full use of their muscles and joints after an injury.

What are some injuries and disorders of the muscular system?

Like other systems, the muscular system can suffer injury or disease. As a result, muscles may lose normal function. Some muscle diseases are hereditary. Diseases that affect muscle function can also affect other body systems. For example, myocarditis is an inflammation of the heart muscle that can cause heart failure and harm the cardiovascular system.

Muscle Strain and Tears

A *strain* is a muscle injury in which a muscle is overstretched or torn. This can happen when muscles have not been stretched properly or when they are overworked. Strains cause the muscle tissue to swell and can be painful. Strains and tears need rest to heal.

Muscular Dystrophy

Muscular dystrophy is a hereditary disease that causes skeletal muscle to become weaker over time. It affects how muscle proteins form. A person with muscular dystrophy has poor balance and difficulty walking or doing other everyday activities.

Tendinitis

Tendons connect muscles to bones. Tendons can become inflamed or even torn when muscles are overused. This painful condition is called *tendinitis*. Tendinitis needs rest to heal. It may also be treated with medicines that reduce swelling.

17 Contrast What is the difference between a muscle strain and tendinitis?

_____

_____

_____

Think Outside the Book

18 Plan With a classmate, research the recommendations for regular physical activity. Then design a poster to show how people can fit 30–60 minutes of physical activity into their daily lives.

What are some benefits of exercise?

Exercising is one of the best things you can do to keep your body healthy. *Exercise* is any activity that helps improve physical fitness and health. Exercise benefits the muscular system by increasing strength, endurance, and flexibility. Exercise helps other body systems, too. It helps keep your heart, blood vessels, lungs, and bones healthy. Exercise also reduces stress, helps you sleep well, and makes you feel good.

Exercises that raise your heart rate to a certain level for at least 60 minutes improve the fitness of the heart. A fit heart is a more efficient pump. It can pump more blood around the body with each beat. It is also less likely to develop heart disease. Good muscle strength and joint flexibility may help a person avoid injuries. Weight training helps bones stay dense and strong. Dense, strong bones are less likely to break. Thirty to sixty minutes of physical activity every day can help improve the health of people of all ages, from children to older adults.

 **Active Reading** **19 Identify** As you read, underline the characteristics of anaerobic and aerobic exercise.

Muscle Strength

Resistance exercise helps improve muscle strength by building skeletal muscle and increasing muscle power. Resistance exercise involves short bursts of intense effort lasting no more than a few minutes. Resistance exercises are also called *anaerobic exercises* because the muscle cells contract without using oxygen. Lifting weights and doing pushups are examples of anaerobic exercises.

Muscle Endurance

Endurance exercises allow muscles to contract for a longer time without getting tired. Endurance exercises are also called *aerobic exercises* because the muscle cells use oxygen when contracting. Aerobic exercises involve moderately intense activity from about 30 to 60 minutes at a time. Some examples of aerobic exercises are walking, jogging, bicycling, skating, and swimming.

Flexibility

Can you reach down and touch your toes? If a joint can move through a wide range of motions, it has good flexibility. *Flexibility* refers to the full range of motion of a joint. Stretching exercises help improve flexibility of a joint. Having good flexibility can help prevent ligament, tendon, and muscle injuries. Stretching after aerobic or anaerobic exercises may also help prevent injuries.

Visual Summary

To complete this summary, fill in the blanks with the correct word or phrase. Then, use the key below to check your answers. You can use this page to review the main concepts of the lesson.

The Skeletal and Muscular Systems

The skeletal system supports and protects the body and allows for movement.

20 The three main parts of the skeletal system are bones, _____, and _____ .

Joints connect two or more bones.

21 The shoulder is an example of a _____ joint.

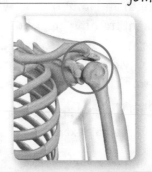

The muscular system allows for movement and flexibility.

22 Muscles work in _____ to move body parts.

Exercise benefits the body in many ways.

23 Aerobic exercises improve muscle _____ .

Anaerobic exercises improve muscle _____ .

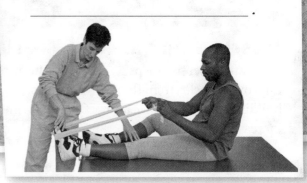

Answers:20 cartilage, ligaments; 21 ball-and-socket; 22 pairs; 23 endurance, strength

24 **Synthesize** Explain why you need both muscles and bones to move your body.

Lesson Review

Vocabulary

Draw a line to connect the following terms to their definitions.

1 skeletal system

2 ligament

3 muscular system

4 joint

5 tendon

A groups of muscles that allow you to move and that move materials inside your body

B a place where two or more bones connect

C bones, cartilage, and the ligaments that hold bones together

D tough strands of tissue that connect muscles to bones

E a type of tough, flexible connective tissue that holds bones together

Key Concepts

6 List What are the functions of the skeletal system?

_____

_____

_____

7 Analyze What are bones made of?

_____

_____

_____

8 Explain How do muscles work in pairs to move the body?

_____

_____

_____

_____

9 Identify What bone disease is caused by a lack of calcium in the diet?

_____

Critical Thinking

Use this graph to answer the following questions.

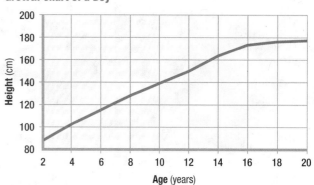

Growth Chart of a Boy

10 Analyze At which points on this graph is bone growing at the fastest rate?

_____

_____

_____

11 Infer At which times on this graph would you expect that the boy's growth plates have stopped creating new bone? Explain your reasoning.

_____

_____

_____

_____

_____

12 Claims • Evidence • Reasoning If aerobic exercise improves heart strength so that it pumps more blood with each beat, what likely happens to the heart rate as the cardiac muscle gets stronger? Use evidence to support your claim and explain your reasoning.

_____

_____

_____

_____

My Notes

The Circulatory and Respiratory Systems

ESSENTIAL QUESTION

How do the circulatory and respiratory systems work?

By the end of this lesson, you should be able to relate the structures of the circulatory and respiratory systems to their functions in the human body.

This micrograph shows red blood cells inside a blood vessel in the lung. The blood cells are picking up oxygen to bring to the rest of the body.

© Houghton Mifflin Harcourt Publishing Company • Image Credits: ©BSIP VEM/SPL/Photo Researchers, Inc.

Engage Your Brain

1 Identify Check T or F to show whether you think each statement is true or false.

T F

☐ ☐ Air is carried through blood vessels.

☐ ☐ The cardiovascular system does not interact with any other body system.

☐ ☐ The respiratory system gets rid of carbon dioxide from the body.

☐ ☐ Smoking cigarettes can lead to lung disease.

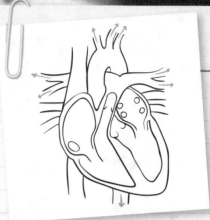

2 Identify What is the name of the organ, shown here, that makes the "lub-dub" sound in your chest?

_____

3 Infer What is the function of this organ?

_____

_____

_____

Active Reading

4 Synthesize You can sometimes tell a lot about the structure of an unknown object by understanding the meaning of its name. Use the meaning of the Latin word and the sentence below to write your own definition of *capillary*.

Latin word	Meaning
capillaris	thin and hairlike

Example sentence
Oxygen that is carried by blood cells moves across the <u>capillary</u> wall and into body cells.

capillary:

_____

_____

_____

Vocabulary Terms

- cardiovascular system
- blood
- lymphatic system
- lymph
- lymph node
- artery
- capillary
- vein
- respiratory system
- pharynx
- larynx
- trachea
- bronchi
- alveoli

5 Apply As you learn the definition of each vocabulary term in this lesson, create your own definition or sketch to help you remember the meaning of the term.

Go with the Flow!

What is the circulatory system?

Active Reading

6 Identify As you read, underline the functions of the cardiovascular system and the lymphatic system.

When you hear the term *circulatory system,* what do you think of? If you said "heart, blood, and blood vessels," you are half right. The term circulatory system describes both the cardiovascular system and the lymphatic system. Both systems interact closely to move fluids around your body and protect it from disease. Your moving blood helps to keep all parts of your body warm. In these ways, the two systems interact to help maintain homeostasis and carry out life processes.

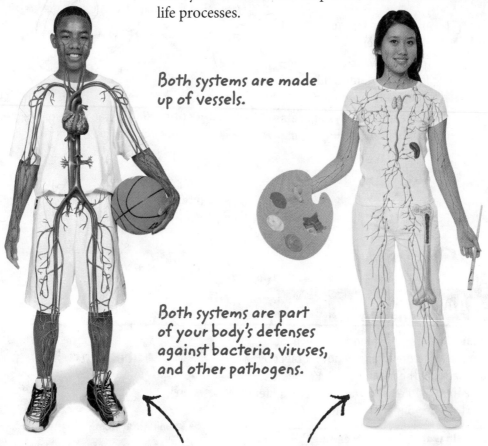

Both systems are made up of vessels.

Both systems are part of your body's defenses against bacteria, viruses, and other pathogens.

The Cardiovascular System

Your heart, blood, and blood vessels make up your **cardiovascular system**, which transports blood around your body. **Blood** is the fluid that carries gases, nutrients, and wastes through the body. The cardiovascular system is a closed circulatory system; the blood is carried in vessels that form a closed loop. The blood maintains homeostasis by transporting hormones, nutrients, and oxygen to cells and by carrying wastes away from cells.

The Lymphatic System

The **lymphatic system** is a group of organs and tissues that collect the fluid that leaks from blood and returns it to the blood. The leaked fluid is called **lymph**. The lymphatic system is an open circulatory system, and lymph can move in and out of the vessels. The lymphatic system is also part of the immune system, which provides defenses against disease. Certain lymph vessels in the abdomen move fats from the intestine and into the blood.

7 Compare Fill in the Venn diagram to compare the structures and functions of both these systems. You can add more details as you read more about these systems in this lesson.

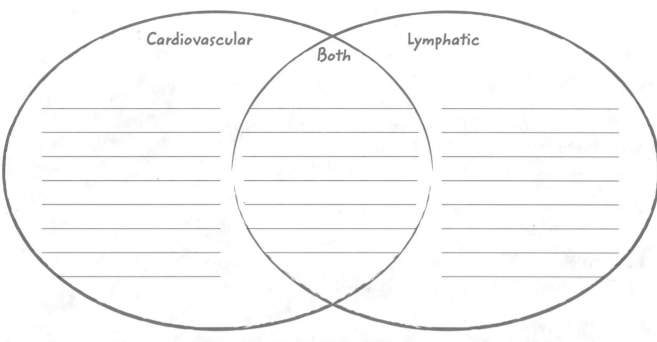

Cardiovascular

Both

Lymphatic

How do the systems interact?

Every time your heart pumps, a little fluid is forced out of the thin walls of the tiniest blood vessels, called *capillaries*. Most of this fluid is reabsorbed by the capillaries, and the remaining fluid is collected by lymph capillaries. *Lymph capillaries* absorb fluid, particles such as dead cells, and pathogens from around body cells. The lymph capillaries carry the fluid, now called *lymph,* to larger lymph vessels. Lymph is returned to the cardiovascular system when it drains into blood vessels at the base of the neck.

The lymphatic system is the place where certain blood cells, called *white blood cells,* mature. Some of these white blood cells stay in the lymphatic system where they attack invading pathogens.

 Active Reading

8 Synthesize How does returning leaked fluid from the blood help maintain homeostasis?

_____

_____

_____

_____

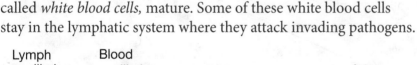

Lymph capillaries   Blood capillaries   Artery

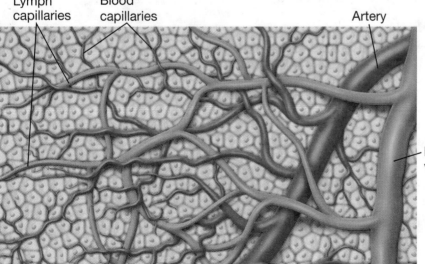

The fluid that leaks from blood capillaries moves into lymph capillaries and is eventually returned to the blood.

Lymphatic vessel

Node Doubt!

What are the parts of the lymphatic system?

As you have read, lymph vessels collect and return fluids that have leaked from the blood. In addition to these vessels, several organs and tissues are part of the lymphatic system.

Active Reading

9 Identify As you read these pages, underline the main function of each part of the lymphatic system.

Lymph Nodes

As lymph travels through lymph vessels, it passes through lymph nodes. **Lymph nodes** are small, bean-shaped organs that remove pathogens and dead cells from lymph. Lymph nodes are concentrated in the armpits, neck, and groin. Infection-fighting blood cells, called *white blood cells,* are found in lymph nodes. When bacteria or other pathogens cause an infection, the number of these blood cells may multiply greatly. The lymph nodes fill with white blood cells that are fighting the infection. As a result, some lymph nodes may become swollen and painful. Swollen lymph nodes might be an early clue of an infection.

Lymph node

Lymph Vessels

Lymph vessels are the thin-walled vessels of the lymphatic system. They carry lymph back to lymph nodes. From the lymph nodes, the fluid is returned to the cardiovascular system through the lymph vessels. The vessels have valves inside them to stop lymph from flowing backward.

Bone Marrow

Bones—part of your skeletal system—are very important to your lymphatic system. *Bone marrow* is the soft tissue inside of bones where blood cells are produced.

Tonsils

Tonsils are small lymphatic organs at the back of the throat and tongue. The tonsils at the back of the throat are the most visible. Tonsils help defend the body against infection. White blood cells in the tonsil tissues trap pathogens. Tonsils in the throat sometimes get infected. An infection of the tonsils is called *tonsillitis*. When tonsils get infected, they may become swollen, as shown here.

Thymus

The *thymus* is an organ in the chest. Some white blood cells made in the bone marrow finish developing in the thymus. From the thymus, the white blood cells travel through the lymphatic system to other areas of the body. The thymus gets smaller as a person gets older. This organ is also a part of the endocrine system.

Spleen

The *spleen* is the largest lymphatic organ. It stores white blood cells and also allows them to mature. As blood flows through the spleen, white blood cells attack or mark pathogens in the blood. If pathogens cause an infection, the spleen may also release white blood cells into the bloodstream.

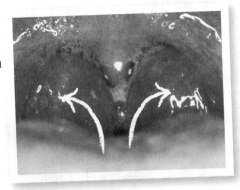

Swollen tonsils

Visualize It!

10 **Predict** A bad case of tonsillitis can sometimes affect a person's breathing. How is this possible?

_____

_____

_____

What are some disorders of the lymphatic system?

Lymphoma is a type of cancer that often begins in a lymph node. It can cause a swelling in the node called a *tumor*. There are many different types of lymphomas. Another disorder of the lymph system is lymphedema (lim•fih•DEE•muh). Lymphedema is a swelling of body tissues caused by a blockage or injury to lymph vessels. Lymph vessels are unable to drain lymph from a certain area, and that area becomes swollen. Filariasis is a disease caused by threadlike worms called *nematodes*. The nematodes may enter lymphatic vessels and block them, preventing lymph from moving around the body. Bubonic plague is a bacterial infection of the lymphatic system. The bacteria can enter the body through the bite of an infected flea. The bacteria grow inside lymph nodes, causing the nodes to swell.

Active Reading

11 **Identify** As you read, underline the names of the lymphatic system diseases discussed here.

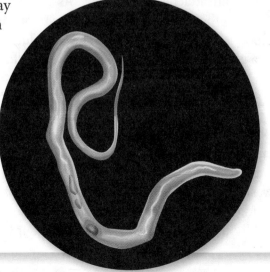

A person gets infected with filarial worms by being bitten by an infected fly. Filariasis is rare in the United States, but is common in some developing countries.

The Heart of the Matter

What are the parts of the cardiovascular system?

Your cardiovascular system is the organ system that carries nutrients, gases, and hormones to body cells and waste products from body cells. It also helps keep the different parts of your body at an even temperature. Your cardiovascular system is made up of the heart, blood vessels, and blood.

Heart

The heart is the pump that sends blood around the body. Your heart is about the size of your fist and is almost in the center of your chest. When heart muscle contracts, it squeezes the blood inside the heart. This squeezing creates a pressure that pushes blood through the body.

Your heart has a left side and a right side. The two sides are separated by a thick wall. The right side of the heart pumps oxygen-poor blood to the lungs. The left side pumps oxygen-rich blood to the body. Each side has an upper chamber and a lower chamber. Each upper chamber is called an *atrium*. Each lower chamber is called a *ventricle*. Blood enters the atria and is pumped down to the ventricles. Flaplike structures called *valves* are located between the atria and the ventricles and in places where large vessels are attached to the heart. As blood moves through the heart, these valves close to prevent blood from going backward. The "lub-dub" sound of a beating heart is caused by the valves closing.

Blood

Blood is a type of connective tissue that is part of the cardiovascular system. It serves as a transport system, providing supplies for cells, carrying chemical messages, and removing wastes so cells can maintain homeostasis. Blood contains cells, fluid, and other substances. It travels through miles and miles of blood vessels to reach every cell in your body.

© Houghton Mifflin Harcourt Publishing Company

> ### Active Reading
>
> **12 Identify** As you read this page, underline the parts of the heart that stop the blood from flowing backward.

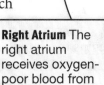

Left Atrium The left atrium receives oxygen-rich blood from the lungs.

Right Atrium The right atrium receives oxygen-poor blood from the body.

Right Ventricle The right ventricle pumps oxygen-poor blood to the lungs.

Left Ventricle The left ventricle pumps oxygen-rich blood to the body.

13 Claims • Evidence • Reasoning How important is it for your heart to keep oxygen-rich blood separate from oxygen-poor blood? Use evidence to support your claim and explain your reasoning.

_____

_____

_____

_____

Blood Vessels

Blood travels throughout your body in tubes called *blood vessels*. The three types of blood vessels are arteries, capillaries, and veins.

An **artery** is a blood vessel that carries blood away from the heart. Arteries have thick walls with a layer of smooth muscle. Each heartbeat pumps blood into your arteries at high pressure, which is your *blood pressure*. This pressure pushes blood through the arteries. Artery walls are strong and stretch to withstand the pressure. Nutrients, oxygen, and other substances must leave the blood to get to your body's cells. Carbon dioxide and other wastes leave body cells and are carried away by blood. A **capillary** is a tiny blood vessel that allows these exchanges between body cells and the blood. The gas exchange can take place because capillary walls are only one cell thick. Capillaries are so narrow that blood cells must pass through them in single file! No cell in the body is more than three or four cells away from a capillary.

Capillaries lead to veins. A **vein** is a blood vessel that carries blood back to the heart. Blood in veins is not under as much pressure as blood in arteries is. Valves in the veins keep the blood from flowing backward. The contraction of skeletal muscles around veins can help blood move in the veins.

Arteries carry oxygen-rich blood away from the heart.

Veins carry oxygen-poor blood back to the heart.

Capillaries deliver oxygen-rich blood to body cells and take oxygen-poor blood away from body cells.

14 Apply Complete the table below by naming the blood vessels and by sketching their function. Your sketch may be a symbol, as shown here.

Type of blood vessel		Vein
Sketch of function	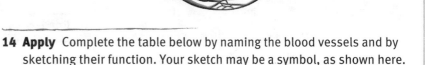	

283

It's in the Blood

What is blood made of?

An adult human body has about 5 liters of blood. Your body probably has a little less than that. Blood is made up of plasma, platelets, and red and white blood cells. Blood is a tissue because it is made of at least two different cell types. If you looked at blood under a microscope, you would see these differently shaped cells and platelets.

The Blood Files

Plasma

The fluid part of the blood is called *plasma*. Plasma is a mixture of water, minerals, nutrients, sugars, proteins, and other substances. This fluid also carries waste. Red blood cells, white blood cells, and platelets are found in plasma.

Platelets

Platelets are tiny pieces of larger cells found in bone marrow. Platelets last for only five to ten days, but they have an important role. When you cut or scrape your skin, you bleed because blood vessels have been cut open. As soon as bleeding starts, platelets begin to clump together in the cut area. They form a plug that helps reduce blood loss. Platelets also release chemicals that react with proteins in plasma. The reaction causes tiny fibers to form. The fibers help create a blood clot.

White Blood Cells

White blood cells help keep you healthy by fighting pathogens such as bacteria and viruses. Some white blood cells squeeze out of blood vessels to search for pathogens. When they find one, they destroy it. Other white blood cells form antibodies. *Antibodies* are chemicals that identify pathogens. White blood cells also keep you healthy by destroying body cells that have died or have been damaged.

White blood cell

Red blood cell

Platelet

Red Blood Cells

Most blood cells are red blood cells. *Red blood cells* are disk-shaped cells that do not have a nucleus. They bring oxygen to every cell in your body. Cells need oxygen to carry out life processes. Each red blood cell has hemoglobin. *Hemoglobin* is an oxygen-carrying protein; it clings to the oxygen molecules you inhale. Red blood cells can then transport oxygen to cells in every part of the body. The disk shape of red blood cells helps them squeeze into capillaries.

15 Predict How would the body be affected if red blood cells had low levels of hemoglobin? Use evidence to support your claim and explain your reasoning.

_____

_____

_____

_____

_____

© Houghton Mifflin Harcourt Publishing Company • Image Credits: (t) ©Davies and Starr/stone/Getty Images; (c) ©Stem Jems/Photo Researchers, Inc.

How does blood move through the body?

Blood is pumped from the right side of the heart to the lungs. From the lungs it returns to the left side of the heart. The blood is then pumped from the left side of the heart to the body. It flows to the tiny capillaries around the body before returning to the right side of the heart. Blood in the arteries that come out of the heart is under great pressure because of the force from the pumping action of the heart. Blood in veins is under much less pressure than arterial blood because veins have larger internal diameters than arteries do. Veins carry larger volumes of blood more slowly.

Blood Moves in Circuits

Blood moves in two loops or circuits around the body. The beating heart moves blood to the lungs and also around the body. The flow of blood between the heart and the lungs is called the *pulmonary circulation*. As blood passes through the lungs, carbon dioxide leaves the blood and oxygen is picked up. The oxygen-rich blood then flows back to the heart, where it is pumped around the rest of the body. The circulation of blood between the heart and the rest of the body is called *systemic circulation*. Oxygen-poor blood returns to the heart from body cells in the systemic circulation.

Active Reading **16 Compare** What is the difference between the pulmonary and systemic circulations?

_____

_____

_____

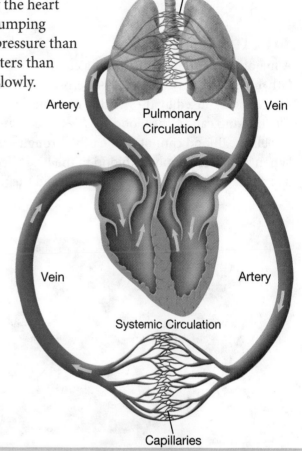

In pulmonary circulation, blood is pumped to the lungs where carbon dioxide leaves the blood and oxygen enters the blood.

Capillaries

Artery

Vein

Pulmonary Circulation

Vein

Artery

Systemic Circulation

Capillaries

In systemic circulation, blood moves around the body.

Visualize It!

17 Apply Put a box around the part of the diagram that shows the pulmonary circulation. Where in the diagram would you find oxygen-poor blood?

_____

_____

_____

How does circulation help maintain body temperature?

The circulation of blood also helps homeostasis. When the brain senses that body temperature is rising, it signals blood vessels in the skin to widen. As the vessels get wider, heat from the blood is transferred to the air around the skin. This transfer helps lower body temperature. When the brain senses that body temperature is normal, it signals the blood vessels to return to normal. When the brain senses the body temperature is getting too low, it signals the blood vessels near the skin to get narrower. This allows the blood to stay close to internal organs to keep them warm.

What are some problems that affect the cardiovascular system?

Cardiovascular disease is the leading cause of death in the United States. Cardiovascular disease can be caused by smoking, poor diet, stress, physical inactivity, or in some cases, heredity. Eating a healthy diet and regular exercise can reduce the risk of developing cardiovascular problems.

Atherosclerosis

A major cause of heart disease is a condition called *atherosclerosis* (ath•uh•roh•skluh•ROH•sis). Atherosclerosis is a hardening of artery walls caused by the buildup of cholesterol and other lipids. The buildup causes the blood vessels to become narrower and less elastic. Blood cannot flow easily through a narrowed artery. When an artery supplying blood to the heart becomes blocked, oxygen cannot reach the heart muscle and the person may have a heart attack.

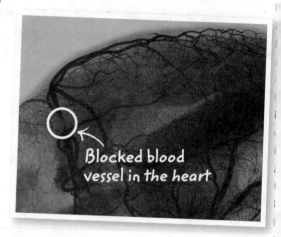

Blocked blood vessel in the heart

Blood pressure checks can help detect illness.

Hypertension

Hypertension is abnormally high blood pressure. Atherosclerosis may be caused in part by hypertension. The higher a person's blood pressure is, the greater their risk of developing cardiovascular problems, such as heart attacks and strokes. Hypertension that is not treated can also cause kidney damage and shorten life expectancy. Regular checkups can help detect problems with blood pressure. Hypertension can be controlled with diet and sometimes with medication.

Heart Attacks and Strokes

A heart attack happens when an artery that supplies blood to the heart becomes blocked and the heart muscle tissue that depends on that blood supply does not get oxygen. Cells and tissues that do not get oxygen get damaged and can die. If enough heart muscle cells are damaged, the heart may stop beating.

A stroke can happen when a blood vessel in the brain becomes blocked or bursts. As a result, that part of the brain receives no oxygen. Without oxygen, brain cells die. Brain damage that occurs during a stroke can affect many parts of the body. People who have had a stroke may experience paralysis or difficulty in speaking.

Think Outside the Book **Inquiry**

18 **Research** Doctors often use an electrocardiogram (EKG) reading to see if there is something wrong with how a person's heart is beating. An EKG is a type of graph that "draws" the pumping activity of the heart. How might graphing the heartbeat help a doctor tell if there is a problem?

Take a Deep Breath

What are the functions of the respiratory system?

Your cells need a constant supply of oxygen to stay alive. Your cells must also be able to get rid of the waste product carbon dioxide, which is toxic to them. Breathing takes care of both of these needs. The **respiratory system** is the group of organs that takes in oxygen and gets rid of carbon dioxide. *Respiration,* or breathing, is the transport of oxygen from outside the body to cells and tissues, and the transport of carbon dioxide and wastes away from cells and to the environment.

 **Active Reading**

19 Identify As you read this page, underline the gas that is needed by your body for cellular respiration.

Takes in Oxygen

When a person inhales, air is drawn into the lungs. Oxygen in the air moves into the blood from the lungs. The oxygen-rich blood flowing away from the lungs is carried to all the cells in the body. Oxygen leaves the capillaries and enters the body cells. Inside each cell, oxygen is used for cellular respiration. During cellular respiration, the energy that is stored in food molecules is released. Without oxygen, body cells would not be able to survive.

Releases Carbon Dioxide

When a person exhales, carbon dioxide is released from the body. Carbon dioxide is a waste product of cellular respiration, and the body needs to get rid of it. Carbon dioxide moves from body cells and into capillaries, where it is carried in the blood all the way to the lungs. Blood that flows to the lungs contains more carbon dioxide than oxygen. The carbon dioxide moves out of the lung capillaries and into the lungs, where it is exhaled.

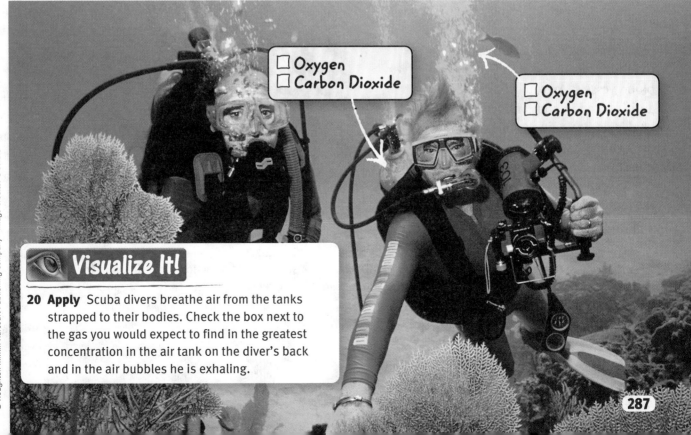

□ Oxygen
□ Carbon Dioxide

□ Oxygen
□ Carbon Dioxide

Visualize It!

20 Apply Scuba divers breathe air from the tanks strapped to their bodies. Check the box next to the gas you would expect to find in the greatest concentration in the air tank on the diver's back and in the air bubbles he is exhaling.

Breathe Easy

What are the parts of the respiratory system?

Breathing is made possible by your respiratory system. Air enters your respiratory system through your nose or mouth when you breathe in. From there, the air moves through a series of tubes to get to your lungs.

Nose, Pharynx, and Larynx

Air enters your respiratory system through your nose and your mouth. From the nose, air flows into the **pharynx** (FAIR•ingks), or throat. The pharynx branches into two tubes. One tube, the *esophagus*, leads to the stomach. The other tube, called the *larynx*, leads to the lungs. The **larynx** (LAIR•ingks) is the part of the throat that holds the vocal cords. When air passes across the vocal cords, they vibrate, making the voice.

Bronchioles and Alveoli

In the lungs, the bronchioles lead to tiny sacs called **alveoli** (singular, *alveolus*). Alveoli are surrounded by blood vessels. Gases in the air move across the thin walls of the alveoli and blood vessels. As you breathe, air is sucked into and forced out of alveoli. Breathing is carried out by the diaphragm and rib muscles. The *diaphragm* is a dome-shaped muscle below the lungs. As you inhale, the diaphragm contracts and moves down. The volume of the chest increases. As a result, a vacuum is created and air is sucked in. Exhaling reverses this process.

Trachea

The larynx is connected to a large tube called the **trachea** (TRAY•kee•uh), or windpipe. Air flows from the larynx through the trachea to the lungs. The trachea splits into two branches called **bronchi** (singular, *bronchus*). One bronchus connects to each lung. Each bronchus branches into smaller tubes called *bronchioles*.

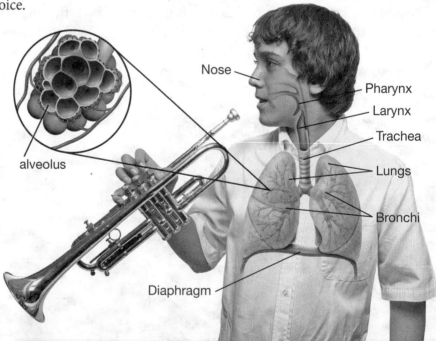

alveolus

Nose

Pharynx

Larynx

Trachea

Lungs

Bronchi

Diaphragm

Visualize It!

21 Apply Draw arrows showing the direction of air flow into the lungs. How would an object blocking a bronchus affect this airflow?

_____

_____

What are some disorders of the respiratory system?

Millions of people suffer from respiratory disorders. These disorders include asthma, pneumonia, emphysema, and lung cancer. Some respiratory problems, such as emphysema and lung cancer, are strongly linked to cigarette smoke. Other respiratory disorders, such as pneumonia, are caused by pathogens, and some are genetic disorders. Depending on the cause, there are many different ways to treat respiratory diseases.

Active Reading

22 Identify As you read, underline the characteristics of the different respiratory disorders.

Asthma

Asthma is a condition in which the airways are narrowed due to inflammation of the bronchi. During an asthma attack, the muscles in the bronchi tighten and the airways become inflamed. This reduces the amount of air that can get into or out of the lungs. Asthma is treated with medicines that open the bronchioles.

Pneumonia

Pneumonia (noo•MOHN•yuh) is an inflammation of the lungs that is usually caused by bacteria or viruses. Inflamed alveoli may fill with fluid. If the alveoli are filled with too much fluid, the person cannot take in enough oxygen and he or she may suffocate. Pneumonia can be treated with medicines that kill the pathogens.

Emphysema

Emphysema (em•fuh•SEE•muh) occurs when the alveoli have been damaged. As a result, oxygen cannot pass across into the blood as well as it could in a normal alveolus. People who have emphysema have trouble getting the oxygen they need and removing carbon dioxide from the lungs. This condition is often linked to long-term use of tobacco.

Visualize It!

23 Compare How are these two lungs different? How can you tell the diseased lung from the healthy lung? Support your claim with evidence.

_____

_____

_____

_____

_____

Think Outside the Book

24 Imagine Pretend you are a lung. The behavior of your body has not been very healthy, and as a result you are sick. Write a plea to your body to help you improve your health. Be sure to include the important functions that you perform and what the body can do to make you healthier.

Emphysema lung

Healthy lung

Visual Summary

To complete this summary, fill in the blanks with the correct word or phrase. Then use the key below to check your answers. You can use this page to review the main concepts of the lesson.

The lymphatic system returns fluid to the blood.

25 The lymph organs found in your throat are called

_____.

Circulatory and Respiratory Systems

The cardiovascular system moves blood throughout the body and carries nutrients and oxygen to body cells.

26 The two gases that the blood carries around the body are

_____ and

_____.

The respiratory system takes oxygen into the body and releases carbon dioxide.

27 Oxygen enters the blood and carbon dioxide leaves the blood in the

_____ of the lungs.

Answers: 25 tonsils; 26 oxygen, carbon dioxide; 27 alveoli

28 Relate Describe how a problem with the respiratory system could directly affect the cardiovascular system.

Lesson Review

Vocabulary

In your own words, define the following terms.

1 blood

_____

_____

2 lymph

_____

_____

3 alveoli

_____

_____

Key Concepts

Fill in the table below.

System	Structures
4 Identify What are the main structures of the lymphatic system?	
5 Identify What are the main structures of the cardiovascular system?	
6 Identify What are the main structures of the respiratory system?	

7 Explain How does blood help maintain homeostasis in the body?

_____

_____

8 Contrast How are arteries and veins different?

_____

_____

9 Relate How might a blockage of the lymph vessels affect the function of the cardiovascular system?

_____

_____

_____

Critical Thinking

Use this image to answer the following questions.

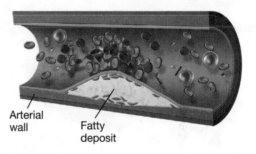

Arterial wall
Fatty deposit

10 Relate To what body system does this structure belong?

_____

11 Predict How might what is happening in this image affect the nervous system?

_____

_____

_____

12 Claims • Evidence • Reasoning Is it important that lymph vessels are spread throughout the body? Use evidence to support your claim and explain your reasoning.

_____

_____

_____

_____

My Notes

Olufunmilayo Falusi Olopade

MEDICAL DOCTOR

Dr. Olufunmilayo Olopade is the head of the University of Chicago's Cancer Risk Clinic. The MacArthur Foundation awarded her $500,000 for her creative work in breast cancer research.

Born in Nigeria, Dr. Olopade began her career as a medical officer at the Nigerian Navy Hospital in Lagos. She later came to Chicago to do cancer research. She became a professor at the University of Chicago in 1991. She founded the Cancer Risk Clinic shortly after this.

Dr. Olopade has found that tumors in African-American women often come from a different group of cells than they do in Caucasian women.

These tumors, therefore, need different treatment. Dr. Olopade designs treatments that address the source of the tumor. More importantly, her treatments try to address the particular risk factors of each patient. These can include diet, heredity, age, and activity. The MacArthur Foundation recognized Dr. Olopade for designing such new and practical treatment plans for patients. Studying cells has provided Dr. Olopade with clues on how to improve the lives of millions of African-American women.

A color-enhanced scanning electron micrograph (SEM) of a breast cancer cell

JOB BOARD

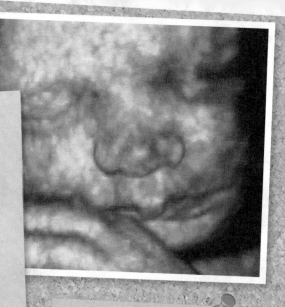

Diagnostic Medical Sonographer

What You'll Do: Operate and take care of the sonogram equipment that uses sound waves to create pictures of inside human bodies that a doctor can interpret.

Where You Might Work: Hospitals, clinics, and private offices that have sonogram equipment.

Education: A two- or four-year undergraduate degree or a special certification program is necessary.

Physical Therapist

What You'll Do: Use exercise, ultrasound, heat, and other treatments when working with patients to help them improve their muscular strength, endurance, and flexibility.

Where You Might Work: Hospitals, clinics, and private physiotherapy offices, as well as some gyms and yoga studios.

Education: A master's degree from an accredited physical therapy program is required.

Prosthetics Technician

What You'll Do: Create, test, fit, maintain, and repair artificial limbs and other prosthetic devices for people who need them.

Where You Might Work: Hospitals with prosthetic divisions and private companies.

Education: Technicians must have an associate, bachelor's, or post-graduate degree in orthotics and prosthetics. Some companies may require additional certification.

Language Arts Connection

Find one report of a new discovery in cancer prevention. Summarize the key points of the discovery in a paragraph. Be sure to include information about what the discovery is, who made it, how the discovery was made, and how it changes what we know about cancer.

The Digestive and Excretory Systems

ESSENTIAL QUESTION

How do your body's digestive and excretory systems work?

By the end of this lesson, you should be able to relate the parts of the digestive and excretory systems to their roles in the human body.

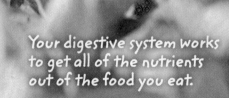

Your digestive system works to get all of the nutrients out of the food you eat.

Lesson Labs

Quick Labs
• Bile Function
• Peristalsis Race
• Mechanical Digestion

S.T.E.M. Lab
• Modeling a Kidney

Engage Your Brain

1 Predict Fill in the blanks with the words that you think best complete the following sentences.

Inside your _____, food is chewed and broken down by teeth and saliva.

The _____ is a muscle inside your mouth that helps you to swallow food and liquids.

If you eat too much food too quickly, you may get a _____ache.

2 Imagine How is a blender like your stomach?

_____

_____

_____

_____

Active Reading

3 Synthesize You can often define an unknown word if you see it used in a sentence. Use the sentence below to make an educated guess about the meaning of the word *enzyme*.

Example sentence
Enzymes in the mouth, stomach, and small intestine help in the chemical digestion of food.

enzyme:

_____

_____

_____

_____

Vocabulary Terms

• digestive system
• enzyme
• esophagus
• stomach
• small intestine
• large intestine
• pancreas
• liver
• excretory system
• kidney
• nephron
• urine

4 Apply As you learn the meaning of each vocabulary term in this lesson, create your own definition or sketch to help you remember the meaning of the term.

You are what you eat!

What is the digestive system?

Your cells need a lot of energy for their daily activities. Cells use nutrients, which are substances in food, for energy, growth, maintenance, and repair. The **digestive system** breaks down the food you eat into nutrients that can be used as building materials and that can provide energy for cells.

The digestive system interacts with other body systems to obtain and use energy from food. Blood, part of the circulatory system, transports nutrients to other tissues. In order to extract energy from nutrients, cells need oxygen. The respiratory system is responsible for obtaining this oxygen from the environment. The nervous system controls and regulates the functioning of the digestive system.

What are the two types of digestion?

Digestion is the process of breaking down food into a form that can pass from the digestive system into the bloodstream. There are two types of digestion: mechanical and chemical.

The Stomach

The deep pits and grooves in the stomach lining help grind food.

Inquiry

6 Infer The stomach lining is made up of deep muscular grooves. How do you think these structures help the stomach to break down food?

_____

_____

_____

_____

© Houghton Mifflin Harcourt Publishing Company • Image Credits: ©Eye of Science/Photo Researchers, Inc.

Mechanical Digestion

Mechanical digestion is the breaking, crushing, and mashing of food. Chewing is a type of mechanical digestion. Chewing creates small pieces of food that are easier to swallow and digest than large pieces are. Mechanical digestion increases the surface area of food for the action of chemical digestion.

Chemical Digestion

Chemical digestion is the process in which large molecules of food are broken down into smaller molecules so that they can pass into the bloodstream. An **enzyme** (EN•zym) is a chemical that the body uses to break down large molecules into smaller molecules. Enzymes act like chemical scissors. They "cut up" large molecules into smaller pieces. Mechanical digestion breaks up food and increases surface area so that enzymes can break nutrients into smaller molecules. Without mechanical digestion, chemical digestion would take days instead of hours!

7 Categorize Decide whether each of these steps in digestion is an example of mechanical digestion or chemical digestion. Then put a check in the correct box.

In your mouth, teeth grind food.

☐ mechanical

☐ chemical

Salivary glands release a liquid called saliva, which helps to break food down.

☐ mechanical

☐ chemical

In the stomach, muscles contract to grind food into a pulpy mixture.

☐ mechanical

☐ chemical

In the small intestine, most nutrients are broken down by enzymes.

☐ mechanical

☐ chemical

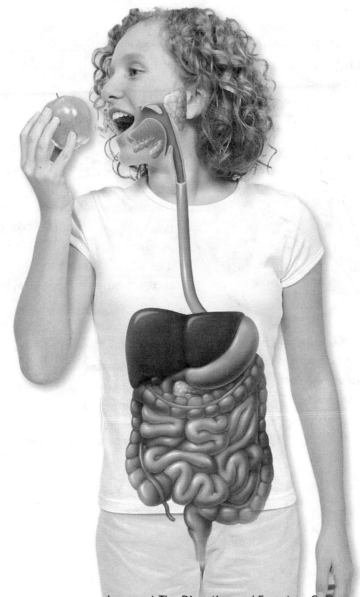

Chew on this

What are the parts of the digestive system?

Has anyone ever reminded you to chew your food? Chewing food is the first part of digestion. After food is chewed and swallowed, pieces of that food move through other organs in the digestive system, where the food is broken down even more.

The Mouth

Digestion begins in the mouth with both mechanical and chemical digestion. Teeth, with the help of strong jaw muscles, break and crush food.

As you chew, food is moistened by a liquid called *saliva*. Glands in your mouth make saliva. Saliva contains many substances, including an enzyme that begins the chemical digestion of starches in food.

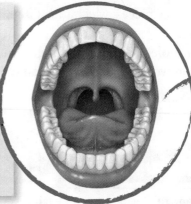

The Esophagus

Once food has been chewed, it is swallowed. The food moves through the throat and into a long tube called the **esophagus** (ih•SAWF•uh•gus). Waves of muscle contractions called *peristalsis* (per•ih•STAWL•sis) move the food into the stomach. The muscles move food along in much the same way as you move toothpaste from the bottom of the tube with your thumbs.

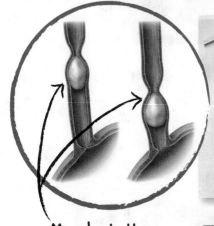

Muscles in the esophagus move this clump of food from your mouth to your stomach.

Visualize It!

9 Claims • Evidence • Reasoning Do you think digestion is more efficient if you are sitting up, slumped over, or lying down? To support your claim, consider the order of organs in the digestive system and their positions in the body. Explain your reasoning.

_____

_____

_____

_____

_____

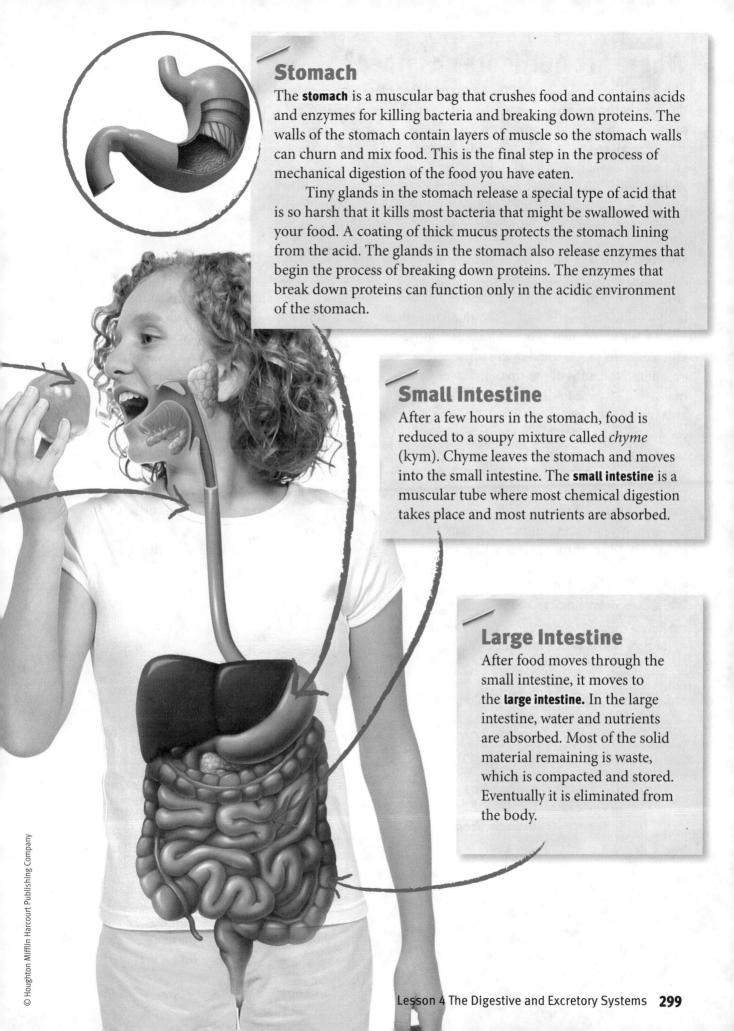

Stomach

The **stomach** is a muscular bag that crushes food and contains acids and enzymes for killing bacteria and breaking down proteins. The walls of the stomach contain layers of muscle so the stomach walls can churn and mix food. This is the final step in the process of mechanical digestion of the food you have eaten.

Tiny glands in the stomach release a special type of acid that is so harsh that it kills most bacteria that might be swallowed with your food. A coating of thick mucus protects the stomach lining from the acid. The glands in the stomach also release enzymes that begin the process of breaking down proteins. The enzymes that break down proteins can function only in the acidic environment of the stomach.

Small Intestine

After a few hours in the stomach, food is reduced to a soupy mixture called *chyme* (kym). Chyme leaves the stomach and moves into the small intestine. The **small intestine** is a muscular tube where most chemical digestion takes place and most nutrients are absorbed.

Large Intestine

After food moves through the small intestine, it moves to the **large intestine.** In the large intestine, water and nutrients are absorbed. Most of the solid material remaining is waste, which is compacted and stored. Eventually it is eliminated from the body.

Where are nutrients absorbed?

The digestion of nutrients in the small intestine takes place with the help of three organs that attach to the small intestine. These organs are the *pancreas*, *liver*, and *gall bladder*.

The **pancreas** (PANG•kree•uhz) makes fluids that break down every type of material found in foods: proteins, carbohydrates, fats, and nucleic acids. The **liver** makes and releases a mixture called *bile* that is then stored in the gall bladder. Bile breaks up large fat droplets into very small fat droplets.

In the Small Intestine

After nutrients are broken down, they are absorbed into the bloodstream and used by the body's cells. The inside wall of the small intestine has three features that allow it to absorb nutrients efficiently: folds, villi, and microvilli.

First, the walls of the small intestine have many folds. These folds increase the surface area inside the intestine wall, creating more room for nutrients to be absorbed. Each fold is covered with tiny fingerlike projections called *villi* (VIL•eye). In turn, the villi are covered with projections called *microvilli*. Microvilli increase the surface area of the villi. Villi contain blood and lymph vessels that absorb nutrients from food as it passes through the small intestine.

In the Large Intestine

The large intestine removes water from mostly-digested food, absorbs vitamins, and turns food waste into semi-solid waste called *feces*.

. Some parts of food, such as the cell walls of plants, cannot be absorbed by the body. Bacteria live in the large intestine that feed off of this undigested food. The bacteria produce vitamins that are absorbed by the large intestine along with most of the water in the undigested food.

The *rectum* is the last part of the large intestine. The rectum stores feces until they can be expelled. Feces pass to the outside of the body through an opening called the *anus*. It takes about 24 hours for a meal to make the full journey through a person's digestive system.

Visualize It!

10 Relate How is the structure and function of this sponge similar to that of the small intestine?

_____

_____

_____

_____

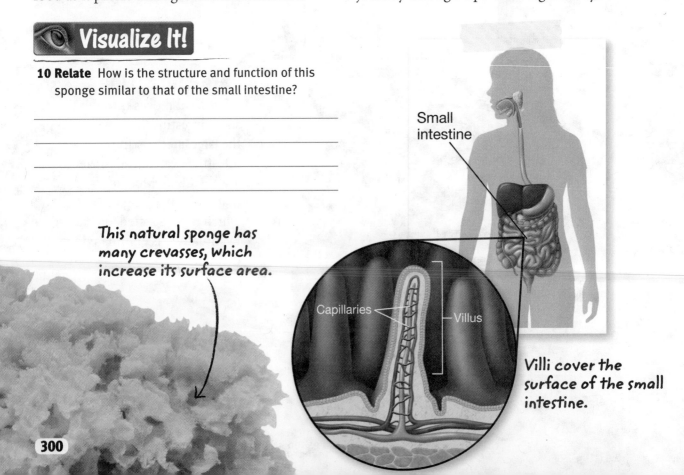

This natural sponge has many crevasses, which increase its surface area.

Small intestine

Capillaries

Villus

Villi cover the surface of the small intestine.

Toxic Waste!

What are the functions of the excretory system?

You have toxic waste in your body! As your cells perform the chemical activities that keep you alive, waste products, such as carbon dioxide and ammonia, are made. These waste products are toxic to cells. If waste builds up in a cell, homeostasis will be disrupted and the cell may die. The **excretory system** eliminates cellular wastes from the body through the lungs, skin, kidneys, and digestive system.

Waste Removal

To Sweat
Your skin is part of the excretory and the integumentary systems. Waste products, such as excess salts, are released through your skin when you sweat.

After you read the text, answer the associated questions below.

11 Identify Sweat releases wastes through your _____.

To Exhale
Your lungs are part of the excretory and respiratory systems. Lungs release water and toxic carbon dioxide when you exhale.

12 List Two waste products that are released when you exhale are _____ and _____.

To Produce Urine and Feces
Kidneys, part of the urinary system, remove all types of cellular waste products from your blood. Your digestive system eliminates feces from your body.

13 Identify The urinary system filters waste out of your _____.

Cleanup crew

What organs are in the urinary system?

The urinary system collects cellular waste and eliminates it from the body in the form of liquid waste. Waste products enter the urinary system through the kidneys.

Active Reading

14 Identify As you read, underline the functions of the organs in the urinary system.

Kidneys

The **kidney** is one of a pair of organs that remove waste from the blood. Inside each kidney are more than 1 million microscopic structures called **nephrons** (NEF•rahnz). Fluid is filtered from the blood into the nephron through a structure called the *glomerulus* (gloh•MEHR•yuh•luhs). Filtered blood leaves the glomerulus and circulates around the tubes that make up the nephron. These structures return valuable salts and ions to the blood. Tubes in the kidneys collect the wastes from the nephrons. Water and the wastes filtered out of the blood form a liquid known as **urine.**

Ureters

Urine forms in the kidneys. From the kidneys, urine travels through the *ureters*. The ureters are tubes that connect the kidneys to the bladder.

Bladder

The urine is transported from the kidneys to the *bladder*. The bladder is a saclike organ that stores urine. Voluntary muscles hold the urine until it is ready to be released. At that time, the muscles contract and squeeze urine out of the bladder.

Urethra

Urine exits the bladder through a tube called the *urethra*.

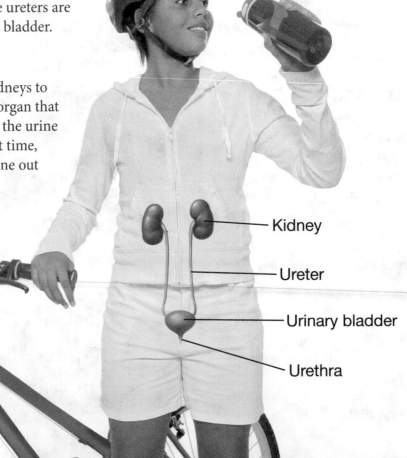

Kidney

Ureter

Urinary bladder

Urethra

Filtering Blood

Nephron

Unfiltered blood enters the kidney and flows into millions of tiny capillaries attached to the nephrons.

Artery

Unfiltered blood

Filtered blood

As blood flows through the capillaries, wastes are drawn out of the blood and into the nephron.

Vein

Ureter

Once the blood has been filtered, it flows back out of the kidney.

Urine is collected from all of the nephrons and then flows out of the kidney through the ureter.

Urine

15 Identify After blood enters the kidneys, name the two paths the fluid takes.

_____

_____

_____

_____

_____

_____

_____

How does the urinary system maintain homeostasis?

Your cells have to maintain a certain level of water and salt in order to function properly. The excretory system interacts with the endocrine system to help maintain homeostasis and carry out life processes. Chemical messengers called *hormones* signal the kidneys to filter more or less water or salt, depending on the levels of water and salt in the body. For example, when you sweat a lot, the water content of your blood can drop. When this happens, a hormone is released that signals the kidneys to conserve more water and make less urine. When your blood has too much water, less of the hormone is released. As a result, the nephrons conserve less water, and more urine is produced by the kidneys.

Household or environmental toxins that enter the body through the skin, lungs, or mouth eventually end up in the bloodstream. When the kidneys are damaged, many toxins can accumulate in the blood. Infections can also affect the kidneys. Bacterial infections can occur when bacteria around the opening of the urethra travel up to the bladder and possibly the kidneys.

Active Reading

16 Explain How does exercise affect the balance of salt and water in your body? Synthesize evidence to support your claim.

_____

_____

_____

_____

_____

_____

_____

_____

_____

_____

Visual Summary

To complete this summary, fill in the blanks with the correct word or phrase. Then, use the answer key to check your answers. You can use this page to review the main concepts of the lesson.

The digestive system breaks down the food you eat into nutrients that provide energy and building materials for cells.

17 The two types of digestion that take place in the mouth are _____ and _____.

Digestion and Excretion

The excretory system removes waste from the body.

18 The _____ remove waste from the blood.

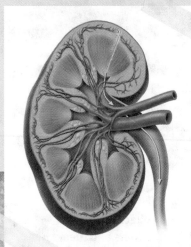

The digestive and excretory systems interact to process the food that you eat.

19 To process this salad, food is broken down by the _____ _____ and wastes are removed by the _____.

20 **Summarize** What types of wastes does the excretory system remove?

Lesson Review

Vocabulary

Fill in the blank with the term that best completes the following sentences.

1 The _____ system helps the body maintain homeostasis by giving it the nutrients it needs to perform different functions.

2 The _____ system eliminates cellular waste through the lungs, skin, and kidneys.

3 The _____ is the name for the hollow muscular organ that stores urine.

Key Concepts

4 Compare What is the difference between mechanical digestion and chemical digestion in the mouth?

_____

_____

_____

_____

5 Describe Starting with the mouth, describe the pathway that food takes through the digestive system.

_____

_____

_____

_____

6 Explain How does the circulatory system interact with the digestive system?

_____

_____

_____

_____

7 Identify Where does urine go after it exits the kidneys?

_____

_____

_____

_____

8 Summarize How do kidneys interact with other body systems to maintain homeostasis?

_____

_____

_____

Use the diagram to answer the following question.

9 Apply Identify the organs numbered below.

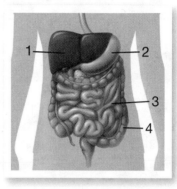

_____

Critical Thinking

10 Relate How would damaged kidneys affect your health? Explain your reasoning.

_____

_____

_____

_____

11 Claims • Evidence • Reasoning Suppose a person has a small intestine that has fewer villi than normal. Would the person most likely be overweight or underweight? State your claim. Summarize evidence to support your claim and explain your reasoning.

_____

_____

_____

_____

_____

My Notes

Lesson 5

The Nervous and Endocrine Systems

ESSENTIAL QUESTION

How do the nervous and endocrine systems work?

By the end of this lesson, you should be able to relate the structures of the nervous and endocrine systems to their functions in the human body.

This sky diver can sense his surroundings and feel the rush of excitement with the help of his nervous and endocrine systems.

© Houghton Mifflin Harcourt Publishing Company • Image Credits: ©Getty Images

Lesson Labs

Quick Labs
• Negative Feedback
• Measuring Reaction Time
Exploration Lab
• Mapping Sensory Receptors

Engage Your Brain

1 Predict Check T or F to show whether you think each statement is true or false.

T F

☐ ☐ The central nervous system allows us to sense the environment.

☐ ☐ The endocrine system functions by sending chemical signals.

☐ ☐ The spinal cord is part of the peripheral nervous system.

☐ ☐ The endocrine system helps regulate our blood sugar after we eat a meal.

2 Describe Think about a situation that makes you feel very nervous or anxious. Describe how this makes you feel inside. What do you think is going on in your body?

_____

_____

_____

_____

_____

Active Reading

3 Apply You can often understand the meaning of a word if you use it in a sentence. Use the following definition to write your own sentence that has the word *gland*.

Definition
gland: a group of cells that make special chemicals for the body

gland:

_____

_____

_____

_____

_____

Vocabulary Terms

• nervous system
• brain
• spinal cord
• neuron
• axon
• dendrite
• endocrine system
• hormone
• gland

4 Apply As you learn the definition of each vocabulary term in this lesson, create your own definition or sketch to help you remember the meaning of the term.

Brainiac!

What is the function of the nervous system?

The **nervous system** is made of the structures that control the actions and reactions of the body in response to stimuli from the environment. Your nervous system has two parts: the central nervous system (CNS) and the peripheral (puh•RIFF•uh•rahl) nervous system (PNS).

The CNS Processes Information

The brain and the spinal cord make up the CNS. The **brain** is the body's central command organ. It constantly receives impulses from all over the body. Your **spinal cord** allows your brain to communicate with the rest of your body. Your nervous system is mostly made up of specialized cells that send and receive electrical signals.

The PNS Connects the CNS to Muscles and Organs

Your PNS connects your CNS to the rest of your body. The PNS has two main parts—the sensory part and the motor part. Many processes that the brain controls happen automatically—you have no control over them. These processes are called *involuntary*. For example, you could not stop your heart from beating even if you tried. However, some of the actions of your brain you can control—these are *voluntary*. Moving your arm is a voluntary action.

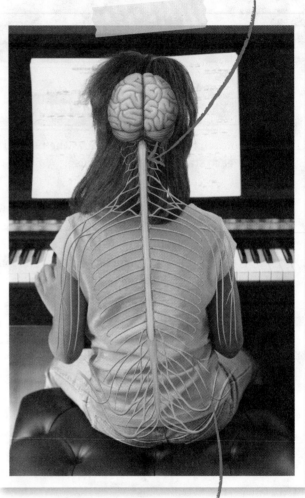

The CNS is shown in yellow.

The PNS is shown in green.

Parts of the CNS

_____

and

_____

The CNS and PNS are both made of

Parts of the PNS

_____

and

5 Compare Fill in the Venn diagram to compare and contrast the structure of the CNS and the PNS.

What are the parts of the CNS?

The CNS is made up of the brain and the spinal cord.

The Brain

The three main areas of the brain are the cerebrum, the cerebellum, and the brain stem. The largest part of the brain is the cerebrum. The cerebrum is where you think and problem-solve, and where most of your memories are stored. It controls voluntary movements and allows you to sense touch, light, sound, odors, taste, pain, heat, and cold. The second largest part of your brain is the cerebellum. It processes information from your body. This allows the brain to keep track of your body's position and coordinate movements. The brain stem connects your brain to your spinal cord. The medulla is part of the brain stem. It controls involuntary processes, such as blood pressure, body temperature, heart rate, and involuntary breathing.

6 Identify List a function of each part of the brain shown here.

Cerebrum

_____

_____

_____

Cerebellum

_____

_____

_____

Brain stem

_____

_____

_____

The Spinal Cord

The spinal cord is made of bundles of nerves. A *nerve* is a collection of nerve cell extensions bundled together with blood vessels and connective tissue. Nerves are everywhere in your body. The spinal cord is surrounded by protective bones called *vertebrae.*

Special cells in your skin and muscles carry sensory information to the spinal cord. The spinal cord carries these impulses to the brain. The brain interprets these impulses as warmth, pain, or other sensations and sends information back to the spinal cord. Different cells in the spinal cord then send impulses to the rest of the body to create a response.

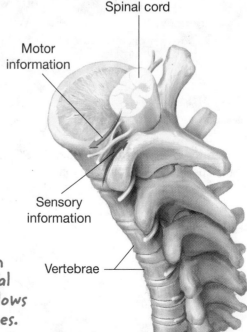

Spinal cord

Motor information

Sensory information

Vertebrae

Sensory information (red) flows in from the environment to the spinal cord. Motor information (blue) flows out from the spinal cord to muscles.

You've Got Nerves!

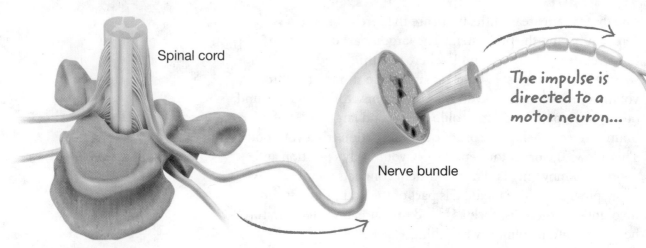

Spinal cord

The impulse is directed to a motor neuron...

Nerve bundle

If you notice that your shoe is untied, your brain interprets this information and sends an impulse down the spinal cord.

How do signals move through the nervous system?

Your nervous system works by receiving information from the environment and translating that information into electrical signals. Those electrical signals are sent from the brain to the rest of the body by special cells called *neurons*. A **neuron** is a cell that moves messages in the form of fast-moving electrical energy. These electrical messages are called *impulses*.

Signals move through the central and peripheral nervous systems with the help of glial (GLEE•uhl) cells. Glial cells do not transmit nerve impulses, but they protect and support neurons. Without glial cells, neurons would not work properly. Your brain has about 100 billion neurons, but there are about 10 to 50 times more glial cells in your brain.

Through Sensory and Motor Neurons

Neurons carry information from the body to the brain, and carry instructions from the brain back to the rest of the body. The two groups of neurons are sensory neurons and motor neurons.

Sensory neurons gather information from in and around your body. They then move this information to the brain. Motor neurons move impulses from the brain and spinal cord to other parts of the body. For example, when you are hot, motor neurons move messages from your brain to your sweat glands to tell the sweat glands to make sweat. Sweating cools your body.

Cell body

The Neuron

...and the motor neurons that connect to muscles in your back allow you to bend over and tie your shoe.

Axon

Axon terminal

Muscle fibers

Dendrite

What are the parts of a neuron?

A neuron is made up of a large region called the *cell body,* a long extension called the *axon,* and short branches called *dendrites.* At the end of the axon is the *axon terminal.*

Like other cells, a neuron's cell body has a nucleus and organelles. But neurons have other structures that allow them to communicate with other cells. A **dendrite** (DEHN•dryt) is a usually short, branched extension of the cell body. A neuron may have one, two, or many dendrites. Neurons with many dendrites can receive impulses from thousands of cells at a time. The cell body gathers information from the dendrites and creates an impulse.

Impulses are carried away from the cell body by extensions of the neuron, called an **axon**. A neuron has only one axon, and they can be very short or quite long. Some long axons extend almost 1 m from your lower back to your toes! Impulses move in one direction along the axon.

At the end of an axon is the axon terminal, where a signal is changed from an electrical signal to a chemical signal. This chemical signal, called a *neurotransmitter,* is released into the gap between the neuron and other cells.

Visualize It!

8 Apply In the boxes below, fill in the appropriate neuron parts, structures, or functions.

NEURON PART	STRUCTURE	FUNCTION
Cell body	region containing nucleus and organelles	
	branches of the cell body	gathers information from other cells
Axon		sends impulse away from cell body
	end of an axon	changes electrical signal to chemical signal

That Makes Sense!

What are the main senses?

The body senses the environment with specialized structures called *sensory organs*. These structures include the eyes, the skin, the ears, the mouth, and the nose.

9 Imagine If you were at this amusement park, what do you think you would see, hear, smell, taste, and feel?

_____

_____

An amusement park is full of sensory information! How do we sense it all?

Sight

Your eye allows you to see the size, shape, motion, and color of objects around you. The front of the eye is covered by a clear membrane called the *cornea*. Light from an object passes through an opening called the *pupil*. Light hits the eye's lens, an oval-shaped piece of clear, curved material. Eye muscles change the shape of the lens to focus light onto the retina. The *retina* (RET•nuh) is a layer of light-sensitive photoreceptor cells that change light into electrical impulses. These cells, called *rods* and *cones,* generate nerve impulses that are sent to the brain.

Rays form an upside-down image on the retina at the back of the eye. This image is translated by the brain.

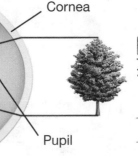

Lens

Cornea

Retina

Pupil

Light enters the eye through the lens. Light rays are bent by the cornea.

> **Visualize It!**
>
> **10 Identify** What part of the eye focuses light on to the retina?
>
> _____
>
> _____

Touch

You feel a tap on your shoulder. The tap produces impulses in sensory receptors on your shoulder. These impulses travel to your brain. Once the impulses reach your brain, they create an awareness called a *sensation*. In this case, the sensation is that of your shoulder being touched. The skin has different kinds of receptors that detect pressure, temperature, pain, and vibration.

Hearing

Ears pick up sound wave vibrations. These sound waves push air particles, creating a wave of sound energy. The sensory cells of your ears turn sound waves into electrical impulses. These electrical impulses then travel to your brain. Each ear has an outer, a middle, and an inner portion. Sound waves reaching the outer ear are funneled toward the middle ear. There, the waves make the eardrum vibrate. The *eardrum* is a thin membrane separating the outer ear from the middle ear. The vibrating eardrum makes three tiny bones in the middle ear vibrate. The last of these bones vibrates against the *cochlea* (KOH•klee•uh), a fluid-filled organ of the inner ear. Inside the cochlea, the vibrations make waves in the fluid. Sensory receptors called *hair cells* move about in the fluid. Movement of the hair cells causes neurons in the cochlea to send electrical impulses. These impulses travel to the brain via the auditory nerve and are interpreted as sound.

The ears also help you maintain balance. Special fluid-filled canals in the inner ear are filled with hair cells that respond to changes in head orientation. These hair cells then send signals to the brain about the position of the head with respect to gravity.

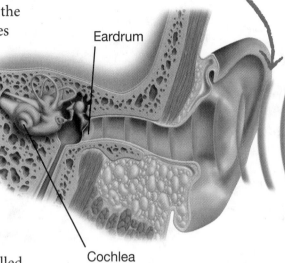

Sound waves enter the ear and cause the eardrum to vibrate. The vibrations are translated by receptors.

Eardrum

Cochlea

Taste

Your tongue is covered with taste buds. These taste buds contain clusters of *taste cells* that respond to signals in dissolved molecules in food. Taste cells react to five basic tastes: sweet, sour, salty, bitter, and savory. Your sense of taste can protect you from eating something that could be harmful.

Smell

The nose is your sense organ for smell. Receptors for smell are located in the upper part of your nasal cavity. Sensory receptors called *olfactory cells* react to chemicals in the air. These molecules dissolve in the moist lining of the nasal cavity and trigger an impulse in the receptors. The nerve impulses are sent to the brain, where they are interpreted as an odor. Your senses of taste and smell work together to allow you to taste a variety of food flavors. Both senses detect chemical cues in the environment.

Olfactory cells

11 Apply If you have a cold that causes congestion in your sinuses, how might that affect your sense of smell? Support your claim with evidence.

_____

_____

_____

_____

Molecules in the air enter your nose. There, they bind to receptors in the top of your nasal cavity.

Keep Your Cool!

What is the function of the endocrine system?

Your **endocrine system** controls body functions and helps maintain homeostasis by using hormones. A **hormone** is a chemical messenger made in one cell or tissue that causes a change in another cell or tissue in a different part of the body. Hormones are produced by endocrine glands or tissues. A **gland** is a group of cells that make special chemicals for your body. Unlike direct signals of the nervous system, the signals sent by the endocrine system are indirect because they cycle through the whole body.

How do hormones work?

Hormones travel through the bloodstream. They travel from the endocrine gland where they are made and can reach every cell in the body. However, hormones affect only the cells that have specific *receptors*. Each hormone has its own receptor and affects only cells that have that receptor. These cells are called *target cells*. Many cells throughout the body have the same receptors, so hormones are able to perform many functions at the same time in different cells.

Active Reading

12 Identify As you read, underline the structure which allows hormones to affect only certain cells.

Visualize It!

13 Apply Explain the difference between an endocrine cell and a target cell.

_____

_____

When you are surprised, a hormone called adrenaline makes you more alert.

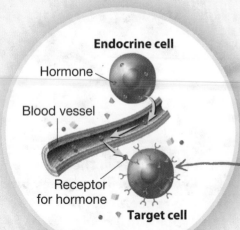

Endocrine cell

Hormone

Blood vessel

Receptor for hormone

Target cell

Hormones are released from an endocrine cell and travel through the bloodstream to bind to a receptor on a target cell. Sometimes a target cell is very far away!

What glands make up the endocrine system?

Your body has several endocrine glands or tissues that make up the endocrine system.

- Your pituitary gland is very important because it secretes hormones that affect other glands. It also stimulates growth and sexual development.
- The hypothalamus is a gland in the brain that controls the release of hormones from the pituitary gland.
- The pineal gland, also in the brain, produces hormones essential in the control of sleep, aging, reproduction, and body temperature.
- Hormones from the thyroid control your metabolism.
- The parathyroid gland controls calcium levels in the blood.
- Hormones made in the reproductive organs (ovaries or testes) control reproduction.
- Other endocrine glands include the pancreas and adrenal glands. The pancreas regulates blood sugar levels and the adrenal glands control the body's fight or flight response in dangerous situations.

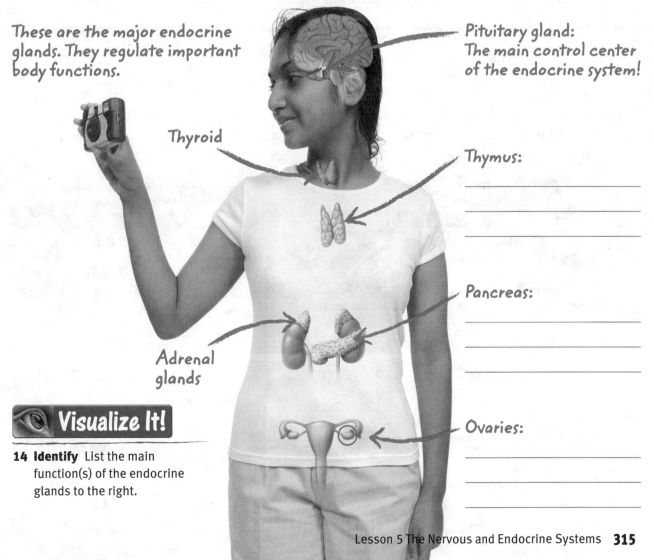

These are the major endocrine glands. They regulate important body functions.

Thyroid

Pituitary gland:
The main control center of the endocrine system!

Thymus:
_____
_____
_____

Pancreas:
_____
_____
_____
_____

Adrenal glands

Ovaries:
_____
_____
_____

Visualize It!

14 Identify List the main function(s) of the endocrine glands to the right.

Feed⬅Back

How are hormone levels controlled?

The endocrine system keeps the body's internal environment in homeostasis. It does this by increasing or decreasing the amount of hormones in the bloodstream, some of which may have opposite effects on body cells. Such a process is called a feedback mechanism. A *feedback mechanism* is a cycle of events in which information from one step controls or affects a previous step.

By Feedback Mechanisms

There are two types of feedback, positive and negative. In negative feedback, the effects of a hormone in the body cause the release of that hormone to be turned down. For example, when you eat food, your blood sugar levels go up. Insulin is released and blood sugar levels are lowered. Once this happens, the lower blood sugar levels tell the pancreas to stop releasing insulin. In other words, when the proper level of blood sugar is reached, the insulin-releasing cells are turned off.

In positive feedback, the effects of a hormone stimulate the release of more of that hormone. For example, the hormone oxytocin stimulates contractions of the uterus. When a fetus matures in the uterus, both it and the mother produce oxytocin. The oxytocin stimulates contractions, and these contractions stimulate more oxytocin to be released. The contractions expel a baby from the mother's uterus at birth.

Active Reading

15 Compare Describe the difference between negative and positive feedback.

_____

_____

_____

_____

_____

Negative Feedback

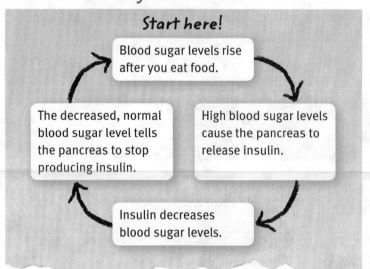

In negative feedback, hormone levels are kept from rising too high.

Positive Feedback

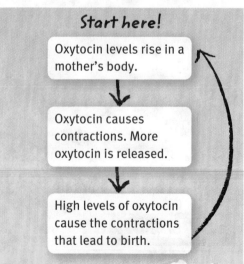

In positive feedback, the level of hormones continues to rise.

What are disorders of the endocrine and nervous systems?

The endocrine system and nervous system are both responsible for sending messages around our bodies. If a problem developed with one or more of these systems, other systems of the body would need to adjust to compensate for this loss.

Hormone Imbalances

Disorders of the endocrine system occur when an endocrine gland makes too much or not enough of a hormone. For example, a person whose pancreas does not make enough insulin has a condition called *type 1 diabetes*. This condition causes an imbalance of the blood sugar. A person who has diabetes may need daily injections of insulin to keep blood sugar levels within safe limits. Some patients receive their insulin automatically from a small pump worn next to the body. New technology allows people with type 1 diabetes to intake insulin using an inhaler.

Think Outside the Book

16 **Compare** Many systems you use every day send messages, such as e-mail, a thermostat, and TV remote controls. Research how one of these systems sends and receives messages. Make a chart to compare this system to the endocrine system.

17 **Describe** How does the insulin pump help a person with type 1 diabetes maintain homeostasis?

_____

_____

_____

_____

_____

This machine injects insulin into a person's bloodstream when insulin levels are low.

Nerve Damage

Disorders of the nervous system include Parkinson's disease, multiple sclerosis, and spinal cord injury. In Parkinson's disease, the cells that control movement are damaged. Multiple sclerosis affects the brain's ability to send signals to the rest of the body.

A spinal cord injury may block information to and from the brain. For example, impulses coming from the feet and legs may be blocked. People with such an injury cannot sense pain in their legs. The person would also not be able to move his or her legs, because impulses from the brain could not get past the injury site.

Visual Summary

To complete this summary, fill in the blank to answer the question. Then, use the key below to check your answers. You can use this page to review the main concepts of the lesson.

The nervous system gathers information and responds by sending electrical signals.

18 Nerve cells called _____ carry electrical messages called _____.

The endocrine system controls conditions in your body by sending chemical messages.

19 Hormones have specific actions by attaching to _____ on target cells.

Sending Signals

Hormones are controlled by feedback mechanisms.

20 _____ feedback is when higher levels of a hormone turn off the production of that hormone.

Start here!

Blood sugar levels rise after you eat food.

High blood sugar cause the pancreas to release insulin.

Insulin decreases blood sugar levels.

The decreased, normal blood sugar level tells the pancreas to stop producing insulin.

Answers: 18 neurons, impulses; 19 receptors; 20 Negative

21 **Claims • Evidence • Reasoning** Describe how both your nervous and endocrine systems would be involved if you walked into a surprise party and were truly surprised. Synthesize evidence to support your claim and explain your reasoning.

Lesson Review

Vocabulary

Use a term from the section to complete each sentence below.

1 The _____ is made up of the brain and spinal cord.

2 Glands in the _____ send messages to target cells.

3 Use *gland* and *hormone* in the same sentence.

_____

_____

_____

4 Use *hormone* and *feedback mechanism* in the same sentence.

_____

_____

_____

Key Concepts

5 Identify Describe the function of the PNS and the CNS.

_____

_____

_____

6 Apply What are the parts of a neuron?

_____

_____

_____

7 Identify How are the messages of the endocrine system moved around the body?

_____

_____

_____

_____

8 Identify What is the main sense organ for each of the five senses?

_____

_____

_____

Critical Thinking

The images below show how an eye responds to different light levels. Use the image to answer the following question.

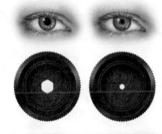

9 Interpret The pupil opens and closes automatically in response to light. What part of your nervous system controls this response?

_____

10 Infer Explain whether this is a voluntary or involuntary action.

_____

_____

_____

11 Claims • Evidence • Reasoning How would your body be affected if your pituitary gland was not working properly? State your claim. Summarize evidence to support your claim and explain your reasoning.

_____

_____

_____

_____

_____

My Notes

Engineering Design Process

Skills	Objectives
✔ Identify a need	• Identify a market need.
Conduct research	• Design an assistive device.
✔ Brainstorm solutions	• Draw a prototype.
✔ Select a solution	
Build a prototype	
Test and evaluate	
Redesign to improve	
✔ Communicate results	

Designing a Device

The human body is an amazing machine, but sometimes it can use a little help. *Assistive devices* are devices that are designed for use by people with disabilities. Creating assistive devices to meet the needs of targeted groups of individuals is known as market needs. Some of these devices are integrated with the body, some are worn on the body, and some are tools that people use. Major categories of assistive devices include communication devices, hygiene (HY•jeen) or medication aids, vision aids, hearing aids, mobility aids, and eating aids. These devices include wheelchairs or grab bars, pacemakers, and internal insulin (IN•suh•lin) pumps. Also, hand railings help people climb stairs, shower handles help people get in and out of the shower, and sidewalk bumps help the visually impaired. These are all examples of ways that engineering is applied to life science.

1 Describe Look at the photo on this page. What examples of assistive devices do you see?

_____

_____

_____

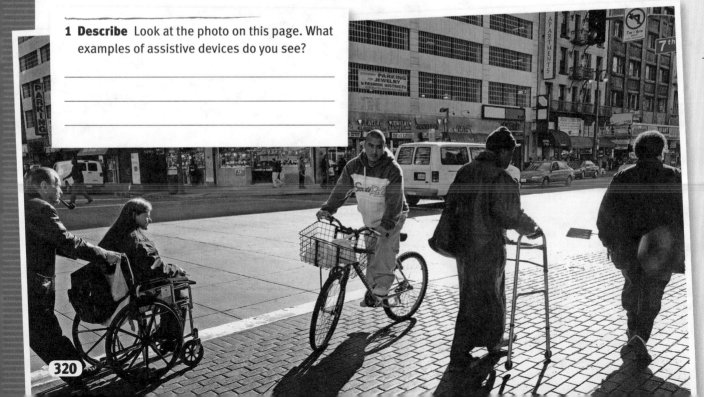

We Can All Use a Little Help

Some of the better-known assistive devices, such as wheelchairs or crutches, help with injuries or disabilities. For example, if you break your leg, your doctor will likely give you crutches to help you to get around while you heal. But many assistive or adaptive devices just simplify daily tasks. Small tools such as buttonhooks help people button their shirts, long-handled shoehorns make it easier to put on shoes, and special utensils make eating easier. Many adaptive devices are also integrated into your everyday environment. For example, some people wear glasses or contact lenses to improve their vision or get hearing aids to help their hearing.

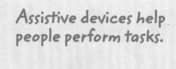

Assistive devices help people perform tasks.

2 Explain For one of the devices shown above, state what the assistive device is and how it is helpful.

_____

_____

_____

_____

 You Try It! ----→

Now it's your turn to design an assistive device.

✋ You Try It!

Now it's your turn to design a realistic assistive device that people need. You will think about what people might need to do, decide which is the most promising idea, draw a prototype of your device, and present your idea to your class.

1 Identify a Need

A Imagine a need for each category of assistive device given below. Think of people you know of who need an assistive device for a daily task. Consider what an older person might need, or someone who is physically disabled.

Grasping	Hygiene	Communication	Mobility	Eating

B To find which idea has the biggest potential impact, make a Pugh chart from the following model. Rank each idea from 1 to 10, with 10 indicating the best fit with the criterion indicated in the criteria column. Find the total for each column.

Criteria	Grasping	Hygiene	Communication	Mobility	Eating
Frequency of use 1 = not often 10 = very often					
Number of users 1 = few 10 = many					
Product lifetime 1 = long 10 = short					
Total					

2 Brainstorm Solutions

In your group, brainstorm ideas for assistive devices that would address the biggest market identified in your Pugh chart.

_____

_____

(3) Select a Solution

With the members of your group, decide on the best idea from your brainstorming session. Then, in the space below, draw a prototype of your chosen idea, and list the materials needed to make it. Be as detailed as possible (use extra paper if necessary).

(4) Communicate Results

Summarize the information about your device. Describe the need that the device addresses, who the users would be, the device itself and how it works, and any other things you think are important to explain your device to another person. Then, as a group, use the summary information to create a poster of your idea to present to the class.

_____

_____

_____

_____

_____

The Reproductive System

ESSENTIAL QUESTION

How does your reproductive system work?

By the end of this lesson, you should be able to relate the structure of the reproductive system to its function in the human body.

Many pregnant women do exercises, such as yoga or other stretches, to stay healthy as their baby develops.

 Engage Your Brain

1 Predict Have you met a woman who was pregnant? Write a short answer describing what type of development you think is going on inside a pregnant woman.

_____
_____
_____
_____
_____
_____
_____

2 Apply Name five things that have changed about you from your fifth to your tenth birthday.

_____
_____
_____
_____
_____
_____

 Active Reading

3 Explain You may be familiar with the eggs that farmers collect from chickens. Females of many species, including humans, produce eggs as part of the reproductive cycle. How do you think a human egg is similar to a chicken egg? How do you think they are different?

_____
_____
_____
_____
_____
_____
_____

Vocabulary Terms

• sperm	• vagina
• testes	• embryo
• penis	• placenta
• egg	• umbilical cord
• ovary	• fetus
• uterus	

4 Apply As you learn the definition of each vocabulary term in this lesson, create your own definition or sketch to help you remember the meaning of the term.

Reproduction

What are the main functions of the male reproductive system?

The male reproductive system functions to produce sperm and deliver sperm to the female reproductive system. **Sperm** are the male cells that are used for reproduction. Each sperm cell carries 23 chromosomes, half of the chromosomes of other body cells. The male reproductive system also produces hormones.

Hormones are chemical messengers that control many important body functions, such as growth, development, and sex-cell production. The **testes** (singular, *testis*) are the main organs of the male reproductive system. These organs produce *testosterone,* the male sex hormone. Testosterone causes male characteristics to develop, such as facial hair and a deep voice.

The testes also make sperm. After sperm mature, they are stored in the *epididymis* (EH•puh•DIH•duh•miss). They leave the epididymis through a tube called the *vas deferens* and mix with fluids from several glands. This mixture of sperm and fluids is called *semen*. To leave the body, semen passes through the *urethra,* the tube that runs through the penis. The **penis** is the organ that delivers semen into the female reproductive system.

Male Reproductive System

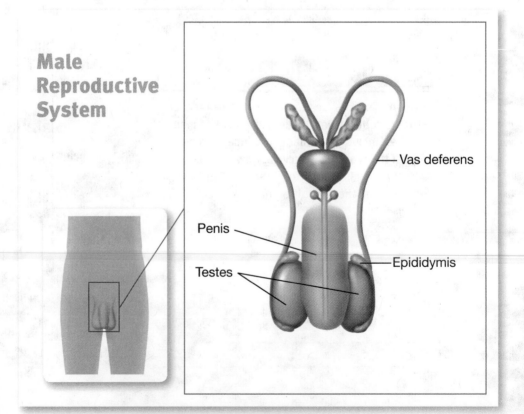

Vas deferens

Penis

Epididymis

Testes

What are the main functions of the female reproductive system?

The female reproductive system produces hormones and eggs, and provides a place to nourish a developing human. An **egg** is the female sex cell. Like sperm, egg cells have 23 chromosomes, only half the number of other body cells.

The female reproductive system produces the sex hormones *estrogen* and *progesterone*. These hormones control the development of female characteristics, such as breasts and wider hips. They also regulate the development and release of eggs, and they prepare the body for pregnancy.

An **ovary** is the reproductive organ that produces eggs. At sexual maturity, females have hundreds of thousands of immature eggs in their ovaries. Eggs are produced through the process of meiosis. During a female's lifetime, usually about 400 of her eggs will mature and be released from the ovaries.

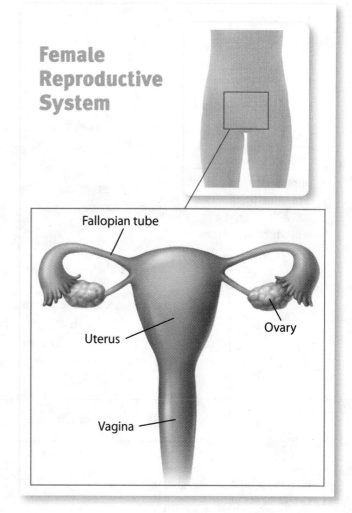

Female Reproductive System

Fallopian tube

Uterus

Ovary

Vagina

---

6 Summarize Fill in the chart below to summarize the structures of the male and female reproductive systems.

Sex	Sex cell	Organ that produces sex cell	Other reproductive organs
Male			
Female			

---

7 Contrast What makes sperm cells and egg cells different from almost all other types of body cells?

_____

_____

_____

Fertile ground

How are eggs released?

A woman's reproductive system goes through changes that produce an egg, release the egg, and prepare the body for pregnancy. These changes are called the *menstrual cycle* and usually take about one month. About halfway through the cycle, an egg is released from the ovary. The egg travels through one of the *fallopian tubes,* a pair of tubes that connect each ovary to the uterus. The **uterus** is the organ in which a fertilized egg develops into a baby. When a baby is born, it passes through the **vagina**, the canal between the uterus and the outside of the body.

If an egg is not fertilized, it is shed with the lining of the uterus. The monthly discharge of blood and tissue from the uterus is called *menstruation.* When menstruation ends, the lining of the uterus thickens and the cycle begins again.

Active Reading

8 Summarize As you read, underline the path an egg takes through the female reproductive system.

9 Number Place a number in the circles to order the steps of the menstrual cycle.

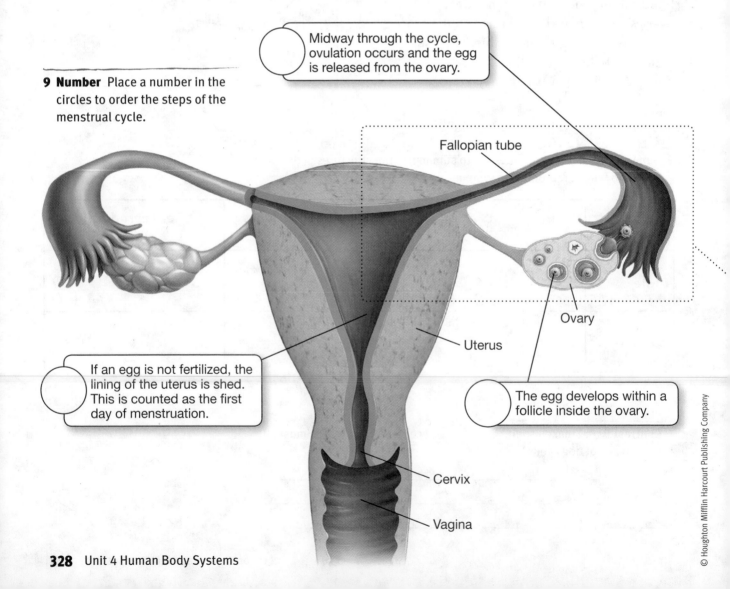

Midway through the cycle, ovulation occurs and the egg is released from the ovary.

Fallopian tube

Ovary

Uterus

If an egg is not fertilized, the lining of the uterus is shed. This is counted as the first day of menstruation.

The egg develops within a follicle inside the ovary.

Cervix

Vagina

© Houghton Mifflin Harcourt Publishing Company

How are eggs fertilized?

When sperm enter the female reproductive system, a few hundred make it through the uterus into a fallopian tube. There, the sperm release enzymes that help dissolve the egg's outer covering.

When a sperm enters an egg, the egg's membrane changes to stop other sperm from entering. During fertilization, the egg and sperm combine to form one cell. Once cell division occurs, the fertilized egg becomes an **embryo**. The genetic material from the father and the mother combine and a unique individual begins to develop. Usually, only one sperm gets through the outer covering of the egg. Sometimes, the fertilized egg splits, resulting in identical twins; sometimes, two eggs are fertilized by two sperm, resulting in fraternal twins. However, if more than one sperm enter the egg, which is rare, it is called *polyspermy* and usually results in the egg not surviving. After fertilization, the embryo travels from the fallopian tube to the uterus over five to six days, and attaches to the thickened and nutrient-rich lining of the uterus.

Inquiry

10 Claims • Evidence • Reasoning Sometimes more than one egg is released at a time. What do you think would happen if two eggs were released and both were fertilized? State your claim and support it with evidence. Explain your reasoning.

_____

_____

_____

_____

_____

11 Summarize Determine what happens if an egg is fertilized and if it is not fertilized, and fill in both of the boxes below.

Was the egg fertilized?

yes →

no →

Steps of Fertilization

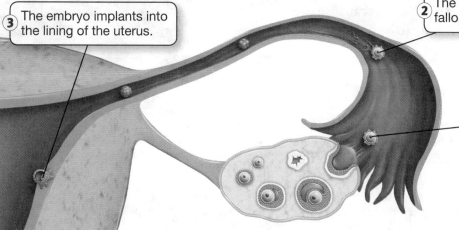

③ The embryo implants into the lining of the uterus.

② The egg is fertilized in the fallopian tube by a sperm.

① The egg is released from the ovary.

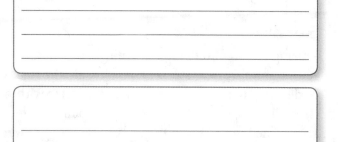

Happy Birthday!

What are the stages of pregnancy?

A normal pregnancy lasts about nine months. These nine months are broken down into three 3-month periods, called *trimesters*.

Active Reading **12 Identify** Underline three things that take place during each trimester.

First Trimester

Soon after implantation, the placenta begins to grow. The **placenta** is a network of blood vessels that provides the embryo with oxygen and nutrients from the mother's blood and carries away wastes. The embryo is surrounded by the *amnion,* a sac filled with fluid that protects the embryo. The embryo connects to the placenta by the **umbilical cord**. After week 10, the embryo is called a **fetus**. Many organs, such as the heart, liver, and brain, form. Arms and legs, as well as fingers and toes, also form during this trimester.

Second Trimester

During the second trimester, joints and bones start to form. The fetus's muscles grow stronger. As a result, the fetus can make a fist and begins to move. The fetus triples its size within a month and its brain begins to grow rapidly. Eventually, the fetus can make faces. The fetus starts to make movements the mother can feel. Toward the end of the trimester, the fetus can breathe and swallow.

Third Trimester

During the third trimester, the fetus can respond to light and sound outside the uterus. The brain develops further, and the organs become fully functional. Bones grow and harden, and the lungs completely develop. By week 32, the fetus's eyes can open and close. By the third trimester the fetus can also dream. After 36 weeks, the fetus is almost ready to be born. A full-term pregnancy usually lasts about 40 weeks.

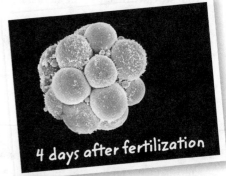

4 days after fertilization

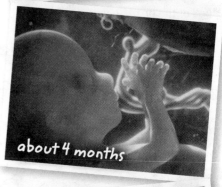

about 4 months

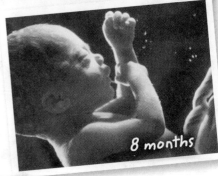

8 months

How are babies born?

As birth begins, the mother's uterus starts a series of muscular contractions called *labor*. Usually, these contractions push the fetus through the mother's vagina, and the baby is born. The umbilical cord is tied and cut. All that will remain of the place where the umbilical cord was attached is the navel. Finally, the mother pushes out the placenta, and labor is complete.

What changes occur during infancy and childhood?

Development during infancy and childhood includes gaining control of skeletal muscles and learning to speak. Generally, infancy is the stage from birth to age 2. During infancy, babies grow quickly and baby teeth appear. The nervous system develops, and babies become more coordinated and start to walk. Many babies begin to say words by age 1. During this time, the body is growing rapidly. Childhood lasts from age 2 to puberty. Baby teeth are replaced by permanent teeth. Children learn to speak fluently and their muscles become more coordinated, allowing them to run, jump, and perform other activities.

What changes occur during adolescence and adulthood?

The stage from puberty to adulthood is *adolescence*. During adolescence, a person's reproductive system becomes mature. In most boys, puberty takes place between the ages of 9 and 16. During this time, the young male's body becomes more muscular, his voice becomes deeper, and body and facial hair appear. In most girls, puberty takes place between the ages of 9 and 15. During this time, the amount of fat in the hips and thighs increases, the breasts enlarge, body hair appears, and menstruation begins.

During adulthood, a person reaches physical and emotional maturity. A person is considered a young adult from about age 20 to age 40. Beginning around age 30, changes associated with aging begin. The aging process continues into middle age (between 40 and 65 years old). During this time, hair may turn gray, athletic abilities will decline, and skin may wrinkle. A person more than 65 years old is considered an older adult. Exercising and eating well-balanced diets help people stay healthy as they grow older.

Do the Math

Everyone grows as they age, but does the amount you grow change as you get older?

Sample Problem

To calculate growth rate, divide the difference in height by the difference in age. For example, the growth rate between the ages of one and five for the girl shown below is:

$$(102\ cm - 71\ cm) \div (5\ years - 1\ year) = 8\ cm/year$$

You Try It

13 Calculate Determine the growth rate for the girl between the ages of 14 and 19. Is the amount of growth greater between ages 1 and 5 or between ages 14 and 19?

1 year, 71 cm

5 years, 102 cm

14 years, 160 cm

19 years, 163 cm

Think Outside the Book

14 Research Learning a new language can be easier for young children. This phenomenon is known as a "critical period." Research critical periods for language and write a short report describing what you learned.

Infections

What causes STIs?

Sexually transmitted infections (STIs) are infections that are passed from one person to another during sexual contact. STIs can be caused by viruses, bacteria, or parasites.

Active Reading **15 Identify** As you read, underline the symptoms of each STI listed below.

Viruses

Acquired immunodeficiency syndrome (AIDS) is caused by the human immunodeficiency virus (HIV). This virus infects and destroys immune system cells. As a result, people with AIDS usually show symptoms of many other illnesses that the immune system of a healthy person usually can fight. Most HIV infections are transmitted through sexual contact.

A much more common, but less deadly, viral STI is genital herpes. Most people with herpes do not have symptoms, but some individuals develop painful sores.

The human papillomavirus (paa•puh•LOH•muh•vy•russ) (HPV) and hepatitis B are two other common viral STIs that are often symptomless. Because some people do not have symptoms, they do not know they are spreading the virus. In the case of hepatitis B, the virus attacks the liver. This can lead to death.

Bacteria and Parasites

A common bacterial STI in the United States is chlamydia. Symptoms include a burning sensation when urinating or a discharge from the vagina or penis. The symptoms for gonorrhea, another bacterial STI, are similar to the symptoms of chlamydia. Both of these infections can be treated with antibiotics. Another STI, syphilis, is caused by the bacterium *Treponema pallidum*. Its symptoms, such as swollen glands, rash and fever, are hard to distinguish from those of other diseases.

Some STIs are caused by parasites. For example, the STI trichomoniasis is caused by the protozoan *Trichomonas vaginalis*. It is the most common curable STI for young women. Symptoms are more common in women and may include a genital discharge and pain during urination. Another parasitic STI is a pubic lice infestation. Pubic lice are tiny insects that feed on blood. The most common symptom of a pubic lice infection is genital itching.

16 Label For each photo below, label the type of infection as a virus, a bacterium, or a parasite.

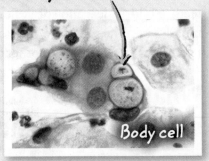

Chlamydia cell

Body cell

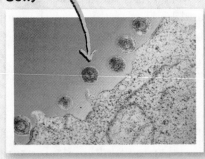

Herpes-infected immune cells

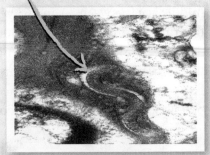

Syphilis cell

Seeing Double

Multiple births occur when two or more babies are carried during the same pregnancy. In humans, the most common type of multiple births occurs when the mother gives birth to two children, or twins. About 3% of all births in the United States result in twins.

Identical Twins
Identical twins form when a single sperm fertilizes a single egg. The developing embryo then divides in two. Identical twins are always the same gender and are genetically identical.

Fraternal Siblings
Fraternal siblings form when two sperm fertilize two or more separate eggs. Fraternal siblings can be the same gender or different genders and are as different genetically as any ordinary siblings.

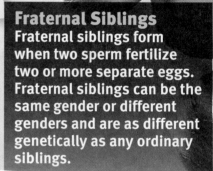

Triplets
While twinning is the most common type of multiple birth, other multiples still occur. About 0.1% of all births are triplets.

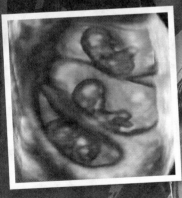

Extend

Inquiry

17 Infer Based on how identical twins form, infer how identical triplets could develop. Explain your reasoning.

18 Research Describe some shared behavioral traits or language between twins and give an example.

19 Create Illustrate how fertilized eggs develop into fraternal triplets. You may choose to make a poster, make a model, or write a short story.

Visual Summary

To complete this summary, circle the correct word. Then, use the key below to check your answers. You can use this page to review the main concepts of the lesson.

The male reproductive system makes hormones and sperm cells.

20 Sperm are produced in the penis / testes.

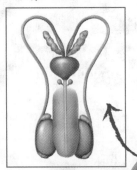

The female reproductive system makes hormones and egg cells, and protects a developing baby if fertilization occurs.

21 Eggs are produced in the ovary / vagina.

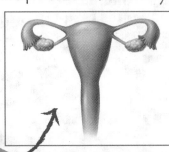

Reproduction and Development

A baby goes through many changes as it develops into an adult.

22 During pregnancy, a growing baby gets oxygen and nourishment from an organ called the embryo / placenta.

Sexually transmitted infections (STIs) are caused by viruses, bacteria, and parasites.

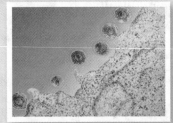

23 STIs are spread through the air / sexual contact.

Answers: 20 testes; 21 ovary; 22 placenta; 23 sexual contact

24 **Apply Concepts** Why does the egg's covering change after a sperm has entered the egg? Support your claim with evidence.

Lesson Review

Vocabulary

1 Use *uterus* and *vagina* in the same sentence.

_____

_____

_____

2 Use *sperm* and *egg* in the same sentence.

_____

_____

_____

Key Concepts

3 Compare Compare the functions of the male and female reproductive systems.

_____

_____

_____

_____

_____

4 Summarize Summarize the processes of fertilization and implantation.

_____

_____

_____

_____

_____

5 Identify Explain what causes STIs and how they are transmitted.

_____

_____

_____

_____

_____

6 Explain How does a fetus get nourishment up until the time it is born?

_____

_____

Use the graph to answer the following question.

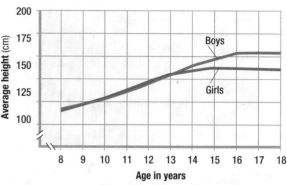

Growth Rates in Boys and Girls

Source: Centers for Disease Control and Prevention

7 Interpret At what age is the difference between the average height of boys and girls greatest? Estimate this difference to the nearest centimeter.

_____

_____

Critical Thinking

8 Claims • Evidence • Reasoning How might cancer of the testes affect a man's ability to make sperm? State your claim. Summarize evidence to support your claim and explain your reasoning.

_____

_____

_____

_____

_____

_____

9 Apply Explain the difference between identical twins and fraternal twins. Include in your answer how they form and their genetic makeup.

_____

_____

_____

_____

_____

My Notes

Unit 4 Big Idea

The human body is made up of systems that have different functions, and these systems interact to carry out life processes.

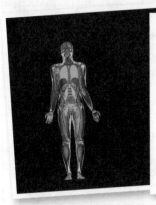

Lesson 1
ESSENTIAL QUESTION
How do the body systems interact to maintain homeostasis?

Describe the functions of the human body systems, including how they interact to maintain homeostasis.

Lesson 2
ESSENTIAL QUESTION
How do your skeletal and muscular systems work?

Explain how the skeletal and muscular systems interact to allow movement of the body.

Lesson 3
ESSENTIAL QUESTION
How do the circulatory and respiratory systems work?

Relate the structures of the circulatory and respiratory systems to their functions in the human body.

Lesson 4
ESSENTIAL QUESTION
How do your body's digestive and excretory systems work?

Relate the parts of the digestive and excretory systems to their roles in the human body.

Lesson 5
ESSENTIAL QUESTION
How do the nervous and endocrine systems work?

Relate the structures of the nervous and endocrine systems to their functions in the human body.

Lesson 6
ESSENTIAL QUESTION
How does your reproductive system work?

Relate the structure of the reproductive system to its function in the human body.

Connect ESSENTIAL QUESTIONS
Lessons 5 and 6

1 Explain How does the endocrine system regulate the function of the reproductive system in males and females?

_____

_____

_____

_____

Think Outside the Book

2 Synthesize Choose one of these activities to help synthesize what you have learned in this unit.

☐ Using what you learned in lessons 1 through 6, choose a human body system and create a poster presentation to explain its structures and functions.

☐ Using what you learned in lessons 2, 3, 4, and 5, write a short story that explains which body systems are involved when a person eats an apple.

Unit 4 Review

Name _____

Vocabulary

Fill in each blank with the term that best completes the following sentences.

1 _____ is the maintenance of a stable environment inside the body.

2 The _____ are the specialized tubes in the kidneys in which waste is collected from the blood.

3 A place where two or more bones are connected is called a(n) _____.

4 The _____ is the body system that controls growth, metabolism, and regulates reproduction through hormones.

5 The _____ is the female reproductive organ that produces egg cells.

Key Concepts

Read each question below, and circle the best answer.

6 Which of these statements correctly describes a key difference between aerobic activity and anaerobic activity?

  A Aerobic activity is intense and of short duration, while anaerobic activity involves moderate effort over a long period of time.

  B Muscles do not use oxygen during aerobic activity, but they do during anaerobic activity.

  C Aerobic activity increases muscle endurance, while anaerobic activity increases muscle strength.

  D Lifting weights is an aerobic activity, while jogging is an anaerobic activity.

7 Which of these body systems is made up of the tissues and organs responsible for collecting fluid that leaks from the blood and returning it to the blood?

  A excretory system   C endocrine system

  B cardiovascular system   D lymphatic system

8 The diagram below shows the main parts of the respiratory system.

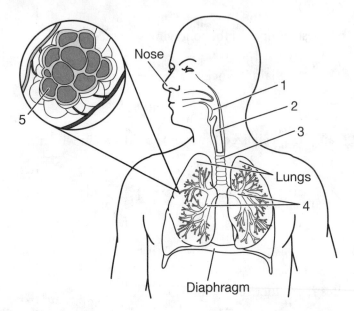

Which of these correctly names the parts of the respiratory system numbered 1 through 5 in the diagram above?

A 1. larynx, 2. pharynx, 3. trachea, 4. bronchi, 5. alveoli

B 1. pharynx, 2. larynx, 3. trachea, 4. bronchi, 5. alveoli

C 1. pharynx, 2. larynx, 3. bronchi, 4. trachea, 5. alveoli

D 1. larynx, 2. trachea, 3. pharynx, 4. alveoli, 5. bronchi

9 Which of these correctly maps the circulation of blood from the heart through the blood vessels and back to the heart?

A heart → arteries → capillaries → veins → heart

B heart → veins → capillaries → arteries → heart

C heart → capillaries → arteries → veins → capillaries → heart

D heart → arteries → capillaries → veins → capillaries → heart

10 Which of the following sentences best describes the esophagus?

A It produces bile that helps the digestive system break down fats.

B It is a muscular tube that moves food from the mouth to the stomach.

C It releases enzymes into the small intestine that aid in chemical digestion.

D It is a muscular bag that churns food and produces acid and enzymes for chemical digestion.

11 The diagram below shows two important parts of the human digestive system.

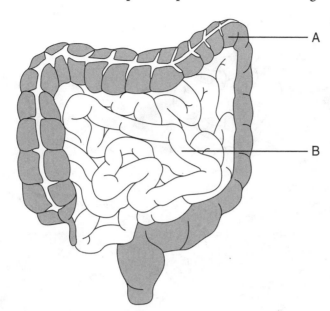

Which of these statements is correct?

A Part A absorbs most of the nutrients from digested food into the bloodstream.

B The pancreas releases enzymes into part A to aid in chemical digestion.

C As food digests, it moves through part B first, then through part A.

D The inside of part A is covered with finger-like projections called villi.

12 Which of the following is a correct statement about the role of the kidney in homeostasis?

A The kidney helps to keep smooth muscle contracting efficiently.

B The kidney filters wastes, such as sodium, from the blood.

C The kidney stores bile, which breaks down fats in the intestine.

D The kidney interacts with the endocrine system to help the body react to stimuli that occur outside the body.

13 Which of these glands of the endocrine system would you suspect has a problem if someone has an abnormal level of sugar in the blood?

A pineal gland   **C** pancreas

B parathyroid   **D** pituitary gland

14 Which of these pictures shows a nerve cell?

A

C

B
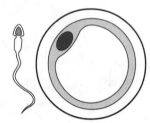

D
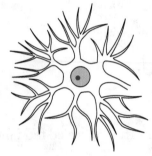

15 Which development occurs in the second trimester of pregnancy?

A The eyes of the fetus first open and blink.

B The embryo becomes a fetus.

C The embryo moves from the fallopian tube to the uterus.

D Contractions in the uterus move the fetus from the uterus through the vaginal canal.

16 Which of these is a function of the testes?

A to produce egg cells

B to produce a hormone that causes facial hair to grow

C to produce a hormone that causes growth of wider hips

D to deliver semen into the female reproductive system

Critical Thinking

Answer the following questions in the space provided.

17 The diagram below shows some of the muscles and bones of the arm.

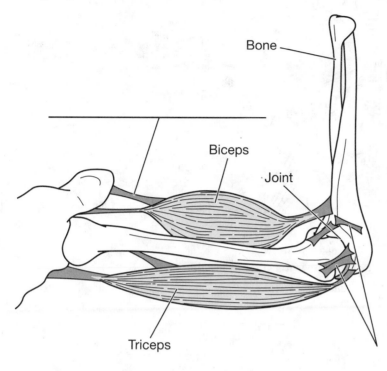

Bone

Biceps

Joint

Triceps

Fill in the blank lines in the diagram above to label the two types of connective tissue shown, then describe the function of each below.

_____

_____

_____

18 What is the difference between pulmonary circulation and systemic circulation? Use evidence to support your claim and explain your reasoning.

_____

_____

_____

_____

_____

_____

_____

19 The diagram below shows the two main parts of the human nervous system.

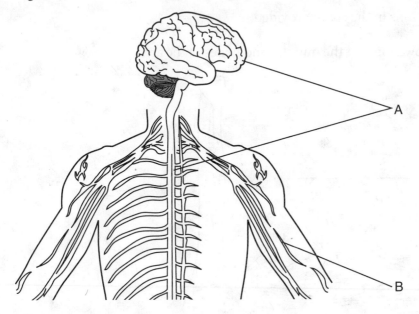

Write the names for the two parts of the nervous system labeled A and B.
Then describe the main functions of each part.

A Name: _____

  Function: _____

B Name: _____

  Function: _____

Connect **ESSENTIAL QUESTIONS**
Lessons 1, 2, 3, and 5

Answer the following question in the space provided.

20 When you burn yourself after touching something hot, you pull your hand away
quickly. How do your skeletal, muscular, circulatory, endocrine, and nervous
systems interact to make you react and to start healing your burn? Use evidence
that you learned in lessons 1, 2, 3, and 5 to support your claim.

_____

_____

_____

_____

_____

_____

_____

Interactions of Living Things

© Houghton Mifflin Harcourt Publishing Company • Image Credits: (bkgd) ©Comstock/age fotostock; (br) ©Millard H. Sharp/Photo Researchers, Inc.

Big Idea

Organisms interact with each other and with the nonliving parts of their environment.

S7L4., S7L4.a, S7L4.b, S7L4.c

Fish and sponges
in a coral reef

What do you think?

Ecosystems consist of living things that depend on one another to survive. How might these fish depend on a coral reef? How might this bird depend on a dragonfly population? As you explore the unit, gather evidence to help you state and support claims to answer these questions.

Eastern bluebirds
feed on insects.

Unit 5
Interactions of Living Things

CITIZEN SCIENCE
Sharing Spaces

Wetlands provide living space for many kinds of birds. Ospreys are large birds of prey that eat mostly fish. They often nest on telephone poles and other man-made structures. Yellow-rumped warblers are small birds that live in trees and eat insects and berries.

① Ask A Question

How can organisms affect each other and a whole ecosystem?

An ecosystem is made up of all the living and nonliving things in an environment. Ospreys and yellow-rumped warblers are part of the same ecosystem. With your teacher and your classmates, brainstorm ways in which ospreys and yellow-rumped warblers might affect each other.

Yellow-rumped warbler

② Think About It

A Look at the photos of the ospreys in their environment. List at least two resources they need to survive and explain how the ospreys get them.

_____

_____

_____

B What are two ways nonliving things could affect yellow-rumped warblers?

_____

_____

_____

Osprey nest

③ Apply Your Knowledge

A List the ways in which yellow-rumped warblers and ospreys share resources.

_____

_____

_____

B Yellow-rumped warblers have a diet that consists mainly of insects and berries. Make a list of other organisms you know that might compete with the warblers for these same food resources.

_____

_____

_____

_____

C Describe a situation that could negatively affect both the osprey population and the yellow-rumped warbler population.

_____

_____

_____

Take It Home

Are ecologists looking for people to report observations in your community? Contact a university near your community to see if you can help gather information about plants, flowers, birds, or invasive species. Then, share your results with your class. See *ScienceSaurus®* for more information about ecosystems.

Introduction to Ecology

ESSENTIAL QUESTION

How are different parts of the environment connected?

By the end of this lesson, you should be able to analyze the parts of an environment.

S7L4.a Interactions in ecosystems

This rain forest is an ecosystem. Hornbills are organisms in the ecosystem that use the trees for shelter.

Lesson Labs

Quick Labs
• Which Abiotic and Biotic Factors Are Found in an Ecosystem?
• Which Biome?

Field Lab
• What's in an Ecosystem?

 Engage Your Brain

1 Describe In your own words, write a list of living or nonliving things that are in your neighborhood.

_____

_____

_____

_____

_____

_____

_____

_____

2 Relate Write a photo caption that compares the ecosystem shown below and the ecosystem shown on the previous page.

_____

_____

_____

_____

 Active Reading

3 Synthesize You can often define an unknown word or term if you know the meaning of its word parts. Use the word parts and sentence below to make an educated guess about the meaning of the term *abiotic factor*.

Word part	Meaning
a-	without
bio-	life

Example sentence
In an ecosystem, rocks are an example of an <u>abiotic factor</u> since they are not a living part of the environment.

abiotic factor:

_____

_____

Vocabulary Terms

• ecology
• biotic factor
• abiotic factor
• population
• species

• community
• ecosystem
• biome
• niche
• habitat

4 Apply As you learn the definition of each vocabulary term in this lesson, create your own definition or sketch to help you remember the meaning of the term.

The Web of Life

How are all living things connected?

Organisms need energy and matter to live. Interactions between organisms cause an exchange of energy and matter. This exchange creates a web of life in which all organisms are connected to one another and to their environment. **Ecology** is the study of how organisms interact with one another and with their environment.

Through the Living Environment

Each individual organism has a role to play in the flow of energy and matter. In this way, organisms are connected to all other organisms. Relationships among organisms affect each one's growth and survival. A **biotic factor** is an interaction between organisms in an area. Competition is one way that organisms interact. For example, different kinds of plants might compete for water in the desert.

This desert includes all of the organisms that live there, and all of the living and nonliving things that they need to survive.

This horse is a part of the living environment.

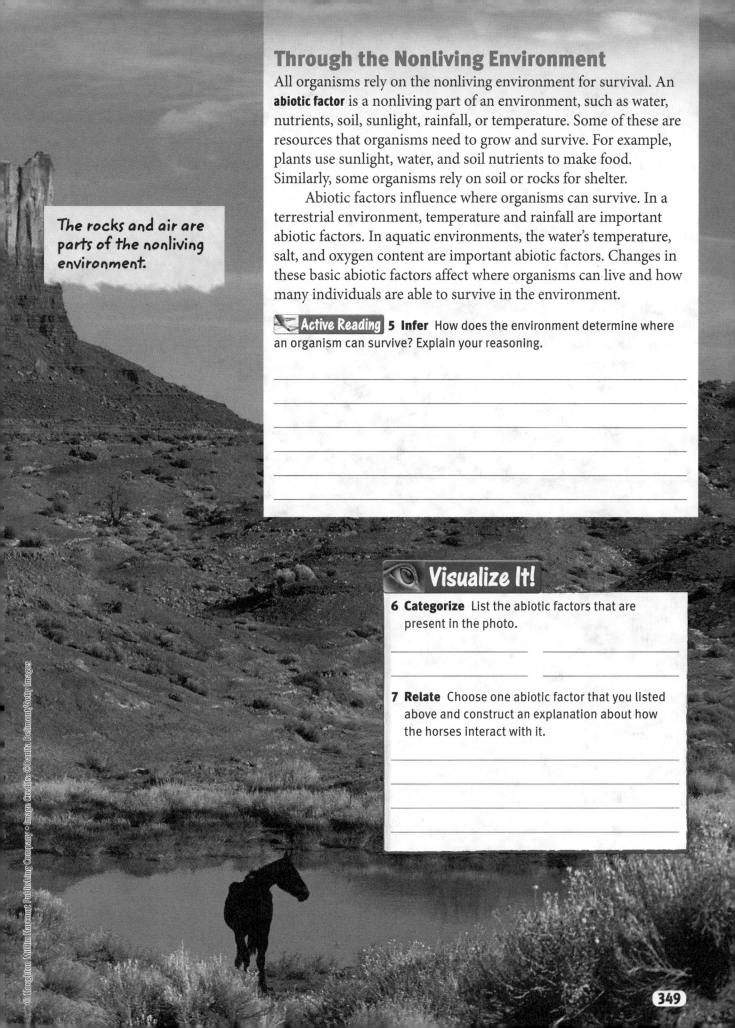

The rocks and air are parts of the nonliving environment.

Through the Nonliving Environment

All organisms rely on the nonliving environment for survival. An **abiotic factor** is a nonliving part of an environment, such as water, nutrients, soil, sunlight, rainfall, or temperature. Some of these are resources that organisms need to grow and survive. For example, plants use sunlight, water, and soil nutrients to make food. Similarly, some organisms rely on soil or rocks for shelter.

Abiotic factors influence where organisms can survive. In a terrestrial environment, temperature and rainfall are important abiotic factors. In aquatic environments, the water's temperature, salt, and oxygen content are important abiotic factors. Changes in these basic abiotic factors affect where organisms can live and how many individuals are able to survive in the environment.

Active Reading **5 Infer** How does the environment determine where an organism can survive? Explain your reasoning.

_____

_____

_____

_____

_____

Visualize It!

6 Categorize List the abiotic factors that are present in the photo.

_____   _____

_____   _____

7 Relate Choose one abiotic factor that you listed above and construct an explanation about how the horses interact with it.

_____

_____

_____

_____

Stay Organized!

What are the levels of organization in the environment?

The environment can be organized into different levels. These levels range from a single organism to all of the organisms and their surroundings in an area. The levels of organization get more complex as more of the environment is considered.

Active Reading 8 **Identify** As you read, underline the characteristics of each of the following levels of organization.

Populations

A **population** is a group of individuals of the same species that live in the same place at the same time. A **species** includes organisms that are closely related and can mate to produce fertile offspring. The alligators that live in the Everglades form a population. Individuals within a population often compete with each other for resources.

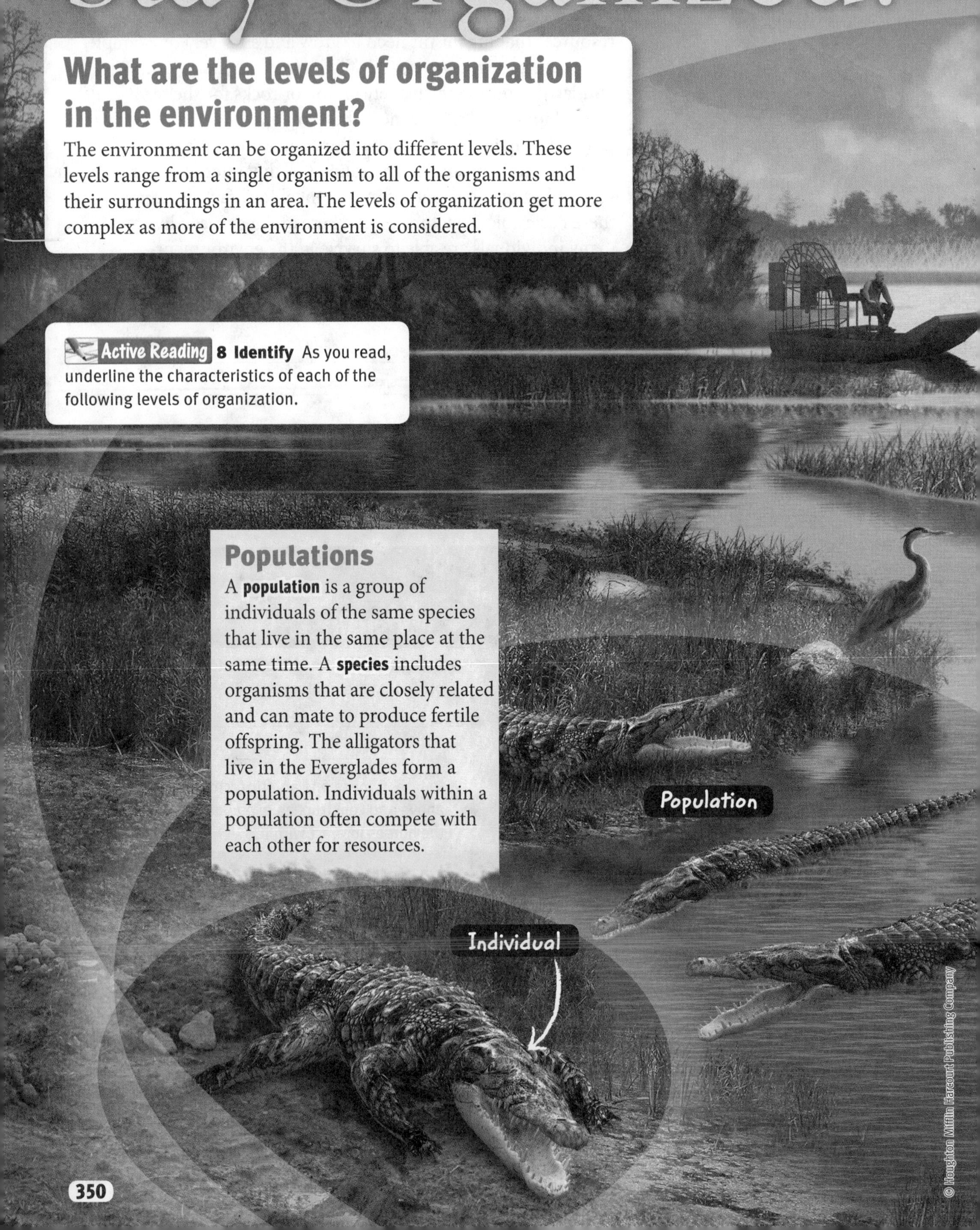

Population

Individual

350

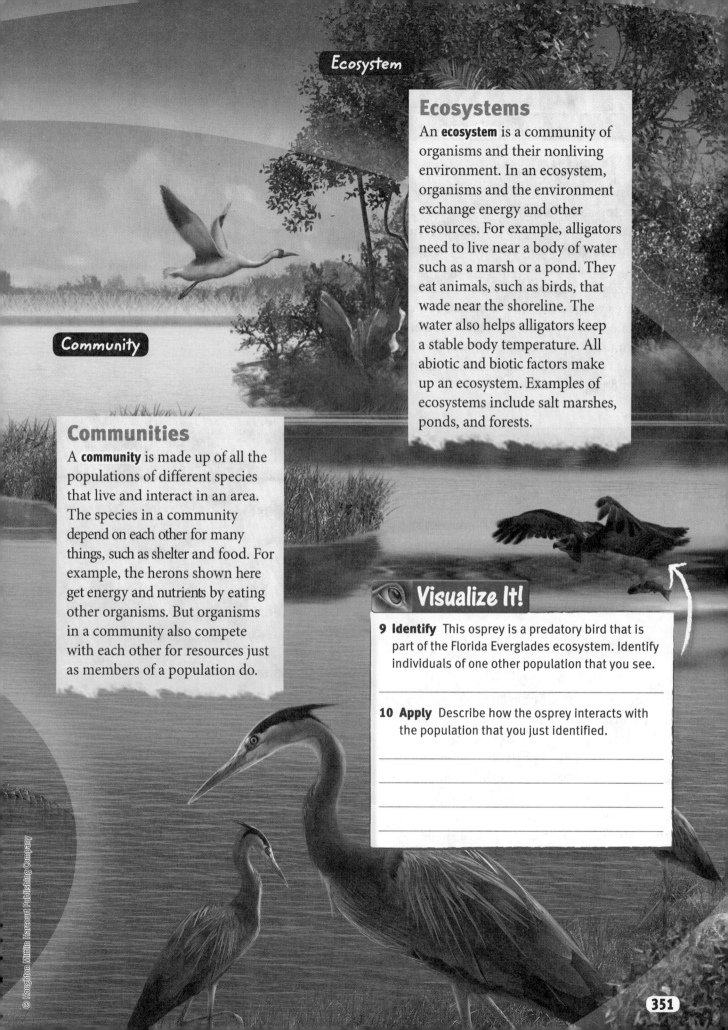

Ecosystem

Community

Ecosystems

An **ecosystem** is a community of organisms and their nonliving environment. In an ecosystem, organisms and the environment exchange energy and other resources. For example, alligators need to live near a body of water such as a marsh or a pond. They eat animals, such as birds, that wade near the shoreline. The water also helps alligators keep a stable body temperature. All abiotic and biotic factors make up an ecosystem. Examples of ecosystems include salt marshes, ponds, and forests.

Communities

A **community** is made up of all the populations of different species that live and interact in an area. The species in a community depend on each other for many things, such as shelter and food. For example, the herons shown here get energy and nutrients by eating other organisms. But organisms in a community also compete with each other for resources just as members of a population do.

Visualize It!

9 Identify This osprey is a predatory bird that is part of the Florida Everglades ecosystem. Identify individuals of one other population that you see.

_____

10 Apply Describe how the osprey interacts with the population that you just identified.

_____

_____

_____

_____

Think Globally!

This temperate rain forest gets a lot of rainfall. The organisms here have adapted to the wet climate.

What is a biome?

Each ecosystem has its own unique biotic and abiotic factors. Some ecosystems have few plants and are cold and dry. Others have forests and are hot and moist. This wide diversity of ecosystems can be organized into categories. Large regions characterized by climate and communities of species are grouped together as **biomes**. A biome can contain many ecosystems. Major land biomes include tundra, taiga, deserts, tropical grasslands (or savannas), temperate grasslands, temperate forests, and tropical rain forests.

What characteristics define a biome?

All of the ecosystems in a biome share some traits. They share climate conditions, such as temperature and rainfall, and have similar communities.

Climate Conditions

Active Reading **11 Identify** As you read, underline the climate factors that characterize biomes.

Temperature is an important climate factor that characterizes biomes. For example, some biomes have a constant temperature. The taiga and tundra have cold temperatures all year. Tropical biomes are warm all year. In other biomes, the temperature changes over the course of a year. Temperate biomes have warm summers and colder winters. In some biomes, major temperature changes occur within a single day. For example, some deserts are hot during the day but cold at night.

Biomes also differ in the amount of precipitation they receive. For example, tropical biomes receive a lot of rainfall, while deserts receive little precipitation. The taiga and tundra have moist summers and dry winters.

Think Outside the Book Inquiry

12 Claims • Evidence • Reasoning
What biome do you live in? Describe your climate and make a list of the living things that are found in natural undeveloped areas nearby. Research which biome has these features. Summarize the evidence that supports your claim and explain your reasoning.

Communities of Living Things

Biomes contain communities of living things that have adapted to the climate of the region. Thus, ecosystems within the same biome tend to have similar species across the globe. Monkeys, vines, and colorful birds live in hot and humid tropical rain forests. Grasses, large mammals, and predatory birds inhabit tropical grasslands on several continents.

Only certain types of plants and animals can live in extreme climate conditions. For example, caribou, polar bears, and small plants live in the tundra, but trees cannot grow there. Similarly, the plant and animal species that live in the desert are also unique. Cacti and certain animal species have adaptations that let them tolerate the dry desert climate.

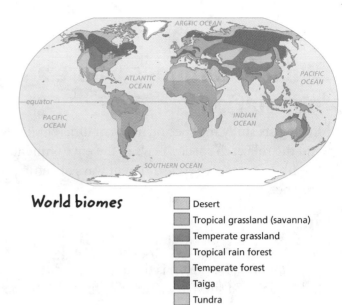

World biomes

- Desert
- Tropical grassland (savanna)
- Temperate grassland
- Tropical rain forest
- Temperate forest
- Taiga
- Tundra

13 Compare The photos below show two different biomes. Use what you learned about the characteristics of biomes to compare these environments, and then explain why they are categorized as different biomes. Write your answers in the space provided.

Compare: _____

_____

_____

_____

_____

_____

_____

Explain: _____

_____

_____

_____

_____

_____

Home Sweet Home

What determines where a population can live?

Ecologists study the specific needs of different kinds of organisms and the role each species plays in the environment. Organisms that live in the same area have different ways of getting the resources they need.

Niche

Each population in an ecosystem plays a specific role. A population's **niche** (NICH) is the abiotic conditions under which individuals can survive and the role they play in the ecosystem. For example, one part of a shark population's niche is eating fish.

A **habitat** is the place where an organism usually lives and is part of an organism's niche. The habitat must provide all of the resources that an organism needs to grow and survive. Abiotic factors, such as temperature, often influence whether a species can live in a certain place. Biotic factors, such as the interactions with other organisms that live in the area, also play a role. For example, the habitat of a shark must include populations of fish it can eat.

Two populations cannot occupy exactly the same niche. Even small differences in habitats, roles, and adaptations can allow similar species to live together in the same ecosystem. For example, green and brown anoles sometimes live on the same trees, but they avoid competition by living in different parts of the trees.

14 Relate How is a habitat like a person's address? How is a niche like a person's job?

_____

_____

_____

_____

_____

_____

_____

Visualize It!

15 Infer Describe the prairie dog's niche. How does it find shelter and impact the environment?

_____

_____

_____

_____

_____

Prairie dogs dig burrows in grassy plains. They eat plants and are hunted by predators such as owls and foxes.

Lizard Invasion

Green anole lizards (*Anolis carolinensis*) have been part of the South Florida ecosystem for a long time. Recently, a closely related lizard, the nonnative brown anole (*Anolis sagrei*), invaded the green anoles' habitat. How do they avoid competing with each other for resources?

Home Base

Green anoles live on perches throughout a tree. Brown anoles live mainly on branches that are close to the ground. If they have to share a tree, green anoles will move away from perches close to the ground. In this way, both kinds of anoles can live in the same tree while avoiding competition with each other.

Intrusive Neighbors

Although brown and green anoles can coexist by sharing their habitats, they do not live together peacefully. For example, brown anoles affect green anoles by eating their young.

Extend

Inquiry

16 Describe How do green and brown anoles avoid competition? Draw a picture of a tree showing both green and brown anoles living in it.

17 Research What are other examples of two species dividing up the parts of a habitat?

18 Claims • Evidence • Reasoning Infer what would happen if the habitats of two species overlapped. Gather evidence to support your claim and explain your reasoning. Present your findings in a format such as a short story, a music video, or a play.

Visual Summary

To complete this summary, circle the correct word. Then use the key below to check your answers. You can use this page to review the main concepts of the lesson.

Ecology and Ecosystems

Ecology is the study of the biotic and abiotic factors in an ecosystem, and the relationships between them.

19 In a desert ecosystem, the sand is a(n) biotic / abiotic factor, and a lizard eating an insect is a(n) biotic / abiotic factor.

Every organism has a habitat and a niche.

20 Horses that live in the desert feed on other organisms that live there, such as low, dry shrubs. In this example, the desert is a habitat / niche and the horses' feeding behavior is part of a habitat / niche.

Biomes are characterized by climate conditions and the communities of living things found within them.

22 Biomes are large / small regions that make up / contain ecosystems.

The environment can be organized into different levels, including populations, communities, and ecosystems.

21 Populations of cacti, together with sand and rocks, are included in a desert community / ecosystem.

Answers: 19 abiotic, biotic; 20 habitat, niche; 21 ecosystem; 22 large, contain

23 **Predict** In the desert ecosystem shown above, name a biotic factor, and describe the effect on the horses if it were removed from the ecosystem.

Lesson Review

Vocabulary

1 Explain how the meanings of the terms *biotic factor* and *abiotic factor* differ.

_____

_____

_____

2 In your own words, write a definition for *ecology*.

_____

_____

_____

3 Explain how the meanings of the terms *habitat* and *niche* differ.

_____

_____

_____

Key Concepts

4 Compare What is the relationship between ecosystems and biomes?

_____

_____

_____

5 Explain Within each biome, how can the environment be organized into levels from complex to simple?

_____

_____

_____

6 Infer How do the populations in a community depend on each other?

_____

_____

_____

7 Identify What factors determine where a population can live?

_____

_____

_____

_____

Critical Thinking

8 Predict What might happen in a tropical rain forest biome if the area received very little rain for an extended period of time?

_____

_____

_____

_____

9 Infer Owls and hawks both eat rodents. They are also found in the same habitats. Since no two populations can occupy exactly the same niche, how can owls and hawks coexist?

_____

_____

_____

_____

Use this graph to answer the following question.

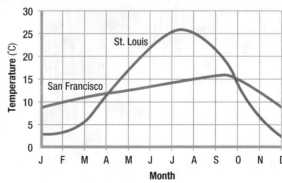

Average Monthly Temperatures

10 Interpret What is the difference in average temperature between the two cities in July?

My Notes

Kenneth Krysko

ECOLOGIST

Snakes have fascinated Dr. Kenneth Krysko since he was four years old. Now he is an ecologist specializing in herpetology—the study of snakes. You can often find him in the Florida Everglades looking for Burmese pythons. He tracks these pythons to help limit the effect they have on Florida ecosystems.

Burmese pythons can grow to be 6 meters long. They are native to southeast Asia and were illegally brought to Florida as pets. Many owners released them into the wild when the snakes grew too large. The snakes breed well in Florida's subtropical climate. And they eat just about any animal they can swallow, including many native species. Dr. Krysko tracks down these invasive pythons. Through wildlife management, molecular genetics, and other areas of study, he works with other scientists to search for ways to reduce the python population.

Dr. Krysko studies many other invasive species, that is, nonnative species that can do harm in Florida ecosystems. He shares what he learns, including ways to identify and deal with invasive species with other ecologists. Along with invasion ecology, he has done research in reproduction and conservation biology. Dr. Krysko also works as a collections manager in the herpetology division at the Florida Museum of Natural History.

Dr. Krysko works to get a handle on what to do about the invasive pythons.

Houghton Mifflin Harcourt Publishing Company • Image Credits: (bkgd) ©Willard Clay/Taxi/Getty Images; (tr) ©Dorling Kindersley/Getty Images; (bl) ©Dr. Kenneth Krysko

JOB BOARD

Park Naturalist

What You'll Do: Teach visitors at state and national parks about the park's ecology, geology, and landscape. Lead field trips, prepare and deliver lectures with slides, and create educational programs for park visitors. You may participate in research projects and track organisms in the park.

Where You Might Work: State and national parks

Education: An advanced degree in science and teacher certification

Other Job Requirements: You need to be good at communicating and teaching. Having photography and writing skills helps you prepare interesting educational materials.

Conservation Warden

What You'll Do: Patrol an area to enforce rules, and work with communities and groups to help educate the public about conservation and ecology.

Where You Might Work: Indoors and outdoors in state and national parks and ecologically sensitive areas

Education: A two-year associate's degree or at least 60 fully accredited college-level credits

Other Job Requirements: To work in the wild, good wilderness skills, map-reading, hiking, and excellent hearing are useful.

Phil McCRORY

Saved by a Hair!

Phil McCrory, a hairdresser in Huntsville, Alabama, asked a brilliant question when he saw an otter whose fur was drenched with oil from the Exxon Valdez oil spill. If the otter's fur soaked up oil, why wouldn't human hair do the same? McCrory gathered hair from the floor of his salon and performed his own experiments. He stuffed hair into a pair of pantyhose and tied the ankles together. McCrory floated this bundle in his son's wading pool and poured used motor oil into the center of the ring. When he pulled the ring closed, not a drop of oil remained in the water! McCrory's discovery was tested as an alternative method for cleaning up oil spills. Many people donated their hair to be used for cleanup efforts. Although the method worked well, the engineers conducting the research concluded that hair is not as useful as other oil-absorbing materials for cleaning up large-scale spills.

Roles in Energy Transfer

ESSENTIAL QUESTION

How does energy flow through an ecosystem?

By the end of this lesson, you should be able to relate the roles of organisms to the transfer of energy in food chains and food webs.

Energy is transferred from the sun to producers, such as kelp. It flows through the rest of the ecosystem.

This fish also needs energy to live. How do you think it gets this energy? From the sun like kelp do?

 S7L4.b Cycling of matter and energy flow in ecosystems

Engage Your Brain

1 Describe Most organisms on Earth get energy from the sun. How is energy flowing through the ecosystem pictured on the opposite page?

_____

_____

_____

_____

_____

2 Predict List two of your favorite foods. Then, explain how the sun's energy helped make those foods available to you.

_____

_____

_____

_____

_____

Active Reading

3 Synthesize You can often define an unknown word if you know the meaning of its word parts. Use the word parts and sentences below to make an educated guess about the meaning of the words _herbivore_ and _carnivore_.

Word part	Meaning
-vore	to eat
herbi-	plant
carni-	meat

Example sentence
A koala bear is an <u>herbivore</u> that eats eucalyptus leaves.

herbivore:

_____

_____

_____

Example sentence
A great white shark is a <u>carnivore</u> that eats fish and other marine animals.

carnivore:

_____

_____

_____

Vocabulary Terms

- producer
- decomposer
- consumer
- herbivore
- carnivore
- omnivore
- food chain
- food web

4 Apply As you learn the definition of each vocabulary term in this lesson, create your own definition or sketch to help you remember the meaning of the term.

Get Energized!

How do organisms get energy?

Energy is all around you. Chemical energy is stored in the bonds of molecules and holds molecules together. The energy from food is chemical energy in the bonds of food molecules. All living things need a source of chemical energy to survive.

Producers Convert Energy Into Food

A **producer**, also called an autotroph, uses energy to make food. Most producers use sunlight to make food in a process called photosynthesis. The sun powers most life on Earth. In photosynthesis, producers use light energy to make food from water, carbon dioxide, and nutrients found in water and soil. The food contains chemical energy and can be used immediately or stored for later use. All green plants, such as grasses and trees, are producers. Algae and some bacteria are also producers. The food that these producers make supplies the energy for other living things in an ecosystem.

Decomposers Break Down Matter

An organism that gets energy and nutrients by breaking down the remains of other organisms is a **decomposer**. Fungi, such as the mushrooms on this log, and some bacteria are decomposers. Decomposers are nature's recyclers. By converting dead organisms and animal and plant waste into materials such as water and nutrients, decomposers help move matter through ecosystems. Decomposers make these simple materials available to other organisms.

These mushrooms are decomposers. They break down the remains of plants and animals.

This plant is a producer. Producers make food using light energy from the sun.

Consumers Eat Other Organisms

A **consumer** is an organism that eats other organisms. Consumers use the energy and nutrients stored in other living organisms because they cannot make their own food. A consumer that eats only plants, such as a grasshopper or bison, is called an **herbivore**. A **carnivore**, such as a badger or this wolf, eats other animals. An **omnivore** eats both plants and animals. A *scavenger* is a specialized consumer that feeds on dead organisms. Scavengers, such as the turkey vulture, eat the leftovers of the meals of other animals or eat dead animals.

This wolf is a consumer. It eats other organisms to get energy.

Consumers

Visualize It!

7 List Beside each image, place a check mark next to the word that matches the type of consumer the animal is.

Name: Hedgehog
What I eat: leaves, earthworms, insects

What am I?
- ☐ herbivore
- ☐ omnivore
- ☐ carnivore

Name: Moose
What I eat: grasses, fruits

What am I?
- ☐ herbivore
- ☐ omnivore
- ☐ carnivore

Name: Komodo dragon
What I eat: insects, birds, mammals

What am I?
- ☐ herbivore
- ☐ omnivore
- ☐ carnivore

8 Infer How might carnivores be affected if the main plant species in a community were to disappear? Give examples to support your claim and explain your reasoning.

_____

_____

_____

_____

_____

Energy Transfer

How is energy transferred among organisms?

Organisms change energy from the environment or from their food into other types of energy. Some of this energy is used for the organism's activities, such as breathing or moving. Some of the energy is saved within the organism to use later. If an organism is eaten or decomposes, the consumer or decomposer takes in the energy stored in the original organism. Only chemical energy that an organism has stored in its tissues is available to consumers. In this way, energy is transferred from organism to organism.

Active Reading **9 Infer** When a grasshopper eats grass, only some of the energy from the grass is stored in the grasshopper's body. How does the grasshopper use the rest of the energy?

_____

_____

This tree gets its energy from the sun.

10 Identify By what process does this tree get its energy?

_____

_____

This ant eats plants like the mesquite tree, and other insects.

11 Apply What type of energy is this ant consuming?

_____

_____

Energy Flows Through a Food Chain

A **food chain** is the path of energy transfer from producers to consumers. Energy moves from one organism to the next in one direction. The arrows in a food chain represent the transfer of energy, as one organism is eaten by another. Arrows represent the flow of energy from the body of the consumed organism to the body of the consumer of that organism.

Producers form the base of food chains. Producers transfer energy to the first, or primary, consumer in the food chain. The next, or secondary, consumer in the food chain consumes the primary consumer. A tertiary consumer eats the secondary consumer. Finally, decomposers recycle matter back to the soil.

Visualize It!

The photographs below show a typical desert food chain. Answer the following four questions from left to right based on your understanding of how energy flows in a food chain.

This hawk eats the lizard. It is at the top of the food chain.

13 Predict If nothing ever eats this hawk, what might eventually happen to the energy that is stored in its body?

_____

_____

This lizard eats mostly insects.

12 Apply What does the arrow between the ant and the lizard represent?

_____

_____

World Wide Webs

How do food webs show energy connections?

Few organisms eat just one kind of food. So, the energy and nutrient connections in nature are more complicated than a simple food chain. A **food web** is the feeding relationships among organisms in an ecosystem. Food webs are made up of many food chains.

The next page shows a coastal food web. Most of the organisms in this food web live in the water. The web also includes some birds that live on land and eat fish. Tiny algae called phytoplankton form the base of this food web. Like plants on land, phytoplankton are producers. Tiny consumers called zooplankton eat phytoplankton. Larger animals, such as fish and squid, eat zooplankton. At the top of each chain are top predators, animals that eat other animals but are rarely eaten. In this food web, the killer whale is a top predator. Notice how many different energy paths lead from phytoplankton to the killer whale.

14 Identify Underline the type of organism that typically forms the base of the food web.

Visualize It!

15 Apply Complete the statements to the right with the correct organism names from the food web.

ENERGY

Energy flows up the food web when

_____ eat puffins.

Puffins are connected to many organisms in the food web.

ENERGY

Puffins get energy by eating

_____ ,

_____ ,

and _____ .

Food Web

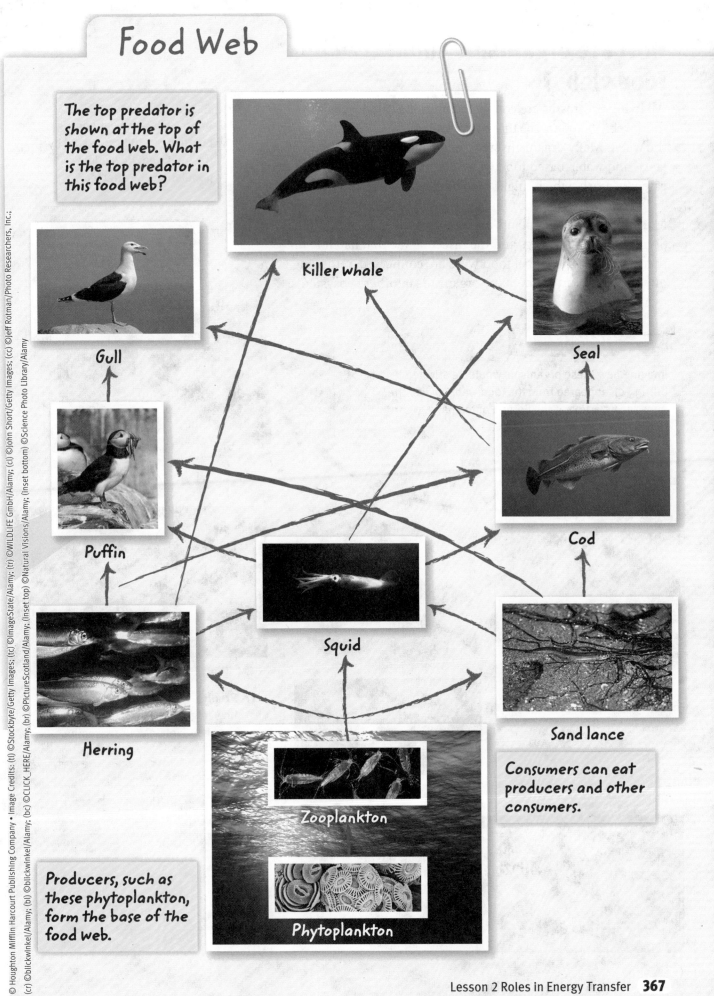

The top predator is shown at the top of the food web. What is the top predator in this food web?

Killer whale

Seal

Gull

Puffin

Cod

Squid

Sand lance

Herring

Consumers can eat producers and other consumers.

Zooplankton

Phytoplankton

Producers, such as these phytoplankton, form the base of the food web.

How are organisms connected by food webs?

All living organisms are connected by global food webs. Global food webs include webs that begin on land and webs that begin in the water. Many organisms have feeding relationships that connect land- and water-based food webs. For example, algae might be eaten by a fish, which might then be eaten by a bird.

Food webs that start on land may also move into the water. Many insects that eat plants on land lay their eggs in the water. Some fish eat these eggs and the insect larvae that hatch from them. Because the global food webs are connected, removing even one organism can affect many organisms in other ecosystems.

18 Infer Gulls don't eat herring but they are still connected by the food web. How might gull populations be affected?

_____
_____
_____
_____

Visualize It!

Imagine how these organisms would be affected if herring disappeared from the food web. Answer the questions starting at the bottom of the page.

■ Gull

■ Puffin

■ Cod

■ Squid

17 Predict With no herring to eat, how might the eating habits of cod change? Explain your reasoning.

_____
_____
_____
_____
_____
_____
_____

Herring

16 Identify Put a check mark next to the organisms that eat herring.

Dangerous Competition

Sometimes species are introduced into a new area. These invasive species often compete with native species for energy resources, such as sunlight and food.

Full Coverage
The kudzu plant was introduced to stop soil erosion, but in the process it outgrew all the native plants, preventing them from getting sunlight. Sometimes it completely covers houses or cars!

Destructive Zebras
The zebra mussel is one of the most destructive invasive species in the United States. They eat by filtering tiny organisms out of the water, often leaving nothing for the native mussel species.

Across the Grass
The walking catfish can actually move across land to get from one pond to another! As a result, sometimes the catfish competes with native species for food.

Extend

Inquiry

19 Relate Describe how the competition between invasive and native species might affect a food web.

20 Describe Give an example of competition for a food resource that may occur in an ecosystem near you.

21 Illustrate Provide an illustration of your example of competition in a sketch or a short story. Be sure to include the important aspects of food webs that you learned in the lesson.

Visual Summary

To complete this summary, circle the correct word. Then use the key below to check your answers. You can use this page to review the main concepts of the lesson.

Energy Transfer
in Ecosystems

Organisms get energy in different ways.

- Producers make their own food.
- Consumers eat other living organisms.
- Decomposers break down dead organisms.

22 Herbivores, carnivores, and omnivores are three types of producers / consumers / decomposers.

Food chains and food webs describe the flow of energy in an ecosystem.

23 All food chains start with producers / consumers / decomposers.

Answers: 22 consumers; 23 producers

24 Model Develop a model or food web that shows how matter and energy cycle through the living and nonliving parts of an ecosystem.

Food Web

Lesson Review

Vocabulary

Fill in the blanks with the term that best completes the following sentences.

1 _____ is the primary source of energy for most ecosystems.

2 A(n) _____ eats mostly dead matter.

3 A(n) _____ contains many food chains.

4 _____ is the process by which light energy from the sun is converted to food.

Key Concepts

5 Describe What are the roles of producers, consumers, and decomposers in an ecosystem?

_____

_____

_____

_____

_____

6 Apply What types of organisms typically make up the base, middle, and top of a food web?

_____

_____

_____

_____

_____

7 Describe Identify the two types of global food webs and describe how they are connected.

_____

_____

_____

_____

_____

Use the figure to answer the following questions.

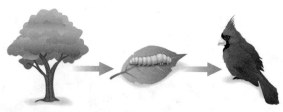

8 Apply Describe the flow of energy in this food chain. Be sure to use the names of the organisms and what role they serve in the food chain (producer, consumer, or decomposer). If an organism is a consumer, identify whether it is an herbivore, carnivore, or omnivore.

_____

_____

_____

_____

9 Apply What do the arrows represent in the figure above?

_____

_____

Critical Thinking

10 Claims • Evidence • Reasoning Give an example of a decomposer, and explain what would happen if decomposers were absent from a forest ecosystem. Provide evidence to support your claim and explain your reasoning.

_____

_____

_____

_____

_____

_____

11 Predict How would a food web be affected if a species disappeared from an ecosystem?

_____

_____

_____

_____

My Notes

Population Dynamics

ESSENTIAL QUESTION

What determines a population's size?

By the end of this lesson, you should be able to explain how population size changes in response to environmental factors and interactions between organisms.

By looking like a snake, this caterpillar may scare off predators. However, the effectiveness of this defense depends on population size. If there are few real snakes, predators won't be fooled for long.

 S7L4.c Factors affecting ecosystems

Lesson Labs

Quick Labs
• What Factors Influence a Population Change?
• Investigate an Abiotic Limiting Factor

Exploration Lab
• How Do Populations Interact?

Engage Your Brain

1 Predict Check T or F to show whether you think each statement is true or false.

T	F	
☐	☐	Plants compete for resources.
☐	☐	Populations of organisms never stop growing.
☐	☐	Animals never help other animals survive.
☐	☐	Living things need the nonliving parts of an environment to survive.

2 Explain When a chameleon eats a butterfly, what happens to the number of butterflies in the population? How could a sudden decrease in butterflies affect chameleons?

_____

_____

_____

Active Reading

3 Synthesize You can often define an unknown word if you know the meaning of its word parts. Use the word parts and sentences below to make an educated guess about the meaning of the words *immigrate* and *emigrate*.

Word part	Meaning
im-	into
e-	out
-migrate	move

Example sentence
Many deer will <u>immigrate</u> to the new park.

immigrate: _____

_____

Example sentence
Birds will <u>emigrate</u> from the crowded island.

emigrate: _____

_____

Vocabulary Terms

• carrying capacity   • competition
• limiting factor   • cooperation

4 Identify This list contains the vocabulary terms you'll learn in this lesson. As you read, circle the definition of each term.

Movin' Out

How can a population grow or get smaller?

Active Reading 5 **Identify** As you read, underline the processes that can cause a population to grow or to get smaller.

A population is a group of organisms of one species that lives in the same area at the same time. If new individuals are added to the population, it grows. The population gets smaller if individuals are removed from it. The population stays at about the same size if the number of individuals that are added is close to the number of individuals that are removed.

By Immigration and Emigration

Populations change in size when individuals move to new locations. *Immigration* occurs when individuals join a population. For example, fruit flies may travel on fruit to a new island. The population of fruit flies on the new island grows as fruit flies immigrate. *Emigration* occurs when individuals leave a population. The population of fruit flies on the original island decreases when fruit flies emigrate.

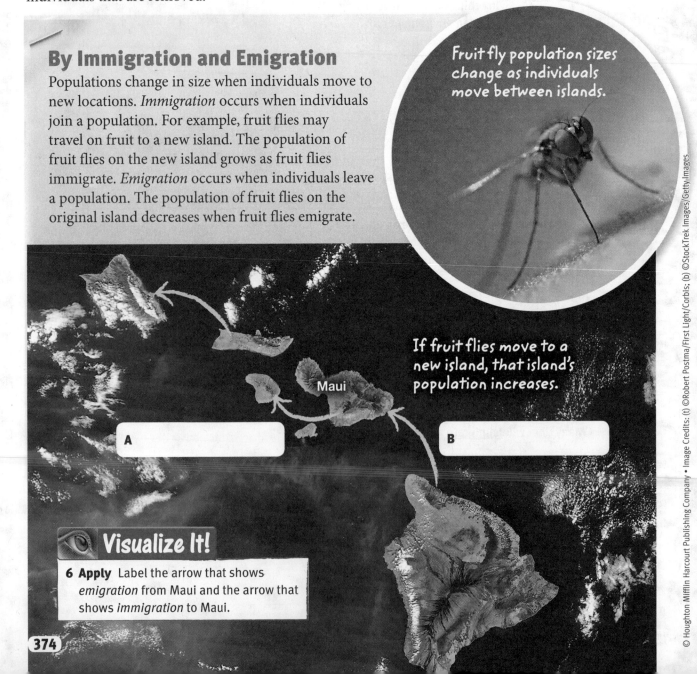

Fruit fly population sizes change as individuals move between islands.

Maui

A

B

If fruit flies move to a new island, that island's population increases.

Visualize It!

6 **Apply** Label the arrow that shows *emigration* from Maui and the arrow that shows *immigration* to Maui.

By Birth and Death

Populations increase as individuals are born. For example, consider a population of 100 deer in a forest. The population will increase if 20 fawns are born that year. But what if 12 deer are killed by predators or disease that year? Populations decrease as individuals die. If 20 deer are added and 12 are lost, the population will have an overall increase. At the end of the year, there will be 108 deer. The number of births compared to the number of deaths helps to determine if a population is increasing or decreasing.

Visualize It!

7 Apply Use the terms *birth*, *death*, and *immigration* to label each way that this population is changing.

An individual being carried off by a predator

A

A wandering male joins the population

B

A mother with nursing babies

C

Know Your Limits

What environmental factors influence population size?

A tropical rain forest can support large populations of trees. A desert, however, will probably support few or no trees. Each environment has different amounts of the resources that living things need, such as food, water, and space.

Resource Availability

The amount of resources in an area influences the size of a population. If important resources are lost from the environment, a population may shrink. The population may grow if the amount of resources in the environment is increased. But if the population continues to grow, the individuals would eventually run out of resources. The **carrying capacity** is the maximum number of individuals of one species that the environment can support. For example, the carrying capacity, or the number of owls that a forest can support, depends on how many mice are available to eat and how many trees are available for the owls to live in.

Deforestation causes a sudden change in resource availability.

Visualize It!

8 Identify Make a list of each population in the image that would be affected by drought.

_____

_____

_____

_____

Animals use plants as food and shelter. Plants depend on sunlight and water as resources.

Changes in the Environment

The carrying capacity can change when the environment changes. For example, after a rainy season, plants may produce a large crop of leaves and seeds. This large amount of food may allow an herbivore population to grow. But what if important resources are destroyed? A population crash occurs when the carrying capacity of the environment suddenly drops. Natural disasters, such as forest fires, and harsh weather, such as droughts, can cause population crashes. The carrying capacity can also be reduced when new competitors enter an area and outcompete existing populations for resources. This would cause existing populations to become smaller or crash.

Active Reading **9 Describe** What are two ways in which the environment can influence population size?

_____

_____

_____

_____

Drought slowly reduces the amount of water available as a resource to different populations.

Think Outside the Book

10 Apply With a classmate, discuss how the immigration of new herbivores might affect the carrying capacity of the local zebra population.

What factors can limit population size?

A part of the environment that keeps a population's size at a level below its full potential is called a **limiting factor**. Limiting factors can be living or nonliving things in an environment.

Abiotic Factors

The nonliving parts of an environment are called *abiotic factors*. Abiotic factors include water, nutrients, soil, sunlight, temperature, and living space. Organisms need these resources to survive. For example, plants use sunlight, water, and carbon dioxide to make food. If there are few rocks in a desert, lizard populations that use rocks for shelter will not become very large.

Biotic Factors

Relationships among organisms affect each one's growth and survival. A *biotic factor* is an interaction between living things. For example, zebras interact with many organisms. Zebras eat grass, and they compete with antelope for this food. Lions prey on zebras. Each of these interactions is a biotic factor that affects the population of zebras.

Think Outside the Book (Inquiry)

11 **Research** With a classmate, choose an animal to research on the Internet. Look for data that show how the availability or scarcity of resources, disease, climate, or human activity have affected the population of that animal. Then, analyze the effects of these factors on entire communities and ecosystems. Share your findings with the class.

Visualize It!

12 **Identify** Label each of the following factors that limits plant population growth as abiotic or biotic.

This plant has a disease.

A

This plant grows between the rocks.

B

Herbivores are eating this leaf.

C

A Fungus Among Us!

In many parts of the world, frog populations are shrinking. We now know that many of these frogs have died because of a fungal infection.

Meet the fungus

Chytrid fungi [KY•trid FUHN•jy] live in water. They are important decomposers. One of them, called Bd, infects frogs.

Stop the Spread

Bd is found in wet mud. If you go hiking in muddy places, washing and drying your boots can help stop Bd from spreading.

Deadly Disease

Frogs take in oxygen and water through their skin. Bd interferes with this process. The fungus also affects an infected frog's nervous system.

Extend

Inquiry

13 Describe How does Bd fungus harm frogs?

14 Recommend Imagine that an endangered frog lives near an area where Bd was just found. How could you help protect that frog species? Make a claim about how your idea would help the frogs. Summarize evidence to support your claim and explain your reasoning.

15 Apply Design an experiment to test whether using soap or using bleach is the better way to clean boots to prevent Bd contamination. What are the independent and dependent variables? Remember to include a control in designing your experiment.

Teamwork

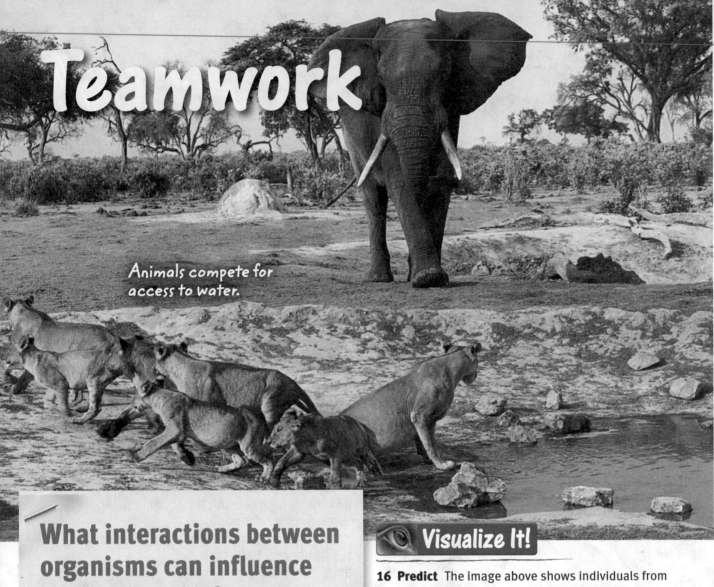

Animals compete for access to water.

What interactions between organisms can influence population size?

As living things try to gather the resources they need, they often interact with each other. Sometimes interactions help one individual and harm another. At other times, all of the organisms benefit by working together.

Competition

When two or more individuals or populations try to use the same limited resource, such as food, water, shelter, space, or sunlight, it is called **competition**. Competition can happen among individuals within a population. The elk in a forest compete with each other for the same food plants. This competition increases in winter when many plants die. Competition also happens among populations. For example, different species of trees in a forest compete with each other for sunlight and space.

16 Predict The image above shows individuals from two populations competing for access to water.

What would happen to the size of the lion population if elephants usually won this competition?

_____

_____

_____

What would happen to each population if lions usually won this competition?

_____

_____

_____

Active Reading **17 Identify** As you read, underline how cooperation can influence population dynamics.

Cooperation

Cooperation occurs when individuals work together. Some animals, such as killer whales, hunt in groups. Emperor penguins in Antarctica stay close together to stay warm. Some populations have a structured social order that determines how the individuals work with each other. For example, ants live in colonies in which the members have different jobs. Some ants find food, others defend the colony, and others take care of the young. Cooperation helps individuals get resources, which can make populations grow.

18 Compare Make an analogy between an ant colony and a sports team. How does each group work together to achieve a goal? Explain your reasoning.

_____
_____
_____
_____
_____
_____
_____

These ants cooperate to protect aphids that produce a substance that ants eat.

Visual Summary

To complete this summary, fill in the blanks with the correct word or phrase. Then use the key below to check your answers. You can use this page to review the main concepts of the lesson.

Populations grow due to birth and immigration and get smaller due to death and emigration.

19 If more individuals are born in a population than die or emigrate, the population will _____.

Both populations and individuals can compete or cooperate.

21 Some birds warn other birds when predators are close. This type of interaction is called

_____.

The carrying capacity is the maximum number of individuals of one species an environment can support.

20 If the amount of resources in an environment decreases, the carrying capacity for a population will probably

_____.

Answers: 19 grow; 20 decrease; 21 cooperation

22 Synthesize Describe how a change in the environment could lead to increased immigration or emigration.

_____

Lesson Review

Vocabulary

Circle the term that best completes the following sentences.

1 Individuals joining a population is an example of *emigration / immigration*.

2 A part of the environment that prevents a population from growing too large is a(n) *abiotic / limiting / biotic* factor.

3 Individuals *cooperate / compete* when they work together to obtain resources.

Key Concepts

4 Identify What is a limiting factor?

_____

_____

_____

_____

5 Describe How do limiting factors affect the carrying capacity of an environment?

_____

_____

_____

_____

_____

_____

6 Explain Give one example of how cooperation can help organisms survive.

_____

_____

_____

7 Provide Name two factors that increase population size and two factors that decrease population size.

_____

_____

_____

Critical Thinking

Use the illustration to answer the following questions.

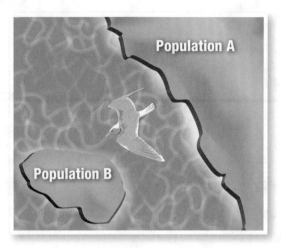

8 Infer What might cause birds in Population A to immigrate to the island?

_____

_____

_____

9 Predict How will the level of competition among birds in Population B change if many birds from Population A join Population B?

_____

_____

_____

10 Conclude Explain how a change in the environment could cause a population crash.

_____

_____

_____

11 Claims • Evidence • Reasoning How does population size relate to resource availability in an environment? Explain your reasoning.

_____

_____

_____

_____

My Notes

Interactions in Communities

ESSENTIAL QUESTION

How do organisms interact?

By the end of this lesson, you should be able to predict the effects of different interactions in communities.

These birds, called tickbirds, eat ticks and flies on a rhinoceros. This behavior helps the rhino. The ticks are also parasites that sometimes drink the rhino's blood!

 S7L4.a Interactions in ecosystems
S7L4.c Factors affecting ecosystems

✋ Lesson Labs

Quick Labs
- Prey Coloration
- Identifying Predators and Prey

Exploration Lab
- Modeling the Predator-Prey Cycle

🧠 Engage Your Brain

1 Predict Check T or F to show whether you think each statement is true or false.

T	F	
☐	☐	Different animals can compete for the same food.
☐	☐	Parasites help the organisms that they feed on.
☐	☐	Some organisms rely on each other for necessities such as food or shelter.
☐	☐	Organisms can defend themselves against predators that try to eat them.

2 Explain Draw an interaction between two living things that you might observe while on a picnic. Write a caption to go with your sketch.

✏️ Active Reading

3 Synthesize You can often define an unknown word if you know the meaning of its word parts. Use the word parts and sentence below to make an educated guess about the meaning of the word *symbiosis*.

Word part	Meaning
bio-	life
sym-	together

Example sentence
The relationship between a sunflower and the insect that pollinates it is an example of <u>symbiosis</u>.

symbiosis:

_____

_____

_____

Vocabulary Terms

- **predator**
- **prey**
- **symbiosis**
- **mutualism**
- **commensalism**
- **parasitism**
- **competition**

4 Apply As you learn the meaning of each vocabulary term in this lesson, create your own definition or sketch to help you remember the meaning of the term.

Feeding Frenzy!

How do predator and prey interact?

Every organism lives with and affects other organisms. Many organisms must feed on other organisms in order to get the energy and nutrients they need to survive. These feeding relationships establish structure in a community.

Predators Eat Prey

In a predator–prey relationship, an animal eats another animal for energy and nutrients. The **predator** eats another animal. The **prey** is an animal that is eaten by a predator. An animal can be both predator and prey. For example, if a warthog eats a lizard, and is, in turn, eaten by a lion, the warthog is both predator and prey.

Predators and prey have adaptations that help them survive. Some predators have talons, claws, or sharp teeth, which provide them with deadly weapons. Spiders, which are small predators, use their webs to trap unsuspecting prey. Camouflage (CAM•ah•flaj) can also help a predator or prey to blend in with its environment. A tiger's stripes help it to blend in with tall grasses so that it can ambush its prey, and the wings of some moths look just like tree bark, which makes them difficult for predators to see. Some animals defend themselves with chemicals. For example, skunks and bombardier beetles spray predators with irritating chemicals.

This lion is a predator. The warthog is its prey.

Adaptations of Predators and Prey

Most organisms wouldn't last a day without their adaptations. This bald eagle's vision and sharp talons allow it to find and catch prey.

sharp talons

Predators and Prey Populations Are Connected

Predators rely on prey for food, so the sizes of predator and prey populations are linked together very closely. If one population grows or shrinks, the other population is affected. For example, when there are a lot of warthogs to eat, the lion population may grow because the food supply is plentiful. As the lion population grows, it requires more and more food, so more and more warthogs are hunted by the lions. The increased predation may cause the warthog population to shrink. If the warthog population shrinks enough, the lion population may shrink due to a shortage in food supply. If the lion population shrinks, the warthog population may grow due to a lack of predators.

This lion is hunting down the antelope. If most of the antelope are killed, the lions will have less food to eat.

6 Compare Fill in the Venn diagram to compare and contrast predators and prey.

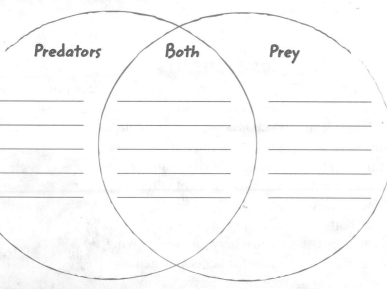

Predators   Both   Prey

Think Outside the Book

7 Apply Choose a predator and think about what it eats and how it hunts. Then do one of the following:
- Write a nomination for the predator to be "Predator of the Year."
- Draw the predator and label the adaptations that help it hunt.

Don't be surprised if this "leaf" walks away—it's actually an insect.

Visualize It!

8 Analyze How might this insect's appearance help keep it from getting eaten?

_____

_____

_____

_____

_____

Living Together

What are the types of symbiotic relationships?

A close long-term relationship between different species in a community is called **symbiosis** (sim•bee•OH•sis). In symbiosis, the organisms in the relationship can benefit from, be unaffected by, or be harmed by the relationship. Often, one organism lives in or on the other organism. Symbiotic relationships are classified as mutualism, commensalism, or parasitism.

Active Reading **9 Identify** As you read, underline examples of symbiotic relationships.

Mutualism

A symbiotic relationship in which both organisms benefit is called **mutualism**. For example, when the bee in the photo drinks nectar from a flower, it gets pollen on its hind legs. When the bee visits another flower, it transfers pollen from the first flower to the second flower. In this interaction, the bee is fed and the second flower is pollinated for reproduction. So, both organisms benefit from the relationship. In this example, the mutualism benefits the bee and the two parent plants that are reproducing.

Bees pollinate flowers. This is an example of mutualism.

Commensalism

A symbiotic relationship in which one organism benefits while the other is unaffected is called **commensalism.** For example, orchids and other plants that often live in the branches of trees gain better access to sunlight without affecting the trees. In addition, the tree trunk shown here provides a living space for lichens, which do not affect the tree in any way. Some examples of commensalism involve protection. For example, certain shrimp live among the spines of the fire urchin. The fire urchin's spines are poisonous but not to the shrimp. By living among the urchin's spines, the shrimp are protected from predators. In this relationship, the shrimp benefits and the fire urchin is unaffected.

Lichens can live on tree bark.

10 Compare How does commensalism differ from mutualism?

_____

_____

_____

_____

12 Claims • Evidence • Reasoning
Observe and take notes about how the organisms in your area interact with one another. Describe what would happen if one of these organisms disappeared. Write down three effects that you can think of. Summarize evidence to support your claim and explain your reasoning.

parasite

host

Parasitism

A symbiotic relationship in which one organism benefits and another is harmed is called **parasitism** (PAR•uh•sih•tiz•uhm). The organism that benefits is the *parasite*. The organism that is harmed is the *host*. The parasite gets food from its host, which weakens the host. Some parasites, such as ticks, live on the host's surface and feed on its blood. These parasites can cause diseases such as Lyme disease. Other parasites, such as tapeworms, live within the host's body. They can weaken their host so much that the host dies.

11 Summarize Using the key, complete the table to show how organisms are affected by symbiotic relationships.

Symbiosis	Species 1	Species 2
Mutualism	+	
	+	0
Parasitism		

Key + organism benefits
0 organism not affected
− organism harmed

Let the Games Begin!

Why does competition occur in communities?

In a team game, two groups compete against each other with the same goal in mind—to win the game. In a biological community, organisms compete for resources. **Competition** occurs when organisms fight for the same limited resource. Organisms compete for resources such as food, water, sunlight, shelter, and mates. If an organism doesn't get all the resources it needs, it could die.

Sometimes competition happens among individuals of the same species. For example, different groups of lions compete with each other for living space. Males within these groups also compete with each other for mates.

Competition can also happen among individuals of different species. Lions mainly eat large animals, such as zebras. They compete for zebras with leopards and cheetahs. When zebras are scarce, competition increases among animals that eat zebras. As a result, lions may steal food or compete with other predators for smaller animals.

Active Reading

13 Identify Underline each example of competition.

14 Predict In the table below, fill in the missing cause and effect of two examples of competition in a community.

Cause	Effect
A population of lions grows too large to share their current territory.	
	Several male hyenas compete to mate with the females present in their area.

Many organisms rely on the same water source.

Think Outside the Book Inquiry

15 Research With a classmate, choose an animal to research. Identify the animal's competitors within its natural ecosystem. Look for and analyze data that show how competition affects the animal's ability to get the resources it needs, and how this impacts on the animal's population within an ecosystem.

Strange Relationships

Glow worms? Blind salamanders? Even creepy crawlers in this extreme cave community interact in ways that help them meet their needs. How do these interactions differ from ones in your own community?

Guano Buffet

Cave swiftlets venture out of the cave daily to feed. The food they eat is recycled as bird dung, or guano, which piles up beneath the nests. The guano feeds many cave dwellers, such as insects. As a result, these insects never have to leave the cave!

A Blind Hunter

Caves are very dark and, over generations, these salamanders have lost the use of their eyes for seeing. Instead of looking for food, they track prey by following water movements.

Sticky Traps

Bioluminescent glow worms make lines of sticky beads to attract prey. Once a prey is stuck, the worm pulls in the line to feast.

Extend

Inquiry

16 Identify Name the type of relationship illustrated in two of the examples shown above.

17 Research Name some organisms in your community and the interactions they have.

18 Create Illustrate two of the interactions you just described by doing one of the following:
- make a poster
- write a song
- write a play
- draw a graphic novel

Visual Summary

To complete this summary, fill in the blanks with the correct word or phrase. Then, use the key below to check your answers. You can use this page to review the main concepts of the lesson.

Organisms interact in feeding relationships.

19 Predators eat

_____.

Organisms interact in symbiosis—very close relationships between two species.

Mutualism:

Commensalism:

Parasitism:

20 A parasite gets nourishment from its

_____.

Interactions
in Communities

Organisms interact in competition.

21 Organisms compete for resources such as

_____

_____

_____

_____

Competition can occur between:

Members of the same species

Members of different species

Answers: 19 prey; 20 host; 21 food, mates, shelter, and water.

22 Synthesize Build an explanation about how interactions can be both beneficial and harmful to the organisms in a community. Give examples and evidence to support your claims.

Lesson Review

Vocabulary

Fill in the blank with the term that best completes the following sentences.

1 A(n) _____ is an animal that kills and eats another animal, known as prey.

2 A long-term relationship between two different species within a community is called

_____.

3 _____ occurs when organisms fight for limited resources.

Key Concepts

Fill in the table below.

Example	Type of symbiosis
4 Identify Tiny organisms called mites live in human eyelashes and feed on dead skin, without harming humans.	
5 Identify Certain bacteria live in human intestines, where they get food and also help humans break down their food.	

6 Describe Think of an animal and list two resources that it might compete for in its community. Then describe what adaptations the animal has to compete for these resources.

_____

_____

_____

_____

_____

7 Explain What is the relationship between the size of a predator population and the size of a prey population?

_____

_____

Critical Thinking

Use this graph to answer the following question.

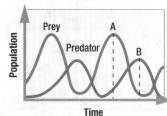

Predator and Prey Populations Over Time

8 Analyze At which point (A or B) on this graph would you expect competition within the predator population to be the highest? Explain your reasoning.

_____

_____

_____

9 Infer Think of a resource, and predict what happens to the resource when competition for it increases.

_____

_____

10 Describe Identify a nearby community, such as a forest, a pond, or your own backyard. Think about the interactions among and between the organisms and the nonliving things. Construct an explanation to describe an interaction and identify the type of relationship. Summarize evidence to support your claim and explain your reasoning.

_____

_____

_____

My Notes

Lesson 1

ESSENTIAL QUESTION
How are different parts of the environment connected?

Analyze the parts of an environment.

Lesson 3

ESSENTIAL QUESTION
What determines a population's size?

Explain how population size changes in response to environmental factors and interactions between organisms.

Lesson 2

ESSENTIAL QUESTION
How does energy flow through an ecosystem?

Relate the roles of organisms to the transfer of energy in food chains and food webs.

Lesson 4

ESSENTIAL QUESTION
How do organisms interact?

Predict the effects of different interactions in communities.

Connect ESSENTIAL QUESTIONS
Lessons 1 and 3

1 Explain Do organisms compete for abiotic resources? Explain your answer.

_____

_____

_____

_____

Think Outside the Book

2 Synthesize Choose one of these activities to help synthesize what you have learned in this unit.

☐ Using what you learned in lessons 2 and 3, write a short story that describes what might happen in a food web when a new species is introduced to an ecosystem.

☐ Using what you learned in lessons 1 through 4, choose an ecosystem and explain three interactions that might occur within it. In your poster presentation, use the terms *cooperation, competition, predator,* and *prey.*

Unit 5 Review

Name _____

Vocabulary

Check the box to show whether each statement is true or false.

T	F	
☐	☐	**1** <u>Competition</u> occurs when organisms try to use the same limited resource.
☐	☐	**2** <u>Biomes</u> are characterized by temperature, precipitation, and the plant and animal communities that live there.
☐	☐	**3** A <u>habitat</u> is the role of a population in its community, including its environment and its relationship with other species.
☐	☐	**4** A <u>food chain</u> is the feeding relationships among all of the organisms in an ecosystem.
☐	☐	**5** A <u>limiting factor</u> is an environmental factor that increases the growth of a population.

Key Concepts

Read each question below, and circle the best answer.

6 A small fish called a cleaner wrasse darts in and out of a larger fish's mouth, removing and eating parasites and dead tissue. Which term best describes the relationship between the cleaner wrasse and the large fish?

A mutualism

B commensalism

C parasitism

D competition

7 Bees have a society in which different members have different responsibilities. The interaction among bees is an example of what type of behavior?

A cooperation

B competition

C consumerism

D commensalism

8 After a mild winter with plenty of food, a deer population grew rapidly. What most likely happened to the wolf population in that same ecosystem?

A It was unaffected.

B It grew.

C It shrank.

D It became extinct.

9 The diagram below shows an aquatic ecosystem.

What is one abiotic factor shown in this diagram?

A the snails

C the crab

B the water

D the tree roots

10 Which of the following is an example of a biotic limiting factor for a population?

A water availability

C disease

B climate

D natural disasters

11 Which of the following is the most likely reason that a population might crash?

A The competition for the same resource suddenly drops.

B The number of prey suddenly increases.

C The number of predators suddenly decreases.

D The carrying capacity of the environment suddenly drops.

12 Grizzly bears are classified in the order Carnivora. Their diet consists of roots, tubers, berries, nuts, fungi, insects, rodents, and fish. What ecological role best describes grizzly bears?

A carnivores

C herbivores

B omnivores

D producers

13 The graph below shows the size of a squirrel population over 20 years.

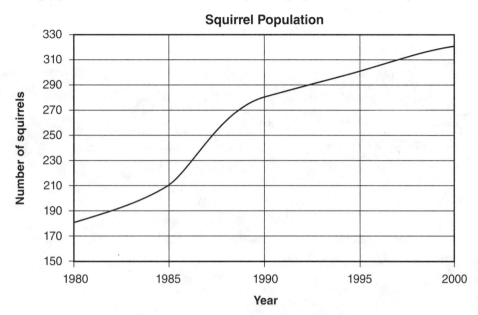

Squirrel Population

The trend displayed on the graph could be a result of what factor?

A emigration

C increased death rate

B immigration

D scarce resources

Critical Thinking

Answer the following questions in the space provided.

14 The diagram below shows how a manatee gets its energy.

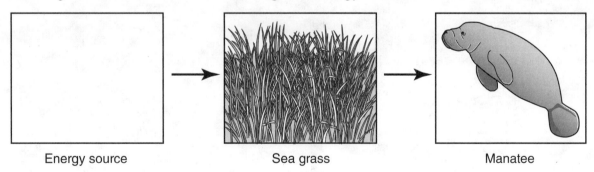

Energy source   Sea grass   Manatee

What provides the energy for the sea grass, the manatee, and most life on Earth? _____

What role does the sea grass play in this food chain? _____

According to this diagram, what type of consumer is the manatee? _____

15 Use the diagram to help you answer the following question.

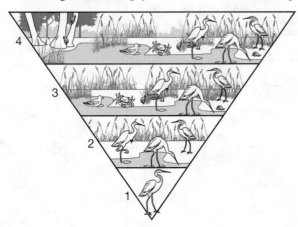

Imagine there is a decrease in food availability for the wading birds. Build an explanation about how the different levels of organization shown in the diagram will be affected.

_____

_____

_____

Connect ESSENTIAL QUESTIONS
Lessons 2 and 4

Answer the following question in the space provided.

16 The diagram below shows an example of a food web.

What traits do the prey animals shown here have in common that help them survive?

_____

What important ecological group is missing from this food web? _____

What might happen if the rabbit population suddenly shrank due to disease?

_____

_____

Earth's Biomes and Ecosystems

Big Idea
Matter and energy together support life within an environment.

S7L4., S7L4.b, S7L4.c, S7L4.d

Mangroves

Roseate spoonbill

What do you think?
Mangroves and roseate spoonbills are both found in Florida. How do organisms like these get and use matter and energy? State your claim and provide evidence to support your reasoning.

Unit 6
Earth's Biomes and Ecosystems

CITIZEN SCIENCE
It's Alive!

This garden is home to many vegetables and other plants.

(1) Think About It

What role do plants play in your life?

_____

_____

_____

_____

_____

_____

_____

② Ask A Question

How do plants use matter and energy?

As a class, design a plan for a garden plot or window box garden in which the class can grow a variety of plants. Remember that plants have different growing periods and requirements.

Sketch It!

Draw your plan to show where each plant will be placed.

③ Apply Your Knowledge

A What do your plants need in order to grow?

_____

_____

_____

B Which of the things you listed above are examples of matter? Which are examples of energy?

_____

_____

_____

_____

C Create and care for your classroom garden and observe the plant growth.

Take It Home

Describe an area in your community that is used for growing food. If there is no such area, initiate a plan to plant in an area that you think could be used. See *ScienceSaurus*® for more information about plants.

Terrestrial Biomes

ESSENTIAL QUESTION

What are terrestrial biomes?

By the end of this lesson, you should be able to describe the characteristics of different biomes that exist on land.

The North American prairie is an example of a grassland biome. It is home to grazing animals such as the bison.

Herds of thousands of bison used to roam the prairies. Bison became rare as people hunted them and developed the prairie into farmland.

 S7L4.c Factors affecting ecosystems

 **S7L4.d** Terrestrial biomes and aquatic ecosystems

Lesson Labs

Quick Labs
- Climate Determines Plant Life
- Identify Your Terrestrial Biome

Field Lab
- Survey of a Biome's Biotic and Abiotic Factors

Engage Your Brain

1 Compare How are the two biomes in the pictures at right different from each other?

_____
_____
_____
_____
_____

2 Infer Which of these biomes gets more rain? Provide evidence to support your reasoning.

_____
_____
_____
_____
_____
_____
_____
_____

Active Reading

3 Word Parts Parts of words that you know can help you find the meanings of words you don't know. The suffix *-ous* means "possessing" or "full of." Use the meanings of the root word and suffix to write the meaning of the term *coniferous tree*.

Root Word	Meaning
conifer	tree or shrub that produces cones

coniferous tree:

_____
_____
_____

Vocabulary Terms

- biome
- tundra
- taiga
- coniferous tree
- desert
- grassland
- savanna
- temperate grassland
- temperate forest
- deciduous tree
- tropical rain forest

4 Apply As you learn the definition of each vocabulary term in this lesson, create your own definition or sketch to help you remember the meaning of the term.

Home Sweet Biome

The taiga is a northern latitude biome that has low average temperatures, nutrient-poor soil, and coniferous trees.

What is a biome?

If you could travel Earth from pole to pole, you would pass through many different biomes. A **biome** is a region of Earth where the climate determines the types of plants that live there. The types of plants in a biome determine the types of animals that live there. Tundra, taiga, deserts, tropical grasslands (or savannas), temperate grasslands, temperate forests, and tropical rain forests are all types of terrestrial, or land, biomes.

What makes one biome different from another?

Each biome has a unique community of plants and animals. The types of organisms that can live in a biome depend on the biome's climate and other abiotic, or nonliving, factors.

Climate

Climate is the main abiotic factor that characterizes a biome. Climate describes the long-term patterns of temperature and precipitation in a region. The position of a biome on Earth affects its climate. Biomes that are closer to the poles receive less annual solar energy and have colder climates. Biomes that are near the equator receive more annual solar energy and have warmer climates. Biomes that are close to oceans often have wet climates.

Earth's Major Terrestrial Biomes

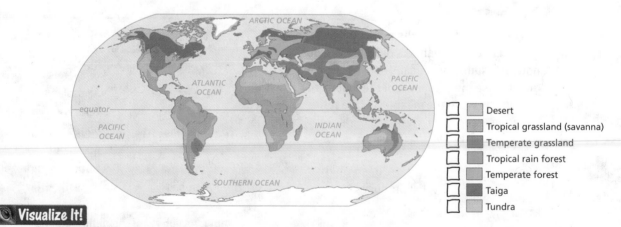

- ☐ Desert
- ☐ Tropical grassland (savanna)
- ☐ Temperate grassland
- ☐ Tropical rain forest
- ☐ Temperate forest
- ☐ Taiga
- ☐ Tundra

Visualize It!

5 Predict Find the locations of the major terrestrial biomes on the map. Underline the names of two biomes that would have some of the coldest temperatures. Place a check mark next to the names of two biomes that would have some of the warmest temperatures.

Other Abiotic Factors

Other abiotic factors that characterize a biome include soil type, amount of sunlight, and amount of water that is available. Abiotic factors affect which organisms can live in a biome.

Plant and Animal Communities

Adaptations are features that allow organisms to survive and reproduce. Plants and animals that live in a particular biome have adaptations to its unique conditions. For example, animals that live in biomes that are cold all year often grow thick fur coats. Plants that live in biomes with seasonal temperature changes lose their leaves and become inactive in winter. Plants that live in warm, rainy biomes stay green and grow all year long.

6 Identify As you read, underline the abiotic factors besides climate that characterize a biome.

Visualize It!

7 Infer Place a check mark in each box to predict the average temperature range for each of the biomes shown.

☐ Warm All Year
☐ Cool All Year
☐ Seasonal Temperatures

☐ Warm All Year
☐ Cool All Year
☐ Seasonal Temperatures

☐ Warm All Year
☐ Cool All Year
☐ Seasonal Temperatures

Life in a Biome

How are ecosystems related to biomes?

Most biomes stretch across huge areas of land. Within each biome are smaller areas called ecosystems. Each *ecosystem* includes a specific community of organisms and their physical environment. A temperate forest biome can contain pond or river ecosystems. Each of these ecosystems has floating plants, fish, and other organisms that are adapted to living in or near water. A savanna biome can contain areas of small shrubs and trees. These ecosystems have woody plants, insects, and nesting birds.

 **Visualize It!**

Three different ecosystems are shown in this temperate forest biome. Different organisms live in each of these ecosystems.

8 Identify List three organisms that you see in the picture that are part of each ecosystem within the biome.

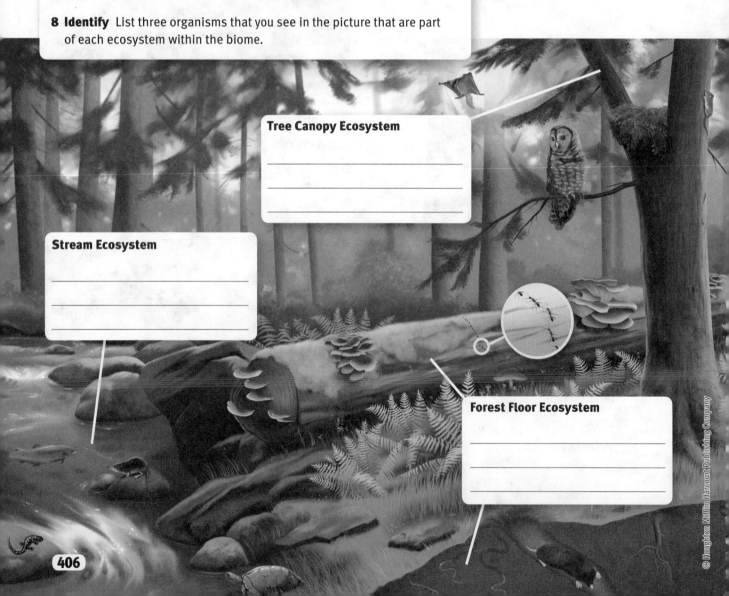

Tree Canopy Ecosystem

_____

_____

Stream Ecosystem

_____

_____

Forest Floor Ecosystem

_____

_____

What are the major terrestrial biomes?

There are seven major terrestrial biomes. They are tundra, taiga, desert, tropical grassland, or savanna, temperate grassland, temperate forest, and tropical rain forest.

Active Reading 9 **Identify** Underline the abiotic features that characterize tundra and taiga biomes.

Tundra

Tundra has low average temperatures and very little precipitation. The ground contains permafrost, a thick layer of permanently frozen soil beneath the surface. Tundra is found in the Arctic and in high mountain regions. Tundra plants include mosses and woody shrubs. These plants have shallow roots, since they cannot grow into the permafrost. Tundra winters are dark, cold, and windy. Animals such as musk oxen have thick fur and fat deposits that protect them from the cold. Some animals, such as caribou, migrate to warmer areas before winter. Ground squirrels hibernate, or become dormant, underground.

Taiga

Taiga is also called the *boreal forest*. **Taiga** has low average temperatures like those in the tundra biome, but more precipitation. The soil layer in taiga is thin, acidic, and nutrient-poor. Taiga biomes are found in Canada and northern Europe and Asia. Taiga plants include **coniferous trees**, which are trees that have evergreen, needlelike leaves. These thin leaves let trees conserve water and produce food all year long. Migratory birds live in taiga in summer. Wolves, owls, and elk live in taiga year-round. Some animals, such as snowshoe hares, experience a change in fur color as the seasons change. Hares that match their surroundings are not seen by predators as easily.

Visualize It!

10 **Describe** Below each picture, describe how organisms that you see are adapted to the biome in which they live.

Tundra

Taiga

_____

_____

_____

_____

Desert

Desert biomes are very dry. Some deserts receive less than 8 centimeters (3 inches) of precipitation each year. Desert soil is rocky or sandy. Many deserts are hot during the day and cold at night, although some have milder temperatures. Plants and animals in this biome have adaptations that let them conserve water and survive extreme temperatures. Members of the cactus family have needlelike leaves that conserve water. They also contain structures that store water. Many desert animals are active only at night. Some animals burrow underground or move into shade to stay cool during the day.

 Active Reading

11 Identify As you read, underline the characteristics of deserts.

Visualize It!

12 Describe How do the adaptations of the desert tortoise, the saguaro cactus, and the kangaroo rat help them make use of available resources in the biome? Use specific data as evidence to support your claims.

_____

_____

_____

_____

Desert Tortoise

A tortoise can crawl into shade or retreat into its shell to avoid the heat. A tortoise has thick skin that prevents water loss.

Saguaro Cactus

A cactus has needlelike leaves to conserve water. A cactus contains structures to store water.

Kangaroo Rat

A rat is active at night when it is cooler. A rat stays in burrows to avoid the heat of the day.

Tropical Grassland

Temperate Grassland

Tropical Grassland (Savanna)

A **grassland** is a biome that has grasses and few trees. *Tropical grasslands*, or **savannas**, have high average temperatures throughout the year. These grasslands, such as the African savanna, also have wet and dry seasons. Thin soils support grasses and some trees in this biome. Grazing animals, such as antelope and zebras, feed on grasses. Predators such as lions hunt grazing animals. Animals in savannas migrate to find water during dry seasons. Plants in savannas are adapted to survive periodic fires.

Temperate Grassland

Temperate grasslands have moderate precipitation, hot summers, and cold winters. These grasslands, such as the North American prairie, have deep soils that are rich in nutrients. Grasses are the dominant plants in this biome. Bison, antelope, prairie dogs, and coyotes are common animals. Periodic fires sweep through temperate grasslands. These fires burn dead plant material and kill trees and shrubs. Grasses and other nonwoody plants are adapted to fire. Some of these plants regrow from their roots after a fire. Others grow from seeds that survived the fire.

Visualize It!

13 Describe Write captions to explain how fire shapes a temperate grassland biome.

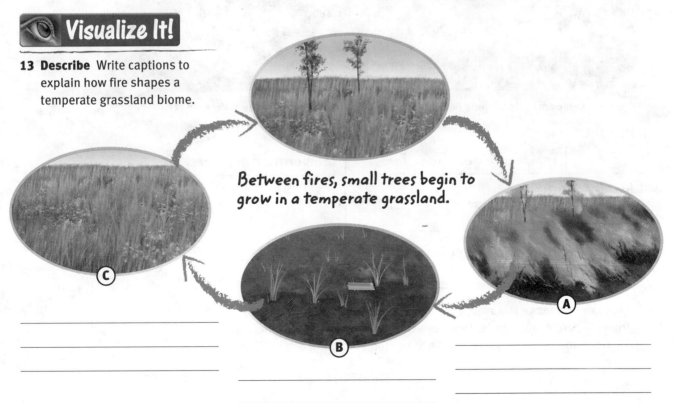

Between fires, small trees begin to grow in a temperate grassland.

Ⓒ

Ⓑ

Ⓐ

_____

_____

_____

Temperate Forest

A **temperate forest** is a biome dominated by trees and other woody vegetation that has a moderate climate, well-defined seasons, and a distinct winter. It is also distinguished by a frost-free growing season of four to six months. Although temperate forests are widely found in North America, Asia, and Europe, there are two different kinds of these biomes that are distinguished by the types of trees that grow there.

Temperate deciduous forests have **deciduous trees**, which are broadleaf trees that drop their leaves as winter approaches. Fallen leaves decay and add organic matter to the soil, making it nutrient-rich. Songbirds nest in these forests during summer, but many migrate to warmer areas before winter. Animals such as chipmunks and black bears hibernate during winter. Deer and bobcats are active year-round. These forests have moderate precipitation, hot summers, and cold winters, and are located in the northeastern United States, East Asia, and much of Europe.

Temperate rain forests are home to coniferous trees, which are trees that have needle-shaped or scale-like leaves. The forest floor is covered with mosses and ferns and contains nutrient-rich soil. Plants grow throughout the year in the temperate rain forest. Animals in this biome include spotted owls, shrews, elk, and cougars. Temperate rain forests exist in the Pacific Northwest and western coast of South America.

👁 Visualize It!

14 Summarize Gather information to complete the table below with the characteristics of each temperate forest biome.

Temperate Deciduous Forest

Temperate Rain Forest

	Temperate Deciduous Forest	Temperate Rain Forest
Climate		
Soil		
Plants		
Animals		

15 Claims • Evidence • Reasoning What abiotic factors differentiate temperate deciduous forests from temperate rain forests? How does climate impact on these differences? State your claim. Then provide evidence from the table to support your claim and explain your reasoning.

_____

_____

_____

Tropical Rain Forest

Tropical rain forests are located near Earth's equator. This biome is warm throughout the year. It also receives more rain than any other biome on Earth. The soil in tropical rain forests is acidic and low in nutrients. Even with poor soil, tropical rain forests have some of the highest biological diversity on Earth. Dense layers of plants develop in a tropical rain forest. These layers block sunlight from reaching the forest floor. Some plants such as orchids grow on tree branches instead of on the dark forest floor. Birds, monkeys, and sloths live in the upper layers of the rain forest. Leaf-cutter ants, jaguars, snakes, and anteaters live in the lower layers.

16 Claims • Evidence • Reasoning How does the availability of resources in each layer of a tropical rain forest affect the organisms that live there? Support your answer with evidence.

Visual Summary

To complete this summary, fill in the answers to the questions. Then, use the key below to check your answers. You can use this page to review the main concepts of the lesson.

Terrestrial Biomes

A biome is a region of Earth characterized by a specific climate and specific plants and animals.

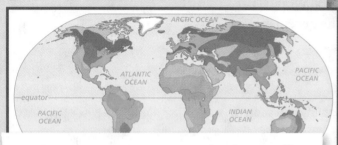

17 What are the major terrestrial biomes?

_____

_____

_____

Plants and animals are adapted to the conditions in their biome.

19 The plant below is adapted to what conditions?

_____

_____

_____

Each biome can contain many ecosystems.

18 How are ecosystems different from biomes?

_____

_____

_____

Sample answers: 17 tundra, taiga, desert, tropical grassland (savanna), temperate grassland, temperate forest, tropical rain forest; 18 Ecosystems are smaller areas within biomes that include communities of organisms and their nonliving environment.; 19 dry conditions

20 Compare Create a list of 3-5 questions about factors, such as location or water, that affect patterns across biomes. Answer your questions using information from various sources. Then, synthesize the differences between terrestrial biomes.

Lesson Review

Vocabulary

Define Draw a line to connect the following terms to their definitions.

1 a region that has a specific climate and a specific community of plants and animals

A taiga

2 a region with low average temperatures and little precipitation

B climate

3 long-term temperature and precipitation patterns in a region

C biome

Key Concepts

4 Identify What are the abiotic factors that help to characterize a biome?

_____

_____

_____

5 Describe Describe a savanna biome.

_____

_____

_____

_____

6 Explain How does climate determine the organisms that live in a biome?

_____

_____

_____

7 Summarize Why can many ecosystems exist in one biome? Explain your reasoning.

_____

_____

_____

_____

_____

Critical Thinking

Use the Venn diagram to answer the following questions.

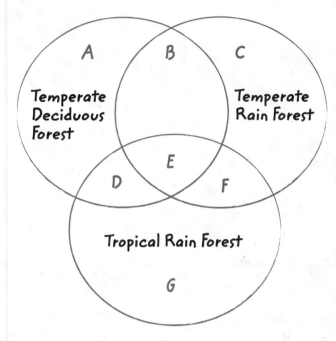

8 Infer In which space on the Venn diagram would you write *coniferous trees*?

_____

9 Analyze What is common among all three types of forests in the diagram?

_____

_____

_____

_____

10 Relate What biome do you think you live in? Explain your answer.

_____

_____

_____

_____

_____

_____

My Notes

Aquatic Ecosystems

ESSENTIAL QUESTION

What are aquatic ecosystems?

By the end of this lesson, you should be able to describe the characteristics of marine, freshwater, and other aquatic ecosystems.

S7L4.d Terrestrial biomes and aquatic ecosystems

Coral reefs are coastal ocean ecosystems that are located in many tropical areas. Coral reefs have some of the highest biological diversity on Earth.

Engage Your Brain

1 Predict Check T or F to show whether you think each statement is true or false.

T	F	
☐	☐	Wetlands can protect areas close to shorelines from flooding.
☐	☐	Most ponds contain both salt water and fresh water.
☐	☐	Plants and animals cannot live in fast-moving waters.
☐	☐	The deep ocean is colder and darker than other marine ecosystems.

2 Predict How do you think organisms like this squid are adapted to life in the deep ocean?

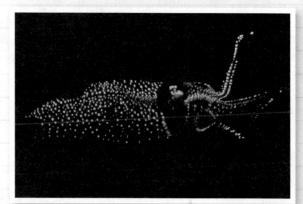

_____

_____

_____

Active Reading

3 Synthesize You can often define an unknown word if you know the meaning of its word parts. Use the word parts and sentence below to make an educated guess about the meaning of the word *wetland*.

Word part	Meaning
wet-	having water or liquid on the surface
-land	solid part of Earth's surface

Example sentence:
Many species of birds and mammals rely on <u>wetlands</u> for food, water, and shelter.

wetland: _____

_____

_____

Vocabulary Terms

• wetland   • estuary

4 Identify As you read, place a question mark next to any words that you don't understand. When you finish reading the lesson, go back and review the text you marked. Work with a classmate to define the words that are still unclear.

Splish Splash

What are the major types of aquatic ecosystems?

Have you ever gone swimming in the ocean, or fishing on a lake? Oceans and lakes support many of the aquatic ecosystems on Earth. An *aquatic ecosystem* includes any water environment and the community of organisms that live there.

The three main types of aquatic ecosystems are freshwater ecosystems, estuaries, and marine ecosystems. Freshwater ecosystems can be found in rivers, lakes, and wetlands. Marine ecosystems are found in oceans. Estuaries exist where rivers and oceans meet along coastlines.

What abiotic factors affect aquatic ecosystems?

Abiotic factors are the nonliving things in an environment. The major abiotic factors that affect aquatic ecosystems include water temperature, water depth, amount of light, oxygen level, water pH, salinity (salt level), and the rate of water flow. An aquatic ecosystem may be influenced by some of these factors but not others. For example, a river would be influenced by rate of water flow but not typically by salinity.

Visualize It!

5 Identify Fill in the major types of aquatic ecosystems in the picture.

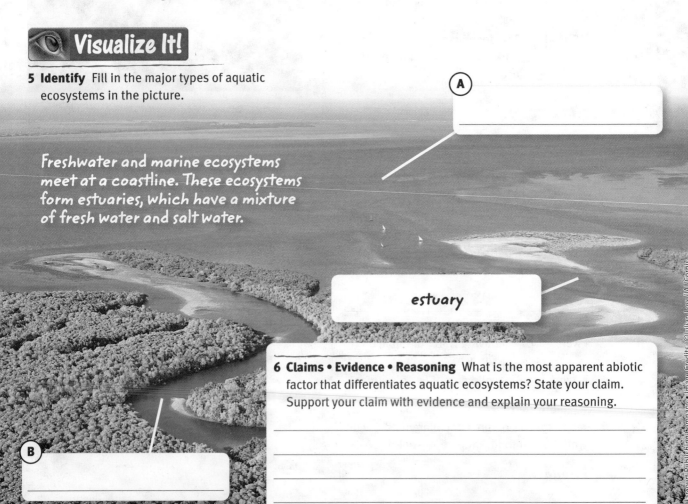

Freshwater and marine ecosystems meet at a coastline. These ecosystems form estuaries, which have a mixture of fresh water and salt water.

A _____

estuary

B _____

6 Claims • Evidence • Reasoning What is the most apparent abiotic factor that differentiates aquatic ecosystems? State your claim. Support your claim with evidence and explain your reasoning.

_____
_____
_____
_____

Where are examples of freshwater ecosystems found?

Freshwater ecosystems contain water that has very little salt in it. Freshwater ecosystems are found in lakes, ponds, wetlands, rivers, and streams. Although freshwater ecosystems seem common, they actually contain less than one percent of all the water on Earth.

In Lakes and Ponds

Lakes and ponds are bodies of water surrounded by land. Lakes are larger than ponds. Some plants grow at the edges of these water bodies. Others live underwater or grow leaves that float on the surface. Protists such as algae and amoebas float in the water. Frogs and some insects lay eggs in the water, and their young develop there. Clams, bacteria, and worms live on the bottom of lakes and ponds and break down dead materials for food. Frogs, turtles, fish, and ducks have adaptations that let them swim in water.

Active Reading

7 Identify As you read, underline the names of organisms that live in or near lakes and ponds.

Visualize It!

8 Describe Pick a plant and animal in the picture. Describe how each is adapted to a pond.

Plant

_____

_____

_____

Animal

_____

_____

_____

_____

© Houghton Mifflin Harcourt Publishing Company

In Wetlands

A **wetland** is an area of land that is saturated, or soaked, with water for at least part of the year. Bogs, marshes, and swamps are types of wetlands. Bogs contain living and decomposing mosses. Many grasslike plants grow in marshes. Swamps have trees and vines. Plants that live in wetlands are adapted to living in wet soil.

Wetlands have high species diversity. Common wetland plants include cattails, duckweed, sphagnum moss, sedges, orchids, willows, tamarack, and black ash trees. Animals found in wetlands include ducks, frogs, shrews, herons, and alligators. Water collects and slowly filters through a wetland. In this way, some pollutants are removed from the water. Since wetlands can hold water, they also protect nearby land and shore from floods and erosion.

Think Outside the Book Inquiry

9 Apply Use library and Internet resources to put together an identification guide to common wetland plants.

 **Visualize It!**

Wetland

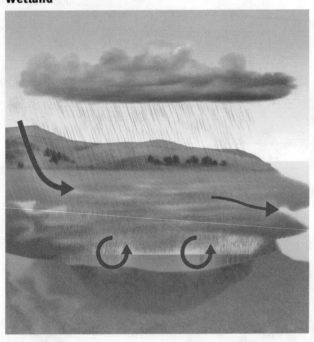

Development That Replaced Wetland

10 Claims • Evidence • Reasoning What can happen when a wetland is replaced by a development in an area? State your claim. Gather evidence to support your claim and explain your reasoning.

_____

_____

_____

_____

_____

_____

In Rivers and Streams

Water moves in one direction in a stream. As water moves, it interacts with air and oxygen is added to the water. A large stream is called a river. Rivers and streams are home to many organisms, including fish, aquatic insects, and mosses. Freshwater ecosystems in streams can have areas of fast-moving and slow-moving water. Some organisms that live in fast-moving water have adaptations that let them resist being washed away. Immature black flies can attach themselves to rocks in a fast-moving stream. Rootlike rhizoids let mosses stick to rocks. In slow-moving waters of a stream, water striders are adapted to live on the water's surface.

The slope of a river's channel and the river's depth determine how quickly water moves.

Visualize It!

11 Match Match the correct captions to the pictures showing areas of fast-moving and slow-moving water.

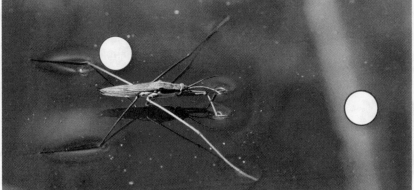

A Water striders move across the surface of a pool of water in a river.

B Rocks form small waterfalls in areas of some streams.

C Aquatic plants can live below the surface of a river.

D Mosses can grow on the surface of rocks even in fast-moving water.

Inquiry

12 Infer Why might stream water have more oxygen in it than pond water does? Explain your reasoning.

Where River Meets Sea

What is an estuary?

An **estuary** is a partially enclosed body of water formed where a river flows into an ocean. Because estuaries have a mixture of fresh water and salt water, they support ecosystems that have a unique and diverse community of organisms. Seagrasses, marsh grasses, mangrove trees, fish, oysters, mussels, and water birds all live in estuaries. Fish and shrimp lay eggs in the calm waters of an estuary. Their young mature here before moving out into the ocean. Many birds feed on the young shrimp and fish in an estuary.

Organisms in estuaries must be able to survive in constantly changing salt levels due to the rise and fall of tides. Some estuary grasses, such as smooth cordgrass, have special structures in their roots and leaves that let them get rid of excess salt.

👁 Visualize It!

13 Describe Fill in the rest of the name tags for each estuary organism. List at least one way the organism uses an estuary to survive.

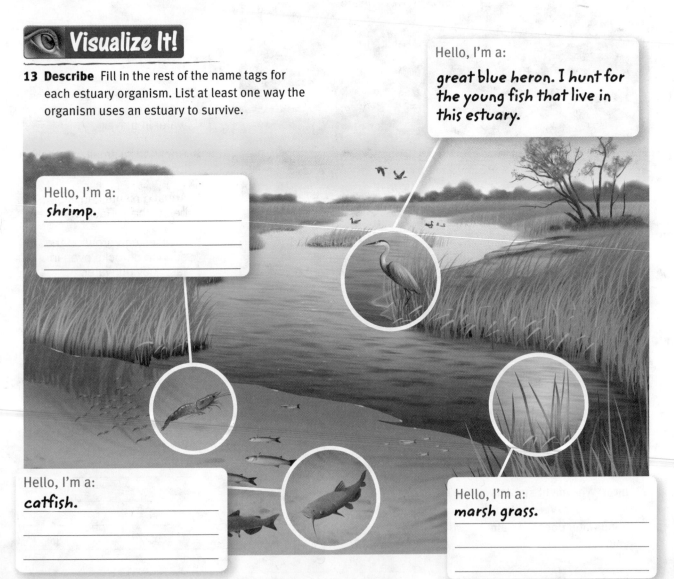

Hello, I'm a:
great blue heron. I hunt for the young fish that live in this estuary.

Hello, I'm a:
shrimp.
_____
_____

Hello, I'm a:
catfish.
_____
_____

Hello, I'm a:
marsh grass.
_____
_____

Protecting Estuaries

Why are estuaries important? The mixture of salt water and nutrient-rich fresh water in an estuary supports breeding grounds for birds, commercial fish, and shellfish such as crabs and shrimp. The grasses in estuaries also protect coastal areas from erosion and flooding.

Oil Spill!

In 2010, a major oil spill occurred in the Gulf of Mexico. Oil flowed into the ocean for almost three months.

Coastal Damage

Estuaries along the northern Gulf Coast were affected. Oil killed birds and other animals. It soaked seagrasses and damaged fish and shellfish nurseries.

Cleaning Up

A large cleanup effort began after the spill. Continuing work will be important to restore ecosystems and protect fishing and tourism jobs in the area.

Extend

14 Explain What are the economic benefits from estuaries?

15 Research Find out about another damaged estuary ecosystem. How has the estuary been restored?

16 Hypothesize Form a hypothesis about how the loss of estuaries can increase erosion along shorelines.

By the Beautiful Sea

The open ocean is vast and contains a variety of life forms. The ocean's largest, fastest, and deepest-diving organisms are found here.

Where are examples of marine ecosystems found?

Marine ecosystems are saltwater ecosystems. They cover more than 70 percent of Earth's surface. Marine ecosystems are found in the coastal ocean, the open ocean, and the deep ocean. Different abiotic, or nonliving, factors affect each marine ecosystem.

In and Along Coastal Oceans

Marine ecosystems in and along coastal oceans include the intertidal zone and the neritic zone. The intertidal zone is the land between high and low tides that includes beaches and rocky shores. Organisms that live in this zone are often adapted to changing water depth, wave action, exposure to air, and changing salinity. Crabs and seagrasses live on beaches. Barnacles and anemones live in tidal pools on rocky shores.

The neritic zone is the underwater zone from the shore to the edge of the continental shelf. Light reaches the bottom of the neritic zone, allowing algae and many plants to live there. Coral reefs and kelp forests are found in the neritic zone. Coral reefs are located mainly in warm tropical areas. They support many species of colorful fish, anemones, and coral. Kelp forests are found in cold, nutrient-rich waters. Kelp forests support brown and red algae, shrimp, fish, brittle stars, and sea otters.

Visualize It!

17 List Below each photo, list abiotic factors that differentiate the coastal ecosystems shown.

Sandy Beach	Rocky Shore	Coral Reef	Kelp Forest

A	B	C	D

_____
_____
_____

In Open Oceans

The open ocean includes all surface waters down to a depth of about 2,000 meters (6,562 feet). Ecosystems at the surface are often dominated by tiny floating organisms called *plankton*. Organisms that are adapted to dark and cold conditions live at greater depths. Because the open ocean is so large, the majority of sea life is found there. Animals found in open ocean ecosystems include sharks, whales, dolphins, fish, and sea turtles. Ecosystems in the bathyal zone, which extends from the edge of the continental shelf to its base, are also considered open ocean ecosystems.

In Deep Oceans

The deep ocean has the coldest and darkest conditions. Deep ocean ecosystems include those in the abyssal zone, which is the part of the ocean below 2,000 meters (6,562 feet). Some species that live in the deep ocean have bioluminescence, which lets them produce a glowing light to attract mates or prey. Female anglerfish attract prey using bioluminescent structures that act as bait.

No light can reach the deep ocean, so no photosynthesis can happen there. Organisms in the deep ocean must get energy in other ways. Some feed on the organic material that is constantly falling from shallower ocean depths. Microorganisms living near hydrothermal vents use chemicals in the water as an energy source.

Active Reading

18 Infer How do organisms in the deep ocean get energy to live?

_____

_____

Hydrothermal vents release super-hot, acidic water in the deep ocean. Microorganisms called *archaea* convert chemicals from the vents into food using chemosynthesis. Archaea, tube worms, crabs, clams, and shrimp are part of hydrothermal vent communities.

Think Outside the Book Inquiry

19 Research Write at least three questions that can help you differentiate between the three aquatic ecosystems found in the Wassaw National Wildlife Area in Georgia.

20 Synthesize Using the questions you developed for the previous activity, use multiple sources to research the ecosystems found in the Wassaw National Wildlife Area. Then, create a poster that describes each ecosystem.

Visual Summary

To complete this summary, fill in the answer to each question. Then, use the key below to check your answers. You can use this page to review the main concepts of the lesson.

Aquatic Ecosystems

Freshwater ecosystems contain still or moving fresh water.

21 Where are freshwater ecosystems found?

_____

_____

An estuary is an ecosystem that forms where a river empties into an ocean.

23 Which abiotic factor would likely have the greatest effect on an estuary?

_____

_____

Marine ecosystems are located in or near oceans.

22 Where are ecosystems found in the ocean?

_____

_____

Sample answers: 21 In lakes, ponds, wetlands, rivers, and streams; 22 In the coastal ocean, open ocean, and deep ocean; 23 changing salinity

24 Research Find one example of each of the three main aquatic ecosystems. Read about the location, climate, food sources, and wildlife found in each ecosystem. Using evidence from your research sources, describe how the biotic and abiotic factors are similar and different among the ecosystems.

Lesson Review

Vocabulary

Fill in the blank with the term that best completes the following sentences.

1 A(n) _____ is a partially enclosed body of water formed where a river flows into an ocean.

2 A(n) _____ is an area of land that is covered or saturated with water for at least part of the year.

Key Concepts

3 Identify What kinds of organisms live in estuaries?

_____

_____

_____

_____

_____

4 Describe What types of adaptations would be needed by organisms that live in a river?

_____

_____

_____

_____

_____

5 Describe Describe the characteristics of the four zones found in the ocean.

_____

_____

_____

_____

_____

_____

_____

_____

Critical Thinking

Use the photo to answer the following question.

6 Predict Organisms in the aquatic ecosystem in the picture must be adapted to which abiotic factors? Provide evidence to support your answer.

_____

_____

_____

_____

_____

7 Draw Draw an organism that is adapted to the abyssal zone of the ocean, and label its adaptations.

8 Analyze Salt water is denser than fresh water. What ecosystem would be most affected by this fact? Explain your answer.

_____

_____

_____

_____

My Notes

Interpreting Circle Graphs

Scientists display data in tables and graphs in order to organize it and show relationships. A *circle graph*, also called a *pie graph*, is used to show and compare the pieces of a whole.

Tutorial

In a circle graph, the entire circle represents the whole, and each piece is called a *sector*. Follow the instructions below to learn how to interpret a circle graph.

1 Evaluating Data Data on circle graphs may be given in one of two ways: as values (such as dollars, days, or numbers of items) or as percentages of the whole.

2 Changing Percentage to Value The word *percent* means "per hundred," so 25% means 25 per 100, or 25/100. To find the total volume represented by a sector, such as the volume of fresh water in surface water, multiply the whole value by the percent of the sector, and then divide by 100.

$$35{,}030{,}000 \text{ km}^3 \times \frac{0.3}{100} = 105{,}090 \text{ km}^3 \text{ of Earth's}$$
fresh water is in surface water.

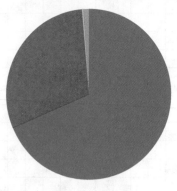

Distribution of Fresh Water (in values)

- ■ Icecaps and Glaciers 24,065,610 km³
- ■ Ground Water 10,544,030 km³
- ■ Surface Water 105,090 km³
- ■ Other 315,270 km³

Source: Gleick, P. H., 1996: Water resources. In Encyclopedia of Climate and Weather, ed. by S. H. Schneider, Oxford University Press, New York, vol. 2, pp.817-823

---

3 Changing Value to Ratio The sum of the sectors, 35,030,000 km³, is the whole, or total value. Divide the value of a sector, such as the icecaps and glaciers sector, by the value of the whole. Simplify this fraction to express it as a ratio.

$$\frac{24{,}065{,}610 \text{ km}^3}{35{,}030{,}000 \text{ km}^3} \approx \frac{25}{35} = \frac{5}{7}$$

About $\frac{5}{7}$ of Earth's fresh water is in icecaps and glaciers.

This ratio can be expressed as $\frac{5}{7}$, 5:7, or 5 to 7.

4 Changing Value to Percentage The whole circle graph is 100%. To find the percentage of a sector, such as the world's fresh water that is found as groundwater, divide the value of the sector by the value of the whole, and then multiply by 100%.

$$\frac{10{,}544{,}030 \text{ km}^3}{35{,}030{,}000 \text{ km}^3} \times 100\% = 30.1\% \text{ of Earth's fresh water is}$$
groundwater.

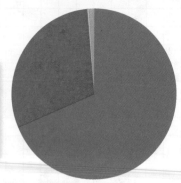

Distribution of Fresh Water (in percentages)

- ■ Icecaps and Glaciers 68.7%
- ■ Ground Water 30.1%
- ■ Surface Water 0.3%
- ■ Other 0.9%

Source: Gleick, P. H., 1996: Water resources. In Encyclopedia of Climate and Weather, ed. by S. H. Schneider, Oxford University Press, New York, vol. 2, pp.817-823

You Try It!

Use the circle graphs below to answer the following questions.

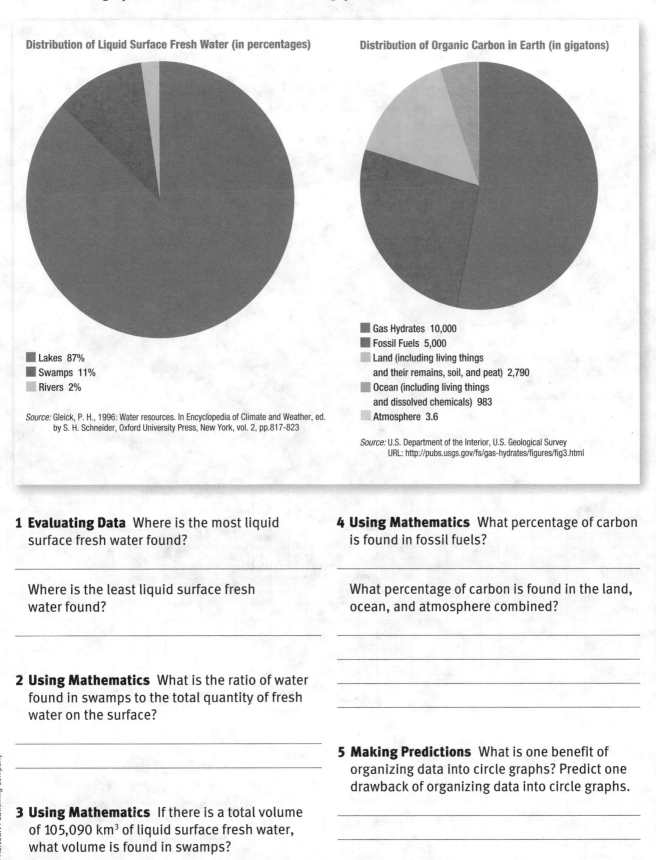

Distribution of Liquid Surface Fresh Water (in percentages)

- Lakes 87%
- Swamps 11%
- Rivers 2%

Source: Gleick, P. H., 1996: Water resources. In Encyclopedia of Climate and Weather, ed. by S. H. Schneider, Oxford University Press, New York, vol. 2, pp.817-823

Distribution of Organic Carbon in Earth (in gigatons)

- Gas Hydrates 10,000
- Fossil Fuels 5,000
- Land (including living things and their remains, soil, and peat) 2,790
- Ocean (including living things and dissolved chemicals) 983
- Atmosphere 3.6

Source: U.S. Department of the Interior, U.S. Geological Survey URL: http://pubs.usgs.gov/fs/gas-hydrates/figures/fig3.html

1 Evaluating Data Where is the most liquid surface fresh water found?

_____

Where is the least liquid surface fresh water found?

_____

2 Using Mathematics What is the ratio of water found in swamps to the total quantity of fresh water on the surface?

_____

_____

3 Using Mathematics If there is a total volume of 105,090 km³ of liquid surface fresh water, what volume is found in swamps?

_____

_____

4 Using Mathematics What percentage of carbon is found in fossil fuels?

_____

What percentage of carbon is found in the land, ocean, and atmosphere combined?

_____

_____

_____

5 Making Predictions What is one benefit of organizing data into circle graphs? Predict one drawback of organizing data into circle graphs.

_____

_____

_____

_____

Energy and Matter in Ecosystems

ESSENTIAL QUESTION

How do energy and matter move through ecosystems?

By the end of this lesson, you should be able to explain the flow of energy and the cycles of matter in ecosystems.

Living things get energy from food. Plants can make their own food, but people have to eat other organisms.

 S7L4.b Cycling of matter and energy flow in ecosystems

Engage Your Brain

1 Predict Organisms get energy from food. Underline the organisms in the list below that get food by eating other organisms.

Lizard	Butterfly
Pine tree	Cactus
Grass	Mountain lion
Salamander	Bluebird
Turtle	Moss

2 Diagram Choose a nearby ecosystem, and draw a diagram below of the flow of energy from the sun to the organisms in the ecosystem.

 Active Reading

3 Apply Many scientific words, such as *energy*, also have everyday meanings. Use context clues to write your own definition for each meaning of the word *energy*.

You could feel the <u>energy</u> in the crowd during the homecoming game.

_____

_____

When she had the flu, Eliza slept all day because she felt completely drained of <u>energy</u>.

_____

_____

The brightly colored painting was full of <u>energy</u>.

_____

_____

Vocabulary Terms
• **matter**
• **energy**
• **law of conservation of energy**
• **law of conservation of mass**
• **energy pyramid**
• **water cycle**
• **nitrogen cycle**
• **carbon cycle**

4 Apply As you learn the definition of each vocabulary term in this lesson, create your own definition or sketch to help remember the meaning of the term.

Soak Up the Sun

How do organisms get energy and matter?

To live, grow, and reproduce, all organisms need matter and energy. **Matter** is anything that has mass and takes up space. Organisms use matter in chemical processes, such as digestion and breathing. For these processes to occur, organisms need energy. **Energy** is the ability to do work and enables organisms to use matter in life processes. Organisms have different ways of getting matter and energy from their environment.

From the Sun

Organisms called *producers* use energy from their surroundings to make their own food. In most ecosystems, the sun is the original source of energy. Producers, like most plants and algae, use sunlight to convert water and carbon dioxide into sugars. In a few ecosystems, producers use chemical energy instead of light energy to make food. Producers take in matter, such as carbon dioxide, nitrogen, and water from air and soil.

From Other Organisms

Consumers are organisms that get energy by eating producers or other consumers. They get materials such as carbon, nitrogen, and phosphorus from the organisms they eat. So, consumers take in both energy and matter when they eat other organisms.

Active Reading

5 Identify As you read, underline the characteristics of producers and consumers.

Roots help trees get matter, such as water and nutrients, from the soil.

6 Infer Use this table to identify where producers and consumers get energy and matter.

Type of organism	How it gets energy	How it gets matter
Producer		
Consumer		

What happens to energy and matter in ecosystems?

Ecosystems are made up of biotic and abiotic factors. Biotic factors, such as plants and animals, are all the living things in an ecosystem. Abiotic factors, such as sunlight and nutrients, are nonliving parts of an ecosystem that are required for living things to survive. All ecosystems need both biotic and abiotic factors to be balanced.

Energy and matter are constantly moving through ecosystems. Organisms need energy and matter for many functions, such as moving, growing, and reproducing. Some producers use carbon dioxide and water to make sugars, from which they get energy. They also collect materials from their environment for their life processes. Consumers get energy and matter for their life processes by eating other organisms. During every process, some energy is lost as heat. And, matter is returned to the physical environment as wastes or when organisms die.

Energy and Matter Are Conserved

The **law of conservation of energy** states that energy cannot be created or destroyed. Energy changes forms. Some producers change light energy from the sun to chemical energy in sugars. When sugars are used, some energy is given off as heat. Much of the energy in sugars is changed to another form of chemical energy that cells can use for life functions. The **law of conservation of mass** states that mass cannot be created or destroyed. Instead, matter moves through the environment in different forms.

Energy and Matter Leave Ecosystems

Ecosystems do not have clear boundaries, so energy and matter can leave them. Matter and energy can leave an ecosystem when organisms move. For example, some birds feed on fish in the ocean. When birds fly back to land, they take the matter and energy from the fish out of the ocean. Matter and energy can leave ecosystems in moving water and air. Even though the matter and energy enter and leave an ecosystem, they are never destroyed.

Visualize It!

7 Analyze How might energy and matter leave the ecosystem shown in the picture above? Provide evidence to support your reasoning.

_____

_____

_____

_____

8 Compare Use the Venn diagram to relate how energy and matter move through ecosystems.

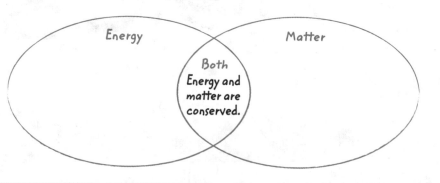

Energy

Matter

Both
Energy and matter are conserved.

Cycle *and* Flow

How does energy move through an ecosystem?

Energy enters most ecosystems as sunlight, which some producers use to make food. Primary consumers, such as herbivores, get energy by consuming producers. Secondary consumers, such as carnivores, get energy by eating primary consumers, and so on up the food chain. An organism uses most of the energy it takes in for life processes. However, some energy is lost to the environment as heat. A small amount of energy is stored within an organism. Only this stored energy can be used by a consumer that eats the organism.

An **energy pyramid** is a tool that can be used to trace the flow of energy through an ecosystem. The pyramid's shape shows that there is less energy and fewer organisms at each level. At each step in the food chain, energy is lost to the environment. Because less energy is available, fewer organisms can be supported at higher levels. The bottom level—the producers—has the largest population and the most energy. The other levels are consumers. At the highest level, consumers will have the smallest population because of the limited amount of energy available to them.

The amount of energy available and population size decrease as you go up the energy pyramid.

Tertiary consumers

Secondary consumers

Primary consumers

Producers

© Houghton Mifflin Harcourt Publishing Company

Visualize It!

9 Analyze Describe how energy flows through each level in this energy pyramid. Is all the matter and energy from one level transferred to the next level?

_____

_____

_____

_____

_____

_____

_____

_____

How does matter move through an ecosystem?

Matter cycles through an ecosystem. For example, water evaporates from Earth's surface into the atmosphere and condenses to form clouds. After forming clouds, water falls back to Earth's surface, completing a cycle.

Carbon and nitrogen also cycle through an ecosystem. Producers take in compounds made of carbon and nitrogen from the physical environment. They use these compounds for life processes. Primary consumers get matter by consuming producers.

Secondary consumers eat primary consumers. The matter in primary consumers is used in chemical processes by secondary consumers. In this way, carbon and nitrogen flow from producers through all levels of consumers.

Consumers do not use all of the matter that they take in. Some of the matter is turned into waste products. Decomposers, such as bacteria and fungi, break down solid waste products and dead organisms, returning matter to the physical environment. Producers can then reuse this matter for life processes, starting the cycles of matter again.

All of these cycles can take place over large areas. Matter leaves some ecosystems and enters other ecosystems. For example, water that evaporates from a lake in the middle of a continent can later fall into an ocean. Because matter can enter and leave an ecosystem, it is called an *open system*.

Active Reading **10 Identify** What is the role of decomposers in the cycling of matter?

_____
_____
_____

Visualize It!

11 Analyze Describe how water is moving through the ecosystem on this page.

_____
_____
_____
_____
_____
_____

What is the water cycle?

The movement of water between the oceans, atmosphere, land, and living things is known as the **water cycle**. Three ways water can enter the atmosphere are evaporation, transpiration, and respiration. During *evaporation*, the sun's heat causes water to change from liquid to vapor. Plants release water vapor from their leaves in *transpiration*. Organisms release water as waste during *respiration*.

In *condensation*, the water vapor cools and returns to liquid. The water that falls from the atmosphere to the land and oceans is *precipitation*. Rain, snow, sleet, and hail are forms of precipitation. Most precipitation falls into the ocean. The precipitation that falls on land and flows into streams and rivers is called *runoff*. Some precipitation seeps into the ground and is stored underground in spaces between or within rocks. This water, called *groundwater*, will slowly flow back into the soil, streams, rivers, and oceans.

12 Explain How does water from the atmosphere return to Earth's surface?

_____

_____

_____

_____

_____

Visualize It!

13 Label Use the terms *evaporation*, *transpiration*, and *respiration* to correctly complete the diagram. Be sure the arrow for each term leads from the proper source.

Condensation

Precipitation

Water vapor in air

A

B

C

Runoff

Groundwater

The water cycle describes how water travels from Earth's surface to the atmosphere and back.

What is the nitrogen cycle?

Organisms need nitrogen to build proteins and DNA for new cells. The movement of nitrogen between the environment and living things is called the **nitrogen cycle**. Most of Earth's atmosphere is nitrogen gas. But most organisms cannot use nitrogen gas directly. However, bacteria in the soil are able to change nitrogen gas into forms that plants can use. This process is called *nitrogen fixation*. Lightning can also fix nitrogen into usable compounds. Plants take in and use fixed nitrogen. Consumers can then get the nitrogen they need by eating plants or other organisms.

When organisms die, decomposers break down their remains. Decomposition releases a form of nitrogen into the soil that plants can use. Finally, certain types of bacteria in the soil can convert nitrogen into a gas, which is returned to the atmosphere.

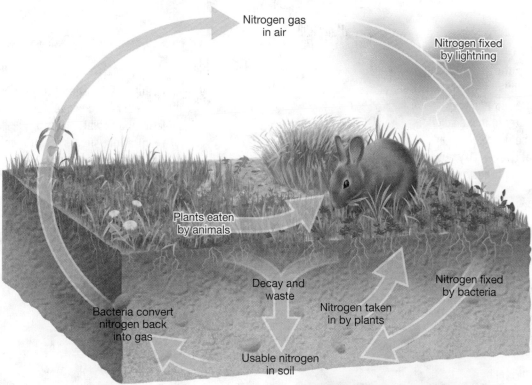

Nitrogen gas
in air

Nitrogen fixed
by lightning

Plants eaten
by animals

Decay and
waste

Nitrogen fixed
by bacteria

Nitrogen taken
in by plants

Bacteria convert
nitrogen back
into gas

Usable nitrogen
in soil

In the nitrogen cycle, nitrogen gas is converted into usable nitrogen by bacteria and lightning. Plants take in the usable nitrogen. Consumers get the nitrogen they need from the organisms they eat.

Visualize It! Inquiry

14 Claims • Evidence • Reasoning What would happen to the ecosystem if there were no nitrogen-fixing bacteria? Provide evidence to support your claim and explain your reasoning.

_____

_____

_____

_____

_____

What is the carbon cycle?

Carbon is an important building block of organisms. It is found in sugars, which store the chemical energy that organisms need to live. It also is found in the atmosphere (as carbon dioxide gas), in bodies of water, in rocks and soils, in organisms, and in fossil fuels. Carbon moves through organisms and between organisms and the physical environment in the **carbon cycle**.

Active Reading **15 List** Identify five places where carbon may be found.

_____

_____

_____

Respiration

Photosynthesis

Photosynthesis

During photosynthesis, producers in the water and on land take in light energy from the sun and use carbon dioxide and water to make sugars. These sugars contain carbon and store chemical energy. Oxygen gas is also a product of photosynthesis.

Respiration

Cellular respiration occurs in producers and consumers on land and in water. During respiration, sugars are broken down to release energy. The process uses oxygen gas. Energy, carbon dioxide, and water are released.

carbon in organisms

carbon dioxide dissolved in water

Visualize It!

16 Relate Briefly describe how carbon enters and exits a consumer, such as the sheep shown in this diagram.

_____

_____

_____

_____

_____

Combustion

Combustion is the burning of materials, including wood and fossil fuels. Burning once-living things releases carbon dioxide, water, heat, and other materials into the environment. It may also produce pollution.

carbon dioxide in air

Combustion

Photosynthesis

Respiration

carbon in organisms

Decomposition

Decomposition

Decomposition is the breakdown of dead organisms and wastes. Decomposers get energy from this material by respiration. Decomposition returns carbon dioxide, water, and other nutrients to the environment.

carbon in fossil fuels

Fossil Fuels

Fossil fuels formed from decomposing organisms that were buried deeply millions of years ago. Fossil fuels are burned during combustion, releasing carbon dioxide into the air.

Think Outside the Book (Inquiry)

17 Apply With a partner, choose an ecosystem with which you are familiar. Create a model to show how matter cycles and how energy flows among biotic and abiotic factors of that ecosystem.

Visual Summary

To complete this summary, fill in the blanks with the correct word or phrase. Then use the key below to check your answers. You can use this page to review the main concepts of the lesson.

Energy and Matter in Ecosystems

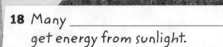

Organisms get energy and matter from different sources.

18 Many _____ get energy from sunlight.

19 _____ get energy by eating other organisms.

Water moves between Earth's surface and the atmosphere in the water cycle.

20 Water that flows over the surface of the ground is called _____.

Nitrogen moves from the atmosphere, to organisms, and back to the atmosphere in the nitrogen cycle.

21 _____ is the process by which bacteria turn nitrogen gas into compounds plants can use.

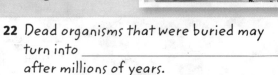

Carbon cycles through organisms, into the physical environment, and back again.

22 Dead organisms that were buried may turn into _____ after millions of years.

23 Carbon from this material reenters the atmosphere by _____.

Answers: 18 producers; 19 Consumers; 20 runoff; 21 Nitrogen fixation; 22 fossil fuels; 23 combustion

24 **Explain** If energy and matter cannot be destroyed, what happens to energy and matter when an organism is eaten? Explain your reasoning.

Lesson Review

Vocabulary

Fill in the blanks with the term that best completes the following sentences.

1 The ability to do work is called _____.

2 _____ is anything that has mass and takes up space.

3 A(n) _____ can be used to trace the flow of energy through an ecosystem.

Key Concepts

4 Describe Explain the difference between a producer, a consumer, and a decomposer.

_____

_____

_____

5 Compare How are the law of conservation of energy and the law of conservation of mass similar?

_____

_____

_____

_____

_____

6 Explain Why do organisms need nitrogen?

_____

_____

_____

_____

Critical Thinking

7 Analyze In an ecosystem, which would have a larger population: producers or primary consumers? Explain.

_____

_____

_____

Use the graph to answer the following questions.

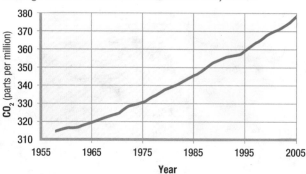

Average Carbon Dioxide Levels at Mauna Loa, Hawaii

Source: *NOAA 2004*

8 Analyze What process of the carbon cycle is likely causing the increase in carbon dioxide levels shown in the graph above?

_____

_____

9 Identify What is the most likely source of the increase in carbon dioxide in the atmosphere shown in the graph above?

_____

10 Evaluate If people planted huge numbers of trees and other plants, how might the carbon dioxide levels in the graph above change? Use data from the graph to support your reasoning.

_____

_____

_____

_____

_____

_____

11 Apply Water is traveling up a tree carrying nutrients. Use the water cycle to explain how that water later becomes groundwater.

_____

_____

_____

_____

My Notes

Changes in Ecosystems

ESSENTIAL QUESTION ·

How do ecosystems change?

By the end of this lesson, you should be able to describe how natural processes change ecosystems and help them develop after a natural disturbance.

Ecosystems are always changing. Many changes in ecosystems are due to natural disturbances. This forest fire in Yellowstone National Park was caused by lightning.

Lesson Labs

Quick Labs
- Measuring Species Diversity
- Investigate Evidence of Succession

Field Lab
- Predicting How Succession Follows a Human Disturbance

Engage Your Brain

1 Predict Check T or F to show whether you think each statement is true or false.

T	F	
☐	☐	Some damaged ecosystems can recover after a disturbance.
☐	☐	Ecosystems only change slowly after natural disturbances.
☐	☐	Changes in ecosystems proceed in a fairly predictable way after a disturbance occurs.
☐	☐	Ecosystems eventually stop changing.

2 Describe Use the picture below to describe how beavers change their environment.

_____

_____

_____

Active Reading

3 Synthesize A compound term is a term made from two or more words. The term *pioneer species* is a compound term. Use the definitions and sentence below to make an educated guess about the meaning of the compound term *pioneer species*.

Word	Meaning
pioneer	the first ones to do something
species	a group of very similar organisms

Example sentence
Lichens and other <u>pioneer species</u> break down rock and leave organic matter that mix together to make soil.

Vocabulary Terms

- eutrophication
- pioneer species
- succession
- biodiversity

4 Identify As you read, create a reference card for each vocabulary term. On one side of the card, write the term and its meaning. On the other side, draw a picture that illustrates or makes a connection to the term. These cards can be used as bookmarks in the text. You can also refer to the cards while studying.

pioneer species:

_____

_____

Lesson 4 Changes in Ecosystems **441**

© Houghton Mifflin Harcourt Publishing Company • Image Credits: (bg) ©David R. Frazier Photolibrary, Inc./Photo Researchers, Inc.; (tr) ©William Smithey Jr./Photographer's Choice/Getty Images

Nothing Stays the Same

How quickly do ecosystems change?

Ecosystems and organisms are constantly changing and responding to changes in the environment. Changes in climate, development of disease, and human activity all impact an ecosystem and affect what resources are available to organisms. Most ecosystem changes are gradual. Some are sudden and irregular.

Active Reading 5 **Describe** As you read, underline one slow change and one sudden change in an ecosystem.

Ecosystems May Change Slowly

Some changes happen slowly. Over time, a pond can develop into a meadow. **Eutrophication** (yoo•trohf•ih•KAY•shuhn) is the process in which organic matter and nutrients slowly build up in a body of water. The nutrients increase the growth of plants and microorganisms. When these organisms die, decaying matter sinks to the bottom of the pond. This organic matter can eventually fill the pond and become soil that grasses and other meadow plants can grow in.

Ecosystem changes can also be caused by seasonal or long-term changes in climate.

Ecosystems May Change Suddenly

Ecosystems can suddenly change due to catastrophic natural disturbances. A hurricane's strong winds can blow down trees and destroy vegetation in a few hours. Lightning can start a forest fire that rapidly clears away plants and alters animal habitats. A volcano, such as Washington's Mount St. Helens, can erupt and cause massive destruction to an ecosystem. But destruction is not the end of the story. Recovery brings new changes to an ecosystem and the populations that live in it.

In 2006, some surviving American chestnut trees were found in F. D. Roosevelt State Park near Warm Springs, Georgia. This was remarkable because in 1904 the fungus *Cryphonectria parasitica* was accidentally introduced to America through the import of Japanese chestnut trees. By 1940, most mature American chestnut trees had died because of the disease.

Ecosystems can change rapidly due to the spread of disease. Entire species can be destroyed through diseases spread by the introduction of non-native species, migration patterns, or even globalization.

The table below lists examples of the impact diseases have had on species and ecosystems in the United States.

Species	Disease	Source	Effect
American chestnut tree	Chestnut blight	Import of Japanese chestnut trees	Almost 4 billion trees died within 40 years
Dutch elm tree	Dutch elm disease	Migration of elm bark beetles	Loss of over half of the elm trees in northern U.S.
Citrus trees	Yellow dragon disease	Globalization—Asian citrus psyllid (insect)	80% reduction in citrus production in affected areas

Sources: College of Environmental Science and Forestry of the State University of New York, National Wildlife Federation, World Health Organization

6 Synthesize How does the introduction of non-native species affect ecosystems? What recommendations would you give to minimize this impact? Provide specific data to support your answer.

_____

_____

_____

Ruin and Recovery

Ecosystems can change very fast. The volcanic eruption of Mount St. Helens in southern Washington devastated the mountain on May 18, 1980, killing 57 people. The hot gas and debris also killed native plant and animal species and damaged 596 square kilometers (230 square miles) of forest.

1979

Today

A Changed Landscape

The eruption changed the ecosystem dramatically. Trees fell and forests burned. Much of the ice and snow melted. The water mixed with ash and dirt that covered the ground. Thick mud formed and slid down the mountain. Flowing mud removed more trees and changed the shape of the landscape.

Road to Recovery

How did the ecosystem recover? Snow patches and ice protected some species. Some small mammals were sheltered in burrows. With the trees gone, more sunlight reached the ground. Seeds sprouted, and the recovery began.

Extend

Inquiry

7 Explain How do sudden catastrophes such as the eruption of Mount St. Helens change the landscape of ecosystems? Support your claim with evidence and explain your reasoning.

8 Research Find out about how natural catastrophic events, such as volcanic eruptions, can affect the climate on Earth.

9 Hypothesize Form a hypothesis based on your research in question 8 about how changes in climate can lead to changes in ecosystems.

What are the two types of ecological succession?

Ecosystems can develop from bare rock or cleared land. This development is the result of slow and constructive gradual changes. The slow development or replacement of an ecological community by another ecological community over time is called **succession**.

Primary Succession

A community may start to grow in an area that has no soil. This process is called *primary succession*. The first organisms to live in an uninhabited area are called **pioneer species**. Pioneer species, such as lichens, grow on rock and help to form soil in which plants can grow.

👁 Visualize It!

10 Label Write a title for each step of primary succession.

A _____

A slowly retreating glacier exposes bare rock where nothing lives, and primary succession begins.

B _____

Acids from lichens break down the rock into particles. These particles mix with the remains of dead lichens to make soil.

C _____

After many years, there is enough soil for mosses to grow. The mosses replace the lichens. Insects and other small organisms begin to live there, enriching the soil.

D _____

As the soil deepens, mosses are replaced by ferns. The ferns may slowly be replaced by grasses and wildflowers. If there is enough soil, shrubs and small trees may grow.

E _____

After hundreds or even thousands of years, the soil may be deep and fertile enough to support a forest.

Secondary Succession

Succession also happens to areas that have been disturbed but that still have soil. Sometimes an existing ecosystem is damaged by a natural disaster, such as a fire or a flood. Sometimes human activity is involved, for example, when farmland is cleared but left unmanaged. An ecosystem may also be affected by a disease that kills one or more species. In any case, if soil is left intact, the original community may regrow through a series of stages called *secondary succession*.

Think Outside the Book

12 Describe Find an example of secondary succession in your community, and make a poster that describes each stage.

11 Identify Underline one or two distinctive features of each stage of secondary succession.

A

The first year after a farmer stops growing crops or the first year after some other major disturbance, wild plants start to grow. In farmland, crabgrass often grows first.

B

By the second year, new wild plants appear. Their seeds may have been blown into the field by the wind, or they may have been carried by insects or birds. Horseweed is common during the second year.

C

In 5 to 15 years, small conifer trees may start growing among the weeds. The trees continue to grow, and after about 100 years, a forest may form.

D

As older conifers die, they may be replaced by hardwoods, such as oak or maple trees, if the climate can support them.

It's a Balancing Act

What are two signs of a mature ecosystem?

In the early stages of succession, only a few species live and grow in an area. As the ecosystem matures, more species become established.

Climax Species

Succession can happen over decades or over hundreds of years. A community of producers forms first. These organisms are followed by decomposers and consumers. Over time, a stable, balanced ecosystem develops.

As a community matures, it may become dominated by well-adapted *climax species*. The redwoods in a temperate rain forest are a climax species. An ecosystem dominated by climax species is stable until the ecosystem is disturbed.

Biodiversity

As succession moves along, richer soil, nutrients, and other resources become available. This increase in resource availability lets more species become established. By the time climax species are established, the resources in the area support many different kinds of organisms. The number and variety of species that are present in an area is referred to as **biodiversity**.

A diverse forest is more stable and less likely to be destroyed by sudden changes, such as an insect invasion. Most plant-damaging insects attack only one kind of plant. The presence of a variety of plants can reduce the impact of the insects. Even if an entire plant species dies off, other similar plant species may survive.

Active Reading **13 Summarize** How is biodiversity beneficial to an ecosystem?

_____

_____

_____

Rain forests are not just found at the equator. Temperate rain forests along the Pacific Northwest host a diversity of life. Temperate rain forests are often dominated by conifers. Rain forests can receive 350 cm or more of rain annually.

Ferns and other small plants live on the wet, shady forest floor.

Shorter trees and shrubs form an understory. The plants of the forest provide food and shelter for animals such as birds and mammals.

A desert is very different from a rain forest, but it can also be an example of a mature ecosystem. Deserts receive as little as 8 cm of rain per year. But a desert has climax species well-adapted to its dry climate. These species form a balanced ecosystem.

Large cactuses are climax species in deserts.

Desert plants are adapted to live in hot, dry conditions and provide food and shelter for animals.

14 Compare Use the Venn diagram to compare and contrast deserts and rain forests.

Rain Forest Ecosystem

Both

Desert Ecosystem

Visual Summary

To complete this summary, fill in the blanks with the correct word or phrase. Then use the key below to check your answers. You can use this page to review the main concepts of the lesson.

Changes in Ecosystems

Ecosystems are always changing.

Ecosystems can change rapidly or slowly.

15 A pond fills in with organic matter during _____.

Secondary succession occurs in damaged ecosystems that still have soil.

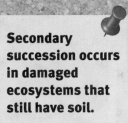

17 Soil in damaged ecosystems enables _____ to grow right away.

Primary succession begins with bare rock.

16 In primary succession, _____ grow on bare rock.

Mature ecosystems include many kinds of diverse organisms living in balance.

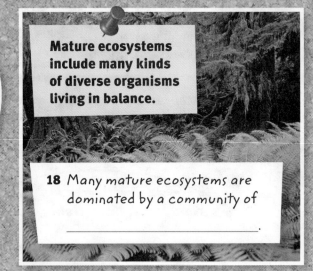

18 Many mature ecosystems are dominated by a community of _____.

Answers: 15 eutrophication; 16 lichens; 17 plants; 18 climax species

19 Claims • Evidence • Reasoning How is diversity related to changes in ecosystems? Provide examples and evidence to support your claim and explain your reasoning.

Lesson Review

Vocabulary

Fill in the blank with the term that best completes the following sentences.

1 _____ are the first organisms to live in an uninhabited area.

2 _____ is the number and variety of species that are present in an area.

3 The gradual development or replacement of one ecological community by another is called

_____ .

Key Concepts

4 Describe Explain how eutrophication can change an aquatic ecosystem into a terrestrial ecosystem.

_____

_____

_____

_____

_____

_____

5 Compare What is the major difference between primary and secondary succession?

_____

_____

_____

_____

6 Summarize Explain the important role a pioneer species plays in succession.

_____

_____

_____

_____

_____

_____

Critical Thinking

Use the diagram to answer the following questions.

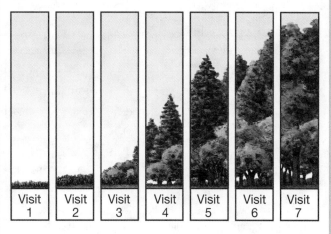

7 Analyze Between visits 1 and 7, what kind of ecological succession is shown? Explain your answer.

_____

_____

_____

_____

8 Predict If a fire occurs at visit 5, what kind of ecological succession is more likely to occur thereafter?

_____

_____

_____

9 Synthesize How might biodiversity help an ecosystem recover from a volcanic eruption? Provide evidence to support your claim.

_____

_____

_____

_____

My Notes

Engineering Design Process

Skills

Identify a need

✓ Conduct research

Brainstorm solutions

✓ Select a solution

✓ Build a prototype

✓ Test and evaluate

✓ Redesign to improve

✓ Communicate results

Objectives

- Explain the flow of energy in an ecosystem.
- Build and analyze a closed ecosystem.

Design an Ecosystem

An ecosystem is a community of living things (biotic factors) that interact with each other and with nonliving things (abiotic factors) in a specific area. Abiotic factors, such as temperature, sunlight, water, and minerals, determine which species can live in an ecosystem. Biotic factors, or populations of organisms in an ecosystem, can be classified by their function. Some producers, such as algae and green plants, make their own food by using sunlight through a process called photosynthesis. Consumers can be carnivores, herbivores, or omnivores. Decomposers, such as fungi and some bacteria, are consumers that break down dead plants and animals and recycle them as nutrients that other organisms can use.

1 Identify On the illustration of the ecosystem, label A through D as a producer, a consumer, or a decomposer.

A

B

Energy in Ecosystems

A food web is the feeding relationship among organisms within an ecosystem. Energy and nutrients are transferred within a food web as organisms feed. Producers form the base of the food web. When producers, such as plants, are consumed, only one tenth of the energy they get from the sun is passed up the food web to primary consumers. The primary consumers, for example herbivores, use the energy they get from plants to grow, reproduce, and live. In turn, when herbivores are eaten, only about one tenth of the energy is passed to secondary consumers, which are carnivores. The decreasing amounts of energy transferred to higher levels is shown by the energy pyramid here.

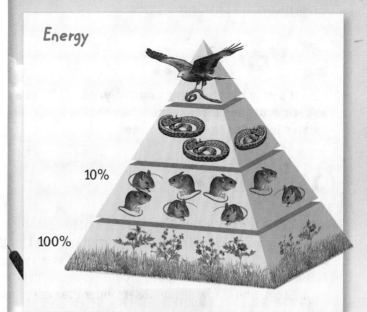

Energy

10%

100%

2 Infer In this example, what percentage of the energy that was available in the grass would reach the snakes? What percentage would reach the eagle? Explain your reasoning.

_____

_____

_____

C

D

You Try It!

Now it's your turn to design a self-contained aquatic ecosystem.

Engineering Design Process

✋ You Try It!

Now it's your turn to create and analyze a model of a self-contained aquatic ecosystem. Your ecosystem should allow the occupants to survive just from the light provided.

① Conduct Research

Write down the biotic factors that you want to put into your ecosystem. Use fast-growing plants to provide oxygen and food for the animals. Draw a simple diagram describing the flow of energy from your abiotic factor to the biotic factors (both producers and consumers) in the ecosystem. Show how decomposers enter the ecosystem.

_____

_____

_____

You Will Need

✔ one-gallon glass jar with tight-fitting lid or sealable clear plastic container

✔ fresh water; can use tap water, but water from natural source is preferable

✔ gravel

✔ aquatic plants and animals to be selected by students

✔ light source if needed

✔ decorative aquarium items (optional)

② Select a Solution

Based on the flow of energy and biomass in an ecosystem, determine the rough proportion of producers and consumers needed in the ecosystem you are designing. Write down how many plants to animals you think that you will need. Explain your reasoning.

_____

_____

_____

③ Build a Prototype

Follow these steps to build a prototype of your system.

- Clean your container, and record its mass.
- Put enough gravel in to cover the bottom.
- Fill the container with water, and add decorative items.
- Let the water and decorative items settle for at least 24 hours to allow the chemicals in the water to evaporate and the water to come to room temperature.
- Add your plants, and wait 24 hours.

- Before releasing the animals into the tank, float the containers holding the animals in the water in the tank for a few hours. This allows the animals to adjust to the temperature of the water in the tank.
- Close the lid tightly to prevent evaporation, and then record the mass of your ecosystem.
- Store your ecosystem where it will receive indirect sunlight.

(4) Test and Evaluate

List five things that you think would be important to record before
you close your system completely. Keep a journal in which you
record daily observations of your ecosystem for several weeks.

_____

_____

_____

_____

_____

(5) Redesign to Improve

After observing your system and keeping a journal for several
weeks, what would you change about your system?

_____

_____

_____

_____

_____

_____

_____

(6) Communicate Results

Summarize the observations you made in your journal. Do your observations
reflect the judgments in your initial diagram about how energy flows from
biotic to abiotic factors in the ecosystem? Consider these questions:
What things do you think made your ecosystem successful or unsuccessful?
What things, if any, would you change to improve your ecosystem even
more? Finally, make a report of your ecosystem to present to the class.

_____

_____

_____

_____

_____

_____

_____

Human Activity and Ecosystems

ESSENTIAL QUESTION

How do human activities affect ecosystems?

By the end of this lesson, you should be able to describe the effects of human activities on ecosystems, and explain the role of conservation in protecting natural resources.

Human activities can disturb habitats and wildlife. Coastal developments may prevent species such as leatherback sea turtles from reproducing.

 S7L4.c Factors affecting ecosystems

 Lesson Labs

Quick Labs
- Biodiversity All Around Us
- Investigate the Acidity of Water

Field Lab
- Field Investigation of Plant Quantity and Diversity

Engage Your Brain

1 Explain Think about what you see as you go to and from school. What is one example of human activity that you would change if you could?

_____

Why and how would you make this change?

_____
_____
_____
_____

2 Describe Write your own caption to this photo.

_____
_____
_____

Active Reading

3 Synthesize Many English words have their roots in other languages. Use the Latin words below to make an educated guess about the meaning of the words *urbanization* and *biodiversity*.

Latin word	Meaning
urbanus	city
divertus	diverse
bio	life

Example sentence
The population of Los Angeles increased during the 20th century because of <u>urbanization</u>.

urbanization:

_____
_____

Example sentence
The <u>biodiversity</u> of our food crops has decreased over the last several decades.

biodiversity:

_____
_____

Vocabulary Terms

- urbanization
- biodiversity
- eutrophication
- stewardship
- conservation

4 Identify As you read, place a question mark next to any words that you don't understand. After you finish reading the lesson, go back and review the text that you marked. If the information is still confusing, consult a classmate or your teacher.

Growing Pains

How do humans negatively affect ecosystems?

Human activities can change and even harm ecosystems. An *ecosystem* is all of the living and nonliving things within a given area. Changing one thing in an ecosystem can affect many other things, because everything in an ecosystem is connected.

Humans can affect ecosystems through pollution. *Pollution* is caused by any material or condition that harms the environment. For example, factories and automobiles burn fossil fuels. This releases harmful chemicals into the environment. Farms that produce our food may also burn fossil fuels and release chemicals, such as pesticides or fertilizers, into the environment.

Even simple actions can harm ecosystems. For example, the trash we throw out may end up in a landfill. Landfills take up space and may contain harmful materials like batteries. Toxic metals in batteries can leak into soil or groundwater, with drastic consequences for organisms and ecosystems.

5 Relate Identify a form of pollution that you observe in your community. How does it affect the people and animals living there?

_____

_____

Tons of garbage are put into landfills every day.

As cities and suburbs expand closer to natural areas, wildlife may wander into our backyards and onto our streets.

By Depleting Resources

Earth's population has increased from 1 billion to more than 7 billion people in the last 200 years. The growing human population has created a greater need for natural resources. This need has created problems for ecosystems. Cutting down trees removes a resource that many organisms need for food and shelter. The loss of many trees in an area can affect shade and local temperatures. These changes can disturb ecosystems.

The overuse of resources causes them to be depleted, or used up. *Resource depletion* occurs when a large fraction of a resource has been used up. Fresh water was once a renewable resource. But in some areas, humans use fresh water faster than it can be replenished.

By Destroying Habitats

Human population growth in and around cities is called **urbanization** (er•buh•nih•ZAY•shuhn). Urban growth often destroys natural habitats. Roads can divide habitats and prevent animals from safely roaming their territory. If animals cannot interact with each other and their surroundings, the ecosystem will not thrive.

An ecosystem may be converted into housing and shopping areas that further shrink habitats. This can bring humans and wildlife into contact. Deer, raccoons, and even coyotes have become common sights in some suburban areas.

Every habitat has its own number and variety of organisms, or **biodiversity**. If a habitat is damaged or destroyed, biodiversity is lost. Because living things are connected with each other and with their environment, loss of biodiversity affects the entire ecosystem.

An open-pit mine like this one is one way that humans remove minerals from the ground. Minerals are nonrenewable resources.

Cutting down forests destroys habitats and affects the physical features of the ecosystem.

Disease is largely an environmental issue. Sixty percent of infectious diseases that affect humans are zoonotic—they originate in animals. And more than two thirds of those originate in wildlife. The table below lists some of these zoonotic diseases.

7 Synthesize How might the destruction of animal habitats through urbanization and deforestation affect human populations? Provide specific data from the table.

Disease	Main Hosts	Usual Mode of Transmission
Lyme Disease	Deer (deer tick)	Tick bites
Rabies	Bats, foxes, raccoons	Bite of infected animal
West Nile Fever	Mosquitoes	Mosquito bite
Zika	Mosquitoes	Mosquito bite

Sources: www.gov.uk; Yale School of Forestry & Environmental Studies, 2016

_____

_____

Think Outside the Book Inquiry

6 Apply Do research to find out what the environment around your school looked like 100 years ago.

Water, Water Everywhere?

How do humans impact oceans?

Oceans support a variety of ecosystems that together contain nearly half of Earth's species. Pollution from human activities damages ocean ecosystems and threatens marine biodiversity.

Point-source pollution comes from one source. Oil spills, such as the one shown above, are an example of this. Spilled oil pollutes open waters and coastal habitats. *Nonpoint-source pollution* comes from many sources. For example, chemicals such as fertilizers and pesticides may be washed into oceans, where they harm many marine organisms.

Raw sewage and trash are frequently dumped into marine habitats. Plastic bags and packaging are dangerous to marine animals. Some animals mistake bags for food or become tangled in packaging. Dumping trash in the ocean is illegal. Many people and agencies work hard to enforce laws that protect the oceans.

Visualize It!

9 Predict Compare these pictures. What is one problem that could arise if a sea turtle sees the plastic bag underwater?

_____

_____

Jellyfish have translucent, sac-like bodies. Sea turtles and dolphins eat jellyfish.

Underwater, plastic bags look like jellyfish.

Image Credits: (t) ©Andy Levin/Photo Researchers, Inc.; (bl) ©Gary Bell/Corbis Documentary/Getty Images; (br) ©F.Bettex-Mysterra.org/Alamy

Through Fishing and Overfishing

A greater demand for seafood from the growing human population has led to *overfishing* of some ocean species. Many fish species cannot reproduce fast enough to replace individuals that are harvested for food. When large numbers of a single fish population are caught, the remaining population may be too small to successfully reproduce. If the population cannot replace itself, it can become locally extinct. The local loss of a species can disturb ocean food webs and threaten ecosystem stability.

Through Coastal Development

The growing human population also has led to increased coastal development. That means building homes and businesses on and near beaches and wetlands. Sadly, this can destroy the very coastlines we want to be near. Roads and shopping centers divide habitats. Increased human activity increases pollution both on shore and in coastal waters.

In some places, development has almost completely replaced natural coastlines. For example, construction of new homes and businesses is rapidly destroying mangrove forests. Mangroves are unique trees found only in certain coastal regions. Mangrove forests play a key role in maintaining coastlines. The thick roots stabilize the sandy soil and prevent erosion. The trees are home to a wide range of species.

Human activity has also damaged coral reefs, but people and scientists are working to correct this damage. Coral reefs are vital ecosystems because so many species live in or around them. To replace this lost habitat, scientists have created artificial reefs. First, different fish species will find safety in the structures. Next, algae and soft corals begin to grow. Over time, hard corals grow and other sea life can be seen. Artificial reefs preserve the reef food web and stabilize the ecosystem.

Overfishing means that the rate at which fish are caught exceeds the rate at which the species can reproduce.

10 List What are three ways that human activities affect ocean ecosystems?

_____

_____

_____

Artificial reefs, such as sunken ships or other human-made objects, are being used to make up for the loss of natural coral reefs.

How do humans affect freshwater ecosystems?

Active Reading

11 Identify As you read, number the steps involved in the formation of acid rain.

Human activities have decreased the amount of water, or *water quantity*, in many river ecosystems. Dams and river channelization are two examples of this. Dams block the flow of river water. That means there is less water downstream of the dam. Channelization is used to straighten rivers to improve travel and other activities. However, changing the natural course of a river also changes the amount of water in it. Differences in water levels can change water temperature and chemistry. These changes can affect the reproduction and survival of many river species.

Human activities can also decrease *water quality*, or change how clean or polluted the water is, in ecosystems. Pollution disturbs water quality. Animal waste and fertilizer from farms contain nutrients that can enter ponds and lakes as runoff. An increase in the amount of nutrients, such as nitrates, in an aquatic ecosystem is called **eutrophication** (yoo•trohf•ih•KAY•shuhn). The extra nutrients cause overgrowth of algae. The excess algae die and decompose, using up the pond's dissolved oxygen. As dissolved oxygen levels decrease, fish begin to die. If eutrophication continues, the pond ecosystem will not recover.

Water quality is also affected by air pollution. For example, some freshwater ecosystems are affected by acid rain. Burning fossil fuels releases chemicals into the air. Some of these combine with rain to form acids. Small amounts of acid in rain cause its pH to fall below its normal value of 5.6. Acid rain can damage both aquatic and terrestrial ecosystems.

Eutrophication causes overgrowth of algae and can disrupt pond ecosystems.

© Houghton Mifflin Harcourt Publishing Company • Image Credits: ©James Leighton/Corbis

Exotic Species

An organism that makes a home for itself in a new place outside its native home is an *exotic species*. Exotic species often thrive in new places because they are free from the predators found in their native homes. Exotic species that outcompete native species for resources, such as food or space, are known as *invasive* exotic species.

European rabbits were introduced into Australia by human activity. They were brought into this country in 1859 for sport hunting. With plenty of space and food—and no predators—Australia's rabbit population exploded.

The rabbits threatened the survival of many native Australian animals and plants. Many efforts were made to control the rabbit population. Their dens were poisoned. Rabbit-proof fences were built. Rabbits were even "herded" by cowboys.

So far, all efforts to remove rabbits have failed. There are still more than 200 million rabbits in Australia.

Extend

Inquiry

12 Explain Based on the data presented on the page, how does human activity such as the introduction of exotic species contribute to habitat destruction?

13 Hypothesize Form a hypothesis about a method that might be effective in controlling an invasive exotic species. Gather evidence to support the reasoning for your hypothesis.

14 Research Identify a non-native plant species that has been introduced into the United States. Explain where the species came from, how or why it was brought to the United States, and how it has affected the ecosystem.

Save It!

![Active Reading]
15 Identify As you read, underline the definition of stewardship.

How do humans protect ecosystems?

There are many ways that humans can protect ecosystems. One way is by using Earth's resources in a careful manner. The careful and responsible management of a resource is called **stewardship**. The resources of an ecosystem include all of its living and nonliving parts.

By Maintaining Biodiversity

The organisms in an ecosystem depend on each other and interact with each other in a vast interconnected food web. Each species has a place in this web and a role to play. The loss of a species or introduction of an exotic species creates gaps in the web. This can disrupt species interactions. Protecting habitats and helping species survive protects the biodiversity in an ecosystem. The greater the biodiversity, the healthier the ecosystem.

16 State What are two ways that humans can help maintain biodiversity in ecosystems?

_____

_____

_____

You can reduce pollution by participating in a local cleanup project.

You can protect habitats by staying on marked trails when visiting national parks and forests.

By Conserving Natural Resources

Humans can protect ecosystems through conservation. **Conservation** is the protection and wise use of natural resources. Practicing conservation means using fewer natural resources and reducing waste. It also helps prevent habitat destruction.

The "three Rs" are three ways to conserve resources.

- *Reduce* what you buy and use—this is the first goal of conservation.
- *Reuse* what you already have. For example, carry water in a reusable bottle and lunch in a reusable lunch bag.
- *Recycle* by recovering materials from waste and by always choosing to use recycling bins.

You can practice conservation every day by making wise choices. Even small changes make a difference!

17 Synthesize Suppose you wanted to stop eating fast food to cut down on excess fat and sodium. How might this benefit the environment as well?

_____

_____

_____

_____

You can help prevent water shortages by turning off the water as you brush your teeth.

You can reduce pesticide use by supporting responsible agriculture.

You can reduce the use of fossil fuels by turning off lights and supporting alternative energy sources.

Visual Summary

To complete this summary, fill in the blanks with the correct word. Then use the key below to check your answers. You can use this page to review the main concepts of the lesson.

Human Activity and Ecosystems

Human demand for resources and land can destroy habitats and disturb ecosystems.

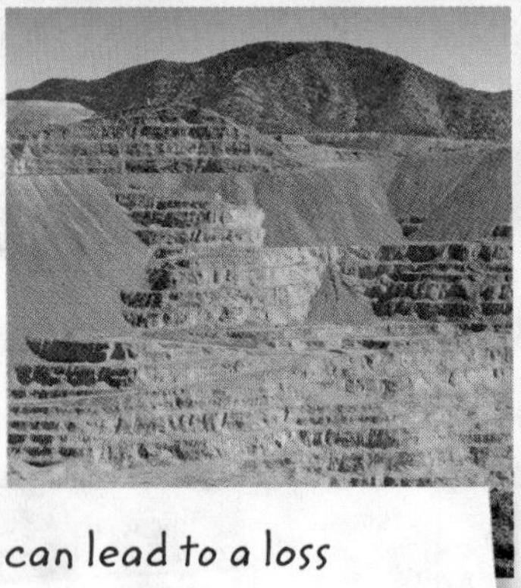

18 Habitat destruction can lead to a loss of ______________________.

Dumping trash and chemicals into waterways can damage aquatic ecosystems.

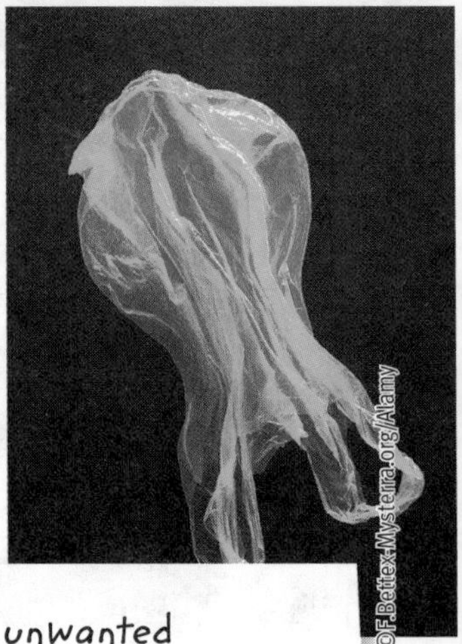

19 Materials that cause unwanted changes in the environment cause ______________________.

Conservation and stewardship help protect ecosystems.

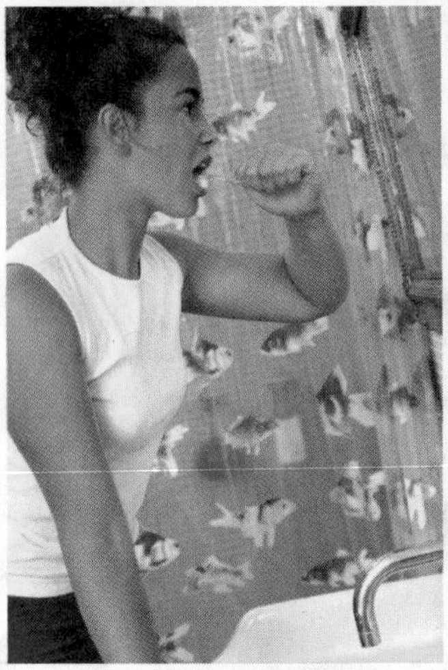

20 The protection and wise use of natural resources is called ______________________.

Answers: 18 biodiversity; 19 pollution; 20 conservation

21 Claims • Evidence • Reasoning Imagine that everyone in the United States chose to ride bicycles rather than drive cars. What effect would this have on your local ecosystem? State your claim and provide evidence to support your reasoning.

Lesson Review

Vocabulary

In your own words, define the following terms.

1 eutrophication

_____

_____

2 stewardship

_____

_____

3 urbanization

_____

_____

Key Concepts

4 Illustrate Name two ways that humans affect terrestrial ecosystems.

_____

_____

5 Describe Explain the difference between an *exotic species* and an *invasive exotic species*.

_____

_____

_____

_____

6 Summarize What is pollution?

_____

_____

_____

_____

7 Identify What are two ways to practice conservation?

_____

_____

_____

_____

Critical Thinking

Use this table to answer the following questions.

Human Population Growth

Human population	Year
1 billion	1804
2 billion	1927
3 billion	1960
4 billion	1974
5 billion	1987
6 billion	1999
7 billion	2011
Projected	
8 billion	2026

8 Calculate How many years did it take for the population to double from 1 billion to 2 billion?

_____

9 Calculate How many years did it take for the population to double from 3 billion to 6 billion?

_____

10 Hypothesize If Earth's population continues to increase without limit, how might this affect natural ecosystems? Explain your reasoning.

_____

_____

_____

_____

_____

_____

11 Synthesize Some detergents contain phosphates, chemicals that act like fertilizers. If wastewater from washing machines enters a local lake, will the fish population increase or decrease? Explain your answer.

_____

_____

_____

_____

My Notes

Unit 6 ⟨Big Idea⟩ Matter and energy together support life within an environment.

Lesson 1

ESSENTIAL QUESTION
What are terrestrial biomes?

Describe the characteristics of different biomes that exist on land.

Lesson 4

ESSENTIAL QUESTION
How do ecosystems change?

Describe how natural processes change ecosystems and help them develop after a natural disturbance.

Lesson 2

ESSENTIAL QUESTION
What are aquatic ecosystems?

Describe the characteristics of marine, freshwater, and other aquatic ecosystems.

Lesson 5

ESSENTIAL QUESTION
How do human activities affect ecosystems?

Describe the effect of human activities on ecosystems, and explain the role of conservation in protecting natural resources.

Lesson 3

ESSENTIAL QUESTION
How do energy and matter move through ecosystems?

Explain the flow of energy and the cycles of matter in ecosystems.

Think Outside the Book

2 Synthesize Choose one of these activities to help synthesize what you have learned in this unit.

☐ Using what you learned in lessons 1 and 2, create a brochure that describes the characteristics of the biome in which you live. In your brochure list what aquatic systems, if any, can also be found where you live.

☐ Using what you learned in lessons 1, 2, and 3, choose a biome or aquatic ecosystem and draw or make a collage of an energy pyramid that might be found in it. Label each tier of the energy pyramid and identify the species shown.

Connect ESSENTIAL QUESTIONS
Lessons 4 and 5

1 Explain How might human activity cause secondary succession? In your answer, identify each stage of secondary succession.

_____

_____

_____

_____

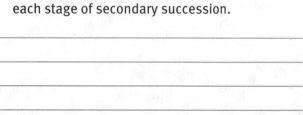

Unit 6 Review

Name _____

Vocabulary

Fill in each blank with the term that best completes the following sentences.

1 The _____ states that energy cannot be created or destroyed.

2 A(n) _____ is a community of organisms at a major regional or global level.

3 A(n) _____ tree has leaves that drop in the winter as an adaptation to cold temperatures.

4 _____ is an increase in the ratio or density of people living in urban areas rather than rural areas.

5 A(n) _____ is one of the first species of organisms to live in an area.

Key Concepts

Read each question below, and circle the best answer.

6 Where do producers, such as trees, get the energy that they need to survive?

  A from the sun   **C** from the organisms they eat

  B from the air   **D** from the remains of organisms

7 What are the ocean zones of a marine ecosystem, from most shallow to deepest?

  A intertidal, neritic, bathyal, abyssal

  B abyssal, neritic, intertidal, bathyal

  C neritic, intertidal, bathyal, abyssal

  D bathyal, abyssal, intertidal, neritic

8 Resource depletion, pollution, and habitat loss are all environmental problems caused by what factor?

  A acid rain   **C** introduced species

  B eutrophication   **D** human activities

9 Below is an energy pyramid diagram.

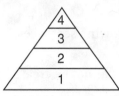

Energy Pyramid

Why is the level at 4 so much smaller than the level at 1?

A Organisms gain energy as the food chain moves down the pyramid.

B Fewer organisms are supported as you move down the pyramid.

C Only the energy that is used is available to organisms at a higher level.

D Only the energy that is stored is available to organisms at a higher level.

10 What element can be changed by lightning into a form that plants can use?

A oxygen

C phosphorous

B carbon

D nitrogen

11 Below is a diagram of the carbon cycle.

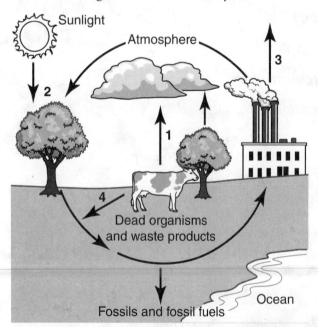

Which number corresponds to combustion and the release of CO_2, water, and the loss of energy as heat into the environment?

A 1

C 3

B 2

D 4

12 What is an adaptation that allows some animals to survive in the tundra?

   A living underground   **C** being active at night only

   B having thick layers of fur   **D** living within the upper branches of trees

13 Some grass species need fire in order for their seeds to germinate. Why might this adaptation be useful for grasses?

   A Fire allows trees to grow and provide shade for the grasses.

   B The hot temperature of the fire helps the grasses grow faster.

   C Seeds can germinate in an area that has been cleared by a fire.

   D Fire discourages grazing by large animals so grass can grow higher.

Critical Thinking

Answer the following questions in the space provided.

14 Draw a diagram of the water cycle and label it with the terms given below.

In the space provided, identify what each term means.

Precipitation: _____

Evaporation: _____

Transpiration: _____

Condensation: _____

15 The picture below shows a terrestrial ecosystem that experiences annual flooding.

Is this ecosystem more likely a result of primary succession or secondary succession? _____

Predict what would happen if a fast growing non-native species of plant was introduced to this ecosystem.

_____

_____

Connect **ESSENTIAL QUESTIONS**
Lessons 2 and 5

Answer the following question in the space provided.

16 Below is an example of an aquatic food web common in mangrove forests.

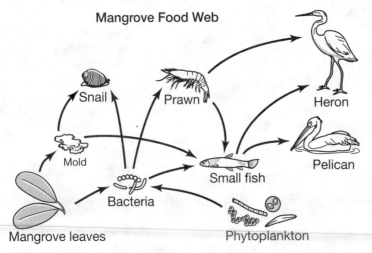

Mangrove Food Web

Mangroves commonly grow in estuaries. What are the characteristics of an estuary? _____

What might happen if the prawns and fish shown in the diagram were fished to near extinction? _____

_____

21st Century Skills
⟨Technology⟩
and Coding⟩

This breathtaking image of Earth was taken from the International Space Station, an international laboratory orbiting Earth. The operation of the International Space Station is controlled by 52 computers and millions of lines of computer code. Its many high-tech features include solar panels that power the laboratory and a human-like robotic astronaut.

This is Robonaut 2, a robot designed to do routine maintenance at the International Space Station.

Data Driven

What is computer science?

If you like computer technology and learning about how computers work, computer science might be for you. *Computer science* is the study of computer technology and how data is processed, stored, and accessed by computers. Computer science is an important part of many other areas, including science, math, engineering, robotics, medicine, game design, and 3D animation.

Computer technology is often described in terms of *hardware*, which are the physical components, and *software*, which are the programs or instructions that a computer runs. Computer scientists must understand how hardware and software work together. Computer scientists may develop new kinds of useful computer software. Or they may work with engineers to improve existing computer hardware.

The first electronic computer, the computer ENIAC (Electronic Numerical Integrator And Computer), was developed at the University of Pennsylvania in 1946.

The integrated circuit (IC), first developed in the 1950s, was instrumental in the development of small computer components.

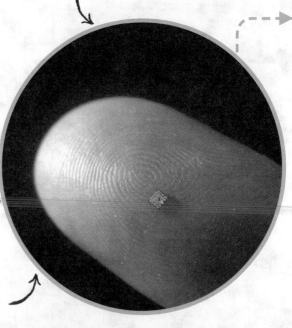

The development of the IC made it possible to reduce the overall size of computers and their components and to increase their processing speed.

How has computer technology changed over time?

Modern, digital computer technology is less than 100 years old. Yet in that short amount of time, it has advanced rapidly. The earliest digital computers could perform only a limited number of tasks and were the size of an entire room. Over the decades, engineers continued to develop smaller, faster, and more powerful computers. Today's computers can process hundreds of millions of instructions per second!

Computer scientists and engineers think about what people want or need from computer technology. The most advanced hardware is not useful if people do not know how to use it. So computer scientists and engineers work to create software that is reliable, useful, and easy to use. Today's tablet computers, cell phones, and video game consoles can be used without any special training.

Advances in digital computer technology have helped make computers cheaper and easier to operate, which has allowed many more people to work and play with them.

1 Compare Are modern computers simpler or more complex than early computers? Explain.

_____

_____

Computer Logic

What do computer scientists do?

Many people enjoy developing computer technology for fun. Learning how to create mobile phone games or Internet-enabled gadgets can be rewarding hobbies. For some people, that hobby may one day become a career in computer science. Working in computer science is a bit like solving a puzzle. Applying knowledge of how computers work to solve real-world problems requires collaboration, creativity, and logical, step-by-step thinking.

This is a kayak folded up.

They collaborate across many disciplines

Computers are valuable tools in math and science because they can perform complex calculations very quickly. Computers are useful to many other fields, too. For example, animators use computer technology to create realistic lighting effects in 3D animated films. Mechanics use computers to diagnose problems in car systems. For every field that relies on special software or computer technology, there is an opportunity for computer scientists and engineers to collaborate and develop solutions for those computing needs. Computer scientists must be able to define and understand the problems presented to them and to communicate and work with experts in other fields to develop the solutions.

Computational origami is a computer program used to model the ways in which different materials, including paper, can be folded. It combines computer science and the art of paper folding to create new technologies, such as this kayak.

Tracking software helps biologists study animal behavior.

satellite →

satellite data receiving center

satellite data processing center

transmitter

They help solve real-world problems

Some computer scientists carry out theoretical research. Others apply computer science concepts to develop software. Theoretical computer science and practical software development help solve real-world problems. For example, biologists need ways to safely and accurately track endangered animals. Computer science theories on artificial intelligence and pattern recognition have been applied to advanced animal-tracking technologies, such as satellite transmitters and aerial cameras. New kinds of image processing software now allow biologists to analyze the collected data in different ways.

They use logical, step-by-step thinking

Computers perform tasks given to them, and they do this very well. But in order to get the results they expect, computer scientists and programmers must write very accurate instructions. Computer science and programming requires logical thinking, deductive reasoning, and a good understanding of cause-and-effect relationships. When designing software, computer scientists must consider every possible user action and how the computer should respond to each action.

2 Explain How is computer science helping this scientist do her research?

_____

_____

_____

_____

Transmitters can be attached to animals to help track their movements.

Up to <Code>

How is computer software created?

Imagine that you are using a computer at the library to learn more about the history of electronic music. You use the library's database application to start searching for Internet resources. You also do a search to look for audio recordings. Finally, you open a word processor to take notes on the computer. Perhaps without realizing it, you've used many different pieces of software. Have you ever wondered how computer software is created?

Computer software is designed to address a need

Computer software can help us to learn more about our world. It can be useful to business. Or it can simply entertain us. Whatever its purpose, computer software should fulfill some human want or need. The first steps in creating software are precisely defining the need or want being addressed and planning how the software will work.

Computer software source code is written in a programming language

The instructions that tell a computer how to run video games, word processors, and other kinds of software are not written in a human language. They are written in a special programming language, or *code.* Javascript, C++, and Python are examples of programming languages. Programming languages—like human languages—must follow certain rules in order to be understood by the computer. A series of instructions written in a programming language is called *source code.*

Identifying what need a computer program addresses is one of the first development steps.

Source code is revised

Sometimes, programmers make mistakes in their code. Many programming environments have a feature that alerts the programmer to certain errors, such as spelling mistakes in commands, missing portions of code, or logical errors in the sequence of instructions. However, many mistakes go undetected, too. Some errors may cause the program to function incorrectly or not at all. When this happens, the programmer must identify the error, correct it, and test the software again.

Computer software is user tested, and revised

Once the software is created, it must be tested thoroughly to make sure it does not fail or behave in unexpected ways. It must also be tested to ensure that it meets users' needs. The creators of a piece of software might observe how people use it. Or they might ask users to provide feedback on certain features and test the software again.

3 Identify This source code contains an error. Infer where the error is located. What does this code "tell" the computer to do? Write your answers below.

_____

_____

_____

_____

```
13
14  # Scores are not tied, so check
15  # which player wins the round
16 ▾ if player1_score > player2_score:
17      print ("Player 1 wins!")
18 ▾ else:
19      prnt ("Player 2 wins!")
20

! Syntax error, line 19
```

Test running a program is important for finding and fixing errors in the code.

Play it Safe

How should I work with computers?

It is easy to lose track of time when you're sitting in front of a computer or game console. It's also easy to forget that things you say or do online can be seen and shared by many different people. Here are some tips for using computers safely and responsibly.

✓ Maintain good posture

Time can pass by quickly when you are working on a computer or another device. Balance computer time with other activities, including plenty of physical activity. When you are sitting at a computer, sit upright with your shoulders relaxed. Your eyes should be level with the top of the monitor and your feet should be flat on the ground.

✓ Observe electrical safety

Building your own electronics projects can be fun, but it's important to have an understanding of circuits and electrical safety first. Otherwise, you could damage your components or hurt yourself. The potential for an electrical shock is real when you open up a computer, work with frayed cords, use ungrounded plugs, or attempt to replace parts without understanding how to do so safely. Ask an adult for help before starting any projects. Also, avoid using a connected computer during thunderstorms.

head and neck in a straight, neutral position

shoulders are relaxed

wrists are straight

feet are flat on the ground

Good posture will help you avoid the aches and injuries related to sitting in front of a computer for a long time.

✓ Handle and maintain computers properly

Be cautious when handling and transporting electronic devices. Dropping them or spilling liquids on them could cause serious damage. Keep computers away from dirt, dust, liquids, and moisture. Never use wet cleaning products unless they are specifically designed for use on electronics. Microfiber cloths can be used to clear smudges from device screens. Spilled liquids can cause circuits to short out and hardware to corrode. If a liquid spills on a device, unplug it and switch it off immediately, remove the battery and wipe up as much of the liquid inside the device as possible. Don't switch the device back on until it is completely dry.

✓ Do not post private information online

Talk to your family about rules for Internet use. Do not use the Internet to share private information such as photographs, your phone number, or your address. Do not respond to requests for personal details from people you do not know.

✓ Treat yourself and others with respect

It is important to treat others with respect when on the Internet. Don't send or post messages online that you wouldn't say to someone in person. Unfortunately, not everyone acts respectfully while online. Some people may say hurtful things to you or send you unwanted messages. Do not reply to unwanted messages. Alert a trusted adult to any forms of contact, such as messages or photos, that make you feel uncomfortable.

4 Apply Fill in the chart below with a suitable response to each scenario.

SCENARIO	YOUR RESPONSE
You receive a text message from an online store asking for your home address.	
You've been lying down in front of a laptop, and you notice that your neck is feeling a little sore.	
You need to take a laptop computer with you on your walk to school.	
You want to try assembling a robotics kit with a friend.	
Someone posts unfriendly comments directed at you.	

Career in Computing: Game Programmer

What do video game programmers do?

Creating your own universe with its own set of rules is fun. Just ask a programmer who works on video games!

What skills are needed in game programming?

A programmer should know how to write code, but there are other important skills a programmer needs as well. An understanding of physics and math is important for calculating how objects move and interact in a game. Game programmers usually work on a team with other people, such as artists, designers, writers, and musicians. They must be able to communicate effectively, and ideally, the programmer should understand the other team members' roles.

How can I get started with game development?

You don't need a big budget or years of experience to try it out. There are books, videos, and websites that can help you get started. When you're first experimenting with game development, start small. Try making a very simple game like Tic-Tac-Toe. Once you've mastered that, you can try something more complex.

5 Brainstorm Why would working on a team be important to the game development process?

_____

_____

_____

Resources

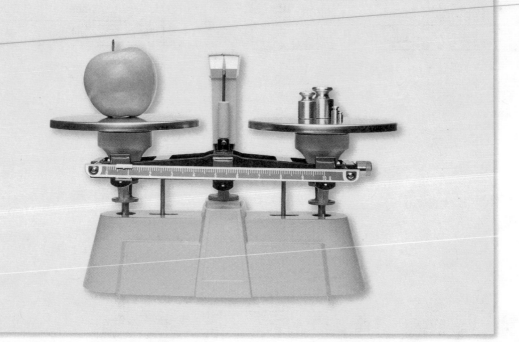

Glossary

Pronunciation Key

Sound	Symbol	Example	Respelling	Sound	Symbol	Example	Respelling
ă	a	pat	PAT	ŏ	ah	bottle	BAHT'l
ā	ay	pay	PAY	ō	oh	toe	TOH
âr	air	care	KAIR	ô	aw	caught	KAWT
ä	ah	father	FAH·ther	ôr	ohr	roar	ROHR
är	ar	argue	AR·gyoo	oi	oy	noisy	NOYZ·ee
ch	ch	chase	CHAYS	ŏŏ	u	book	BUK
ĕ	e	pet	PET	ōō	oo	boot	BOOT
ĕ (at end of a syllable)	eh	settee lessee	seh·TEE leh·SEE	ou	ow	pound	POWND
ĕr	ehr	merry	MEHR·ee	s	s	center	SEN·ter
ē	ee	beach	BEECH	sh	sh	cache	CASH
g	g	gas	GAS	ŭ	uh	flood	FLUHD
ĭ	i	pit	PIT	ûr	er	bird	BERD
ĭ (at end of syllable)	ih	guitar	gih·TAR	z	z	xylophone	ZY·luh·fohn
ī	y eye (only for a complete syllable)	pie island	PY EYE·luhnd	z	z	bags	BAGZ
				zh	zh	decision	dih·SIZH·uhn
				ə	uh	around broken focus	uh·ROWND BROH·kuhn FOH·kuhs
îr	ir	hear	HIR	ər	er	winner	WIN·er
j	j	germ	JERM	th	th	thin they	THIN THAY
k	k	kick	KIK				
ng	ng	thing	THING	w	w	one	WUHN
ngk	ngk	bank	BANGK	wh	hw	whether	HWETH·er

A

abiotic factor (ay·by·AHT·ik FAK·ter) an environmental factor that is not associated with the activities of living organisms (349)

factor abiótico factor ambiental que no está asociado con las actividades de los seres vivos

active transport (AK·tiv TRANS·pohrt) the movement of substances across the cell membrane that requires the cell to use energy (131)

transporte activo movimiento de sustancias a través de la membrana celular que requiere que la célula gaste energía

adaptation (ad·ap·TAY·shuhn) a characteristic that improves an individual's ability to survive and reproduce in a particular environment (21)

adaptación característica que mejora la capacidad de un individuo para sobrevivir y reproducirse en un determinado ambiente

allele (uh·LEEL) one of the alternative forms of a gene that governs a characteristic, such as hair color (198)

alelo de las formas alternativas de un gen que rige un carácter, como por ejemplo, el color del cabello

alveolus (al·VEE·uh·luhs) tiny, thin-walled, capillary-rich sac in the lungs where the exchange of oxygen and carbon dioxide takes place; also called air sac (288)

alveolo saco diminuto ubicado en los pulmones, de paredes delgadas y rico en capilares, donde ocurre el intercambio de oxígeno y dióxido de carbono

Animalia (an·uh·MAYL·yuh) a kingdom made up of complex, multicellular organisms that lack cell walls, can usually move around, and quickly respond to their environment (61)

Animalia reino formado por organismos pluricelulares complejos que no tienen pared celular, normalmente son capaces de moverse y reaccionan rápidamente a su ambiente

Archaea (ar·KEE·uh) a domain made up of prokaryotes, most of which are known to live in extreme environments, that are distinguished from other prokaryotes by differences in their genetics and in the makeup of their cell walls (58)

Archaea dominio compuesto por procariotes, la mayoría de los cuales viven en ambientes extremos, que se distinguen de otros procariotes por su genética y por la composición de su pared celular

artery (AR·tuh·ree) a blood vessel that carries blood away from the heart to the body's organs (283)

arteria vaso sanguíneo que transporta la sangre del corazón a los órganos del cuerpo

asexual reproduction (ay·SEHK·shoo·uhl ree·pruh·DUHK·shuhn) reproduction that does not involve the union of sex cells and in which one parent produces offspring that are genetically identical to the parent (8, 186)

reproducción asexual reproducción que no implica la unión de células sexuales, en la que un solo progenitor produce descendencia que es genéticamente igual al progenitor

atom (AT·uhm) the smallest unit of an element that maintains the properties of that element (90)

átomo unidad más pequeña de un elemento que conserva las propiedades de ese elemento

axon (AK·sahn) an elongated extension of a neuron that carries impulses away from the cell body (311)

axón extensión alargada de una neurona que transporta impulsos hacia fuera del cuerpo de la célula

B

Bacteria (bak·TIR·ee·uh) a domain made up of prokaryotes that usually have a cell wall and that usually reproduce by cell division (58)

Bacteria dominio compuesto por procariotes que por lo general tienen pared celular y se reproducen por división celular

biodiversity (by·oh·dih·VER·sih·tee) the number and variety of organisms in a given area during a specific period of time (446, 457)

biodiversidad número y variedad de organismos que se encuentran en un área determinada durante un período específico de tiempo

biome (BY·ohm) a large region characterized by a specific type of climate and certain types of plant and animal communities (352, 404)

bioma región extensa caracterizada por un tipo de clima específico y ciertos tipos de comunidades de plantas y animales

biotechnology (by·oh·tek·NAHL·uh·jee) the use and application of living things and biological processes (234)

biotecnología uso y aplicación de seres vivos y procesos biológicos

biotic factor (by·AHT·ik FAK·ter) an environmental factor that is associated with or results from the activities of living organisms (348)

factor biótico factor ambiental que está asociado con las actividades de los seres vivos o que resulta de ellas

blood (BLUHD) the fluid that carries gases, nutrients, and wastes through the body and that is made up of platelets, white blood cells, red blood cells, and plasma (278)
sangre líquido que transporta gases, nutrientes y desechos por el cuerpo y que está formado por plaquetas, glóbulos blancos, glóbulos rojos y plasma

brain (BRAYN) the organ that is the main control center of the nervous system (308)
encéfalo órgano que es el centro principal de control del sistema nervioso

bronchus (BRAHNG·kuhs) one of the two main branches of the trachea that lead directly to the lungs—plural, bronchi (288)
bronquio una de las dos ramificaciones principales de la tráquea que conducen directamente a los pulmones

capillary (KAP·uh·lehr·ee) a tiny blood vessel that allows an exchange between blood and cells in tissue (283)
capilar diminuto vaso sanguíneo que permite el intercambio entre la sangre y las células de los tejidos

carbohydrate (kar·boh·HY·drayt) a class of molecules that includes sugars, starches, and fiber; contains carbon, hydrogen, and oxygen (93)
carbohidrato clase de moléculas entre las que se incluyen azúcares, almidones y fibra; contiene carbono, hidrógeno y oxígeno

carbon cycle (KAR·buhn SY·kuhl) the movement of carbon from the nonliving environment into living things and back (436)
ciclo del carbono movimiento del carbono del ambiente inanimado a los seres vivos y de los seres vivos al ambiente

cardiovascular system (kahr·dee·oh·VAS·kyuh·ler SIS·tuhm) a collection of organs that transport blood throughout the body; the organs in this system include the heart, the arteries, and the veins (278)
aparato cardiovascular conjunto de órganos que transportan la sangre a través del cuerpo; los órganos de este sistema incluyen el corazón, las arterias y las venas

carnivore (KAR·nuh·vohr) an organism that eats animals (363)
carnívoro organismo que se alimenta de animales

carrying capacity (KAIR·ee·ing kuh·PAS·ih·tee) the largest population that an environment can support at any given time (376)
capacidad de carga población más grande que un ambiente puede sostener en cualquier momento dado

cell (SEL) in biology, the smallest unit that can perform all life processes; cells are covered by a membrane and contain DNA and cytoplasm (6, 80)
célula en biología, la unidad más pequeña que puede realizar todos los procesos vitales; las células están cubiertas por una membrana y tienen ADN y citoplasma

cell cycle (SEL SY·kuhl) the life cycle of a cell (166)
ciclo celular ciclo de vida de una célula

cell membrane (SEL MEM·brayn) a phospholipid layer that forms a cell's surface and acts as a barrier between the inside of a cell and the cell's external environment (84)
membrana celular capa de fosfolípidos que cubre la superficie de la célula y funciona como una barrera entre el interior de la célula y el ambiente exterior de la célula

cell wall (SEL WAWL) a rigid structure that surrounds the cell membrane and provides support to the cell (104)
pared celular estructura rígida que rodea la membrana celular y le brinda soporte a la célula

cellular respiration (SEL·yuh·luhr res·puh·RAY·shuhn) the process by which cells use oxygen to produce energy from food (128, 146)
respiración celular proceso por medio del cual las células utilizan oxígeno para producir energía a partir de los alimentos

chlorophyll (KLOHR·uh·fil) a green pigment that captures light energy for photosynthesis (145)
clorofila pigmento verde que capta la energía luminosa para la fotosíntesis

chloroplast (KLOHR·uh·plast) an organelle found in plant and algae cells where photosynthesis occurs (105)
cloroplasto organelo que se encuentra en las células vegetales y en las células de las algas, en el cual se lleva a cabo la fotosíntesis

chromosome (KROH·muh·sohm) in a eukaryotic cell, one of the structures in the nucleus that are made up of DNA and protein; in a prokaryotic cell, the main ring of DNA (165)
cromosoma en una célula eucariótica, una de las estructuras del núcleo que está hecha de ADN y proteína; en una célula procariótica, el anillo principal de ADN

clone (KLOHN) an organism, cell, or piece of genetic material that is genetically identical to one from which it was derived; to make a genetic duplicate (237)
clon organismo, célula o muestra de material genético que es genéticamente idéntico a; clonar (verbo) producir un duplicado genético aquel del cual deriva

codominance (koh·DAHM·uh·nuhns) a condition in which two alleles are expressed such that the phenotype of a heterozygous individual is a combination of the phenotypes of the two homozygous parents (203)
codominancia condición en la que dos alelos se expresan de tal manera que el fenotipo de un individuo heterocigoto es una combinación de los fenotipos de los dos progenitores homocigotos

commensalism (kuh·MEN·suh·liz·uhm) a relationship between two organisms in which one organism benefits and the other is unaffected (388)
comensalismo relación entre dos organismos en la que uno se beneficia y el otro no se ve afectado

community (kuh·MYOO·nih·tee) all of the populations of species that live in the same habitat and interact with each other (351)
comunidad todas las poblaciones de especies que viven en el mismo hábitat e interactúan entre sí

competition (kahm·pih·TISH·uhn) ecological relationship in which two or more organisms depend on the same limited resource (380, 390)
competencia relación ecológica en la que dos o más organismos dependen del mismo recurso limitado

coniferous tree (kuh·NIF·er·uhs TREE) cone-bearing trees that usually keep their leaves or needles during all the seasons of the year (407)
árbol conífero árboles que producen conos o piñas y que generalmente conservan sus hojas o agujas durante todas las estaciones del año

conservation (kahn·ser·VAY·shuhn) the wise use of and preservation of natural resources (463)
conservación uso inteligente y preservación de los recursos naturales

consumer (kuhn·SOO·mer) an organism that eats other organisms or organic matter (363)
consumidor organismo que se alimenta de otros organismos o de materia orgánica

cooperation (koh·ahp·uh·RAY·shuhn) an interaction between two or more living things in which they are said to work together (381)
cooperación interacción entre dos o más seres vivos en la cual se dice que trabajan juntos

cytokinesis (sy·toh·kuh·NEE·sis) the division of the cytoplasm of a cell (167)
citocinesis división del citoplasma de una célula

cytoplasm (sy·toh·PLAZ·uhm) the region of the cell within the membrane that includes the fluid, the cytoskeleton, and all of the organelles except the nucleus (84)
citoplasma región de la célula dentro de la membrana que incluye el líquido, el citoesqueleto y todos los organelos excepto el núcleo

cytoskeleton (sy·toh·SKEL·ih·tn) the cytoplasmic network of protein filaments that plays an essential role in cell movement, shape, and division (101)
citoesqueleto red citoplásmica de filamentos de proteínas que desempeña un papel esencial en el movimiento, la forma y la división de la célula

deciduous tree (dih·SIJ·oo·uhs TREE) trees that lose their leaves at the end of the growing season (410)
árbol caducifolio árboles que pierden sus hojas al temporada final de la de crecimiento

decomposer (dee·kuhm·POH·zer) an organism that gets energy by breaking down the remains of dead organisms or animal wastes and consuming or absorbing the nutrients (362)
descomponedor organismo que, para obtener energía, desintegra los restos de organismos muertos o los desechos de animales y consume o absorbe los nutrientes

dendrite (DEN·dryt) branchlike extension of a neuron that receives impulses from neighboring neurons (311)
dendrita extensión ramificada de una neurona que recibe impulsos de las neuronas vecinas

desert (DEZ·ert) a region characterized by a very dry climate and extreme temperatures (408)
desierto región que se caracteriza por tener un clima muy seco y temperaturas extremas

diffusion (dih·FYOO·zhuhn) the movement of particles from regions of higher concentration to regions of lower concentration (130)
difusión movimiento de partículas de regiones de mayor concentración a regiones de menor concentración

digestive system (dy·JES·tiv SIS·tuhm) the organs that break down food so that it can be used by the body (296)
aparato digestivo órganos que descomponen los alimentos de modo que el cuerpo los pueda usar

DNA (dee·en·AY) deoxyribonucleic acid, a molecule that is present in all living cells and that contains the information that determines the traits a living thing inherits and needs to live (8, 165, 220)
ADN ácido desoxirribonucleico, una molécula que está presente en todas las células vivas y que contiene la información que determina los caracteres que un ser vivo hereda y necesita para vivir

domain (doh·MAYN) in a taxonomic system, one of the three broad groups that all living things fall into (58)
dominio en un sistema taxonómico, uno de los tres amplios grupos al que pertenecen todos los seres vivos

dominant (DAHM·uh·nuhnt) in genetics, describes an allele that is fully expressed whenever the allele is present in an individual (199)
dominante en genética, término que describe un alelo que se expresa por completo cada vez que el alelo está presente en un individuo

E

ecology (ee·KAHL·uh·jee) the study of the interactions of living organisms with one another and with their environment (348)
ecología estudio de las interacciones de los seres vivos entre sí mismos y entre sí mismos y su ambiente

ecosystem (EE·koh·sis·tuhm) a community of organisms and their abiotic, or nonliving, environment (351)
ecosistema comunidad de organismos y su ambiente abiótico, o inanimado

egg (EG) a sex cell produced by a female (327)
óvulo célula sexual producida por una hembra

embryo (EM·bree·oh) in humans, a developing individual from first division after fertilization through the 10th week of pregnancy (329)
embrión en los seres humanos, un individuo en desarrollo desde la primera división después de la fecundación hasta el final de la décima semana de embarazo

endocrine system (EN·duh·krin SIS·tuhm) a collection of glands and groups of cells that secrete hormones that regulate growth, development, and homeostasis; includes the pituitary, thyroid, parathyroid, and adrenal glands, the hypothalamus, the pineal body, and the gonads (314)
sistema endocrino conjunto de glándulas y grupos de células que secretan hormonas, las cuales regulan el crecimiento, el desarrollo y la homeostasis; incluye las glándulas pituitaria, tiroides, paratiroides y suprarrenales, el hipotálamo, el cuerpo pineal y las gónadas

endocytosis (en·doh·sy·TOH·sis) the process by which a cell membrane surrounds a particle and encloses the particle in a vesicle to bring the particle into the cell (132)
endocitosis proceso por medio del cual la membrana celular rodea una partícula y la encierra en una vesícula para llevarla al interior de la célula

endoplasmic reticulum (en·doh·PLAZ·mik ri·TIK·yuh·luhm) a system of membranes that is found in a cell's cytoplasm and that assists in the production, processing, and transport of proteins and in the production of lipids (103)
retículo endoplásmico sistema de membranas que se encuentra en el citoplasma de la célula y que tiene una función en la producción, el procesamiento y el transporte de proteínas y en la producción de lípidos

energy (EN·er·jee) the ability to cause change (430)
energía capacidad de producir un cambio

energy pyramid (EN·er·jee PIR·uh·mid) a triangular diagram that shows an ecosystem's loss of energy, which results as energy passes through the ecosystem's food chain; each row in the pyramid represents a trophic (feeding) level in an ecosystem, and the area of a row represents the energy stored in that trophic level (432)
pirámide de energía diagrama triangular que muestra la pérdida de energía que ocurre en un ecosistema a medida que la energía pasa a través de la cadena alimenticia del ecosistema; cada de la pirámide representa un nivel trófico (de alimentación) en el ecosistema, y el área de la fila representa la energía almacenada en ese nivel trófico

enzyme (EN·zym) a type of protein that speeds up metabolic reactions in plants and animals without being permanently changed or destroyed (297)
enzima tipo de proteína que acelera las reacciones metabólicas en las plantas y los animales sin ser modificada permanentemente ni ser destruida

esophagus (ih·SAHF·uh·guhs) a long, straight tube that connects the pharynx to the stomach (298)
esófago conducto largo y recto que conecta la faringe con el estómago

estuary (ES·choo·ehr·ee) an area where fresh water mixes with salt water from the ocean (420)
estuario área donde el agua dulce de los ríos se mezcla con el agua salada del océano

Eukarya (yoo·KAIR·ee·uh) in a modern taxonomic system, a domain made up of all eukaryotes; this domain aligns with the traditional kingdoms Protista, Fungi, Plantae, and Animalia (59)
Eukarya en un sistema taxonómico moderno, un dominio compuesto por todos los eucariotes; este dominio coincide con los reinos tradicionales Protista, Fungi, Plantae y Animalia

eukaryote (yoo·KAIR·ee·oht) an organism made up of cells that have a nucleus enclosed by a membrane; eukaryotes include protists, animals, plants, and fungi, but not archaea or bacteria (85)
eucariote organismo cuyas células tienen un núcleo contenido en una membrana; entre los eucariotes se encuentran protistas, animales, plantas y hongos, pero no arqueas ni bacterias

eutrophication (yoo·trohf·ih·KAY·shuhn) an increase in the amount of nutrients, such as nitrates, in a marine or aquatic ecosystem (442, 460)
eutrofización aumento en la cantidad de nutrientes, tales como nitratos, en un ecosistema marino o acuático

evolution (ev·uh·LOO·shuhn) the process by which inherited characteristics within a population change over generations such that new species sometimes arise (16)

evolución proceso por medio del cual las características heredadas dentro de una población cambian con el transcurso de las generaciones, de manera tal que a veces surgen nuevas especies

excretory system (EK·skrih·tohr·ee SIS·tuhm) the system that collects and excretes nitrogenous wastes and excess water from the body in the form of urine (301)

aparato excretor sistema que recolecta y elimina del cuerpo los desperdicios nitrogenados y el exceso de agua en forma de orina

exocytosis (ek·soh·sy·TOH·sis) the process in which a cell releases a particle by enclosing the particle in a vesicle that then moves to the cell surface and fuses with the cell membrane (132)

exocitosis proceso por medio del cual una célula libera una partícula encerrándola en una vesícula que luego se traslada a la superficie de la célula y se fusiona con la membrana celular

extinction (ek·STINGK·shuhn) the death of every member of a species (23, 41)

extinción muerte de todos los miembros de una especie

fertilization (fer·tl·ih·ZAY·shuhn) the union of a male and female gamete to form a zygote (188)

fecundación unión de un gameto masculino y uno femenino para formar un cigoto

fetus (FEE·tuhs) a developing human from the end of the 10th week of pregnancy until birth (330)

feto ser humano en desarrollo desde el final de la décima semana de embarazo hasta el nacimiento

food chain (FOOD CHAYN) the pathway of energy transfer through various stages as a result of the feeding patterns of a series of organisms (365)

cadena alimenticia vía de transferencia de energía a través de varias etapas que ocurre como resultado de los patrones de alimentación de una serie de organismos

food web (FOOD WEB) a diagram that shows the feeding relationships between organisms in an ecosystem (366)

red alimenticia diagrama que muestra las relaciones de alimentación entre los organismos de un ecosistema

fossil (FAHS·uhl) the trace or remains of an organism that lived long ago, most commonly preserved in sedimentary rock (31, 40)

fósil rastros o restos de un organismo que vivió hace mucho tiempo, comúnmente preservados en las rocas sedimentarias

fossil record (FAHS·uhl REK·erd) the history of life in the geologic past as indicated by the traces or remains of living things (31, 40)

registro fósil historia de la vida en el pasado geológico según la indican los rastros o restos de seres vivos

function (FUNGK·shuhn) the special, normal, or proper activity of an organ or part (118)

función actividad especial, normal o adecuada de un órgano o una parte

Fungi (FUHN·jy) a kingdom made up of non-green, eukaryotic organisms that have no means of movement, reproduce using spores, and get food by breaking down substances in their surroundings and absorbing the nutrients (61)

hongos reino formado por organismos eucarióticos no verdes que no tienen capacidad de movimiento, se reproducen por esporas y obtienen alimento al descomponer sustancias de su entorno y absorber los nutrientes

gene (JEEN) one set of instructions for an inherited trait (198)

gen conjunto de instrucciones para un carácter heredado

genetic engineering (juh·NET·ik en·juh·NIR·ing) a technology in which the genome of a living cell is modified for medical or industrial use (236)

ingeniería genética tecnología en la que el genoma de una célula viva se modifica con fines médicos o industriales

genotype (JEEN·uh·typ) the entire genetic makeup of an organism; also the combination of genes for one or more specific traits (199)

genotipo constitución genética completa de un organismo; también, la combinación de genes para uno o más caracteres específicos

genus (JEE·nuhs) the level of classification that comes after family and that contains similar species (56)

género nivel de clasificación que viene después de la familia y que contiene especies similares

geologic time scale (jee·uh·LAHJ·ik TYM SKAYL) the standard method used to divide Earth's long natural history into manageable parts (42)
　　escala de tiempo geológico método estándar que se usa para dividir la larga historia natural de la Tierra en partes manejables

gland (GLAND) a group of cells that make chemicals for use elsewhere in the body (314)
　　glándula grupo de células que producen sustancias químicas para su utilización en otra parte del cuerpo

Golgi complex (GOHL·jee KAHM·pleks) a cell organelle that helps make and package materials to be transported out of the cell (103)
　　aparato de Golgi organelo celular que ayuda a producir y a empacar los materiales que serán transportados al exterior de la célula

grassland (GRAS·land) a region that is dominated by grasses, that has few woody shrubs and trees, that has fertile soils, and that receives moderate amounts of seasonal rainfall (409)
　　pradera región en la que predomina la hierba, tiene algunos arbustos leñosos y árboles, y suelos fértiles, y recibe cantidades moderadas de precipitaciones estacionales

habitat (HAB·ih·tat) the place where an organism usually lives (354)
　　hábitat lugar donde generalmente vive un organismo

herbivore (HER·buh·vohr) an organism that eats only plants (363)
　　herbívoro organismo que solo come plantas

heredity (huh·RED·ih·tee) the passing of genetic material from parent to offspring (196)
　　herencia transmisión de material genético de padres a hijos

homeostasis (hoh·mee·oh·STAY·sis) the maintenance of a constant internal state in a changing environment (7, 126, 258)
　　homeostasis capacidad de mantener un estado interno constante en un ambiente en cambio

homologous chromosomes (hoh·MAHL·uh·guhs KROH·muh·sohmz) chromosomes that have the same sequence of genes and the same structure (174)
　　cromosomas homólogos cromosomas con la misma secuencia de genes y la misma estructura

hormone (HOHR·mohn) a substance that is made in one cell or tissue and that causes a change in another cell or tissue in a different part of the body (314)
　　hormona sustancia que se produce en una célula o un tejido, la cual causa un cambio en otra célula u otro tejido ubicado en una parte diferente del cuerpo

incomplete dominance (in·kuhm·PLEET DAHM·uh·nuhns) a condition in which two alleles are expressed such that the phenotype of a heterozygous individual is an intermediate of the phenotypes of the two homozygous parents (202)
　　dominancia incompleta condición en la que dos alelos están expresados de modo que el fenotipo de un individuo heterocigoto es intermedio entre los fenotipos de sus dos progenitores homocigotos

interphase (IN·ter·fayz) the period of the cell cycle during which activities such as cell growth and protein synthesis occur without visible signs of cell division (166)
　　interfase período del ciclo celular durante el cual las actividades como el crecimiento celular y la síntesis de proteínas existen sin signos visibles de división celular

joint (JOYNT) a place where two or more bones meet (268)
　　articulación lugar donde se unen dos o más huesos

kidney (KID·nee) one of the organs that filter water and wastes from the blood, excrete products as urine, and regulate the concentration of certain substances in the blood (302)
　　riñón uno de los órganos que filtran el agua y los desechos de la sangre, excretan productos como la orina y regulan la concentración de ciertas sustancias en la sangre

large intestine (LAHRJ in·TES·tin) the broader and shorter portion of the intestine, where water is removed from the mostly digested food to turn the waste into semisolid feces, or stool (299)
　　intestino grueso porción más ancha y más corta del intestino, donde el agua se elimina de los alimentos mayormente digeridos para convertir los desechos en heces semisólidas, o excremento

larynx (LAIR·ingks) the part of the respiratory system between the pharynx and the trachea; has walls of cartilage and muscle and contains the vocal cords (288)
　　laringe parte del aparato respiratorio que se encuentra entre la faringe y la tráquea; tiene paredes de cartílago y músculo y contiene las cuerdas vocales

law of conservation of energy (LAW UHV kahn·suhr·VAY·shuhn UHV EN·er·jee) the law that states that energy cannot be created or destroyed, but can be changed from one form to another (431)
ley de la conservación de la energía ley que establece que la energía ni se crea ni se destruye, solo se transforma de una forma a otra

law of conservation of mass (LAW UHV kahn·suhr·VAY·shuhn UHV MAS) the law that states that mass cannot be created or destroyed in ordinary chemical and physical changes (431)
ley de la conservación de la masa ley que establece que la masa no se crea ni se destruye por cambios químicos o físicos comunes

ligament (LIG·uh·muhnt) a type of tissue that holds together the bones in a joint (266)
ligamento tipo de tejido que mantiene unidos los huesos en una articulación

limiting factor (LIM·ih·ting FAK·ter) an environmental factor that prevents an organism or population from reaching its full potential of size or activity (378)
factor limitante factor ambiental que impide que un organismo o una población alcance su máximo potencial de distribución o de actividad

lipid (LIP·id) a fat molecule or a molecule that has similar properties; examples include oils, waxes, and steroids (92)
lípido molécula de grasa o una molécula que tiene propiedades similares; algunos ejemplos son los aceites, las ceras y los esteroides

liver (LIV·er) the largest organ in the body; it makes bile, stores and filters blood, and stores excess sugars as glycogen (300)
hígado órgano más grande del cuerpo; produce bilis, almacena y filtra la sangre, y almacena el exceso de azúcares en forma de glucógeno

lymph (LIMF) the clear, watery fluid that leaks from blood vessels and contains white blood cells; circulates in the lymphatic system; returned to bloodstream through lymph vessels (278)
linfa fluido claro y acuoso que se filtra de los vasos sanguíneos y contiene glóbulos blancos; circula por el sistema linfático; regresa al torrente sanguíneo a través de los vasos linfáticos

lymph node (LIMF NOHD) small, bean-shaped masses of tissue that remove pathogens and dead cells from the lymph; concentrated in the armpits, neck, and groin; high concentration of white blood cells found in lymph nodes (280)
ganglio linfático masas de tejido pequeñas y con forma de frijol que eliminan los patógenos y las células muertas de la linfa; están concentrados en las axilas, el cuello y la ingle; los ganglios linfáticos presentan una alta concentración de glóbulos blancos

lymphatic system (lim·FAT·ik SIS·tuhm) a network of organs and tissues that collect the fluid that leaks from blood and returns it to blood vessels; includes lymph nodes, lymph vessels, and lymph; the place where certain white blood cells mature (278)
sistema linfático red de órganos y tejidos que recolectan el fluido que se filtra de la sangre y lo regresan a los vasos sanguíneos; incluye los ganglios linfáticos, los vasos linfáticos y la linfa; el lugar donde maduran ciertos glóbulos blancos

lysosome (LY·suh·sohm) a cell organelle that contains digestive enzymes (106)
lisosoma organelo celular que contiene enzimas digestivas

matter (MAT·er) anything that has mass and takes up space (430)
materia cualquier cosa que tiene masa y ocupa un lugar en el espacio

meiosis (my·OH·sis) a process in cell division during which the number of chromosomes decreases to half the original number by two divisions of the nucleus, which results in the production of sex cells (gametes or spores) (175)
meiosis proceso de división celular durante el cual el número de cromosomas disminuye a la mitad del número original por medio de dos divisiones del núcleo, lo cual resulta en la producción de células sexuales (gametos o esporas)

mitochondrion (my·toh·KAHN·dree·uhn) in eukaryotic cells, the organelle that is the site of cellular respiration, which releases energy for use by the cell (102)
mitocondria en las células eucarióticas, el organelo donde se lleva a cabo la respiración celular, la cual libera energía para que utilice la célula

mitosis (my·TOH·sis) in eukaryotic cells, a process of cell division that forms two new nuclei, each of which has the same number of chromosomes (129, 167)
mitosis las células eucarióticas, un proceso de división celular que forma dos núcleos nuevos, cada uno de los cuales posee el mismo número de cromosomas

molecule (MAHL·ih·kyool) a group of atoms that are held together by chemical forces; a molecule is the smallest unit of a compound that keeps all the properties of that compound (91)
molécula grupo de átomos unidos por fuerzas químicas; una molécula es la unidad más pequeña de un compuesto que conserva todas las propiedades de ese compuesto

muscular system (MUS·kyuh·ler SIS·tuhm) the organ system whose primary function is movement and flexibility (270)

sistema muscular sistema de órganos cuya función principal es permitir el movimiento y la flexibilidad

mutation (myoo·TAY·shuhn) a change in the nucleotide base sequence of a gene or DNA molecule (20, 225)

mutación cambio en la secuencia de la base de nucleótidos de un gen o de una molécula de ADN

mutualism (MYOO·choo·uh·liz·uhm) a relationship between two species in which both species benefit (388)

mutualismo relación entre dos especies en la que ambas se benefician

natural selection (NACH·uhr·uhl sih·LEK·shuhn) the process by which individuals that are better adapted to their environment survive and reproduce more successfully than less well-adapted individuals do (20)

selección natural proceso por medio del cual los individuos que están mejor adaptados a su ambiente sobreviven y se reproducen con más éxito que los individuos menos adaptados

nephron (NEF·rahn) the unit in the kidney that filters blood (302)

nefrona unidad del riñón que filtra la sangre

nervous system (NER·vuhs SIS·tuhm) the structures that control the actions and reactions of the body in response to stimuli from the environment; it is formed by billions of specialized nerve cells, called neurons (308)

sistema nervioso estructuras que controlan las acciones y reacciones del cuerpo en respuesta a los estímulos del ambiente; está formado por miles de millones de células nerviosas especializadas, llamadas neuronas

neuron (NUR·ahn) a nerve cell that is specialized to receive and conduct electrical impulses (310)

neurona célula nerviosa que está especializada en recibir y transmitir impulsos eléctricos

niche (NICH) the role of a species in its community, including use of its habitat and its relationships with other species (354)

nicho papel que desempeña una especie en su comunidad, incluidos el uso de su hábitat y su relación con otras especies

nitrogen cycle (NY·truh·juhn SY·kuhl) the cycling of nitrogen between organisms, soil, water, and the atmosphere (435)

ciclo del nitrógeno movimiento del nitrógeno entre los organismos, el suelo, el agua y la atmósfera

nucleic acid (noo·KLAY·ik AS·id) a molecule made up of subunits called nucleotides (93)

ácido nucleico molécula formada por subunidades llamadas nucleótidos

nucleotide (NOO·klee·oh·tyd) in a nucleic-acid chain, a subunit that consists of a sugar, a phosphate, and a nitrogenous base (223)

nucleótido en una cadena de ácidos nucleicos, una subunidad formada por un azúcar, un fosfato y una base nitrogenada

nucleus (NOO·klee·uhs) in a eukaryotic cell, a membrane-bound organelle that contains the cell's DNA and has a role in processes such as growth, metabolism, and reproduction of the cell (84)

núcleo en una célula eucariótica, un organelo cubierto por una membrana, el cual contiene el ADN de la célula y participa en procesos tales como el crecimiento, el metabolismo y la reproducción de la célula

omnivore (AHM·nuh·vohr) an organism that eats both plants and animals (363)

omnívoro organismo que come tanto plantas como animales

organ (OHR·guhn) a collection of tissues that carry out a specialized function of the body (116)

órgano conjunto de tejidos que desempeñan una función especializada en el cuerpo

organ system (OHR·guhn SIS·tuhm) a group of organs that work together to perform body functions (117)

aparato (o sistema) de órganos grupo de órganos que trabajan en conjunto para desempeñar funciones corporales

organelle (ohr·guhn·EL) one of the small bodies in a cell's cytoplasm that are specialized to perform a specific function (84)

organelo uno de los cuerpos pequeños del citoplasma de una célula que están especializados para llevar a cabo una función específica

organism (OHR·guh·niz·uhm) a living thing; anything that can carry out life processes independently (80, 114)

organismo ser vivo; cualquier cosa que pueda llevar a cabo procesos vitales independientemente

osmosis (ahz·MOH·sis) the diffusion of water through a semipermeable membrane (130)

ósmosis difusión de agua a través de una membrana semipermeable

ovary (OH·vuh·ree) in the female reproductive system of animals, an organ that produces eggs (327)

ovario en el aparato reproductor femenino de los animales, un órgano que produce óvulos

© Houghton Mifflin Harcourt Publishing Company

P-Q

pancreas (PANG·kree·uhs) the organ that lies behind the stomach and that makes digestive enzymes and hormones that regulate sugar levels (300)
páncreas órgano que se encuentra detrás del estómago y que produce las enzimas digestivas y las hormonas que regulan los niveles de azúcar

parasitism (PAIR·uh·sih·tiz·uhm) a relationship between two species in which one species, the parasite, benefits from the other species, the host, which is harmed (389)
parasitismo relación entre dos especies en la que una, el parásito, se beneficia de la otra, el huésped, la cual resulta perjudicada

passive transport (PAS·iv TRANS·pohrt) the movement of substances across a cell membrane without the use of energy by the cell (130)
transporte pasivo movimiento de sustancias a través de una membrana celular sin que la célula tenga que usar energía

pedigree (PED·ih·gree) a diagram that shows the occurrence of a genetic trait across several generations of a family (214)
pedigrí un diagrama que muestra la incidencia de un carácter genético en varias generaciones de una familia

penis (PEE·nis) the male organ that transfers sperm to a female and that carries urine out of the body (326)
pene órgano masculino que transfiere espermatozoides a una hembra y que lleva la orina hacia el exterior del cuerpo

pharynx (FAIR·ingks) the part of the respiratory system that extends from the mouth to the larynx (288)
faringe parte del aparato respiratorio que va de la boca a la laringe

phenotype (FEE·nuh·typ) an organism's appearance or other detectable characteristic (199)
fenotipo apariencia de un organismo u otra característica perceptible

phospholipid (fahs·foh·LIP·id) a lipid that contains phosphorus and is a structural component of cell membranes (94)
fosfolípido lípido que contiene fósforo y que es un componente estructural de la membrana celular

photosynthesis (foh·toh·SIN·thih·sis) the process by which plants, algae, and some bacteria use sunlight, carbon dioxide, and water to make food (128, 144)
fotosíntesis proceso por medio del cual las plantas, las algas y algunas bacterias utilizan luz solar, dióxido de carbono y agua para producir alimento

pioneer species (py·uh·NIR SPEE·sheez) a species that colonizes an uninhabited area and that starts a process of succession (444)
especie pionera especie que coloniza un área deshabitada y empieza un proceso de sucesión

placenta (pluh·SEN·tuh) the partly fetal and partly maternal organ by which materials are exchanged between a fetus and the mother (330)
placenta órgano parcialmente fetal y parcialmente materno por medio del cual se intercambian materiales entre el feto y la madre

Plantae (PLAN·tee) a kingdom made up of complex, multicellular organisms that are usually green, have cell walls made of cellulose, cannot move, and use the Sun's energy to make sugar by photosynthesis (60)
Plantae reino formado por organismos pluricelulares complejos que normalmente son verdes, tienen una pared celular de celulosa, no tienen capacidad de movimiento y utilizan la energía del Sol para producir azúcar mediante la fotosíntesis

population (pahp·yuh·LAY·shuhn) a group of organisms of the same species that live in a specific geographical area (350)
población grupo de organismos de la misma especie que viven en un área geográfica específica

predator (PRED·uh·ter) an organism that kills and eats all or part of another organism (386)
depredador organismo que mata y se alimenta de otro organismo o de parte de él

prey (PRAY) an organism that is killed and eaten by another organism (386)
presa organismo al que otro organismo mata para alimentarse de él

probability (prahb·uh·BIL·ih·tee) the likelihood that a possible future event will occur in any given instance of the event (212)
probabilidad posibilidad de que ocurra un potencial suceso futuro en cualquier caso dado del suceso

producer (pruh·DOO·ser) an organism that can make its own food by using energy from its surroundings (362)
productor organismo que puede elaborar su propio alimento utilizando la energía de su entorno

prokaryote (proh·KAIR·ee·oht) a single-celled organism that does not have a nucleus or membrane-bound organelles; examples are archaea and bacteria (85)
procariote organismo unicelular que no tiene núcleo ni organelos cubiertos por una membrana, por ejemplo, las arqueas y las bacterias

protein (PROH·teen) a molecule that is made up of amino acids and is needed to build and repair body structures and regulate processes in the body (92)
proteína molécula formada por aminoácidos y que es necesaria para construir y reparar estructuras corporales y para regular procesos del cuerpo

Protista (proh·TIS·tuh) a kingdom of mostly one-celled eukaryotic organisms that are different from plants, animals, archaea, bacteria, and fungi (60)
Protista reino compuesto principalmente por organismos eucarióticos unicelulares que son diferentes de las plantas, animales, arqueas, bacterias y hongos

Punnett square (PUH·nuht SKWAIR) a graphic used to predict the results of a genetic cross (210)
cuadro de Punnett gráfica que se usa para predecir los resultados de una cruza genética

R

ratio (RAY·shee·oh) a comparison of two numbers using division (212)
razón comparación de dos números mediante la división

recessive (ree·SES·iv) describes an allele that will be masked unless the organism is homozygous for the trait (199)
recesivo término que describe un alelo que no se expresa a menos que el organismo sea homocigoto para el carácter

replication (rep·lih·KAY·shuhn) the duplication of a DNA molecule (224)
replicación la duplicación de una molécula de ADN

respiratory system (RES·per·uh·tohr·ee SIS·tuhm) a collection of organs whose primary function is to take in oxygen and expel carbon dioxide; the organs of this system include the lungs, the throat, and the passageways that lead to the lungs (287)
aparato respiratorio conjunto de órganos cuya función principal es asimilar oxígeno y expulsar dióxido de carbono; los órganos de este aparato incluyen los pulmones, la garganta y las vías que llevan a los pulmones

ribosome (RY·buh·sohm) a cell organelle composed of RNA and protein; the site of protein synthesis (102, 227)
ribosoma organelo celular compuesto de ARN y proteína; el lugar donde ocurre la síntesis de proteínas

RNA (ar·en·AY) ribonucleic acid, a molecule that is present in all living cells and that plays a role in protein production (226)
ARN ácido ribonucleico, molécula presente en todas las células vivas y que interviene en la producción de proteínas

S

savanna (SUH·van·uh) a region characterized by wide open spaces, spotty trees, and many scrub-like bushes; it is found between tropical forests and desert biomes, and receives about 35–50 cm of rain during the rainy season; also called tropical grassland (409)
sabana región caracterizada por amplios espacios abiertos, árboles diseminados y muchos matorrales; se encuentra entre los biomas de selva tropical y desierto, y recibe entre 35 y 50 cm de lluvia durante la estación lluviosa; también se denomina pradera tropical

selective breeding (suh·LEK·tiv·BREE·ding) the human practice of breeding animals or plants that have certain desired traits; also called artificial selection (18, 235)
cría selectiva práctica humana de criar animales o cultivar plantas que tienen ciertos caracteres deseados; también se denomina selección artificial

sexual reproduction (SEHK·shoo·uhl ree·pruh·DUHK·shuhn) reproduction in which the sex cells from two parents unite to produce offspring that share traits from both parents (8, 188)
reproducción sexual reproducción en la que se unen las células sexuales de los dos progenitores para producir descendencia que comparte caracteres de ambos progenitores

skeletal system (SKEL·ih·tl SIS·tuhm) the organ system whose primary function is to support and protect the body and to allow the body to move (264)
sistema esquelético sistema de órganos cuya función principal es sostener y proteger el cuerpo y permitir que se mueva

small intestine (SMAWL in·TES·tin) the organ between the stomach and the large intestine where most of the breakdown of food happens and most of the nutrients from it are absorbed (299)
intestino delgado órgano que se encuentra entre el estómago y el intestino grueso en el cual se produce la mayor parte de la descomposición de los alimentos y se absorben la mayoría de los nutrientes

species (SPEE·sheez) a group of organisms that are closely related and can mate to produce fertile offspring (56, 350)
especie grupo de organismos que tienen un parentesco cercano y que pueden aparearse para producir descendencia fértil

sperm (SPERM) the male sex cell (326)
espermatozoide célula sexual masculina

spinal cord (SPY·nuhl KOHRD) a column of nerve tissue running from the base of the brain through the vertebral column (308)
médula espinal columna de tejido nervioso que se origina en la base del cerebro y corre a lo largo de la columna vertebral

stewardship (STOO·erd·ship) the careful and responsible management of a resource (462)
gestión ambiental responsable manejo cuidadoso y responsable de un recurso

stimulus (STIM·yuh·luhs) anything that causes a reaction or change in an organism or any part of an organism (7)
estímulo cualquier cosa que causa una reacción o un cambio en un organismo o cualquier parte de un organismo

stomach (STUHM·uhk) the saclike, digestive organ that is between the esophagus and the small intestine that breaks down food by the action of muscles, enzymes, and acids (299)
estómago órgano digestivo con forma de bolsa, ubicado entre el esófago y el intestino delgado, que descompone los alimentos por la acción de los músculos, las enzimas y los ácidos

structure (STRUHK·cher) the arrangement of parts in an organism (118)
estructura orden y la distribución de las partes de un organismo

succession (suhk·SESH·uhn) the replacement of one type of community by another at a single location over a period of time (444)
sucesión reemplazo de un tipo de comunidad por otro en un mismo lugar a lo largo de un período de tiempo

symbiosis (sim·by·OH·sis) a relationship in which two different organisms live in close association with each other (388)
simbiosis relación en la que dos organismos diferentes viven estrechamente asociados uno con el otro

taiga (TY·guh) a region of evergreen, coniferous forest below the arctic and subarctic tundra regions (407)
taiga región de bosques perennes de coníferas, ubicados debajo de las regiones ártica y subártica de tundra

temperate forest (tem·PUR·ut FOR·ust) a region characterized by trees that lose their leaves during certain months of the year, and moderate temperatures during summer and winter; it receives 75–150 cm of rainfall every year; also called a deciduous forest (410)
bosque templado región caracterizada por árboles que pierden sus hojas durante determinados meses del año y temperaturas moderadas en verano e invierno; recibe entre 75 y 150 cm de lluvia al año; también se denomina bosque caducifolio

temperate grassland (tem·PUR·ut GRAS·land) a region characterized by large areas of grass and shrubs, hot summers, and very cold winters; it receives 55–95 cm of rain per year (409)
pradera templada región caracterizada por grandes extensiones de hierba y arbustos, veranos cálidos e inviernos muy fríos; recibe entre 55 y 95 cm de lluvia al año

tendon (TEN·duhn) a tough connective tissue that attaches a muscle to a bone or to another body part (271)
tendón tejido conectivo duro que une un músculo con un hueso o con otra parte del cuerpo

testes (TES·teez) the primary male reproductive organs, which produce sperm cells and testosterone (singular, testis) (326)
testículos principales órganos reproductores masculinos, los cuales producen espermatozoides y testosterona

tissue (TISH·oo) a group of similar cells that perform a common function (115)
tejido grupo de células similares que llevan a cabo una función común

trachea (TRAY·kee·uh) thin-walled tube that extends from the larynx to the bronchi; carries air to the lungs; also called windpipe (288)
tráquea conducto de paredes delgadas que va de la laringe a los bronquios; transporta el aire a los pulmones

tropical rain forest (TROP·ih·kul RAYN FOR·ust) a region characterized by very warm and humid climate, over 300 cm of rain per year, and a great diversity of living things; found along the equator (411)
selva tropical región que se caracteriza por un clima muy cálido y húmedo, más de 300 cm de lluvia al año y una gran diversidad de seres vivos; se encuentra a lo largo del ecuador

tundra (TUHN·druh) a region found at far northern and far southern latitudes characterized by low-lying plants, a lack of trees, and long winters with very low temperatures (407)
tundra región que se encuentra en latitudes muy al norte o muy al sur y que se caracteriza por plantas bajas, ausencia de árboles e inviernos prolongados con temperaturas muy bajas

umbilical cord (uhm·BIL·ih·kuhl KOHRD) the ropelike structure through which blood vessels pass and by which a developing mammal is connected to the placenta (330)
cordón umbilical estructura con forma de cuerda a través de la cual pasan vasos sanguíneos y por medio de la cual un mamífero en desarrollo está unido a la placenta

urbanization (er·buh·nih·ZAY·shuhn) an increase in the proportion of a population living in urban areas rather than in rural areas (457)
urbanización aumento en la proporción de población en las áreas urbanas

urine (YUR·in) the liquid excreted by the kidneys, stored in the bladder, and passed through the urethra to the outside of the body (302)
orina líquido que excretan los riñones, se almacena en la vejiga y pasa a través de la uretra hacia el exterior del cuerpo

uterus (YOO·ter·uhs) in female placental mammals, the hollow, muscular organ in which an embryo embeds itself and develops into a fetus (328)
útero en los mamíferos placentarios hembras, el órgano hueco y muscular en el que el embrión se incrusta y se desarrolla hasta convertirse en feto

vacuole (VAK·yoo·ohl) a fluid-filled vesicle found in the cytoplasm of plant cells or protozoans (104)
vacuola vesícula llena de líquido que se encuentra en el citoplasma de las células vegetales o de los protozoarios

vagina (vuh·JY·nuh) the female reproductive organ that connects the outside of the body to the uterus (328)
vagina órgano reproductor femenino que conecta el exterior del cuerpo con el útero

variation (vair·ee·AY·shuhn) the occurrence of hereditary or nonhereditary differences between different individuals of a population (20)
variabilidad incidencia de diferencias hereditarias o no hereditarias entre distintos individuos de una población

vein (VAYN) in biology, a vessel that carries blood to the heart (283)
vena en biología, un vaso que lleva sangre al corazón

water cycle (WAW·ter SY·kuhl) the continuous movement of water between the atmosphere, the land, the oceans, and living things (434)
ciclo del agua movimiento continuo del agua entre la atmósfera, la tierra, los océanos y los seres vivos

wetland (WET·land) an area of land that is periodically underwater or whose soil contains a great deal of moisture (418)
pantano terreno que está periódicamente bajo el agua o cuyo suelo contiene una gran cantidad de humedad

Index

Note: Italic page numbers represent illustrative material, such as figures, tables, margin elements, photographs, and illustrations. Boldface page numbers represent page numbers for definitions.

F

fallopian tube, 327, 328, **328**, *328*
family, 57, *57*
feces, 300
feedback mechanism, 316, **316**, *316*
    negative, 316
    positive, 316
fertilization, 188, *188*
fetus, 330
flagella, 85
flexor, 271, *271*
food chain, **364–365**, 365, *365*
food web, 3**66**, *366*, 366–368, **367**, 451
    coastal, 366–367
    global, 368
    land, 368
fossil, 1–3, 27, *27*, *28*, *30*, **40**, *41*
    cast, *30*, 31
    determining age of, 40
    how formed, 31
    stromatolites, 44
    transitional, 31
fossil fuels, 437
fossil record, 31, **31**, 40, *47*
    evolution of multicellular
        organisms, 44
    gaps in, 31
fracture, 269, *269*
fragmentation, 189
Franklin, Rosalind, 221
freshwater ecosystem, **417**, *417*,
    417–419
    lakes and ponds, 418, *418*
    rivers and streams, 419, *419*
    wetlands, 418, *418*, *418*
function, 118, **118**
Fungi, 61, **61**, *61*, 63

G

Galápagos Islands, 16, *16*, 17, 21
gall bladder, 300
gametes, 175
gene, 198, **198**, *198*, 223
    influence on traits, 200
genetic disorder, 225
    from mutations, 225
    inherited, 225
genetic engineering, 236, **236**, *236*, 237
genetic variation, 20–23
genotype, 199, **199**, 210
genus, 57, *57*
geologic time scale, 42, **42**
    Cenozoic, 43, *43*, 47, **47**, *47*
    Mesozoic, 43, *43*, 46
    Paleozoic, 43, 44, **44**, 45
    Precambrian, 43, *43*, 44
gland, 314, **314**, *314*
    adrenal, 315, *315*
    hypothalamus, 315
    pancreas, 315, *315*

pineal, 315
pituitary, 315, *315*
thymus, 315, *315*
thyroid, 315, *315*
gold, 91
Golgi, Camillo, 103
Golgi complex, **98**, *98*, 103, **103**, *103*,
    106, 107
Grant, Rosemary and Peter, 21
grassland, 409, **409**, *409*

H

habitat, 354, **354**
haploid cells, 175, **175**, *175*, 176
heart, 282, **282**, *282*
    atrium, 282
    valves, 282
    ventricle, 282
heart attack, 286
hemoglobin, 284
herbivore, 363, **363**, *363*
heredity, 194–205, 196, **196**
Hershey, Alfred, 221
heterotrophs, 60, **60**, 61, *61*
heterozygous, 198, **198**
hierarchy, 62, **62**
History of Life on Earth, 38–51
    change over time, 41
HIV (human immunodeficiency virus),
    332
HMS *Beagle*, 16
homeostasis, 7, **7**, 126–127, 133, 258,
    258, *258*
    maintaining, 133, 258
    problems with, 259
homologous chromosome, 174, **174**,
    176, *176–177*
Hooke, Robert, 77, 80, 82
    microscope, 77, 82, *82*
hormone, 303, 314, **314**, *314*, 326, 327
host, 389, **389**
Human Body Systems, 252–335
    circulatory and respiratory, *254*,
        276–291
    communication between, 257
    digestive and excretory, *255*,
        294–305
    interaction between, 257
    introduction to, 252–261
    link between structure and function,
        256–257
    nervous and endocrine, *255*,
        306–319
    reproductive, *254*, 324–335
    skeletal and muscular, *254*,
        262–275
    what they do, 254–255
Human Genome Project, 161
human growth changes,
    adolescence, 331
    adulthood, 331
    childhood, 331
    infancy, 331

human immunodeficiency virus (HIV),
    332
human impact on ecosystems, 456–460,
    456–460
    air pollution, 460
    coastal development, 459
    depleting resources, 456
    destroying habitats, 456
    fishing, 459, *459*
    pollution, 456, 458, *458*
hydrogen, 91, 93
hypertension, 286
hypothesis, 110, **110**

I

immigration, 374
incomplete dominance, 202
independent studies, 26
integumentary system, 255, **255**, *255*
interphase, 166, **166**, *168–169*
involuntary, 309

J

Job Board,
    Conservation Warden, 359
    Diagnostic Medical Sonographer,
        293
    Genetic Counselor, 183
    Park Naturalist, 359
    Physical Therapist, 293
    Plant Nursery Manager, 183
    Prosthetics Technician, 293
    Student Research Assistant, 51
    Vet Technician, 51
    Wildlife Photographer, 51
joint, 268
    ball-and-socket, 268, *268*
    fixed, 268
    gliding, 268, *268*
    hinge, 268, *268*
    movable, 268

K

kidney, 302, **302**, *302*
    nephron, 302, **302**, *303*
    urine, 302, **302**, *303*
kingdom, 57, *57*
    Animalia, 61, **61**, *61*
    Fungi, 61, **61**, *61*
    Plantae, 60, **60**, *60*
    Protista, 60, **60**, *60*

L

Ladder of Nature, 62
Lamarck, Jean-Baptiste, 19
large intestine, 298, **298**, *298*, 300
larynx, 288, **288**, *288*

law of conservation of energy, 431, **431**
law of conservation of mass, 431, **431**
ligament, 266, **266**, *267*
limiting factor, 378, **378**
Linnaeus, Carolus, 56, 57, 63
lipid, 92, **92**, 103
liver, 300, **300**
living things, 4–13
  characteristics of, 6–9
  classification of, 52–69
  growth of, 9, *9*
  needs, 9, 10–11
Lyell, Charles, 19
lymph, 278, **278**
lymph node, 280, **280**, *280*
lymphatic disorders, 281
  bubonic plague, 281
  filariasis, 281
  lymphedema, 281
  lymphoma, 281
lymphatic system, 255, **255**, *255*, 278,
  278, 280
  bone marrow, 280, **280**, *280*
  lymph nodes, 280, **280**, *280*
  lymph vessels, 280, **280**, *280*
  spleen, *280*, 281, **281**
  thymus, *280*, 281, **281**
  tonsils, *280*, 281, **281**
lysosome, 106, **106**, *106*, 107

M

Ma (mega annum), 40
Malthus, Thomas, 19
marine ecosystem, 422–432
  coastal ocean, 422
  deep ocean, 423
  open ocean, 423
matter, 430, **430**, *430*
  in ecosystems, 431–433
meiosis, 170–181, **175**, *176–177*
  comparison to mitosis, 178, *178*
  meiosis I, 176
  meiosis II, 177
membrane,
  cell, 84, **84**, *84*, 94, *96*, 101, *101*,
    102, 103, *103*, 106, 107, 130
  nuclear, 101, *101*
Mendel, Gregor, 160, 182, 196–197,
  198, 202
menstruation, 328
Mesozoic era, 43, *43*, 46
  development of many species, 46
  mass extinction, 46
metaphase, 168, **168**, *168*, *176–177*
microscope, 63, 75, *75–77*
  electron, 77
  history of, 76–77
  light, 77
  scanning tunneling, 77
mitochondrion, 102, **102**, *102*, *103*,
  105, *106*, 107
mitosis, 129, **129**, *129*, 161, 162–170,
  166, 167, **167**, *167*

comparison to meiosis, 178, *178*
  phases of, 168
molecule, **91**, *91*, 91–93
Morgan, Thomas Hunt, 161
mouth, 298
multicellular organisms, 6, *6*, 9, 59–61,
  83, 85, 100, 114, **114**, *114*, 127
  evolution of, 44
  levels of organization, 114
multiple births, 183, *183*
muscle, 250–251
  cardiac, 271, *271*
  endurance, 273
  flexibility, 273
  involuntary, 270
  main functions of, 270
  skeletal, 271, *271*
  smooth, 270, **270**
  strain, 272
  strength, 273
  tear, 272
  voluntary, 270
muscular dystrophy, 272
muscular system, 254, **254**, *254*, **270**
  benefits of exercise, 273
  diseases of, 272
  injuries to, 272
mutagens, 225
mutation, 20, **20**, 22, 225, **225**, *225*
  deletion, 225
  insertion, 225
  substitution, 225
mutualism, 388, **388**, *388*

N

natural selection, **20**, 20–22
  adaptation, 21, **21**
  genetic variation, 20, **20**, 21, 22
  overproduction, 20
  selection, 21
naturalist, 16, **16**
nephron, 302, *303*
nerve, 309, **309**, 310, *310*
nerve cell, 256, *256*
nervous system, 255, **255**, *255*
  central, 308, 309
  disorders of, 317
  movement through, 310
  peripheral, 308, 309
neuron, 310, **310**, *311*
  axon, 311, *311*
  axon terminal, 311, *311*
  cell body, 311, *311*
  dendrite, 311, *311*
  motor, 310
  sensory, 310
neurotransmitter, 311
niche, 354, **354**, *354*
nitrogen cycle, 433, 435, **435**, *435*
nuclear membrane, 101, *101*
nucleic acid, 92, 93, **93**
nucleotide, 223, **223**, *223*, *224*
  adenine, 223

cytosine, 223
  guanine, 223
  thymine, 223
nucleus, 84, 85, 101, **101**, *101*, *103*,
  106, 107
nutrients, 136, **136**, *136*
  absorption of, 300

O

observation, 110
omnivore, 363, **363**, *363*
order, 57, *57*
organ, 116, **116**, *116*, 120
  animal, 116, **116**, *117*
  plant, 116, **116**, *116*
organelle, 84, **84**, *84*, 85, 100,
  101–102, 166
  chloroplast, 105
  Golgi complex, 103
  mitochondrion, 102
  ribosome, 102
organism, 8, 9, 11, 18, 80, **80**, 114, **114**
  acquiring traits, 19
  function, 118, 120–121
  multicellular, 6, *6*, 9, 59–61, 83, 85,
    100, 114, **114**, *114*, 120, 127
  structure, 118
  unicellular, 6, *6*, 9, 59–61, 83, 114,
    114, *114*, 120, 127, *127*
organ system, 117, **117**, *117*, 120–121
  cardiovascular, 127
  digestive, 120, 121
  excretory, 120, 121
  respiratory, 120, 121, 127
  vascular, 120, *127*
osmosis, 95, 130
  importance of water, 95, *95*
osteoporosis, 269, *269*
ovary, 327, **327**, *327*, *328*
oxygen, 44, 91, 93, 287
ozone, 44

P–Q

paleontologist, 40, 42
Paleozoic era, 43, 44, **44**, 45
  Carboniferous period, 45, *45*
  development of land life, 45
  evolution during, 45
  mass extinction, 45
pancreas, 300, **300**
parasite, 389, **389**
parasitism, 389
parthenogenesis, 189
passive transport, 130, *131*
pedigree, 214, **214**, *214*
penis, 326, **326**, *326*
People in Science,
  Coble, Michael, 182
  Krysko, Kenneth, 358
  McCrory, Phil, 359
  Olopade, Dr. Olufunmilayo, 292